D0688064

Credit Risk Modeling Using Excel and VBA with DVD

For other titles in the Wiley Finance series
please see www.wiley.com/finance

Credit Risk Modeling Using Excel and VBA with DVD

Gunter Löffler
Peter N. Posch

A John Wiley and Sons, Ltd., Publication

This edition first published 2011

Registered office
John Wiley & Sons Ltd, The Atrium, Southern Gate, Chichester, West Sussex, PO19 8SQ, United Kingdom

For details of our global editorial offices, for customer services and for information about how to apply for permission to reuse the copyright material in this book please see our website at www.wiley.com.

Reprinted December 2012

ISBN 978-0-470-66092-8

A catalogue record for this book is available from the British Library.

Typeset in 10/12pt Times by Aptara Inc., New Delhi, India
Printed in Great Britain by CPI Antony Rowe, Chippenham, Wiltshire

Mundus est is qui constat ex caelo, et terra et mare cunctisque sideribus.
Isidoro de Sevilla

Contents

Preface to the 2nd Edition

It is common to blame the inadequacy of risk models for the fact that the 2007–2008 financial crisis caught many market participants by surprise. On closer inspection, though, it often appears that it was not the models that failed. A good example is the risk contained in structured finance securities such as collateralized debt obligations (CDOs). In the first edition of this book, which was published before the crisis, we already pointed out that the rating of such products is not meant to communicate their systematic risk even though this risk component can be extremely large. This is easy to illustrate with simple, standard credit risk models, and surely we were not the first to point this out. Hence, in terms of risk, an AAA-rated bond is definitely not the same as an AAA-rated CDO. Many institutions, however, appear to have built their investment strategy on the presumption that AAA is AAA regardless of the product.

Recent events therefore do not invalidate traditional credit risk modeling as described in the first edition of the book. A second edition is timely, however, because the first edition dealt relatively briefly with the pricing of instruments that featured prominently in the crisis (CDSs and CDOs). In addition to expanding the coverage of these instruments, we devote more time to modeling aspects that were of particular relevance in the financial crisis (e.g., estimation error). We also examine the usefulness and limitations of credit risk modeling through case studies. For example, we discuss the role of scoring models in the subprime market, or show that a structural default prediction model would have assigned relatively high default probabilities to Lehman Brothers in the months before its collapse. Furthermore, we added a new chapter in which we show how to predict borrower-specific loss given default.

For university teachers, we now offer a set of powerpoint slides as well as problem sets with solutions. The material can be accessed via our homepage `www.loeffler-posch.com`. The hybrid character of the book – introduction to credit risk modeling as well as cookbook for model implementation – makes it a good companion to a credit risk course, at both introductory or advanced levels.

We are very grateful to Roger Bowden, Michael Kunisch and Alina Maurer for their comments on new parts of the book. One of us (Peter) benefited from discussions with a lot of people in the credit market, among them Nick Atkinson, David Kupfer and Marion Schlicker. Georg Haas taught him everything a trader needs to know, and Josef Gruber provided him with valuable insights to the practice of risk management. Several readers of the first edition pointed out errors or potential for improvement. We would like to use this opportunity to thank them again and to encourage readers of the second edition to send us their comments (email: `comment@loeffler-posch.com`). Finally, special thanks to our team at Wiley: Andrew Finch, Brian Burge and our editors Aimee Dibbens and Karen Weller.

At the time of writing it is June. The weather is fine. We are looking forward to devoting more time to our families again.

Preface to the 1st Edition

This book is an introduction to modern credit risk methodology as well as a cookbook for putting credit risk models to work. We hope that the two purposes go together well. From our own experience, analytical methods are best understood by implementing them.

Credit risk literature broadly falls into two separate camps: risk measurement and pricing. We belong to the risk measurement camp. Chapters on default probability estimation and credit portfolio risk dominate chapters on pricing and credit derivatives. Our coverage of risk measurement issues is also somewhat selective. We thought it better to be selective than to include more topics with less detail, hoping that the presented material serves as a good preparation for tackling other problems not covered in the book.

We have chosen Excel as our primary tool because it is a universal and very flexible tool that offers elegant solutions to many problems. Even Excel freaks may admit that it is not their first choice for some problems. But even then, it is nonetheless great for demonstrating how to put models to work, given that implementation strategies are mostly transferable to other programming environments. While we tried to provide efficient and general solutions, this was not our single overriding goal. With the dual purpose of our book in mind, we sometimes favored a solution that appeared more simple to grasp.

Readers surely benefit from some prior Excel literacy, e.g., knowing how to use a simple function such as AVERAGE(), being aware of the difference between SUM(A1:A10) SUM($A1:$A10) and so forth. For less experienced readers, there is an *Excel for beginners* video on the DVD, and an introduction to VBA in the Appendix; the other videos supplied on the DVD should also be very useful as they provide a step-by-step guide more detailed than the explanations in the main text.

We also assume that the reader is somehow familiar with concepts from elementary statistics (e.g., probability distributions) and financial economics (e.g., discounting, options). Nevertheless, we explain basic concepts when we think that at least some readers might benefit from it. For example, we include appendices on maximum likelihood estimation or regressions.

We are very grateful to colleagues, friends and students who gave feedback on the manuscript: Oliver Blümke, Jürgen Bohrmann, André Güttler, Florian Kramer, Michael Kunisch, Clemens Prestele, Peter Raupach, Daniel Smith (who also did the narration of the videos with great dedication) and Thomas Verchow. An anonymous reviewer also provided a lot of helpful comments. We thank Eva Nacca for formatting work and typing video text. Finally, we thank our editors Caitlin Cornish, Emily Pears and Vivienne Wickham.

Any errors and unintentional deviations from best practice remain our own responsibility. We welcome your comments and suggestions: just send an email to comment@loeffler-posch.com or visit our homepage at www.loeffler-posch.com.

We owe a lot to our families. Before struggling to find the right words to express our gratitude we rather stop and give our families what they missed most, our time.

Some Hints for Troubleshooting

We hope that you do not encounter problems when working with the spreadsheets, macros and functions developed in this book. If you do, you may want to consider the following possible reasons for trouble:

- We repeatedly use the Excel Solver. This may cause problems if the Solver Add-in is not activated in Excel and VBA. How this can be done is described in Appendix A2. Apparently, differences in Excel versions can also lead to situations in which a macro calling the Solver does not run even though the reference to the Solver is set.
- In Chapters 10 and 11, we use functions from the *AnalysisToolpak* Add-in. Again, this has to be activated. See Chapter 10 for details.
- Some Excel 2003 functions (e.g., BINOMDIST or CRITBINOM) have been changed relative to earlier Excel versions. We've tested our programs on Excel 2003 and Excel 2010. If you're using an older Excel version, these functions might return error values in some cases.
- All functions have been tested for the demonstrated purpose only. We have not strived to make them so general that they work for most purposes one can think of. For example:

  - some functions assume that the data is sorted in some way, or arranged in columns rather than in rows;
  - some functions assume that the argument is a range, not an array. See Appendix A1 for detailed instructions on troubleshooting this issue.

A comprehensive list of all functions (Excel's and user-defined) together with full syntax and a short description can be found in Appendix A5.

1

Estimating Credit Scores with Logit

Typically, several factors can affect a borrower's default probability. In the retail segment, one would consider salary, occupation and other characteristics of the loan applicant; when dealing with corporate clients, one would examine the firm's leverage, profitability or cash flows, to name but a few items. A scoring model specifies how to combine the different pieces of information in order to get an accurate assessment of default probability, thus serving to automate and standardize the evaluation of default risk within a financial institution.

In this chapter, we show how to specify a scoring model using a statistical technique called *logistic regression* or simply *logit*. Essentially, this amounts to coding information into a specific value (e.g., measuring leverage as debt/assets) and then finding the combination of factors that does the best job in explaining historical default behavior.

After clarifying the link between scores and default probability, we show how to estimate and interpret a logit model. We then discuss important issues that arise in practical applications, namely the treatment of outliers and the choice of functional relationship between variables and default.

An important step in building and running a successful scoring model is its validation. Since validation techniques are applied not just to scoring models but also to agency ratings and other measures of default risk, they are described separately in Chapter 8.

LINKING SCORES, DEFAULT PROBABILITIES AND OBSERVED DEFAULT BEHAVIOR

A score summarizes the information contained in factors that affect default probability. Standard scoring models take the most straightforward approach by linearly combining those factors. Let x denote the factors (their number is K) and b the weights (or coefficients) attached to them; we can represent the score that we get in scoring instance i as

$$\text{Score}_i = b_1 x_{i1} + b_2 x_{i2} + \ldots + b_K x_{iK} \tag{1.1}$$

It is convenient to have a shortcut for this expression. Collecting the bs and the xs in column vectors $\mathbf{b}$ and $\mathbf{x}$ we can rewrite (1.1) to

$$\text{Score}_i = b_1 x_{i1} + b_2 x_{i2} + \ldots + b_K x_{iK} = \mathbf{b}'\mathbf{x}_i, \quad \mathbf{x}_i = \begin{bmatrix} x_{i1} \\ x_{i2} \\ \ldots \\ x_{iK} \end{bmatrix}, \quad \mathbf{b} = \begin{bmatrix} b_1 \\ b_2 \\ \ldots \\ b_K \end{bmatrix} \tag{1.2}$$

If the model is to include a constant b_1, we set $x_{i1} = 1$ for each i.

Assume for simplicity that we have already agreed on the choice of the factors $\mathbf{x}$ – what is then left to determine is the weight vector $\mathbf{b}$. Usually, it is estimated based on observed default

Table 1.1 Factor values and default behavior

			Default indicator for year +1	Factor values from the end of year			
Scoring instance i	Firm	Year	y_i	x_{i1}	x_{i2}		x_{iK}
1	XAX	2001	0	0.12	0.35	...	0.14
2	YOX	2001	0	0.15	0.51	...	0.04
3	TUR	2001	0	−0.10	0.63	...	0.06
4	BOK	2001	1	0.16	0.21	...	0.12
...	...	...	...	...	...	...	...
912	XAX	2002	0	−0.01	0.02	...	0.09
913	YOX	2002	0	0.15	0.54	...	0.08
914	TUR	2002	1	0.08	0.64	...	0.04
...	...	...	...	...	...	...	...
N	VRA	2005	0	0.04	0.76	...	0.03

behavior.[1] Imagine that we have collected annual data on firms with factor values and default behavior. We show such a data set in Table 1.1.[2]

Note that the same firm can show up more than once if there is information on this firm for several years. Upon defaulting, firms often stay in default for several years; in such cases, we would not use the observations following the year in which default occurred. If a firm moves out of default, we would again include it in the data set.

The default information is stored in the variable y_i. It takes the value 1 if the firm defaulted in the year following the one for which we have collected the factor values, and zero otherwise. N denotes the overall number of observations.

The scoring model should predict a high default probability for those observations that defaulted and a low default probability for those that did not. In order to choose the appropriate weights $\mathbf{b}$, we first need to link scores to default probabilities. This can be done by representing default probabilities as a function F of scores:

$$\text{Prob}(\text{Default}_i) = \text{Prob}(y_i = 1) = F(\text{Score}_i) \tag{1.3}$$

Like default probabilities, the function F should be constrained to the interval from zero to one; it should also yield a default probability for each possible score. The requirements can be fulfilled by a cumulative probability distribution function, and a distribution often considered for this purpose is the logistic distribution. The logistic distribution function $\Lambda(z)$ is defined as $\Lambda(z) = \exp(z)/(1 + \exp(z))$. Applied to (1.3) we get

$$\text{Prob}(\text{Default}_i) = \Lambda(\text{Score}_i) = \frac{\exp(\mathbf{b}'\mathbf{x}_i)}{1 + \exp(\mathbf{b}'\mathbf{x}_i)} = \frac{1}{1 + \exp(-\mathbf{b}'\mathbf{x}_i)} \tag{1.4}$$

Models that link information to probabilities using the logistic distribution function are called *logit* models.

[1] In qualitative scoring models, however, experts determine the weights.

[2] Data used for scoring are usually on an annual basis, but one can also choose other frequencies for data collection as well as other horizons for the default horizon.

Table 1.2 Scores and default probabilities in the logit model

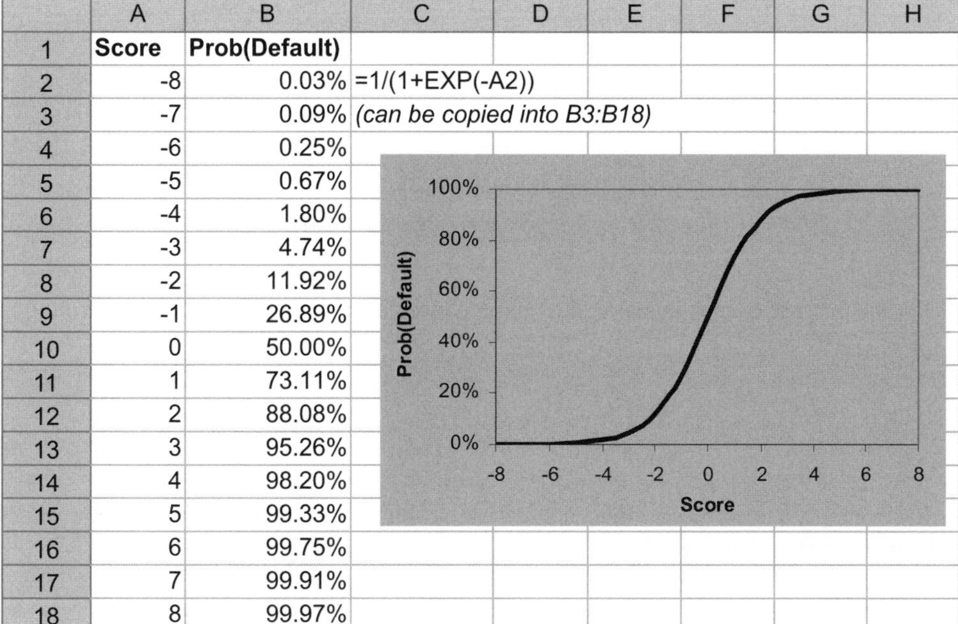

	A	B	C	D	E	F	G	H
1	**Score**	**Prob(Default)**						
2	-8	0.03%	=1/(1+EXP(-A2))					
3	-7	0.09%	*(can be copied into B3:B18)*					
4	-6	0.25%						
5	-5	0.67%						
6	-4	1.80%						
7	-3	4.74%						
8	-2	11.92%						
9	-1	26.89%						
10	0	50.00%						
11	1	73.11%						
12	2	88.08%						
13	3	95.26%						
14	4	98.20%						
15	5	99.33%						
16	6	99.75%						
17	7	99.91%						
18	8	99.97%						

In Table 1.2, we list the default probabilities associated with some score values and illustrate the relationship with a graph. As can be seen, higher scores correspond to a higher default probability. In many financial institutions, credit scores have the opposite property: they are higher for borrowers with a lower credit risk. In addition, they are often constrained to some set interval, e.g., zero to 100. Preferences for such characteristics can easily be met. If we use (1.4) to define a scoring system with scores from -9 to 1, but want to work with scores from 0 to 100 instead (100 being the best), we could transform the original score to $myscore = -10 \times score + 10$.

Having collected the factors $\mathbf{x}$ and chosen the distribution function F, a natural way of estimating the weights $\mathbf{b}$ is the maximum likelihood (ML) method. According to the ML principle, the weights are chosen such that the probability (=likelihood) of observing the given default behavior is maximized (see Appendix A3 for further details on ML estimation).

The first step in maximum likelihood estimation is to set up the likelihood function. For a borrower that defaulted, the likelihood of observing this is

$$\text{Prob}(\text{Default}_i) = \text{Prob}(y_i = 1) = \Lambda(\mathbf{b}'\mathbf{x}_i) \tag{1.5}$$

For a borrower that did not default, we get the likelihood

$$\text{Prob}(\text{No default}_i) = \text{Prob}(y_i = 0) = 1 - \Lambda(\mathbf{b}'\mathbf{x}_i) \tag{1.6}$$

Using a little trick, we can combine the two formulae into one that automatically gives the correct likelihood, be it a defaulter or not. Since any number raised to the power of zero evaluates to one, the likelihood for observation i can be written as

$$L_i = (\Lambda(\mathbf{b}'\mathbf{x}_i))^{y_i}(1 - \Lambda(\mathbf{b}'\mathbf{x}_i))^{1-y_i} \tag{1.7}$$

Assuming that defaults are independent, the likelihood of a set of observations is just the product of the individual likelihoods:[3]

$$L = \prod_{i=1}^{N} L_i = \prod_{i=1}^{N}(\Lambda(\mathbf{b}'\mathbf{x}_i))^{y_i}(1 - \Lambda(\mathbf{b}'\mathbf{x}_i))^{1-y_i} \tag{1.8}$$

For the purpose of maximization, it is more convenient to examine ln L, the logarithm of the likelihood:

$$\ln L = \sum_{i=1}^{N} y_i \ln(\Lambda(\mathbf{b}'\mathbf{x}_i)) + (1 - y_i)\ln(1 - \Lambda(\mathbf{b}'\mathbf{x}_i)) \tag{1.9}$$

It can be maximized by setting its first derivative with respect to **b** to zero. This derivative (like **b**, it is a vector) is given by

$$\frac{\partial \ln L}{\partial \mathbf{b}} = \sum_{i=1}^{N}(y_i - \Lambda(\mathbf{b}'\mathbf{x}_i))\mathbf{x}_i \tag{1.10}$$

Newton's method (see Appendix A3) does a very good job in solving equation (1.10) with respect to **b**. To apply this method, we also need the second derivative, which we obtain as

$$\frac{\partial^2 \ln L}{\partial \mathbf{b}\partial \mathbf{b}'} = -\sum_{i=1}^{N}\Lambda(\mathbf{b}'\mathbf{x}_i)(1 - \Lambda(\mathbf{b}'\mathbf{x}_i))\mathbf{x}_i\mathbf{x}_i' \tag{1.11}$$

ESTIMATING LOGIT COEFFICIENTS IN EXCEL

Excel does not contain a function for estimating logit models, and so we sketch how to construct a user-defined function that performs the task. Our complete function is called LOGIT. The syntax of the LOGIT command is equivalent to the LINEST command: LOGIT(*y*,*x*,[*const*],[*statistics*]), where [] denotes an optional argument.

The first argument specifies the range of the dependent variable, which in our case is the default indicator *y*; the second parameter specifies the range of the explanatory variable(s). The third and fourth parameters are logical values for the inclusion of a constant (1 or omitted if a constant is included, 0 otherwise) and the calculation of regression statistics (1 if statistics are to be computed, 0 or omitted otherwise). The function returns an array, therefore, it has to be executed on a range of cells and entered by [ctrl]+[shift]+[enter].

[3] Given that there are years in which default rates are high, and others in which they are low, one may wonder whether the independence assumption is appropriate. It will be if the factors that we input into the score capture fluctuations in average default risk. In many applications, this is a reasonable assumption.

Table 1.3 Application of the LOGIT command to a data set with information on defaults and five financial ratios

	A	B	C	D	E	F	G	H	I	J	K	L	M	N	O
1	Firm ID	Year	De-fault	WC/ TA	RE/ TA	EBIT/ TA	ME/ TL	S/ TA		CONST	WC/ TA	RE/ TA	EBIT/ TA	ME/ TL	S/ TA
2	1	1999	0	0.50	0.31	0.04	0.96	0.33	b	-2.543	0.414	-1.454	-7.999	-1.594	0.620
3	1	2000	0	0.55	0.32	0.05	1.06	0.33		{=LOGIT(C2:C4001,D2:H4001,1,0)}					
4	1	2001	0	0.45	0.23	0.03	0.80	0.25		*(applies to J2:O2)*					
5	1	2002	0	0.31	0.19	0.03	0.39	0.25							
6	1	2003	0	0.45	0.22	0.03	0.79	0.28							
7	1	2004	0	0.46	0.22	0.03	1.29	0.32							
8	2	1999	0	0.01	-0.03	0.01	0.11	0.25							
9	2	2000	0	-0.11	-0.12	0.03	0.15	0.32							
...															
108	21	1996	1	0.36	0.06	0.03	3.20	0.28							
...															
4001	830	2002	1	0.07	-0.11	0.04	0.04	0.12							

Before delving into the code, let us look at how the function works on an example data set.[4] We have collected default information and five variables for default prediction; Working Capital (WC), Retained Earnings (RE), Earnings Before Interest and Taxes (EBIT) and Sales (S), each divided by Total Assets (TA); and Market Value of Equity (ME) divided by Total Liabilities (TL). Except for the market value, all these items are found in the balance sheet and income statement of the company. The market value is given by the number of shares outstanding multiplied by the stock price. The five ratios are the ones from the widely known Z-score developed by Altman (1968). WC/TA captures the short-term liquidity of a firm, RE/TA and EBIT/TA measure historic and current profitability, respectively. S/TA further proxies for the competitive situation of the company and ME/TL is a market-based measure of leverage.

Of course, one could consider other variables as well; to mention only a few, these could be: cash flows over debt service, sales or total assets (as a proxy for size), earnings volatility, stock price volatility. In addition, there are often several ways of capturing one underlying factor. Current profits, for instance, can be measured using EBIT, EBITDA (=EBIT plus depreciation and amortization) or net income.

In Table 1.3, the data is assembled in columns A to H. Firm ID and year are not required for estimation. The LOGIT function is applied to range J2:O2. The default variable that the LOGIT function uses is in the range C2:C4001, while the factors x are in the range D2:H4001. Note that (unlike in Excel's LINEST function) coefficients are returned in the same order as the variables are entered; the constant (if included) appears as the leftmost variable. To interpret the sign of the coefficient b, recall that a higher score corresponds to a higher default probability. The negative sign of the coefficient for EBIT/TA, for example, means that default probability goes down as profitability increases.

Now let us have a close look at important parts of the LOGIT code. In the first lines of the function, we analyze the input data to define the data dimensions: the total number of observations `N` and the number of explanatory variables (including the constant) `K`. If a

[4] The data is hypothetical, but mirrors the structure of data for listed US corporates.

constant is to be included (which should be done routinely) we have to add a vector of 1s to the matrix of explanatory variables. This is why we call the read-in factors `xraw`, and use them to construct the matrix `x` we work with in the function by adding a vector of 1s. For this, we could use an If-condition, but here we just write a 1 in the first column and then overwrite it if necessary (i.e., if `constant` is zero):

```
Function LOGIT(y As Range, xraw As Range, _
                Optional constant As Byte, Optional stats As Byte)

If IsMissing(constant) Then constant = 1
If IsMissing(stats) Then stats = 0

'Count variables
Dim i As long, j As long, jj As long

'Read data dimensions
Dim K As Long, N As Long
N = y.Rows.Count
K = xraw.Columns.Count + constant

'Adding a vector of ones to the x matrix if constant=1,
'name xraw=x from now on

Dim x() As Double
ReDim x(1 To N, 1 To K)
For i = 1 To N
 x(i, 1) = 1
 For j = 1 + constant To K
  x(i, j) = xraw(i, j - constant)
 Next j
Next i
...
```

The logical value for the constant and the statistics are read in as variables of type byte, meaning that they can take integer values between 0 and 255. In the function, we could therefore check whether the user has indeed input either zero or 1, and return an error message if this is not the case. Both variables are optional, if their input is omitted the constant is set to 1 and the statistics to 0. Similarly, we might want to send other error messages, e.g., if the dimension of the dependent variable y and the one of the independent variables x do not match.

The way we present it, the LOGIT function requires the input data to be organized in columns, not in rows. For the estimation of scoring models, this will be standard, because the number of observations is typically very large. However, we could modify the function in such a way that it recognizes the organization of the data. The LOGIT function maximizes the log-likelihood by setting its first derivative to zero, and uses Newton's method (see Appendix A3) to solve this problem. Required for this process are: a set of starting values for the unknown parameter vector **b**; the first derivative of the log-likelihood (the gradient vector $g()$ given in (1.10)); the second derivative (the Hessian matrix $H()$ given in (1.11)). Newton's method then leads to the following rule:

$$b_1 = b_0 - \left[\frac{\partial^2 \ln L}{\partial b_0 \partial b_0'}\right]^{-1} \frac{\partial \ln L}{\partial b_0} = b_0 - H(b_0)^{-1} g(b_0) \tag{1.12}$$

The logit model has the nice feature that the log-likelihood function is globally concave. Once we have found the root to the first derivative, we can be sure that we have found the global maximum of the likelihood function.

When initializing the coefficient vector (denoted by `b` in the function), we can already initialize the score $\mathbf{b}'\mathbf{x}$ (denoted by `bx`), which will be needed later on:

```
'Initializing the coefficient vector (b) and the score (bx)
Dim b() As Double, bx() As Double
ReDim b(1 To K): ReDim bx(1 To N)
```

Since we only declare the coefficients and the score, their starting values are implicitly set to zero. Now we are ready to start Newton's method. The iteration is conducted within a Do-while loop. We exit once the change in the log-likelihood from one iteration to the next does not exceed a certain small value (like 10^{-11}). Iterations are indexed by the variable `iter`. Focusing on the important steps, once we have declared the arrays `dlnl` (gradient), `Lambda` (prediction $\Lambda(\mathbf{b}'\mathbf{x})$), `hesse` (Hessian matrix) and `lnl` (log-likelihood), we compute their values for a given set of coefficients, and therefore for a given score `bx`. For your convenience, we summarize the key formulae below the code:

```
'Compute prediction Lambda, gradient dlnl,
'Hessian hesse, and log likelihood lnl
For i = 1 To N
 Lambda(i) = 1 / (1 + Exp(-bx(i)))
 For j = 1 To K
  dlnL(j) = dlnL(j) + (y(i) - Lambda(i)) * x(i, j)
  For jj = 1 To K
   hesse(jj, j) = hesse(jj, j) - Lambda(i) * (1 - Lambda(i)) _
                  * x(i, jj) * x(i, j)
  Next jj
 Next j
 lnL(iter) = lnL(iter) + y(i) * Log(Lambda(i)) + (1 - y(i)) _
             * Log(1 - Lambda(i))
Next i
```

$$\text{Lambda} = \Lambda(\mathbf{b}'\mathbf{x}_i) = 1/(1 + \exp(-\mathbf{b}'\mathbf{x}_i))$$

$$\text{dlnl} = \sum_{i=1}^{N} (y_i - \Lambda(\mathbf{b}'\mathbf{x}_i))\mathbf{x}_i$$

$$\text{hesse} = -\sum_{i=1}^{N} \Lambda(\mathbf{b}'\mathbf{x}_i)(1 - \Lambda(\mathbf{b}'\mathbf{x}_i))\mathbf{x}_i\mathbf{x}_i'$$

$$\text{lnl} = \sum_{i=1}^{N} y_i \ln(\Lambda(\mathbf{b}'\mathbf{x}_i)) + (1 - y_i)\ln(1 - \Lambda(\mathbf{b}'\mathbf{x}_i))$$

We have to go through three loops. The function for the gradient, the Hessian and the likelihood each contain a sum for `i=1 to N`. We use a loop from `i=1 to N` to evaluate those sums. Within this loop, we loop through `j=1 to K` for each element of the gradient vector; for the Hessian, we need to loop twice, and so there is a second loop `jj=1 to K`. Note that the gradient and the Hessian have to be reset to zero before we redo the calculation in the next step of the iteration.

With the gradient and the Hessian at hand, we can apply Newton's rule. We take the inverse of the Hessian using the worksheet-Function MINVERSE, and multiply it with the gradient using the worksheet-Function MMULT:

```
'Compute inverse Hessian (=hinv) and multiply hinv with gradient dlnl
hinv = Application.WorksheetFunction.MInverse(hesse)
hinvg = Application.WorksheetFunction.MMult(dlnL, hinv)

If Abs(change) <= sens Then Exit Do
' Apply Newton's scheme for updating coefficients b
For j = 1 To K
 b(j) = b(j) - hinvg(j)
Next j
```

As outlined above, this procedure of updating the coefficient vector b is ended when the change in the likelihood, `abs(ln(iter)-ln(iter-1))`, is sufficiently small. We can then forward b to the output of the function LOGIT.

COMPUTING STATISTICS AFTER MODEL ESTIMATION

In this section, we show how the regression statistics are computed in the LOGIT function. Readers wanting to know more about the statistical background may want to consult Appendix A4.

To assess whether a variable helps explain the default event or not, one can examine a t-ratio for the hypothesis that the variable's coefficient is zero. For the jth coefficient, such a t-ratio is constructed as

$$t_j = b_j/\mathrm{SE}(b_j) \tag{1.13}$$

where SE is the estimated standard error of the coefficient. We take b from the last iteration of the Newton scheme and the standard errors of estimated parameters are derived from the Hessian matrix. Specifically, the variance of the parameter vector is the main diagonal of the negative inverse of the Hessian at the last iteration step. In the LOGIT function, we have already computed the Hessian `hinv` for the Newton iteration, and so we can quickly calculate the standard errors. We simply set the standard error of the jth coefficient to `Sqr(-hinv(j, j)`. t-ratios are then computed using Equation (1.13).

In the logit model, the t-ratio does not follow a t-distribution as in the classical linear regression. Rather, it is compared to a standard normal distribution. To get the p-value of a two-sided test, we exploit the symmetry of the normal distribution:

$$p\text{-value} = 2^*(1\text{-NORMSDIST(ABS}(t))) \tag{1.14}$$

The LOGIT function returns standard errors, t-ratios and p-values in lines two to four of the output if the logical value statistics is set to 1.

In a linear regression, we would report an R^2 as a measure of the overall goodness of fit. In nonlinear models estimated with maximum likelihood, one usually reports the Pseudo-R^2 suggested by McFadden (1974). It is calculated as 1 minus the ratio of the log-likelihood of the estimated model ($\ln L$) and the one of a restricted model that has only a constant ($\ln L_0$):

$$\text{Pseudo-}R^2 = 1 - \ln L / \ln L_0 \tag{1.15}$$

Like the standard R^2, this measure is bounded by zero and one. Higher values indicate a better fit. The log-likelihood $\ln L$ is given by the log-likelihood function of the last iteration of the Newton procedure, and is thus already available. Left to determine is the log-likelihood of the restricted model. With a constant only, the likelihood is maximized if the predicted default probability is equal to the mean default rate $\bar{y}$. This can be achieved by setting the constant equal to the logit of the default rate, i.e., $b_1 = \ln(\bar{y}/(1-\bar{y}))$. For the restricted log-likelihood, we then obtain:

$$\begin{aligned} \ln L_0 &= \sum_{i=1}^{N} y_i \ln(\Lambda(\mathbf{b}'\mathbf{x}_i)) + (1-y_i)\ln(1-\Lambda(\mathbf{b}'\mathbf{x}_i)) \\ &= \sum_{i=1}^{N} y_i \ln(\bar{y}) + (1-y_i)\ln(1-\bar{y}) \\ &= N \cdot [\bar{y}\ln(\bar{y}) + (1-\bar{y})\ln(1-\bar{y})] \end{aligned} \tag{1.16}$$

In the LOGIT function, this is implemented as follows:

```
'ln Likelihood of model with just a constant(lnL0)
 Dim lnL0 As Double, ybar as Double
 ybar = Application.WorksheetFunction.Average(y)
 lnL0 = N * (ybar * Log(ybar) + (1 - ybar) * Log(1 - ybar))
```

The two likelihoods used for the Pseudo-R^2 can also be used to conduct a statistical test of the entire model, i.e., test the null hypothesis that all coefficients except for the constant are zero. The test is structured as a likelihood ratio test:

$$\text{LR} = 2(\ln L - \ln L_0) \tag{1.17}$$

The more likelihood is lost by imposing the restriction, the larger the LR-statistic will be. The test statistic is distributed asymptotically chi-squared with the degrees of freedom equal to the number of restrictions imposed. When testing the significance of the entire regression, the number of restrictions equals the number of variables K minus 1. The function CHIDIST(test statistic, restrictions) gives the p-value of the LR test. The LOGIT command returns both the LR and its p-value.

Table 1.4 Output of the user-defined function LOGIT

b_1	b_2	...	b_K
SE(b_1)	SE(b_2)	...	SE(b_K)
$t_1 = b_1/\mathrm{SE}(b_1)$	$t_2 = b_2/\mathrm{SE}(b_2)$	...	$t_K = b_K/\mathrm{SE}(b_K)$
p-value(t_1)	p-value(t_2)	...	p-value(t_K)
Pseudo-R^2	# iterations	#N/A	#N/A
LR-test	p-value (LR)	#N/A	#N/A
log-likelihood (model)	log-likelihood(restricted)	#N/A	#N/A

The likelihoods ln L and ln L_0 are also reported, as is the number of iterations that was needed to achieve convergence. As a summary, the output of the LOGIT function is organized as shown in Table 1.4.

INTERPRETING REGRESSION STATISTICS

Applying the LOGIT function to our data from Table 1.3 with the logical values for constant and statistics both set to 1, we obtain the results reported in Table 1.5. Let us start with the statistics on the overall fit. The LR test (in J7, p-value in K7) implies that the logit regression is highly significant. The hypothesis 'the five ratios add nothing to the prediction' can be rejected with high confidence. From the three decimal points displayed in Table 1.5, we can deduce that the significance is better than 0.1%, but in fact it is almost indistinguishable from zero (being smaller than 10^{-36}). So we can trust that the regression model helps explain the default events.

Knowing that the model does predict defaults, we would like to know how well it does so. One usually turns to the R^2 for answering this question, but as in linear regression, setting up general quality standards in terms of a Pseudo-R^2 is difficult to impossible. A simple but often effective way of assessing the Pseudo-R^2 is to compare it with the ones from other models

Table 1.5 Application of the LOGIT command to a data set with information on defaults and five financial ratios (with statistics)

	C	D	E	F	G	H	I	J	K	L	M	N	O
1	De-fault y	WC/TA	RE/TA	EBIT/TA	ME/TL	S/TA		CONST	WC/TA	RE/TA	EBIT/TA	ME/TL	S/TA
2	0	0.50	0.31	0.04	0.96	0.33	b	-2.543	0.414	-1.454	-7.999	-1.594	0.620
3	0	0.55	0.32	0.05	1.06	0.33	SE(b)	0.266	0.572	0.229	2.702	0.323	0.349
4	0	0.45	0.23	0.03	0.80	0.25	t	-9.56	0.72	-6.34	-2.96	-4.93	1.77
5	0	0.31	0.19	0.03	0.39	0.25	p-value	0.000	0.469	0.000	0.003	0.000	0.076
6	0	0.45	0.22	0.03	0.79	0.28	Pseudo R² / # iter	0.222	12	#N/A	#N/A	#N/A	#N/A
7	0	0.46	0.22	0.03	1.29	0.32	LR-test / p-value	160.1	0.000	#N/A	#N/A	#N/A	#N/A
8	0	0.01	-0.03	0.01	0.11	0.25	lnL / lnL$_0$	-280.5	-360.6	#N/A	#N/A	#N/A	#N/A
9	0	-0.11	-0.12	0.03	0.15	0.32		{=LOGIT(C2:C4001,D2:H4001,1,1)}					
...	...	...	...	...	...	...		*(applies to J2:O8)*					
108	1	0.36	0.06	0.03	3.20	0.28							
...	...	...	...	...	...	...							
4001	1	0.07	-0.11	0.04	0.04	0.12							

estimated on similar data sets. From the literature, we know that scoring models for listed US corporates can achieve a Pseudo-R^2 of 35% and more.[5] This indicates that the way we have set up the model may not be ideal. In the final two sections of this chapter, we will show that the Pseudo-R^2 can indeed be increased by changing the way in which the five ratios enter the analysis.

When interpreting the Pseudo-R^2, it is useful to note that it does not measure whether the model correctly predicted default probabilities – this is infeasible because we do not know the true default probabilities. Instead, the Pseudo-R^2 (to a certain degree) measures whether we correctly predicted the defaults. These two aspects are related, but not identical. Take a borrower that defaulted although it had a low default probability: If the model was correct about this low default probability, it has fulfilled its goal, but the outcome happened to be out of line with this, thus reducing the Pseudo-R^2. In a typical loan portfolio, most default probabilities are in the range 0.05–5%. Even if we get each single default probability right, there will be many cases in which the observed data (=default) is not in line with the prediction (low default probability) and we therefore cannot hope to get a Pseudo-R^2 close to 1. A situation in which the Pseudo-R^2 would be close to 1 would look as follows: Borrowers fall into one of two groups; the first group is characterized by very low default probabilities (0.1% and less), the second group by very high ones (99.9% or more). This is clearly unrealistic for typical credit portfolios.

Turning to the regression coefficients, we can summarize that three out of the five ratios have coefficients b that are significant on the 1% level or better, i.e., their p-value is below 0.01. If we reject the hypothesis that one of these coefficients is zero, we can expect to err with a probability of less than 1%. Each of the three variables has a negative coefficient, meaning that increasing values of the variables reduce default probability. This is what we would expect: by economic reasoning, retained earnings, EBIT and market value of equity over liabilities should be inversely related to default probabilities. The constant is also highly significant. Note that we cannot derive the average default rate from the constant directly (this would only be possible if the constant were the only regression variable).

Coefficients on working capital over total assets and sales over total assets, by contrast, exhibit significance of only 46.9% and 7.6%, respectively. By conventional standards of statistical significance (5% is most common) we would conclude that these two variables are not or only marginally significant, and we would probably consider not using them for prediction.

If we simultaneously remove two or more variables based on their t-ratios, we should be aware of the possibility that variables might jointly explain defaults even though they are insignificant individually. To test this possibility statistically, we can run a second regression in which we exclude variables that were insignificant in the first run, and then conduct a likelihood ratio test.

This is shown in Table 1.6. Model 1 is the one we estimated in Table 1.5. In model 2, we remove the variables WC/TA and S/TA, i.e., we impose the restriction that the coefficients on these two variables are zero. The likelihood ratio test for the hypothesis $b_{\text{WC/TA}} = b_{\text{S/TA}} = 0$ is based on a comparison of the log-likelihoods $\ln L$ of the two models. It is constructed as

$$\text{LR} = 2[\ln L(\text{model 1}) - \ln L(\text{model 2})]$$

[5] See, e.g., Altman and Rijken (2004).

Table 1.6 Testing joint restrictions with a likelihood ratio test

	C	D	E	F	G	H	I	J	K	L	M	N	O
1	De-fault y	WC/TA	RE/TA	EBIT/TA	ME/TL	S/TA	**Model 1**	CONST	WC/TA	RE/TA	EBIT/TA	ME/TL	S/TA
2	0	0.50	0.31	0.04	0.96	0.33	b	-2.543	0.414	-1.454	-7.999	-1.594	0.620
3	0	0.55	0.32	0.05	1.06	0.33	SE(b)	0.266	0.572	0.229	2.702	0.323	0.349
4	0	0.45	0.23	0.03	0.80	0.25	t	-9.56	0.72	-6.34	-2.96	-4.93	1.77
5	0	0.31	0.19	0.03	0.39	0.25	p-value	0.000	0.469	0.000	0.003	0.000	0.076
6	0	0.45	0.22	0.03	0.79	0.28	Pseudo R^2 / # iter	0.222	12	#N/A	#N/A	#N/A	#N/A
7	0	0.46	0.22	0.03	1.29	0.32	LR-test / p-value	160.1	0.000	#N/A	#N/A	#N/A	#N/A
8	0	0.01	-0.03	0.01	0.11	0.25	$\ln L / \ln L_0$	-280.5	-360.6	#N/A	#N/A	#N/A	#N/A
9	0	-0.11	-0.12	0.03	0.15	0.32		{=LOGIT(C2:C4001,D2:H4001,1,1)}					
10	0	0.06	-0.11	0.04	0.41	0.29		*(applies to J2:O8)*					
11	0	0.05	-0.09	0.05	0.25	0.34	**Model 2**	CONST	RE/TA	EBIT/TA	ME/TL		
12	0	0.12	-0.11	0.04	0.46	0.31	b	-2.318	-1.420	-7.179	-1.616		
13	0	-0.04	0.27	0.05	0.59	0.21	SE(b)	0.236	0.229	2.725	0.325		
14	0	-0.04	0.25	0.03	0.33	0.21	t	-9.84	-6.21	-2.63	-4.97		
15	0	0.00	0.15	0.00	0.16	0.16	p-value	0.000	0.000	0.008	0.000		
16	0	-0.05	0.02	0.01	0.07	0.16	Pseudo R^2 / # iter	0.217	11	#N/A	#N/A		
17	0	-0.03	-0.01	0.02	0.10	0.18	LR-test / p-value	156.8	0.000	#N/A	#N/A		
18	0	-0.03	-0.04	0.02	0.09	0.19	$\ln L / \ln L_0$	-282.2	-360.6	#N/A	#N/A		
19	0	0.02	0.05	0.05	0.55	0.07		{=LOGIT(C2:C4001,E2:G4001,1,1)}					
20	0	0.02	0.08	0.03	0.60	0.09		*(applies to J12:M18)*					
21	0	0.03	0.11	0.04	0.79	0.10							
22	0	0.00	0.12	0.04	0.82	0.09	**LR- Test for b(WC/TA)=b (S/TA)=0 in model 1**						
23	0	0.04	0.14	0.02	0.63	0.12	LR	3.39	=2*(J8-J18)				
24	0	-0.05	0.15	0.04	0.89	0.15	DF	2					
25	0	-0.01	0.14	0.04	0.68	0.11	p-value	18.39%	=CHIDIST(J23,J24)				
...	...	...	...	...	...	...							
4001	1	0.07	-0.11	0.04	0.04	0.12							

and referred to a chi-squared distribution with two degrees of freedom because we impose two restrictions. In Table 1.6 the LR test leads to a value of 3.39 with a *p*-value of 18.39%. This means that if we add the two variables WC/TA and S/TA to model 2, there is a probability of 18.39% that we do not add explanatory power. The LR test thus confirms the results of the individual tests: individually and jointly, the two variables would be considered only marginally significant.

Where do we go from there? In model building, one often follows simple rules based on stringent standards of statistical significance, such as 'remove all variables that are not significant on a 5% level or better'. Such a rule would call to favor model 2. However, it is advisable to complement such rules with other tests. Notably, we might want to conduct an out-of-sample test of predictive performance as described in Chapter 8.

PREDICTION AND SCENARIO ANALYSIS

Having specified a scoring model, we want to use it for predicting probabilities of default. In order to do so, we calculate the score and then translate it into a default probability (see

Table 1.7 Predicting the probability of default

	C	D	E	F	G	H	I	J	K	L	M	N	O	P	Q
1	Default y	WC/ TA	RE/ TA	EBIT/ TA	ME/ TL	S/ TA		CONST	WC/ TA	RE/ TA	EBIT TA	ME/ TL	S/ TA		Default probability
2	0	0.50	0.31	0.04	0.96	0.33	b	-2.543	0.414	-1.454	-7.999	-1.594	0.620		1.16%
3	0	0.55	0.32	0.05	1.06	0.33		{=LOGIT(C2:C4001,D2:H4001,1,0)}							0.91%
4	0	0.45	0.23	0.03	0.80	0.25		*(applies to J2:O2)*							1.75%
5	0	0.31	0.19	0.03	0.39	0.25									3.24%
6	0	0.45	0.22	0.03	0.79	0.28									1.76%
7	0	0.46	0.22	0.03	1.29	0.32									0.82%
8	0	0.01	-0.03	0.01	0.11	0.25									7.10%
9	0	-0.11	-0.12	0.03	0.15	0.32		=1/(1+EXP(-(J$2+SUMPRODUCT(K$2:O$2,D9:H9))))							6.25%
...	...	...	...	...	...	...		*(can be copied into Q2:Q4001)*							...
108	1	0.36	0.06	0.03	3.20	0.28									0.05%
...	...	...	...	...	...	...									...
4001	1	0.07	-0.11	0.04	0.04	0.12									6.74%

Equations (1.1) and (1.4)):[6]

$$\text{Prob}(\text{Default}_i) = \Lambda(\text{Score}_i) = \Lambda(\mathbf{b}'\mathbf{x}_i) = \frac{1}{1+\exp(-\mathbf{b}'\mathbf{x}_i)} \tag{1.18}$$

In Table 1.7, we calculate default probabilities based on the model with all five ratios. For prediction, we just need the coefficients, so we can suppress the statistics by setting the associated logical value in the LOGIT function to zero.

We need to evaluate the score $\mathbf{b}'\mathbf{x}_i$. Our coefficient vector $\mathbf{b}$ is in J2:O2, and the ratio values contained in $\mathbf{x}_i$ can be found in columns D to H, with each row corresponding to one value of i. However, columns D to H do not contain a column of 1s that we had assumed when formulating Score $= \mathbf{b}'\mathbf{x}$. This is just a minor problem, though, as we can multiply the ratio values from columns D to H with the coefficients for those ratios (in K2:O2) and then add the constant given in J2. The default probability can thus be computed via (here for row 9)

=1/(1 + EXP(−(J$2 + SUMPRODUCT(K$2:O$2, D9:H9))))

The formula can be copied into the range Q2:Q4001 because we have fixed the reference to the coefficients with a dollar sign. The observations shown in the table contain just two defaulters (in row 108 and 4001), for the first of which we predict a default probability of 0.05%. This should not be cause for alarm though, for two reasons. First, a borrower can default even if its default probability is very low; second, even though a model may do a good job in predicting defaults on the whole (as evidenced by the LR-test of the entire model, for example) it can nevertheless fail at predicting some individual default probabilities.

[6] Note that in applying Equation (1.18) we assume that the sample's mean default probability is representative of the population's expected average default probability. If the sample upon which the scoring model is estimated is choice-based or stratified (e.g., overpopulated with defaulting firms) we would need to correct the constant b_0 before estimating the PDs; see Anderson (1972) or Scott and Wilde (1997).

Of course, the prediction of default probabilities is not confined to borrowers that are included in the sample used for estimation. On the contrary, scoring models are usually estimated with past data and then applied to current data.

As already used in a previous section, the sign of the coefficient directly reveals the directional effect of a variable. If the coefficient is positive, default probability increases if the value of the variable increases, and vice versa. If we want to say something about the magnitude of an effect, things get somewhat more complicated. Since the default probability is a nonlinear function of all variables and the coefficients, we cannot directly infer a statement such as 'if the coefficient is 1, the default probability will increase by 10% if the value of the variable increases by 10%'.

One way of gauging a variable's impact is to examine an individual borrower and then to compute the change in its default probability that is associated with variable changes. The easiest form of such a scenario analysis is a *ceteris paribus* (c.p.) analysis, in which we measure the impact of changing one variable while keeping the values of the other variables constant. Technically, what we do is change the variables, insert the changed values into the default probability formula (1.18) and compare the result to the default probability before the change.

In Table 1.8, we show how to build such a scenario analysis for one borrower. The estimated coefficients are in row 4 and the ratios of the borrower in row 7. For convenience, we include a 1 for the constant. We calculate the default probability (cell C9) very similarly to the way we did in Table 1.7.

Table 1.8 Scenario analysis – how default probability changes with changes in explanatory variables

	A	B	C	D	E	F	G	H
1		CONST	WC/TA	RE/TA	EBIT/TA	ME/TL	S/TA	
2								
3	**Estimated model**							
4	Coefficients	-2.543	0.414	-1.454	-7.999	-1.594	0.620	
5								
6	**Data for borrower under analysis**							
7	Ratio values	1	0.50	0.31	0.04	0.96	0.33	
8								
9		=> Default prob:	1.16%	=1/(1+EXP(-SUMPRODUCT(B4:G4,B7:G7)))				
10								
11	**Scenario analysis: Default prob's for c.p. changes of individual variables**							
12	Scenario values for variables							
13	better		0.40	0.40	0.08	1.00	0.20	
14	worse		0.60	0.20	-0.02	0.50	0.40	
15								
16	Scenario default probability							
17	better		1.11%	1.01%	0.87%	1.08%	1.07%	
18	worse		1.21%	1.35%	1.91%	2.37%	1.21%	
19			C18: =1/(1+EXP(-(SUMPRODUCT($B$4:$G$4,$B$7:$G$7)+ C$4*(C14-C$7))))					
20			*(can be copied into C17:B18)*					

In rows 13 and 14, we state scenario values for the five variables, and in rows 17 and 18 we compute the associated default probabilities. Recall that we change just the value of one variable. When calculating the score $\mathbf{b}'\mathbf{x}_i$ by multiplying $\mathbf{b}$ and $\mathbf{x}_i$, there is only one element in $\mathbf{x}_i$ affected. We can handle this by computing the score $\mathbf{b}'\mathbf{x}_i$ based on the status quo, and then correcting it for the change assumed for a particular scenario. When changing the value of the second variable from x_{i2} to x_{i2}^*, for example, the new default probability is obtained as

$$\text{Prob}(\text{Default}_i) = \Lambda(\mathbf{b}'\mathbf{x}_i^*) = \Lambda(\mathbf{b}'\mathbf{x}_i + b_2(x_{i2}^* - x_{i2})) \tag{1.19}$$

In cell C18, this is implemented via

```
=1/(1+EXP(−(SUMPRODUCT($B$4:$G$4,$B$7:$G$7)+C$4*(C14-C$7))))
```

We can directly copy this formula to the other cells C17:G17. For example, if the firm manages to increase its profitability EBIT/TA from −2% to 8%, its default probability will move from 1.91% to 0.87%. We could also use the Goal seek functionality or the Solver to find answers to questions such as ‘what change in the variable ME/TL is required to produce a default probability of 1%?’.

An analysis like the one conducted here can therefore be very useful for firms that want to reduce their default probability to some target level, and would like to know how to achieve this goal. It can also be helpful in dealing with extraordinary items. For example, if an extraordinary event has reduced the profitability from its long-run mean to a very low level, the estimated default probability will increase. If we believe that this reduction is only temporary, we could base our assessment on the default probability that results from replacing the currently low EBIT/TA by its assumed long-run average. For a discussion of the predictive quality of scoring models during the financial crisis, see Box 1.1.

Box 1.1 Credit scores and the subprime crisis

The 2007–2008 financial crisis started when losses on defaulted US mortgage loans mounted. Since credit scores play a major role in mortgage loan application decisions, it is important to examine whether credit scoring systems failed to reveal the true risk of borrowers.

Research by Demyanyk and Van Hemert (2010) shows that a statistical analysis of default rates would have revealed that loan quality decreased from 2002 onwards. This decrease, however, was not reflected in the credit scores that were used in the industry. So why did the market not react to the warning signals, and why did credit scores fail to send out such signals? To some extent, mortgage financers seem to have been aware of the increased risk because mortgage rates became more sensitive to risk characteristics. On the other hand, overall mortgage rates were too low, especially for high-risk, subprime borrowers. Although the data showed that riskiness increased over time, the true magnitude of the risks was concealed by rising house prices. As long as house prices were rising, borrowers with financial difficulties could resell their house or refinance themselves because the increase in the value of their houses increased their borrowing capacity.

This does not answer the question of why credit scores failed to indicate the increased risk. Rajan, Seru and Vig (2009) put forward the following explanation: In

Box 1.1 (Continued)

the years before 2007, more and more mortgage loans were securitized, i.e., mortgage financers did not keep the loans on their books but sold them to the capital market. In order to better communicate the risks of the loans to potential investors, mortgage financers increasingly relied on verifiable hard information summarized by credit scores. Soft information, e.g., obtained through an assessment of an applicant's future expenses or his/her probability of job loss, played a lesser and lesser role. This decreased the probability that applicants with negative soft information were declined. Such a structural change can severely affect the performance of scoring models. Scoring functions were estimated based on past data in which soft information played an important role. They were then applied to loan applications for which this was no longer the case. Though their scores remained stable or even improved, average risk of high-risk borrowers increased because they included more and more borrowers with negative soft information. The lesson to be learned is not so much that scoring models performed badly because they missed some pieces of information. Inevitably, models will miss some information. Missing information becomes dangerous if the importance of this information changes over time. A similar effect arises if fraudulent behavior proliferates. If the percentage of applicants who manage to conceal negative information increases, scores may fail to capture an increase of risk. (For an analysis of fraud in mortgage applications, see for example Fitch (2007).)

Several other factors may have been at work in keeping scores high (see Hughes (2008) for an overview). Here, we only want to point out that it does not require fraud to boost one's credit score. Retail scores (see `www.myfico.com` for information on a score widely used in the US) often include information on the payment history and the proportion of credit lines used. Several actions that do not improve credit quality can lead to an improvement of the score: Increase your credit card limit even though there is no need for it, have an extra credit card that you do not use or ask another person to be added as user to that person's credit card. Again, it is conceivable that the increased use of credit scores increased the number of people who legally gamed the system.

To conclude, it is important to note that the meaning and quality of a score can change over time. It can change with the cycle, i.e., when rising house prices mask low credit quality. It can also change because the use of a scoring system changes people's behavior.

TREATING OUTLIERS IN INPUT VARIABLES

Explanatory variables in scoring models often contain a few extreme values. They can reflect genuinely exceptional situations of borrowers, but they can also be due to data errors, conceptual problems in defining a variable or accounting discretion.

In any case, extreme values can have a large influence on coefficient estimates, which could impair the overall quality of the scoring model. A first step in approaching the problem is to examine the distribution of the variables. In Table 1.9, we present several descriptive statistics for our five ratios. Excel provides the functions for the statistics we are interested

Table 1.9 Descriptive statistics for the explanatory variables in the logit model

	H	I	J	K	L	M	N	O	P
1	S/ TA			WC/ TA	RE/ TA	EBIT/ TA	ME/ TL	S/ TA	*Formulae for column O, can be copied in columns K to L*
2	0.33		Average	0.14	0.21	0.05	1.95	0.30	=AVERAGE(H$2:H$4001)
3	0.33		Median	0.12	0.22	0.05	1.14	0.26	=MEDIAN(H$2:H$4001)
4	0.25		Stdev	0.17	0.33	0.03	2.99	0.21	=STDEV(H$2:H$4001)
5	0.25		Skewness	-1.01	-2.55	-4.84	7.75	4.48	=SKEW(H$2:H$4001)
6	0.28		Kurtosis	17.68	17.44	86.00	103.13	71.22	=KURT(H$2:H$4001)
7	0.32		Extreme values / Percentiles						
8	0.25		Min	-2.24	-3.31	-0.59	0.02	0.04	=MIN(H$2:H$4001)
9	0.32		0.50%	-0.33	-1.72	-0.05	0.05	0.06	=PERCENTILE(H$2:H$4001,$J9)
10	0.29		1%	-0.17	-0.92	-0.02	0.08	0.07	
11	0.34		5%	-0.06	-0.25	0.02	0.22	0.10	
12	0.31		95%	0.44	0.65	0.09	5.60	0.68	
13	0.21		99%	0.58	0.90	0.12	14.44	1.05	
14	0.21		99.50%	0.63	0.94	0.13	18.94	1.13	
15	0.16		Max	0.77	1.64	0.20	60.61	5.01	=MAX(H$2:H$4001)

in: arithmetic means (AVERAGE) and medians (MEDIAN), standard deviations (STDEV), skewness (SKEW) and excess kurtosis (KURT),[7] percentiles (PERCENTILE) along with minima (MIN) and maxima (MAX).

A common benchmark for judging an empirical distribution is the normal distribution. The reason is not that there is *a priori* a reason why the variables we use should follow a normal distribution but rather that the normal serves as a good point of reference because it describes a distribution in which extreme events have been averaged out.[8]

A good indicator for the existence of outliers is the excess kurtosis. The normal distribution has excess kurtosis of zero, but the variables used here have very high values ranging from 17.4 to 103.1. A positive excess kurtosis indicates that, compared to the normal, there are relatively many observations far away from the mean. The variables are also skewed, meaning that extreme observations are concentrated on the left (if skewness is negative) or on the right (if skewness is positive) of the distribution.

In addition, we can look at percentiles. For example, a normal distribution has the property that 99% of all observations are within ± 2.58 standard deviations of the mean. For the variable ME/TL, this would lead to the interval $[-5.77, 9.68]$. The empirical 99% confidence interval, however, is $[0.05, 18.94]$, i.e., wider and shifted to the right, confirming the information we acquire by looking at the skewness and kurtosis of ME/TL. Looking at WC/TA, we see that 99% of all values are in the interval $[-0.33, 0.63]$, which is roughly in line with what we would expect under a normal distribution, namely $[-0.30, 0.58]$. In the case of WC/TA, the outlier problem is thus confined to a small subset of observations. This is most evident by looking at the minimum of WC/TA: it is -2.24, which is very far away from the bulk of the observations (it is 14 standard deviations away from the mean, and 11.2 standard deviations away from the 0.5% percentile).

[7] Excess kurtosis is defined as kurtosis minus 3.

[8] The relevant theorem from statistics is the central limit theorem, which says that if we sample from any probability distribution with finite mean and finite variance, the sample mean will tend to the normal distribution as we increase the number of observations to infinity.

Table 1.10 Exemplifying winsorization for the variable WC/TA

	A	B	C	D	E	F
1	WC/TA	WC/TA winsorized				
2	0.501	0.501		Level	2%	
3	0.548	0.521		Lower bound	-0.113	=PERCENTILE(A2:A4001,E2)
4	0.451	0.451		Upper bound	0.521	=PERCENTILE(A2:A4001,1-E2)
5	0.307	0.307				
6	0.447	0.447	=MAX(MIN(A6,E$4),E$3)			
7	0.458	0.458	*(can be copied to B2:B4001)*			
8	0.006	0.006				
9	-0.115	-0.113				
10	0.061	0.061				
11	0.051	0.051				
...	...	....				
4001	0.066	0.066				

Having identified the existence of extreme observations, a clinical inspection of the data is advisable because it can lead to the discovery of correctable data errors. In many applications, however, this will not lead to a complete elimination of outliers; even data sets that are 100% correct can exhibit bizarre distributions. Accordingly, it is useful to have a procedure that controls the influence of outliers in an automated and objective way.

A commonly used technique applied for this purpose is *winsorization*, which means that extreme values are pulled to less extreme ones. One specifies a certain winsorization level α; values below the α-percentile of the variable's distribution are set equal to the α-percentile, values above the $1-\alpha$ percentile are set equal to the $1-\alpha$ percentile. Common values for alpha are 0.5%, 1%, 2% or 5%. The winsorization level can be set separately for each variable in accordance with its distributional characteristics, providing a flexible and easy way of dealing with outliers without discarding observations.

Table 1.10 exemplifies the technique by applying it to the variable WC/TA. We start with a blank worksheet containing only the variable WC/TA in column A. The winsorization level is entered in cell E2. The lower percentile associated with this level is found by applying the PERCENTILE() function to the range of the variable, which is done in E3. Analogously, we get the upper percentile for one minus the winsorization level.

The winsorization itself is carried out in column B. We compare the original value of column A with the estimated percentile values; if the original value is between the percentile values, we keep it. If it is below the lower percentile, we set it to this percentile's value; likewise for the upper percentile. This can be achieved by combining a maximum function with a minimum function. For cell B6, we would write

=MAX(MIN(A6, E$4), E$3)

The maximum condition pulls low values up, the minimum function pulls large values down.

We can also write a function that performs winsorization and requires as arguments the variable range and the winsorization level. It might look as follows:

```
Function WINSOR(x As Range, level As Double)

Dim N As Integer, i As Integer
N = x.Rows.Count

'Obtain percentiles
Dim low, up
low = Application.WorksheetFunction.Percentile(x, level)
up = Application.WorksheetFunction.Percentile(x, 1 - level)

'Pull x to percentiles
Dim result
ReDim result(1 To N, 1 To 1)
For i = 1 To N
    result(i, 1) = Application.WorksheetFunction.Max(x(i), low)
    result(i, 1) = Application.WorksheetFunction.Min(result(i, 1), up)
Next i

WINSOR = result

End Function
```

The function works in much the same way as the spreadsheet calculations in Table 1.10. After reading the number of observations *N* from the input range *x*, we calculate lower and upper percentiles and then use a loop to winsorize each entry of the data range. WINSOR is an array function that has as many output cells as the data range that is inputted into the function. The winsorized values in column B of Table 1.10 would be obtained by entering

=WINSOR(A2:A4002,0.02)

in B2:B4001 and confirming with [ctrl]+[shift]+[enter].

If there are several variables as in our example, we would winsorize each variable separately. In doing so, we could consider different winsorization levels for different variables. As we saw above, there seem to be fewer outliers in WC/TA than in ME/TA, and so we could use a higher winsorization level for ME/TA. We could also choose to winsorize asymmetrically, i.e., apply different levels to the lower and the upper side.

Below we present skewness and kurtosis of our five variables after applying a 1% winsorization level to all variables:

	WC/TA	RE/TA	EBIT/TA	ME/TL	S/TA
Skewness	0.63	−0.95	0.14	3.30	1.68
Kurt	0.01	3.20	1.10	13.48	3.42

Table 1.11 Pseudo-R^2s for different data treatments

	Pseudo-R^2 (%)
Original data	22.2
Winsorized at 1%	25.5
Winsorized at 1% + log of ME/TL	34.0
Original but log of ME/TL	34.9

Both skewness and kurtosis are now much closer to zero. Note that both statistical characteristics are still unusually high for ME/TL. This might motivate a higher winsorization level for ME/TL, but there is an alternative: ME/TL has many extreme values to the right of the distribution. If we take the logarithm of ME/TL, we also pull them to the left, but we do not blur the differences between those beyond a certain threshold as we do in winsorization. The logarithm of ME/TL (after winsorization at the 1% level) has skewness of −0.11 and kurtosis of 0.18, suggesting that the logarithmic transformation works for ME/TL in terms of outliers.

The proof of the pudding is in the regression. Examine in Table 1.11 how the Pseudo-R^2 of our logit regression depends on the type of data treatment.

For our data, winsorizing increases the Pseudo-R^2 by three percentage points from 22.2% to 25.5%. This is a handsome improvement, but taking logarithms of ME/TL is much more important: the Pseudo-R^2 subsequently jumps to around 34%. And one can do even better by using the original data and taking the logarithm of ME/TL rather than winsorizing first and then taking the logarithm.

We could go on and take the logarithm of the other variables. We will not present details here, but instead just mention how this could be accomplished. If a variable takes negative values (this is the case with EBIT/TL, for example), we cannot directly apply the logarithm as we did in the case of ME/TL. Also, a variable might exhibit negative skewness (an example is again EBIT/TL). Applying the logarithm would increase the negative skewness rather than reduce it, which may not be what we want to achieve. There are ways around these problems. We could, for example, transform EBIT/TA by computing −ln(1 − EBIT/TA) and then proceed similarly for the other variables.

As a final word of caution, note that one should guard against data mining. If we fish long enough for a good winsorization or similar treatment, we might end up with a set of treatments that works very well for the historical data on which we optimized it. It may not, however, serve to improve the prediction of future defaults. A simple strategy against data mining is to be restrictive in the choice of treatments. Instead of experimenting with all possible combinations of individual winsorization levels and functional transformations (logarithmic or other), we might restrict ourselves to a few choices that are common in the literature or that seem sensible based on a descriptive analysis of the data.

CHOOSING THE FUNCTIONAL RELATIONSHIP BETWEEN THE SCORE AND EXPLANATORY VARIABLES

In the scoring model (1.1), we assume that the score is linear in each explanatory variable x: $\text{Score}_i = \mathbf{b}'\mathbf{x}_i$. In the previous section, however, we have already seen that a logarithmic transformation of a variable can greatly improve the fit. There, the transformation was motivated as an effective way of treating extreme observations, but it may also be the right one from a conceptual perspective. For example, consider the case where one of our variables is a default probability assessment, denoted by p_i. It could be a historical default rate for the segment of borrower i, or it could originate from models like the ones we discuss in Chapters 2 and 4. In such a case, the appropriate way of entering the variable would be the logit of p_i, which is the inverse of the logistic distribution function:

$$x = \Lambda^{-1}(p) = \ln(p/(1-p)) \quad \Rightarrow \quad \Lambda(x) = p \tag{1.20}$$

because this guarantees that the default prediction equals the default probability we input into the regression.

With logarithmic or logit transformations, the relationship between a variable and the default probability is still monotonic: for a positive coefficient, a higher value of the variable leads to a higher default probability. In practice, however, we can also encounter non-monotonic relationships. A good example is sales growth: Low sales growth may be due to high competition or an unsuccessful product policy, and correspondingly indicate high default risk. High sales growth is often associated with high cash requirements (for advertising and inventories), or may have been bought at the expense of low margins; thus, high sales growth can be symptomatic of high default risk, too. All combined, there might be a U-shaped relationship between default risk and sales growth. To capture this non-monotonicity, one could enter the square of sales growth together with sales growth itself:

$$\text{Prob}(\text{Default}_i) = \Lambda\left(b_1 + b_2 \text{ Sales growth}_i + b_3(\text{Sales growth}_i)^2 + \ldots + b_K x_{iK}\right) \tag{1.21}$$

Similarly, we could try to find appropriate functional representations for variables where we suspect that a linear relation is not sufficient. But how can we guarantee that we detect all relevant cases and then find an appropriate transformation? One way is to examine the relationships between default rates and explanatory variables separately for each variable. Now, how can we go about visualizing these relationships? We can classify the variables into ranges, and then examine the average default rate within a single range. Ranges could be defined by splitting the domain of a variable into parts of equal length. With this procedure, we are likely to get a very uneven distribution of observations across ranges, which could impair the analysis. A better classification would be to define the ranges such that they contain an equal number of observations. This can easily be achieved by defining the ranges through percentiles. We first define the number of ranges M that we want to examine. The first range includes all observations with values below the $(1/M)$ percentile; the second includes all observations with values above the $(1/M)$ percentile but below the $(2/M)$ percentile and so forth.

For the variable ME/TL, the procedure is exemplified in Table 1.12. We fix the number of ranges in F1, and then use this number to define the alpha values for the percentiles (in D5:D24). In column E, we use this information and the function PERCENTILE(x, alpha) to determine the associated percentile value of our variable. In doing so, we use a minimum condition to ascertain that the alpha value is not above 1. This is necessary because the summation process in column L can yield values slightly above 1 (Excel rounds to 15 digit precision).

The number of defaults within a current range is found recursively. We count the number of defaults up to (and including) the current range, and then subtract the number of defaults

Table 1.12 Default rate for percentiles of ME/TL

	A	B	C	D	E	F	G	H	I
1	Default	ME/TL		Number of ranges:		20			
2	0	0.96							
3	0	1.06		alpha	Range bound	Defaults	Obs	Default rate	
4	0	0.80							
5	0	0.39		5%	0.22	46	200	23.0%	
6	0	0.79		10%	0.33	9	200	4.5%	
7	0	1.29		15%	0.44	5	200	2.5%	
8	0	0.11		20%					
9	0	0.15		25%					
10	0	0.41		30%					
11	0	0.25		35%					
12	0	0.46		40%					
13	0	0.59		45%					
14	0	0.33		50%					
15	0	0.16		55%	1.32	2	200		
16	0	0.07		60%	1.50	1	2		
17	0	0.10		65%	1.71	0	2		
18	0	0.09		70%	1.95	4	2		
19	0	0.55		75%	2.24	2	2		
20	0	0.60		80%	2.65	0	2		
21	0	0.79		85%	3.21	1	2		
22	0	0.82		90%	3.89	0	2		
23	0	0.63		95%	5.60	0	2		
24	0	0.89		100%	60.61	1	2		
25	0	0.68							
26	0	0.58							
...	...	...							
4001	1	0.04							

```
D5: =D4+1/F$1
E5: =PERCENTILE(B$2:B$4001,MIN(1,D5))
F5: =SUMIF(B$2:B$4001,"<="&E5,A$2:A$4001)-SUM(F4:F$4)
G5: =COUNTIF(B$2:B$4001,"<="&E5)-SUM(G4:G$4)
H5: =F5/G5
```

Can be copied down into range J5:N24

that are contained in the ranges below. For cell F5, this can be achieved through

$$= \text{SUMIF(B\$2:B\$4001, ``<="\& E5, A\$2:A\$4001)} - \text{SUM(F4:F\$4)}$$

where E5 contains the upper bound of the current range; defaults are in column A, and the variable ME/TL in column B. Summing over the default variable yields the number of defaults because defaults are coded as 1. In an analogous way, we determine the number of observations. We just replace SUMIF by COUNTIF.

What does the graph tell us? Apparently, it is only for very low values of ME/TL that a change in this variable impacts default risk. Above the 20% percentile, there are many ranges with zero default rates, and the ones that see defaults are scattered in a way that does not suggest any systematic relationship. Moving from the 20% percentile upward has virtually no effect on default risk, even though the variable moves largely from 0.5 to 60. This is perfectly in line with the results of the previous section where we saw that taking the logarithm of ME/TL greatly improves the fit relative to a regression in which ME/TL entered linearly. If we enter ME/TL linearly, a change from ME/TL = 60 to ME/TL = 59.5 has the same effect on the score as a change from ME/TL = 0.51 to ME/TL = 0.01 – contrary to what we see in the data. The logarithmic transformation performs better because it reduces the effect of a given absolute change in ME/TL for high levels of ME/TL.

Thus, the examination of univariate relationships between default rates and explanatory variables can give us valuable hints as to which transformation is appropriate. In the case of ML/TE, it supports the logarithmic one; in others it may support a polynomial representation like the one we mentioned above in the sales growth example.

Often, however, which transformation to choose may not be clear, and we may want to have an automated procedure that can be run without us having to look carefully at a set of graphs first. To such end, we can employ the following procedure. We first run an analysis like in Table 1.12. Instead of entering the original values of the variable into the logit analysis, we use the default rate of the range to which they are assigned. That is, we use a data-driven, non-parametric transformation. Note that before entering the default rate in the logit regression, we would apply the logit transformation (1.20) to it.

We will not show how to implement this transformation in a spreadsheet. With many variables, it would involve a lot of similar calculations, making it a better idea to set up a user-defined function that maps a variable into a default rate for a chosen number of ranges. Such a function might look like this:

```
Function XTRANS(defaultdata As Range, x As Range, numranges As Integer)
Dim bound, numdefaults, obs, defrate, N, j, defsum, obssum, i
ReDim bound(1 To numranges), numdefaults(1 To numranges)
ReDim obs(1 To numranges), defrate(1 To numranges)

N = x.Rows.Count

'Determining number of defaults, observations and default rates for
ranges
For j = 1 To numranges

   bound(j) = Application.WorksheetFunction.Percentile(x, j / numranges)

   numdefaults(j) = Application.WorksheetFunction.SumIf(x, "<=" & _
                          bound(j), defaultdata) - defsum
   defsum = defsum + numdefaults(j)

   obs(j) = Application.WorksheetFunction.CountIf(x, "<=" & bound(j)) _
            - obssum
   obssum = obssum + obs(j)

   defrate(j) = numdefaults(j) / obs(j)
Next j

'Assigning range default rates in logistic transformation
Dim transform
ReDim transform(1 To N, 1 To 1)
```

```
For i = 1 To N
    j = 1
    While x(i) - bound(j) > 0
        j = j + 1
    Wend
    transform(i, 1) = Application.WorksheetFunction.Max(defrate(j), _
                        0.0000001)
    transform(i, 1) = Log(transform(i, 1) / (1 - transform(i, 1)))
Next i

XTRANS = transform
End Function
```

After dimensioning the variables, we loop through each range, `j=1` to `numranges`. It is the analog of what we did in range D5:H24 of Table 1.12. That is why we see the same commands: SUMIF to get the number of defaults below a certain percentile, and COUNTIF to get the number of observations below a certain percentile.

In the second loop over $i = 1$ to N, we perform the data transformation. For each observation, we search through the percentiles until we have the one that corresponds to our current observation (`Do While ... Loop`) and then assign the default rate. In the process, we set the minimum default rate to an arbitrarily small value of 0.0000001. Otherwise, we could not apply the logit transformation in cases where the default rate is zero.

To illustrate the effects of the transformation, we set the number of ranges to 20, apply the function XTRANS to each of our five ratios and run a logit analysis with the transformed ratios. This leads to a Pseudo-R^2 of 47.8% – much higher than we received with the original data, winsorization or logarithmic transformation (see Table 1.13).

The number of ranges that we choose will depend on the size of the data set and the average default rate. For a given number of ranges, the precision with which we can measure their default rates will tend to increase with the number of defaults contained in the data set. For large data sets, we might end up choosing 50 ranges while smaller ones may require only 10 or less.

Note that the transformation also deals with outliers. If we choose M ranges, the distribution of a variable beyond its $1/M$ and $1 - 1/M$ percentiles does not matter. As in the case of outlier treatments, we should also be aware of potential data mining problems. The transformation introduces a data-driven flexibility in our analysis, and so we may end up fitting the data without really explaining the underlying default probabilities. The higher the number of ranges, the more careful we should be about this.

Table 1.13 Pseudo-R^2s for different data treatments and transformations

	Pseudo-R^2 (%)
Original data	22.2
Winsorized at 1%	25.5
Winsorized at 1% + log of ME/TL	34.0
Original but log of ME/TL	34.3
Transformation based on default rates	47.8

CONCLUDING REMARKS

In this chapter, we addressed several steps in building a scoring model. The order in which we presented these steps was chosen for reasons of exposition; it is not necessarily the order in which we would approach a problem. A possible frame for building a model might look like as follows:

1. From economic reasoning, compile a set of variables that you believe to capture factors that might be relevant for default prediction. To give an example: the Factor 'Profitability' might be captured by EBIT/TA, EBITDA/TA or Net Income/Equity.
2. Examine the univariate distribution of these variables (skewness, kurtosis, quantiles. . .) and their univariate relationship to default rates.
3. From step 2, determine whether there is a need to treat outliers and nonlinear functional forms. If yes, choose one or several ways of treating them (winsorization, transformation to default rates. . .)
4. Based on steps 1 to 3, run regressions in which each of the factors you believe to be relevant is represented by at least one variable. To select just one variable out of a group that represents the same factor, first consider the one with the highest Pseudo-R^2 in univariate logit regressions.[9] Run regressions with the original data and with the treatments applied in step 3 to see what differences they make.
5. Rerun the regression with insignificant variables from step 4 removed; test the joint significance of the removed variables.

Of course, there is more to model building than going through a small number of steps. Having finished step 5, we may want to fine-tune some decisions that were made in between (e.g., the way in which a variable was defined). We may also reconsider major decisions (such as the treatment of outliers). In the end, model building is an art as much as a science.

NOTES AND LITERATURE

In the econometrics literature, the logit models we looked at are subsumed under the heading of 'binary response or qualitative response models'. Statisticians, on the other hand, often speak of generalized linear models. Expositions can be found in most econometrics textbooks, e.g., Greene, W.H., 2003, *Econometric Analysis*, Prentice Hall. For corrections when the sample's mean probability of default differs from the population's expected average default probability, see Anderson, J.A., 1972, Separate sample logistic discrimination, *Biometrika* 59, 19–35, and Scott, A.J. and Wild, C.J., 1997, Fitting regression models to case-control data by maximum likelihood, *Biometrika* 84, 57–71.

For detailed descriptions of scoring models developed by a rating agency, see: Falkenstein, E., 2000, RiskCalc for private companies. Moody' default model. *Moody's Investor Service*; Sobehart, J., Stein, R., Mikityanskaya, V. and Li, L., 2000, Moody's public firm risk model: A hybrid approach to modeling short term default risk. *Moody's Investor Service*; Dwyer, D., Kocagil, A. and Stein, R., 2004, *Moody's KMV RiskCalc v3.1 model*, Moody's KMV.

Two academic papers that describe the estimation of a logit scoring model are Shumway, T. 2001, Forecasting bankruptcy more accurately: A simple hazard model, *Journal of Business* 74, 101–124 and Altman, R. and Rijken, H., 2004, How rating agencies achieve rating stability, *Journal of Banking and*

[9] For each variable, run a univariate logit regression in which default is explained by only this variable; the Pseudo-R^2s from these regressions give a good indication on the relative explanatory power of individual variables.

Finance 28, 2679–2714. Both papers make use of the financial ratios proposed by Altman, E., 1968, Financial ratios, discriminant analysis and the prediction of corporate bankruptcy, *Journal of Finance* 23, 589–609.

Details on the relationship between scoring models and the subprime crisis are given by Demyanyk, Y. and Van Hemert, O., 2010, Understanding the subprime mortgage crisis, *The Review of Financial Studies*, forthcoming, as well as Rajan, U., Seru, A. and Vig, V., 2009, The failure of models that predict failure: Distance, incentives and defaults, Working Paper. In 2007, Fitch published an analysis by Pendley, M., Costello, G. and Kelsch, M., 2007, The impact of poor underwriting practices and fraud in subprime RMBS performance, *Fitch Special Report*.

For more details on McFadden's Pseudo-R^2, see McFadden, D., 1974, The measurement of urban travel demand, *Journal of Public Economics* 3, 303–328.

APPENDIX

Logit and probit

We have described the estimation of scoring model with logit. A common alternative choice is the probit model, which replaces the logistic distribution in (1.4) by the standard normal distribution. Experience suggests that the choice of the distribution is not crucial in most settings; predicted default probabilities are fairly close. Note, however, that the estimated coefficients differ significantly because the two distributions have different variances. When comparing logit and probit models estimated on the same data set, you should compare default probability estimates or other information that is not affected by scaling.

Marginal effects

Scenario analysis is an intuitive way of understanding the impact of individual variables. An analytical approach would be to calculate the *marginal effect* of a variable. In linear models the marginal effect is equal to the coefficient. In the logit model, however, life is more difficult. The marginal effect is given by the coefficient multiplied by a scale factor:

$$\text{Marginal effect}_i = \text{Scale factor}_i \times b_i = \Lambda(\mathbf{b}'\mathbf{x}_i)(1 - \Lambda(\mathbf{b}'\mathbf{x}_i)) \times b_i \tag{1.22}$$

This scale factor varies with each observation – that is, for each row of our data set we have a different scale factor. To make a statement about average marginal effects, we can use the mean of the x variables to calculate (1.22). Alternatively, we can calculate the scale factor for every observation and then take the average of that.

2

The Structural Approach to Default Prediction and Valuation

Structural models of default risk are cause-and-effect models. From economic reasoning, we identify conditions under which we expect borrowers to default and then estimate the probability that these conditions come about to obtain an estimate of the default probability.

For limited liability companies, default is expected to occur if the asset value (i.e., the value of the firm) is not sufficient to cover the firm's liabilities. Why should this be so? From the identity

$$\text{Asset value} = \text{Value of equity} + \text{Value of liabilities}$$

and the rule that equity holders receive the residual value of the firm, it follows that the value of equity is negative if the asset value is smaller than the value of liabilities. If you have something with negative value, and you can give it away at no cost, you are more than willing to do so. This is what equity holders are expected to do. They exercise the walk-away option that they have because of limited liability and leave the firm to the creditors. As the asset value is smaller than the value of liabilities, creditors' claims are not fully covered, meaning that the firm is in default. The walk-away option can be priced with standard approaches from option pricing theory.

This is why structural models are also called option-theoretic or contingent-claim models. Another common name is Merton models, because Robert C. Merton (1974) first applied option theory to the problem of valuing a firm's liabilities in the presence of default and limited liability.

In this chapter, we first explain how structural models can be used for estimating default probabilities and valuing a firm's liabilities. We then show how to implement structural models in the spirit of the original Merton model. The focus is on the estimation of default probabilities rather than valuation. Then we will implement a widely used alternative model: the CreditGrades approach. With this model we conduct a case study of Lehman Brothers prior to its default in September 2008.

DEFAULT AND VALUATION IN A STRUCTURAL MODEL

The basic premise of structural models is that default occurs if the value of the assets falls below a critical value associated with the firm's liabilities. To clarify the issues, we consider the simple set-up examined by Merton (1974): the firm's liabilities consist of just one zero-coupon bond with principal L maturing in T. There are no payments up until T, and equity holders will wait until T before they decide whether to default or not. (If they defaulted before T they would forego the chance of benefiting from an increase of the asset value). Accordingly, the default probability is then the probability that, at time T, the value of the assets is below the value of the liabilities.

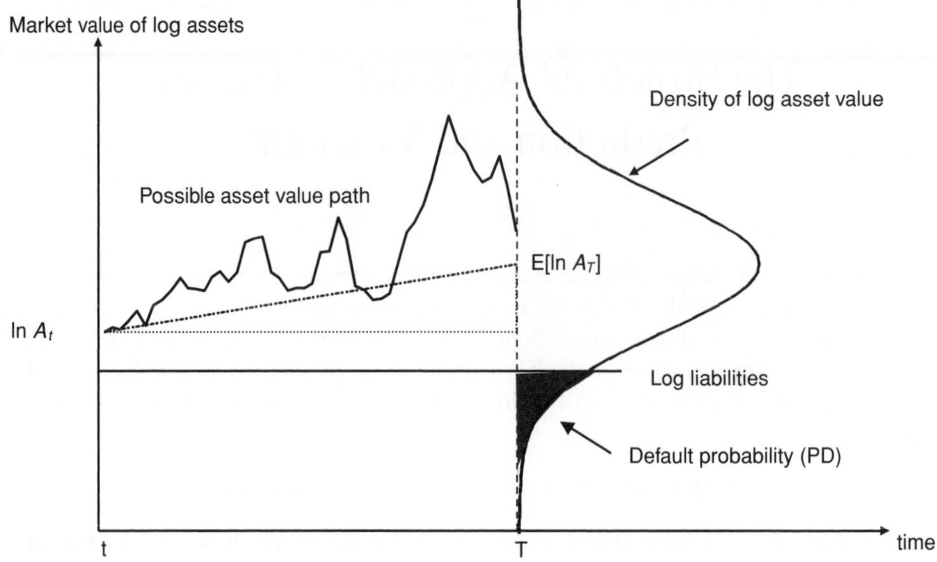

Figure 2.1 Default probability in the Merton model

What is required to determine this probability? In Figure 2.1 we get the firm's liability from the balance sheet (hoping that it is not manipulated). We then need to specify the probability distribution of the asset value at maturity T. A common assumption is that the value of financial assets follows a lognormal distribution, i.e., that the logarithm of the asset value is normally distributed. We denote the per annum variance of the log asset value changes by σ^2. The expected per annum change in log asset values is denoted $\mu - \sigma^2/2$, where μ is the drift parameter.[1] Let t denote today. The log asset value in T thus follows a normal distribution with the following parameters:

$$\ln A_T \sim N\left(\ln A_t + (\mu - \sigma^2/2)(T-t), \quad \sigma^2(T-t)\right) \tag{2.1}$$

If we know L, A_t, μ and σ^2, determining the default probability is an exercise in elementary statistics. In general, the probability that a normally distributed variable x falls below z is given by $\Phi[(z - \mathrm{E}[x])/\sigma(x)]$, where Φ denotes the cumulative standard normal distribution. Applying this result to our case, we get

$$\begin{aligned}\text{Prob(Default)} &= \Phi\left[\frac{\ln L - \ln A_t + (\mu - \sigma^2/2)(T-t)}{\sigma\sqrt{T-t}}\right] \\ &= \Phi\left[\frac{\ln(L/A_t) + (\mu - \sigma^2/2)(T-t)}{\sigma\sqrt{T-t}}\right]\end{aligned} \tag{2.2}$$

[1] A variable X whose logarithm is normal with mean $\mathrm{E}(\ln X)$ and variance σ^2 has expectation $\mathrm{E}[X] = \exp(\mathrm{E}(\ln X) + \sigma^2/2)$. Denoting the expected change of $\ln X$ by $\mathrm{E}(\ln X) = \mu - \sigma^2/2$ rather than by μ has the effect that the expected change of X is $\mathrm{E}[X] = \exp(\mu)$ and thus depends only on the chosen drift parameter, and not on the variance σ^2.

In the literature, one often uses the term *distance to default* (DD). It measures the number of standard deviations the expected asset value A_T is away from the default. We can therefore write

$$DD = \frac{\ln A_t + (\mu - \sigma^2/2)(T - t) - \ln L}{\sigma\sqrt{T - t}}$$

$$=> \text{Prob(Default)} = \Phi[-DD] \tag{2.3}$$

So far, we have not used any option pricing formula. In fact, there is no theoretical reason why we need them to determine default probabilities, but instead a practical one: for a typical firm, we cannot observe the market value of assets. What we can observe are book values of assets, which can diverge from market values for many reasons. If we do not observe asset values, we do not know today's asset value A_t needed for formula (2.2). In addition, we cannot use observed asset values to derive an estimate of the asset volatility σ.

Option pricing theory can help because it implies a relationship between the unobservable (A_t, σ) and observable variables. For publicly traded firms, we observe the market value of equity, which is given by the share price multiplied with the number of outstanding shares. At maturity T, we can establish the following relationship between equity value and asset value (see Figure 2.2): as long as the asset value is below the value of liabilities, the value of equity is zero because all assets are claimed by the bond holders. If the asset value is higher than the principal of the zero-coupon bond, however, equity holders receive the residual value, and their pay-off increases linearly with the asset value.

Mathematically, the pay-off to equity holders can be described as

$$E_T = \max(0, A_T - L) \tag{2.4}$$

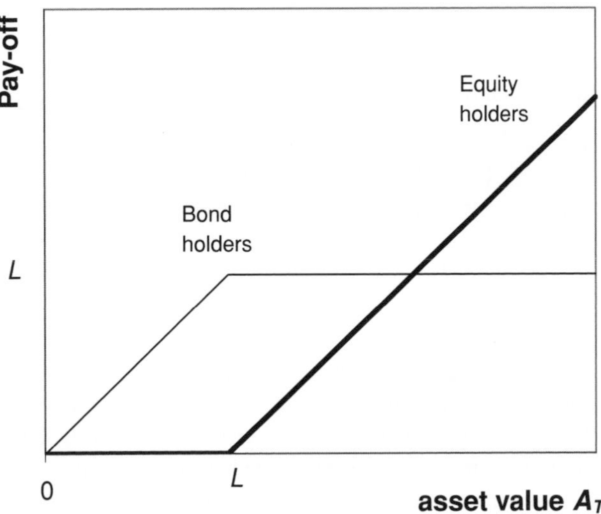

Figure 2.2 Payoff to equity and bond holders at maturity T

This is the pay-off of a European call option. The underlying of the call are the firm's assets; the call's strike is L. The pay-off to bond holders corresponds to a portfolio composed of a risk-free zero-coupon bond with principal L and a short put on the firm's assets, again with strike L.

If the firm pays no dividends, the equity value can be determined with the standard Black-Scholes call option formula:

$$E_t = A_t \cdot \Phi(d_1) - Le^{-r(T-t)}\Phi(d_2) \tag{2.5}$$

$$d_1 = \frac{\ln(A_t/L) + (r + \sigma^2/2)(T-t)}{\sigma\sqrt{T-t}}$$

$$d_2 = d_1 - \sigma\sqrt{T-t} \tag{2.6}$$

where r denotes the logarithmic risk-free rate of return.

Remember our problem of determining the asset value A_t and the asset volatility σ. We now have an equation that links an observable value (the equity value) to these two unknowns (σ enters Equation (2.5) via Equation (2.6)). However, we have only one equation, but two unknown variables. So where do we go from there? We can go back into the past to increase the available information. There are several ways of using this information, and we illustrate two different methods in the next two sections.

IMPLEMENTING THE MERTON MODEL WITH A ONE-YEAR HORIZON

The iterative approach

Rearranging the Black-Scholes formula (2.5), we get

$$A_t = \left[E_t + Le^{-r(T-t)}\Phi(d_2)\right] / \Phi(d_1) \tag{2.7}$$

If we go back in time, say 260 trading days, we get a system of equations:

$$\begin{aligned} A_t &= \left[E_t + L_t e^{-r_t(T-t)}\Phi(d_2)\right] / \Phi(d_1) \\ A_{t-1} &= \left[E_{t-1} + L_{t-1} e^{-r_{t-1}(T-(t-1))}\Phi(d_2)\right] / \Phi(d_1) \\ &\dots \\ A_{t-260} &= \left[E_{t-260} + L_{t-260} e^{-r_{t-260}(T-(t-260))}\Phi(d_2)\right] / \Phi(d_1) \end{aligned} \tag{2.8}$$

For simplicity, we have not added time subscripts to the d_1s and d_2s, whereas we have added them to the other variables that can change over time. Using time-varying interest rates and liabilities is somehow inconsistent with the Merton model, in which both are constant. However, we can hope to come closer to market valuations with this approach, because the latter will be based on the information the market has at a particular date.

Equation system (2.8) is composed of 261 equations in 261 unknowns (the asset values). Have we made any progress? Although it seems as if we have an additional unknown variable, the asset volatility σ, this should not bother us, because this variable can be estimated from a time series of As. Therefore, the system of equations can be solved.

Before applying this procedure to an example firm, however, we have to translate the stylized firm of the Merton model into the real world. Typical firms have many different liabilities maturing at different points in time – from one day to 30 years or more. One solution often found in the literature is the following: assume that the firm has only liabilities that mature in one year. The choice may appear to be ad hoc, and outrageously so. It is largely motivated by convenience. Structural models are often used to produce one-year default probabilities. Had we assumed a maturity of, say, three years, it would not have been obvious how to convert the three-year default probability to a one-year probability.

If we make the ad hoc assumption that the maturity is one year, there is no reason why we should not apply it to every day in the past. On the contrary, it seems natural because firms often have relatively stable maturity structures, i.e., issue new debt when some part of the debt is retired. Setting $(T - t)$ to one for each day within the preceding twelve months, (2.8) simplifies to

$$\begin{aligned} A_t &= \left[E_t + L_t e^{-r_t}\Phi(d_2)\right]/\Phi(d_1) \\ A_{t-1} &= \left[E_{t-1} + L_{t-1} e^{-r_{t-1}}\Phi(d_2)\right]/\Phi(d_1) \\ &\cdots \\ A_{t-260} &= \left[E_{t-260} + L_{t-260} e^{-r_{t-260}}\Phi(d_2)\right]/\Phi(d_1) \end{aligned} \tag{2.9}$$

This system of equations can be solved through the following iterative procedure:

Iteration 0: Set starting values A_{t-a} for each $a = 0, 1, \ldots, 260$. A sensible choice is to set the A_{t-a} equal to the sum of the market value of equity E_{t-a} and the book value of liabilities L_{t-a}. Set σ equal to the standard deviation of the log asset returns computed with the A_{t-a}.

For any further iteration $k = 1, \ldots,$ end

Iteration k: Insert A_{t-a} and σ from the previous iteration into the Black-Scholes formulae d_1 and d_2. Input these d_1 and d_2 into Equation (2.7) to compute the new A_{t-a}. Again use the A_{t-a} to compute the asset volatility.

We go on until the procedure converges. One way of checking convergence is to examine the change in the asset values from one iteration to the next. If the sum of squared differences between consecutive asset values is below some small value (such as 10^{-10}) we stop.

We will now implement this procedure for Enron, three months before its default in December 2001. At that time, this default was the biggest corporate default ever. It also caught many investors by surprise because Enron had decent agency ratings until a few days before default.

We collect quarterly data on Enron's liabilities from the SEC Edgar data base. The one-year US treasury rate serves as the risk-free rate of return[2] and the market value of equity can be obtained from various data providers. When linking the daily data on equity value with the

[2] Data can, for example, be obtained from `www.econstats.com`.

Table 2.1 Using the iterative approach to estimate asset values and asset volatility

	A	B	C	D	E	F	G	H	I	J
1										
2		Market	Liabi-	risk free		Asset values		ln returns	Asset volatility	
3	Date	equity E	lities L	rate r		iter k	iter k+1	iter k	iter k	
4	8/31/00	62716	34797	6.0%		95,490	95,487		28.42%	
5	9/1/00	63039	34797	6.0%		95,797	95,795	0.32%	Sum of squared errors	
6	9/4/00	63039	34797	6.0%		95,805	95,803	0.01%	5.74E-12	
7	9/5/00	63547	34797	6.0%		96,321	96,318	0.54%		
8	9/6/00	62346	3479							
9	9/7/00	61330	3479							
10	9/8/00	62208	3479							
11	9/11/00	63547	3479							
12	9/12/00	63639	3479							
13	9/13/00	63870	3479							
14	9/14/00	64240	3479							
15	9/15/00	66087	3479							
16	9/18/00	66087	34797	5.9%		98,894	98,892	0.02%		
...	...	...								
261	8/27/01	28315	5							
262	8/28/01	28615	5							
263	8/29/01	27970	5							
264	8/30/01	26620	5							
265	8/31/01	26237	51652	3.4%		77,395	75,602	-0.59%		

```
G4: =(B4+C4*EXP(-D4*1)*NORMSDIST(BSd(F4,C4,1,D4,I$4)-
I$4))/NORMSDIST(BSd(F4,C4,1,D4,I$4))
(can be copied into G5:G265)

H5: =ln(F5/F4)
(can be copied into H5:H265)

I4: =STDEV(H5:H265)*260^0.5
I6: =SUMXMY2(F4:F265,G4:G265)
```

```
Sub iterate()
Do While Range("I6") > 10 ^ -10
    'Copy asset values from iteration k+1 to iteration k
    Range("F4:F265") = (Range("G4:G265"))
Loop
End Sub
```

quarterly liability data, we take the most recent, available data. The date of availability is taken to be the filing date stated in the SEC filings. On July 31, 2001, for example, the liability data is from the report for the first quarter of 2001, filed on May 15, 2001. We therefore use only information actually available to the market at our valuation date.

The data and calculations are contained in Table 2.1. We start by entering the initial values for the asset value in column F. Our guess is that the asset value equals the market value of equity plus the (book) value of liabilities. Cell F4, for example, would read = B4 + C4.

Column G contains the system of Equations (2.9). For each day, we compute the asset value using the rearranged Black-Scholes formula. For convenience we write a VBA-function BSd to compute the d_1 as given in Equation (2.6):

```
Function BSd(S, x, h, r, sigma)
'S=value underlying, x=strike, h=time to maturity,
'r=risk-free rate, sigma=volatility underlying
BSd = (Log(S / x) + (r + 0.5 * sigma ^ 2) * h) / (sigma * h ^ 0.5)
End Function
```

Note that the horizon $(T - t)$ is here denoted by h.

In column H, we compute the log returns of the asset values from column F. We use the function STDEV to determine their standard deviation and multiply the result with the square-root of 260 (the number of trading days within a year) to transform it into a per annum volatility (this is an application of the root-T-rule explained in Box 2.1).

Box 2.1 Root-T-rule for scaling standard deviations of return

The percentage price change over T periods from $t = 0$ to $t = T$ can be written as

$$P_T/P_0 = R_{0,T} = R_1 \times R_2 \times R_3 \times \ldots \times R_T$$

where P denotes price and R the simple, gross return. With logarithmic returns $r = \ln(R)$ we have (recall $\ln(xy) = \ln(x) + \ln(y)$)

$$r_{0,T} = r_1 + r_2 + r_3 + \ldots + r_T$$

If the returns are independent across periods, the T-period variance is just the sum of the one-period variances

$$\text{Var}(r_{0,T}) = \text{Var}(r_1) + \text{Var}(r_2) + \text{Var}(r_3) + \ldots + \text{Var}(r_T)$$

If return variances are identical across time, $\text{Var}(r_1) = \text{Var}(r_2) = \ldots = \text{Var}(r_T) = \text{Var}(r_t)$, we can then write

$$\text{Var}(r_{0,T}) = T \times \text{Var}(r_t)$$

For the standard deviation of returns, it follows that

$$\sigma(r_{0,T}) = \sqrt{T}\sigma(r_t)$$

This is the root-T-rule. An example application is the following: we multiply the standard deviation of monthly returns with the square root of 12 to get the annualized standard deviation of returns. The annualized standard deviation is usually called *volatility*.

The iterative procedure is implemented through the macro *iterate*. Its job is very simple: just copy column G into column F as long as the sum of squared differences in asset values (in G and F) is above 10^{-10}. The sum of squared differences is computed in cell I6 using the function SUMXMY2.

For the default probability formula, we need the expected change in asset values. With the asset values obtained in Table 2.1, we can apply the standard procedure for estimating expected returns with the Capital Asset Pricing Model (CAPM). We obtain the beta of the assets with respect to a market index, and then apply the CAPM formula for the return on an asset i:

$$\text{E}[R_i] - R = \beta_i(\text{E}[R_M] - R) \tag{2.10}$$

with R denoting the simple risk-free rate of return ($R = \exp(r) - 1$). We take the S&P 500 index return as a proxy for R_M, the return on the market portfolio. Computations are shown in

Table 2.2 Using estimated asset values and the CAPM to derive an estimate of the drift rate of asset returns

	A	B	C	D	E	F	G	H	I	J
1	**Data**					**Excess returns**			**CAPM calculations**	
2		Asset		risk-free		Asset			(market premium assumed 4%)	
3	Date	value	S&P	rate R		value	S&P			
4	8/31/00	95,487	1517.68	6.18%					Beta	
5	9/1/00	95,795	1520.77	6.23%		0.30%	0.18%		0.293	
6	9/4/00	95,803	1520.77	6.21%		-0.02%	-0.02%		=SLOPE(F5:F265,G5:G265)	
7	9/5/00	96,318	1507.08	6.18%		0.51%	-0.92%		Expected asset return	
8	9/6/00	95,114	1492.25	6.19%		-1.27%	-1.01%		0.046	
9	9/7/00	94,089	1502.51	6.22%		-1.10%	0.66%		=D265+I5*0.04	
10	9/8/00	94,973	1494.50	6.20%		0.92%	-0.56%		Drift rate μ	
11	9/11/00	96,312	1489.26	6.20%		1.39%	-0.37%		0.045	
12	9/12/00	96,414	1481.99	6.17%		0.08%	-0.51%		=LN(1+I8)	
13	9/13/00	96,660	1484.91	6.12%		0.23%	0.17%		F5: =B5/B4-(1+$D4/260)	
14	9/14/00	97,026	1480.87	6.13%		0.36%	-0.30%		*(can be copied to F4:F265)*	
...	...	...	...	...		...	...		G5: =C5/C4-(1+$D4/260)	
265	8/31/01	75,602	1133.58	3.47%		-0.60%	0.39%		*(can be copied to G4:G265)*	

Table 2.2. We copy the asset values from column G of Table 2.1 into column B of Table 2.2 and then add the S&P index values and the risk-free rate of return. In columns F and G, we compute the excess return on the assets and the S&P 500 (excess return is return minus risk-free rate).

By regressing the asset value returns on S&P 500 returns, we obtain an estimate of the asset's beta. This is done in Cell I5 with the function SLOPE. Assuming a standard value of 4% for the market risk premium $E[R_M] - R$, the expected asset return is then 4.6%. This, however, is not the drift rate μ that we use in our formula 2.2. The drift rate μ is for logarithmic returns. We determine μ as ln(1.046).

Now that we have estimates of the asset volatility, the asset value and the drift rate, we can compute the default probability. This is done in Table 2.3. The estimated one-year default probability as of August 31, 2001, is 8.72%.

Table 2.3 Using the estimates to determine the implied default probability

	A	B	C	D
1	**Estimates**			
2	Asset value A_t	75,602	(from Table 2.1)	
3	Asset volatility σ	28.4%	(from Table 2.1)	
4	Asset drift rate μ	4.5%	(from Table 2.2)	
5				
6	**Balance sheet data**			
7	Liabilities L	51,652	(from Table 2.1)	
8				
9	**Default probability calculations**			
10	Distance to default	1.36	=(LN(B2)+(B4-B3^2/2)-LN(B7))/B3	
11	Default probability	8.72%	=NORMSDIST(-B10)	
12				

A solution using equity values and equity volatilities

The iterative solution of the last section used the Black-Scholes formula

$$E_t = A_t \cdot \Phi(d_1) - Le^{-r(T-t)}\Phi(d_2) \tag{2.11}$$

and solved the problem of one equation with two unknowns by examining (2.11) for various dates t.

Another common approach is to use (2.11) for the current date t only, and introduce another equation that also contains the two unknowns. Since equity is a call on the asset value, its riskiness depends on the riskiness of the asset value. Specifically, one can show that the equity volatility σ_E is related to the asset value A_t and the asset volatility σ in the following way:

$$\sigma_E = \sigma\ \Phi(d_1)A_t/E_t \tag{2.12}$$

where d_1 is the standard Black-Scholes d_1 as given in Equation (2.6). If we know the equity value E_t and have an estimate of the equity volatility σ_E, (2.11) and (2.12) are two equations with two unknowns. This system of equations does not have a closed-form solution, but we can use numerical routines to solve it.

In the following, we apply this approach to the case study from the previous section. We use the same data and assumptions, i.e., we set the horizon $T-t$ to one year, we take the equity value E_t from the stock market, set liabilities L equal to book liabilities, and use the one-year yield on US treasuries as the risk-free rate of return. The only new parameter that we need is an estimate of the equity volatility σ_E. We choose to base our estimate on the historical volatility measured over the preceding 260 days. Data and computations are shown in Table 2.4. Daily Enron stock prices are in column B.[3] They are converted to daily log returns in column C. For example the formula reads =LN(B3/B2) for cell C3. By applying the STDEV command to the range containing the returns, we get the standard deviation of daily returns. Multiplying

Table 2.4 Estimating equity volatility from stock prices

	A	B	C	D	E	F
1	Date	Stock Price ($)	Daily log return		Volatility (per annum)	
2	31-Aug-00	84.88			45.65%	
3	1-Sep-00	85.31	0.51%		=STDEV(C3:C263)*260^0.5	
4	4-Sep-00	85.31	0.00%			
5	5-Sep-00	86	0.81%			
6	6-Sep-00	84.38	-1.90%			
7	7-Sep-00	83	-1.65%			
8	8-Sep-00	84.19	1.42%			
9	11-Sep-00	86	2.13%			
10	12-Sep-00	86.13	0.15%			
11	13-Sep-00	86.44	0.36%	=LN(B11/B10)		
12	14-Sep-00	86.94	0.58%	*(can be copied into C3:C263)*		
...	...	...	...			
262	30-Aug-01	35.5	-4.95%			
263	31-Aug-01	34.99	-1.45%			

[3] Prices should be adjusted for stock splits etc.

Table 2.5 Calibrating the Merton model to equity value and equity volatility

	A	B	C	D
1	**Data/Assumptions**			
2	Equity value E_t	26,237		
3	Equity volatility σ_E	45.65%		
4	Liabilities L_t	51,652		
5	Risk free rate r	3.41%		
6	Horizon (T-t)	1		
7				
8	**Unknowns**			
9	Asset Value A_t	76,146	(initial value: =B2+B4)	
10	Asset Volatility σ	15.78%	(initial value: =B3*B2/B9	
11				
12	**Model values from Black-Scholes formulae**			
13	d_1	2.76	=(LN(B9/B4)+(B5+B10^2/2)*B6)/(B10*B6^0.5)	
14	d_2	2.60	=B13-B10*B6^0.5	
15	Equity value E_t	26,237	=B9*NORMSDIST(B13)-B4*EXP(-B5*B6)*NORMSDIST(B14)	
16	Equity volatility σ_E	45.65%	=(B9/B15)*B10*NORMSDIST(B13)	
17				
18	**Objective: minimize deviation data – model**			
19	Squared rel. errors	0.0000000	=(B15/B2-1)^2+(B16/B3-1)^2	
21				
22				
23				
24				
25				
26				
27				
28				
29				
30				
31				
32				
33				
34				
35				

Solver Parameters
Set Target Cell: $B$19
Equal To: Max Min Value of: 0
By Changing Cells: $B$9:$B$10
Subject to the Constraints:
Solve Close Guess Options Add Change Reset All Delete Help

this figure with the square root of 260 gives us the annualized equity volatility (see Box 2.1). The whole formula for cell E2 then reads =STDEV(C3:C263)*260^0.5.

We now have all the data needed to solve the Black-Scholes equation system. This is done in Table 2.5. Our input data is contained in the range B2:B6.

The unknown parameters are in cells B9:B10. It is necessary to assign feasible initial values to them, i.e., values larger than zero. To speed up the numerical search procedure, it is also advisable to choose the initial values such that they are already close to the values that solve the system.

A good choice for the initial asset value in cell B9 is the market value of equity plus the book value of liabilities. An approximation of the unknown asset volatility in cell B10 can be based on Equation 2.12. Solving this equation with respect to σ and assuming $\Phi(d_1) = 1$, we get the approximation

$$\sigma = \sigma_E \, E_t / A_t \tag{2.13}$$

To see why Equation (2.13) is useful, examine when the assumption $\Phi(d_1) = 1$ holds. Through the properties of the normal distribution, $\Phi(d_1)$ lies between 0 and 1. For large d_1, $\Phi(d_1)$ approaches 1. Comparing the equation for d_1 (2.6) with the equation for the distance to default (2.3), we see that they have the same structure, and differ only in the drift rate and the sign of the variance in the numerator. Thus, a large d_1 goes along with a high distance to default, and a low default probability. If this is true – and most firms have default probabilities smaller than 5% – the approximation (2.13) is reasonable.

The option pricing equations are entered in B13:B16. We could again use our Bd1 function. For the sake of variation, we type the formulae for d_1 and d_2 in cells B13 and B14, respectively. The two Black-Scholes equations (2.11) and (2.12) are in cells B15 and B16, respectively.

The equation system is solved if the difference between model values and observed values is zero. That is, we would like to reach B15=B2 and B16=B3 by changing B9 and B10. To arrive at a solution, we can minimize the sum of squared differences between model values and observed values. Since equity value and equity volatility are of different order, it is advisable to minimize the sum of squared *percentage* differences. Otherwise, the numerical routine could be insensitive to errors in equity volatility and stop short of a solution that sets both equations to zero.

The objective function that we are going to minimize thus reads

$$=(\text{Model } E_t/\text{Observed } E_t - 1)^2 + (\text{Model } \sigma_E/\text{Observed } \sigma_E - 1)^2$$

=(B15/B2-1)^2 + (B16/B3-1)^2

which we write in cell B19. We then use the Solver to minimize B19 by changing B9 and B10 (see screenshot in Table 2.5). The precision option of the Solver is set to 0.000001. We also tick the options 'Assume non-negative' and 'Use Automatic Scaling'.

The Solver worked fine in this example – model values are very close to observed equity values, and convergence was quick. In cases where the Solver has approached the solution but stopped before errors were close to zero, try running the Solver again. In cases where the Solver procedure stops because it considers a value of zero for the asset volatility, add the constraint B10≥0.000001 in the Solver window. In some cases, playing around with the objective function might also help.

To compute the default probability, we again need the drift rate of asset returns. We could, for example, obtain it in a fashion similar to the previous section. Apply the calculations from Table 2.5 to a series of dates in the past, obtain a series of asset values, and use the CAPM as in Table 2.2. For simplicity, we do not spell out the calculations but rather use the drift rate obtained in the previous section, which was 4.5%. The default probability can then be determined as in Table 2.3, which gives 0.38%.

Comparing different approaches

The following table summarizes the key results that we obtained with the two different approaches:

	Iterative	2 equations
Asset value	77,395	76,146
Asset volatility	28.23%	15.78%
Default probability	7.35%	0.38%

The iterative procedure and the procedure based on solving a system of two equations yield asset values that are relatively close (the asset value from the 2-equation approach is 1.9% lower than the one from the iterative approach). The asset volatilities, however, differ dramatically, which is also the main reason why the default probabilities differ in the way they do.

This may seem odd because we used the same one-year history of equity prices in both approaches. However, we used them in different ways. In the 2-equation approach, we estimated the equity volatility from those prices. This is a good way of estimating a volatility if we believe it to be constant across time. But equity is a call option in the Merton world, with risk varying if the asset-to-equity ratio A_t/E_t varies (see Equation 2.12). Equivalently, we could also say that equity risk varies with leverage, because leverage can be measured through $(A_t - E_t)/A_t = 1 - E_t/A_t$.

During the time period of the analysis, Enron's asset-to-equity ratio changed dramatically. Using the figures from Table 2.1, it increased from 1.52 in August 2000 to 2.96 in August 2001. Leverage increased from 34% to 66%. The equity volatility measured with past values thus mixes observations from a low volatility regime with the ones from a high volatility regime.

By contrast, in the iterative approach, we model changes in leverage. Recall that we had collected the history of liabilities, which then entered the Black-Scholes equations. We do rely on the assumption that the *asset* volatility is constant across time, but this is an assumption that is also implicitly included in the 2-equation approach (equity volatility is constant if both leverage and asset volatility are constant). For data characterized by large changes in leverage, one can therefore make a case for preferring the iterative approach.

We can also compare our estimates to the ones from a commercial implementation of the Merton model: the EDF^{TM} measure by Moody's KMV (MKMV, see Box 2.2 for a brief description). One element that MKMV adds to the simple Merton approach is calibration of the model outcome to default data. For various reasons (e.g., non-normal asset returns) Merton default probabilities can underestimate the actual default probabilities. MKMV thus uses a historical default database to map model default probabilities into estimates of actual default probabilities. Partly for this reason, EDFs are usually larger than the default probabilities we get from implementations like the ones we followed here.

Box 2.2 The EDF^{TM} measure by Moody's KMV

A commercial implementation of the Merton model is the EDFTM measure by Moody's KMV (MKMV). Important modeling aspects are the following:

- MKMV uses a modified Black-Scholes valuation model that allows for different types of liabilities.
- In the model, default is triggered if the asset value falls below the sum of short-term debt plus a fraction of long-term debt. This rule is derived from an analysis of historical defaults.
- The distance-to-default that comes out of the model is transformed into default probabilities by calibrating it to historical default rates.

For August 2001, the EDF for Enron was roughly 2%,[4] which is larger than the result we get from the 2-equation approach, but smaller than the result from the iterative approach. The latter is somewhat atypical. One reason could be that the critical value that triggers default in the EDF model is not total liabilities, but short-term debt plus a fraction of long-term liabilities. Although this adjustment increases the quality of EDFs on average, it may have led to an underestimation for Enron. Due to off-balance sheet transactions, financial statements understated the Enron's liabilities. By using the total liabilities, we may have unwittingly corrected this bias.

To sum up, the case that we have examined may be somewhat atypical in the sense that a simple implementation of the Merton model yields relatively high default probabilities, which also seem to be close to the true default probability. In many cases and especially for short maturities, a simple Merton approach will produce default probabilities that are very low, such as 0.0000001%, even though we have good reason to believe that they should be much higher. We would then be hesitant to use the model result as an estimate of the actual default probability. Empirical studies, however, show that the results can nonetheless be very useful for ordering firms according to their default risk (see Vassalou and Xing, 2004).

IMPLEMENTING THE MERTON MODEL WITH A *T*-YEAR HORIZON

So far, we have implemented the Merton model by setting debt maturity to one year – an arbitrary, but convenient assumption. Typically, the average maturity of a firm's debt is larger than one year. So can we hope to get better results by aligning the maturity in the model with the actual debt maturities? The answer is not immediately obvious. If the only thing that we change is the horizon (e.g., change cell B6 of Table 2.5 from 1 to 5), we would have failed to model the fact that the firm makes payments before maturity – like regular interest on bonds and loans, or dividends. It may be safe to ignore such interim payments over a horizon of one year. A one-year bond with annual coupon payments is in fact a zero-coupon bond, and firms usually do not pay out large dividends shortly before default. However, for a horizon of several years interim payments should enter our valuation formula in a consistent way.

In the following, we implement such an approach. It maintains the set-up of the Merton model in the sense that there is only one date at which liabilities are due, however, we take interim payments into account. The key steps are as follows:

1. Assume that the firm has issued only one coupon bond with maturity equal to the average maturity of liabilities.
2. Accrue interest and dividend payments to the maturity assumed in step 1; i.e., hypothetically shift their payment dates into the future.
3. Since accrued dividends and interest are assumed to be due at maturity, even though they are actually paid before, treat them as liabilities that have higher priority than the principal of the bond.

We start with step 1. In the balance sheet of a firm, liabilities are split up into current liabilities (maturity less than one year) and long-term liabilities (maturity larger than one year).

[4] See EDF Case Study: Enron, `http://www.moodyskmv.com/research/files/Enron.pdf` (accessed August 18, 2010).

Additional information on maturity can be obtained from the annual report, an examination of outstanding bonds or other sources. Usually, however, this information is not sufficient for precisely determining the average maturity. Here, we follow a simple rule that requires little information: assuming that current (long-term) liabilities have an average maturity of 0.5 (10) years, the average maturity obtains as (L is total liabilities, CL is current liabilities)

$$[0.5 \times CL + 10 \times (L - CL)]/L$$

With the balance sheet from Enron's quarterly report for June 2001, this leads to a maturity of $T - t = 5.53$ years.

Having fixed T, we can proceed to step 2 and compute the value of accrued dividends and interest payments at T. We assume that dividends are paid annually, and that they grow at an annual rate of g. With the dividend just paid (D_0), the end value of the dividend stream, which we denote by D, then obtains as

$$D = \sum_{\tau=t+1}^{T} D_0(1+g)^{\tau-t}\exp(r(T-\tau)) \tag{2.14}$$

From Enron's annual report, the dividend for 2000 was $D_0 = 368$m, up 3.66% on the 1999 dividend. This motivates our assumption of $g = 3\%$. Note that we accrue dividends at the risk-free rate r, which we take to be the yield of five-year treasuries. Using the risk-free rate seems ad hoc, because dividends are risky, but it has some justification because dividends will be treated senior to debt, and so it is probably a better choice than the yield on Enron's debt.

Interest payments are treated in a similar fashion. Assuming that they are due annually, and that the coupon rate is c, the end value of interest payments (denoted by I) is

$$I = \sum_{\tau=t+1}^{T} c \cdot L \cdot \exp(r(T-\tau)) \tag{2.15}$$

We could infer the coupon rate by examining the coupons on Enron bonds outstanding at t. Here, we just assume a value $c = 4\%$.

Now we can move to step 3. As in the first two sections, the analysis will rest on the option pricing formula that returns equity value as a function of the asset value, liabilities and asset volatility. To understand how equity should be valued, we examine the pay-off to equity holders at maturity T. Assuming that accrued dividends D have priority over the principal L, and that accrued interest I and accrued dividends have equal priority, we can distinguish three regimes (A_T is the asset value at maturity):

- $A_T < D + I$: Firm is in default, and asset value is not sufficient to cover claims from dividends and interest. The equity holders receive their share $D/(D+I)A_T$.
- $L + D + I > A_T > D + I$: Asset value suffices to cover claims from dividends and interest, but the firm is in default because the principal L is not fully covered. Equity holders receive only accrued dividends D.
- $A_T > L + D + I$: Asset value suffices to cover all claims. Equity holders receive $A_T - L - I$. Note that this includes the dividend claims D. Explicitly stated equity holders receive $D + (A_T - L - I - D) = A_T - L - I$.

Table 2.6 Pay-off structure if accrued dividends and interest have priority over other liabilities L

	A	B	C	D
1	**Example data**			
2	Accrued dividends D	100		
3	Accrued interest I	50		
4	Liabilities L	250		
5				
6	**Payoffs**			
7	Asset Value A_T	Payoff Equity		
8	0	0	=IF(A8<B$2+B$3,B$2/(B$2+B$3)*A8, IF(B$2+B$3+B$4>A8,B$2,A8-B$3-B$4))	
9	50	33.33	*(can be copied into B8:B28)*	
10	100	66.67		
11	150	100		
12	200	100		
13	250	100		
14	300	100		
15	350	100		
16	400	100		
17	450	150		
18	500	200		
19	550	250		
20	600	300		
21	650	350		
22	700	400		
23	750	450		
24	800	500		
25	850	550		
26	900	600		
27	950	650		
28	1000	700		

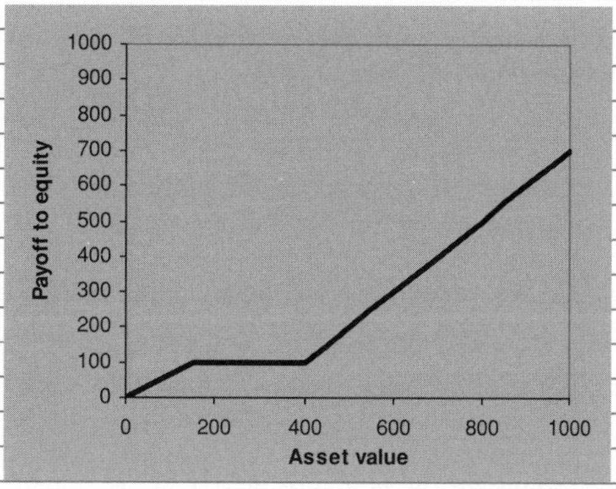

The pay-off structure is shown in Table 2.6 for example values for D, I and L.

Carefully inspecting the pay-off structure, it is an exercise in financial engineering to replicate the pay-off to equity with a portfolio of call options and direct investments in the underlying assets. Specifically, equity is equivalent to

a share of $D/(D+I)$ in the assets, plus
a share of $D/(D+I)$ in a short call on assets with strike $D+I$, plus a call on assets with strike $L+D+I$
$=$ equity value.

Here is a graphical depiction:

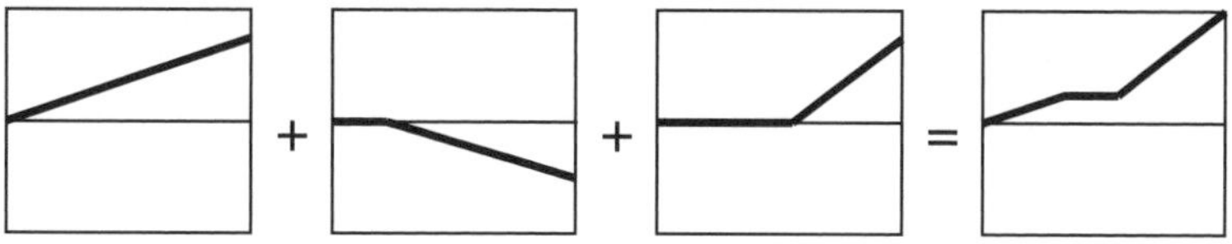

We can then use the standard Black-Scholes option pricing formula to model today's value of equity. We obtain

$$E_t = A_t \cdot \Phi(d_1) - (L + D + I)\, e^{-r(T-t)}\Phi(d_2) + \frac{D}{D+I}(A_t - A_t\Phi(k_1) + (D+I)e^{-r(T-t)}\Phi(k_2)) \tag{2.16}$$

with

$$d_1 = \frac{\ln(A_t/(L+D+I)) + (r+\sigma^2/2)(T-t)}{\sigma\sqrt{T-t}}$$

$$d_2 = d_1 - \sigma\sqrt{T-t} \tag{2.17}$$

$$k_1 = \frac{\ln(A_t/(D+I)) + (r+\sigma^2/2)(T-t)}{\sigma\sqrt{T-t}}$$

$$k_2 = k_1 - \sigma\sqrt{T-t} \tag{2.18}$$

As before, we can derive a second equation relating equity volatility to asset volatility

$$\sigma_E = \sigma\frac{A_t}{E_t}\left(N(d_1) + \frac{D}{D+I}(1 - N(k_1))\right) \tag{2.19}$$

and determine the unknowns A_t and σ by solving (2.16) and (2.19).

In Table 2.7, the approach is applied to Enron. Dividends and interest are accrued in E1:G12 using Equations (2.14) and (2.15), respectively.

The starting value for the asset value is equity value plus book value of liabilities; the starting value for the asset correlation is equity correlation times E_t/A_t. Cells B19:B24 contain the formulae (2.16) to (2.19). We then use the Solver to minimize the squared percentage errors between the observed values (for equity value and volatility) and their model counterparts.

We also determine the default probability (cell B29). Assuming the drift rate to be 4.5% as in the previous section, we get a default probability of 31.37%. Note that this is a default probability over a horizon of 5.5 years. Within our framework, it is not obvious how to convert it to an annual default probability, because the model does not allow interim defaults. To get some indication, we can derive an annual default probability under the assumption that default probabilities are constant across time. This leads to

$$\text{Prob(default p.a.)} = 1 - (1 - 0.3137)^{1/5.5} = 6.58\%$$

When comparing this figure to the previous results, note that there are several effects at work. The assumptions about dividends and interest are not the only difference between the multi-year approach and the one-year approach. The sensitivity of the default probability to a given asset drift and a given asset volatility also changes with the horizon. This is evident from the results. The asset volatility in Table 2.7 is closer to the one we received from the one-year, 2-equation approach. The default probability, on the other hand, is closer to the one from the iterative approach.

Table 2.7 Calibrating the multi-period model to equity value and equity volatility

	A	B	C	D	E	F	G	H
1	**Data/Assumptions**				**Value of payouts at T**			
2	Equity value E_t	26,237			Year	Dividends	Interest	
3	Equity volatility σ_E	45.65%			1	464	1,979	
4	Liabilities L_t	51,652			2	457	1,893	
5	Risk free rate r	4.47%			3	450	1,810	
6	Horizon (T-t)	5.53			4	443	1,731	
7	Coupon rate c	4%			5	437	1,655	
8	Dividend D_0	368			6	0	0	
9	Dividend growth g	3%			7	0	0	
10	Accrued div D	2,252	=SUM(F3:F12)		8	0	0	
11	Accrued int I	9,069	=SUM(G3:G12)		9	0	0	
12					10	0	0	
13								
14	**Unknowns**							
15	Asset Value A_t	69,835	(initial value: =B2+B4)					
16	Asset Volatility σ	20.59%	(initial value: =B3*B2/B15)					
17								
18	**Model**							
19	d_1	0.97	=(LN(B15/(B4+B10+B11))+(B5+B16^2/2)*B6)/(B16*B6^0.5)					
20	d_2	0.48	=B19-B16*B6^0.5					
21	k_1	4.51	=(LN(B15/(B10+B11))+(B5+B16^2/2)*B6)/(B16*B6^0.5)					
22	k_2	4.00	=B21-B16*B6^0.5					
23	Equity value E_t	26,237	=B15*NORMSDIST(B19)-(B4+B10+B11)*EXP(-B5*B6)*NORMSDIST(B20)+B10/(B10+B11)*(B15-B15*NORMSDIST(B21)+EXP(-B5*B6)*(B10+B11)*NORMSDIST(B22))					
24	Equity volatility σ_E	45.65%	=B16*B15/B23*(NORMSDIST(B19)+B10/(B10+B11)*(1-NORMSDIST(B21)))					
25								
26	**Objective: minimize deviation data – model**							
27	Squared rel. errors	0.00000%	=(B23/B2-1)^2+(B24/B3-1)^2					
28								
29	Prob (default)	31.37%	=NORMSDIST(-(LN(B15/(B4+B10+B11))+(0.045-B16^2/2)*B6)/(B16*B6^0.5))					

F12: =(E12<=B$6)*B$8*(1+B$9)^E12*
EXP(B$5*(B$6-E12))
G12: =(E12<=B$6)*B$7*B$4*
EXP(B$5*(B$7-E12))
(can be copied into F3:F11 and G3:G11, respectively)

CREDIT SPREADS

With the estimates from Table 2.7, we can also determine the yield on Enron's liabilities. In our model, the firm has just one bond that pays $L + I$ at maturity (if the firm is not in default). The current value of the bond B_t is the payment in T discounted at the yield y. We also know that it is equal to the asset value minus the equity value. Therefore, we have

$$B_t = A_t - E_t = \frac{L + I}{(1 + y)^{T-t}} \tag{2.20}$$

Solving for the yield y we get

$$y = \left(\frac{L + I}{A_t - E_t}\right)^{1/(T-t)} - 1 = 6.17\% \tag{2.21}$$

Here, we have inserted the results from Table 2.7. The spread s (i.e., the difference between the corporate bond yield and the risk-free rate) is

$$s = y - R = y - (\exp(r) - 1) = 1.60\% \tag{2.22}$$

In accordance with the relatively large default probability, we get a spread that is typical of relatively risky debt, which appears to be sensible.

In empirical studies, however, spreads produced by Merton models are often found to be lower than observed market spreads. One reason could be that the Merton model tends to underestimate default risk (see the discussion in the previous section). In addition, market spreads compensate investors for the illiquidity and tax disadvantages of corporate bonds, i.e., factors that are separate from default risk.

CREDITGRADES

In this section we implement a widely used alternative structural modeling approach called CreditGrades (CG, hereafter). In this model default occurs if the asset value of the firm drops below a random barrier. The randomness of the barrier is the main difference to the models presented so far. It captures the fact that we usually do not know the level of a firm's liabilities until the firm defaults. (Balance sheet information is only available at a quarterly frequency, and it could be distorted or manipulated.) In addition, the CG model assumes that default can occur at any time, whereas default in the classical Merton model occurs only at maturity. The CG approach is illustrated in Figure 2.3, which can be compared to Figure 2.1.

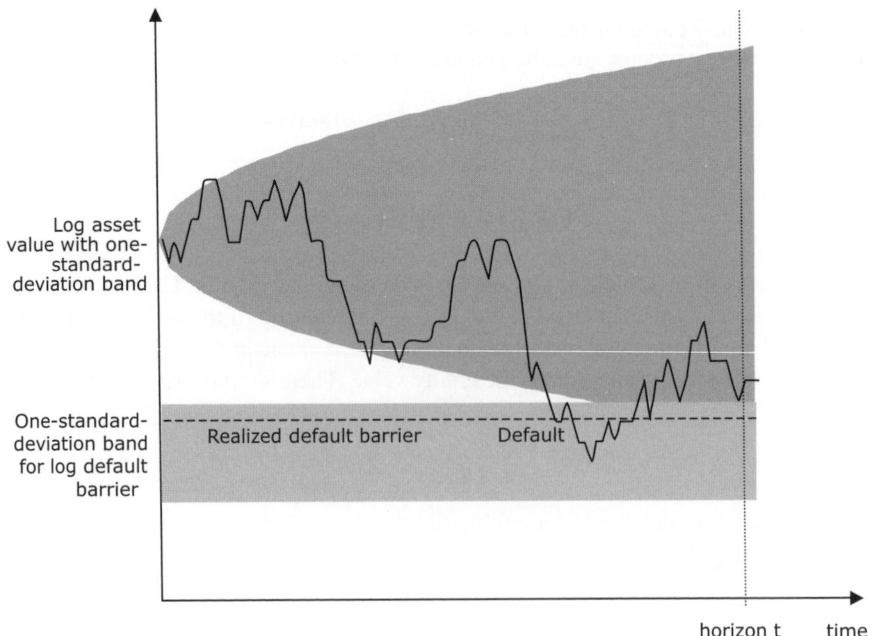

Figure 2.3 Illustration of the CreditGrades model

We follow the CG documentation and express the relevant firm variables on a per-share basis. We denote today's asset value per-share by A. As above, asset values are assumed to follow a lognormal distribution. The random default barrier is given as

$$\text{default barrier} = \Lambda\ D$$

where D is today's debt-per-share. Λ represents the uncertainty in recovery values and is a random variable, which is assumed to follow a lognormal distribution with mean $\overline{\Lambda}$ and standard deviation λ, independent of the asset value process.[5] As in the classical Merton model, we need to estimate today's asset value, its volatility and its drift rate. In CG, they are determined as follows.

The drift rate is set to zero. This is justified if firms tend to maintain a constant leverage over time. Assets may rise at some rate but if debt rises at the same rate, the distance to the default barrier remains constant and we can describe the situation by assuming a zero drift for both assets and debt.

For the initial asset value, the CG model suggests the approximation $A = S + \overline{\Lambda}D$ where S is the firm's stock price. This choice is based on an inspection of boundary cases; details can be found in Finger *et al.* (2002, p. 10). The asset volatility is set to

$$\sigma = \sigma_E \frac{S}{S + \overline{\Lambda}D}$$

where σ_E is equity volatility. This expression is an approximation of the theoretical relationship between asset volatility and equity volatility that we also used in previous sections (see Equations (2.12 and 2.13)).

Moving on, one can derive an approximation for the probability that the firm survives until time t, as seen from today ($t = 0$):

$$Prob(Survival\ to\ t) = \Phi\left(-\frac{\alpha_t}{2} + \frac{\log(d)}{\alpha_t}\right) - d\Phi\left(-\frac{\alpha_t}{2} - \frac{\log(d)}{\alpha_t}\right) \tag{2.23}$$

with

$$d = \frac{S + \overline{\Lambda}D}{\overline{\Lambda}D}\exp(\lambda^2) \quad \text{and} \quad \alpha_t^2 = \left(\sigma_E \frac{S}{S + \overline{\Lambda}D}\right)^2 t + \lambda^2$$

As shown by Kiesel and Veraart (2008), it is also possible to derive an exact solution which would be straightforward to implement with the tools presented in this book.[6]

Next, we describe how the parameters of Equation (2.23) are specified in the CG model. The number of shares used for computing per-share figures is the number of common shares plus the number of preferred shares. The number of common shares can be determined by dividing the company's market capitalization by the current stock price; the number of preferred shares is calculated by dividing the book value of preferred shares by the price of common stock from

[5] In order to comply with our previous notation we changed some symbols from the CreditGrades technical document. In the original CG model our Λ is called L and they use A_t to denote our α_t.

[6] The exact solution involves the bivariate normal distribution, which can be evaluated with a function used in Chapter 6.

the reporting date of the book value. Furthermore, the number of preferred shares is capped at half the number of common shares.

The debt-per-share measure D is calculated by dividing liabilities by the number of shares. For industrial firms this is done by calculating the financial debt as the sum of short-term borrowings, long-term borrowings and one half times the sum of other short-term liabilities and other long-term liabilities. The latter two are weighted by $^1/_2$ to correct for their inclusion of non-financial liabilities such as deferred taxes or provisions. 'Accounts payable' is not included in the financial debt calculation. Liabilities of subsidiaries are fully included in a consolidated balance sheet even though the parent may own less than 100% of the subsidiary. To adjust for this effect, the final debt measure is found by reducing the financial debt by $\min\{0.5 \times \text{financial debt, minority interest}\}$.

For financial firms and companies with large financial subsidiaries the debt calculation is adjusted by either excluding the financial subsidiary or changing the whole financial debt calculation procedure. For banks some authors suggest eliminating the short-term borrowings. Another way to obtain an estimate for the debt-per-share ratio is to compare the leverage ratios of the company with its peers.

The recovery rate $\overline{\Lambda}$ and its volatility λ can be based on recovery statistics published by rating agencies, e.g., see Chapter 7, Table 7.6. CG proposes $\overline{\Lambda} = 0.5$ and $\lambda = 0.3$. Equity volatility can be estimated as described above (see Table 2.4). Alternatively, option implied volatilities can be used.

Several modifications are possible. When leverage data is difficult to obtain or if market conditions change quickly, a promising extension can be to use additional information in order to back out an implied leverage.[7] Recall that the survival probability of Equation (2.23) depends on the debt-per-share. The basic idea is to back out an implied debt-per-share from market observed credit default swap (CDS) spreads and insert it into Equation (2.23) in place of balance sheet information.[8]

We move on to implement the CG model in Excel. All calculations can be done in the spreadsheet, with VBA merely adding convenience. We start with a simple example and later extend the methodology to a case study of Lehman.

In Table 2.8 we estimate the CreditGrades model for John Wiley & Sons as of December 09. The parameters for the global recovery Λ and the volatility of the default barrier $\overline{\Lambda}$ are set to 50% (cell B4) and 30% (cell B5) respectively. The time horizon can be specified in cell B6.

From the SEC filings we obtain the balance sheet information needed to calculate the financial debt: the short-term borrowings (cell B10), long-term borrowings (B11) and the other short-term (B12) and long-term (B13) liabilities.

Both the preferred equity and minority interest (cells B14/B15) are zero for Wiley. The financial debt is then given in cell B17 as the sum of the former, with a weighting of $^1/_2$ on other liabilities:

```
=B10+B11+0.5*(B12+B13).
```

[7] See Hull, Nelken and White (2005) for a discussion of implied leverage in the Merton model.

[8] See Chapter 10 of this book for an extensive discussion of CDS and implied probabilities. See Equation (2.A2) in the Appendix of this chapter for a closed form solution of a CDS spread under the CG model. Another approach to market implied leverage is the use of two at-the-money option prices to estimate both the implied asset volatility and implied leverage using the option pricing formula (2.A1).

Table 2.8 Calibrating the CreditGrades model

	A	B	C	D	E	F	G
1	**CreditGrades Model**	for	John Wiley & Sons		at Dec 2009		
2							
3	**Parameters**						
4	Global recovery $\bar{\Lambda}$	50%					
5	Volatility of the barrier	30%					
6	Time (yrs)	1					
7							
8		**Company Information**					
9	**Balance Sheet**			**Market**			
10	Short Term Borrowings	78.75		Market Cap (in Mio)	2,461		
11	Long Term Borrowings	774.43		Stock Price S	41.88		
12	Other Short Term Liab.	215.77		# Common Shares (in Mio)	58.77	=E10/E11	
13	Other Long Term Liab.	359.81		#Preferred Shares	-	=MIN(0.5*E12,B14/E10)	
14	Preferred Equity	-		#Shares	58.77	=E12+E13	
15	Minority Interest	-					
16				Hist. Vola (200D)	30%		
17	Financial Debt	1,140.97	=B10+B11+0.5*(B12+B13)	ATM impl. Vola	33%		
18	Debt	1,140.97	=B17-MIN(0.5*B17,B15)	Used vola	33%		
19	Debt-per-share D	19.41	=B18/E14	Risk-free rate over T	2.93%		
20							
21							
22		**CreditGrades Calculation**					
23							
24	S+ $\bar{\Lambda}$ D	51.59	=E11+B4*B19				
25	d	5.81	=(B24*EXP(B5^2))/(B4*B19)				
26	α	0.40	=(((E18*E11)/(B24))^2*B6+B5^2)^0.5				
27							
28	Prob(Survival)	99.997%	=NORMSDIST(-(B26/2)+(LN(B25)/B26))-B25*NORMSDIST(-(B26/2)-(LN(B25)/B26))				
29	PD	0.003%	=1-B28				
30							

The final debt variable is found by subtracting the minority interest capped at $^1/_2$ of the financial debt. Cell B18 therefore reads:

=B17-MIN(0.5*B17,B15).

Before estimating the debt-per-share variable D, we need to estimate the number of shares. We divide the market capitalization (cell E10) by the stock price (E11) in cell E12. Since there are no preferred shares outstanding the total number of shares in E14 is the sum of common shares and zero. Debt-per-share in cell B19 is simply the debt divided by the number of shares: =B18/E14.

We specify the volatility measure in cell E18 as the option implied volatility of 33%.[9]

[9] Cells E16–E17 present both the 30 days historical volatility and the option implied volatility. In cell E18 we enter our assumed volatility.

In cell B24 we calculate the asset value according to the CG approximation introduced above. When calculating the parameter d according to Equation (2.23) we can refer to cell B24. Thus d is defined as

=(B24*EXP(B5^2))/(B4*B19)

The final auxiliary parameter α is determined in cell B26 according to Equation (2.23):

=(((E18*E11)/(B24))^2*B6 + B5^2)^0.5

Now we estimate the probability of survival in cell B28 according to Equation (2.23). The survival probability over the next year is 99.997%. This implies a one-year default probability of 0.003%.

In the following case study we will show the calculation of a time series of CreditGrade survival probabilities for one company, Lehman Brothers. As mentioned before, the adjustments necessary when dealing with financial companies are not standard. The estimation of the debt-per-share variable should be adjusted in order not to overweight short-term borrowings. Furthermore, the volatility of the barrier is usually set to a lower level, e.g., 10% as proposed by Veraart (2004). Here we show that these simple adjustments are sufficient to obtain a timely credit assessment.[10] When dealing with time series it is convenient to comprise the calculation into one function; here `CG_PS(S, sigma_E, D, Lambda, sigma_B, t)` will directly estimate the survival probability according to Equation (2.23):[11]

```
Function CG_PS(S, sigma_E, D, Lambda, sigma_B, t)
'S= stock price, sigma_E=equity vola, D=Debt-per-share
'Lambda=global recovery, s_B=vola of barrier, t=time
Dim d1, alpha
d1 = (S + Lambda * D) * Exp(sigma_B ^ 2) / (Lambda * D)
alpha = (((sigma_E * S) / (S + Lambda * D)) ^ 2 * t + sigma_B ^ 2) ^ 0.5
CG_PS = Application.NormSDist(-(alpha / 2) + (Log(d1) / alpha)) - _
        d1 * Application.NormSDist(-(alpha / 2) - (Log(d1) / alpha))
End Function
```

Now let us look into the balance sheet of Lehman. We calculate the debt-per-share ratios from each quarterly report between Q4 2003 and Q2 2008 (Lehman defaulted in September 2008) and report the numbers in Table 2.9.[12]

Using end-of-quarter stock prices and historical volatilities over 90 days, we estimate the one-year probabilities of default for Lehman setting $\lambda = 10\%$ and $\overline{\Lambda} = 50\%$ (see Figure 2.4).

S&P rated Lehman Brothers at A+ from October 05 to June 08 when it downgraded the company to an A flat rating. According to S&P's yearly default studies, these rating categories translate into a yearly historical default rate of 0.05–0.07%; the CreditGrades implied PD is

[10] In the Appendix to this chapter, we further demonstrate how the debt-per-share can be implied by CDS data.

[11] In the VBA code we cannot distinguish between the capital lambda Λ and the small λ, thus we denote the latter by sigma_B.

[12] Note that Lehman undertook two stock splits (2:1), one in September 2000, the other in June 2006. The share prices we use adjust for these splits.

Table 2.9 Case study on Lehman Brothers

	A	B	C	D	E	F
1	Global recovery $\overline{\Lambda}$	50%				
2	Volatility of the barrier λ	10%				
3	Time (yrs) t	1				
4	Date	Share Price	Debt-per-Share	Hist. 30D Vola (%)	S&P Rating	CG 1yr PD (%)
5		(adj.)				
6	**Q42003**	36.1	70.0	25.3	A+	0.00
7	**Q12004**	[illegible]	[illegible]	[illegible]	[illegible]	[illegible]
8	**Q22004**	[illegible]	[illegible]	[illegible]	[illegible]	[illegible]
9	**Q32004**	[illegible]	[illegible]	[illegible]	[illegible]	[illegible]
10	**Q42004**	41.9	94.4	22.0	A+	0.00
11	**Q12005**	45.6	110.3	18.8	A+	0.00
12	**Q22005**	46.1	113.8	23.7	A+	0.00
13	**Q32005**	52.8	121.7	20.2	A+	0.00
14	**Q42005**	63.0	106.1	25.2	A	0.00
15	**Q12006**	73.0	126.9	23.0	A	0.00
16	**Q22006**	66.6	157.0	29.0	A	0.02
17	**Q32006**	63.8	121.6	27.9	A	0.00
18	**Q42006**	73.7	137.9	29.0	A	0.01
19	**Q12007**	73.3	179.4	30.8	A	0.05
20	**Q22007**	73.4	194.8	27.6	A	0.03
21	**Q32007**	54.8	235.0	34.9	A	1.04
22	**Q42007**	62.6	239.9	54.5	A	5.24
23	**Q12008**	51.0	219.8	78.4	A	17.43
24	**Q22008**	36.8	127.8	99.9	A	27.41

F6 =(1-CG_PS(B6,D6/100,C6,B$1,B$2,B$3))*100
(can be copied down to F24)

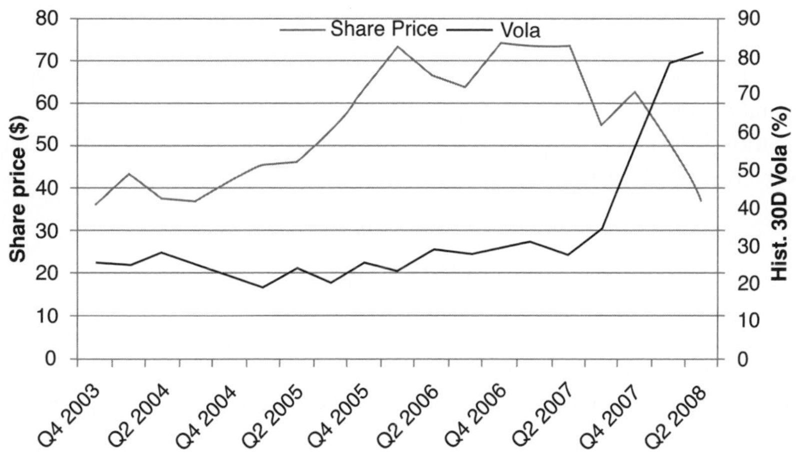

Figure 2.4 Share price and historical volatility for Lehman Brothers

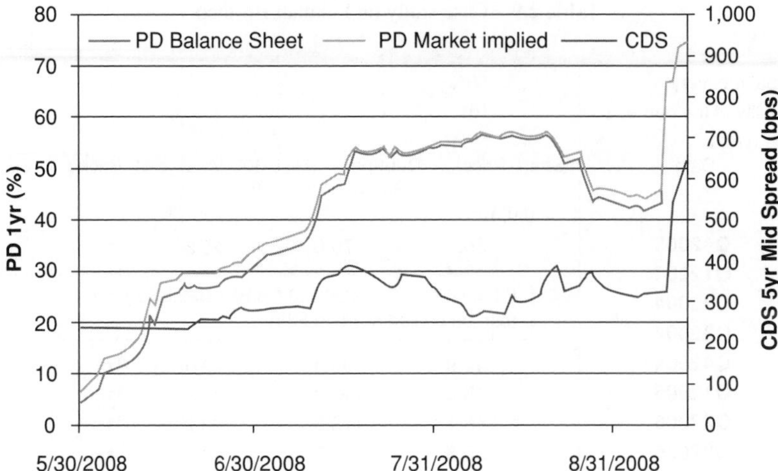

Figure 2.5 Comparing PD from the CreditGrades model with different specifications and the CDS spread for Lehman Brothers

lower during Q4 2003–Q4 2006,[13] and in Q1 2007 the model matches the 0.05%. In 2007, the decline of the stock price paired with the increase of the volatility results in sharper PD estimates implying S&P ratings between BBB and BB–.[14] In 2008, CreditGrades implies PDs of 17–27% per year, indicating a CCC/C level and thus pre-default. However, in the second quarter of 2008 one might have believed in a model error, rather than an early warning. Let us look at the CDS levels at that time together with the CreditGrades PDs in Figure 2.5.

At the end of the second quarter 2008, when Lehman published its last quarterly report, the Lehman CDS trades around 230 basis points. Assuming that the CDS spread correctly prices the default risk, we obtain a market-implied debt-per-share ratio of \$62.[15] Using this implied debt-per-share ratio lowers the PD implied by CreditGrades compared to the use of balance sheet information, but it is still large enough to create serious concerns about the solvency of Lehman. The subsequent increase of both PD measures is driven by the increasing stock volatility and the decrease of the stock price, predictors that are particularly useful in such crisis scenarios. Concluding, we find that CreditGrades is able to provide quite timely credit signals, even in difficult cases.

APPENDIX

Here we collect some equations of the CreditGrades model mentioned in the main text. The formulae can be used to estimate the implied asset volatility and implied barrier. Furthermore we give the CDS spread formula for estimating the implied debt-per-share from observed CDS

[13] Increasing the global recovery parameter, e.g., to 60%, as examined for financials by Veraart (2004), improves the match to the rating implied PDs during that period.

[14] In early 2007 the historical volatility climbed from around 30% to 50%. With option implied volatility this pattern is even more pronounced. The stock price started dipping two quarters later.

[15] See the Appendix to this chapter.

spreads. To start, the price of an European put option under the CG framework is given as[16]

$$P(S,t,B) = X\exp(-r(T-t))\Phi(a_1,a_2) - S\Phi(a_5) + I(B,\sigma,S,X) \tag{2.A1}$$

where X is the strike, T the maturity of the option, B the random default barrier, $\Phi(x,y)$ the integral over the normal distribution density from x to y and $\Phi(x)$ the corresponding integral over $[-\infty, x]$. I is given as

$$\begin{aligned} I(Ba,\sigma,S,x) = {} & -X\exp(-r(T-t)\Phi(a_3,a_4)) + S(1-\Phi(a_4)) \\ & + Ba\exp(rt)(\Phi(a_2)-\Phi(a_4)-\Phi(a_5)+\Phi(a_6)) \\ & - \frac{S}{Ba}X\exp(-rT)\Phi(a_3,a_4) + 2X\exp\left(\frac{z}{2}-r(T-t)\right) \\ & \times \int_{z/\sqrt{2\tau}}^{\infty} \sqrt{2\pi}^{-1}\exp\left(-\frac{S^2}{2}\right)\exp\left(-\frac{z^2}{8s^2}\right)ds \end{aligned}$$

where

$$\begin{aligned} a_{1,3} &= \pm\frac{0.5\sigma^2(T-t)-\sigma\eta}{\sigma\sqrt{T-t}} \\ a_{2,5} &= -\frac{\sigma(\eta-\eta_X)\mp 0.5\sigma^2(T-t)}{\sigma\sqrt{T-t}} \\ \sigma_{4,6} &= -\frac{\sigma(\eta+\eta_X)\pm 0.5\sigma^2(T-t)}{\sigma\sqrt{T-t}} \end{aligned}$$

which depend on the distance to default measures

$$\begin{aligned} \eta &= \frac{1}{\sigma}\log\left(1+\frac{S}{Ba\exp(rt)}\right) \\ \eta_X &= \frac{1}{\sigma}\log\left(1+\frac{X}{Ba\exp(rt)}\right) \end{aligned}$$

With two at-the-money put prices $P_{1,2}$ we can use Equation (2.A1) to solve for the implied asset volatility and the implied barrier. However here it is easier to solve

$$\sigma_{1,2} = \sigma\left(1+\frac{Ba}{X_{1,2}-S}\log\left(\frac{X_{1,2}}{S}\right)\right)$$

[16] See Finger *et al.* (2002).

Converting the survival probability into a credit spread we specify R as the recovery rate of the underlying credit[17] and obtain[18]

$$s = r(1-R)\frac{1 - PS_0 + \exp\left(r\frac{\sigma^2\Lambda}{\sigma^2}\right)\left(G\left(t+\frac{\sigma^2\Lambda}{\sigma^2}\right) - G\left(\frac{\sigma^2\Lambda}{\sigma^2}\right)\right)}{PS_0 - PS_t\exp(-rt) - \exp\left(r\frac{\sigma^2\Lambda}{\sigma^2}\right)\left(G\left(t+\frac{\sigma^2\Lambda}{\sigma^2}\right) - G\left(\frac{\sigma^2\Lambda}{\sigma^2}\right)\right)} \quad (2.A2)$$

where the function G is given as

$$G(x) = d^{\sqrt{\frac{1}{2}+\frac{2r}{\sigma^2}\Lambda}+\frac{1}{2}}\,\Phi\left(-\frac{\log(d)}{\sigma\sqrt{x}} - \sqrt{\frac{1}{4}+\frac{2r}{\sigma}}\sigma\sqrt{x}\right)$$

$$+d^{-\sqrt{\frac{1}{4}+\frac{2r}{\sigma}}+\frac{1}{2}}\,\Phi\left(-\frac{\log(d)}{\sigma\sqrt{x}} + \sqrt{\frac{1}{4}+\frac{2r}{\sigma}}\sigma\sqrt{x}\right)$$

In VBA we define the corresponding functions as

```
Function CG_G(x, d1, r, sigma)
Dim z
z = (0.25 + (2 * r / sigma ^ 2)) ^ (0.5)
CG_G = d1 ^ (z + 0.5) * Application.NormSDist(-Log(d1) / _
      (sigma * x ^ 0.5) - z * sigma * x ^ 0.5) + d1 ^ (-z + 0.5) _
       * Application.NormSDist(-Log(d1) / (sigma * x ^ 0.5) + _
       z * sigma * x ^ 0.5)
End Function
```

and the main function

```
Function CG_CDS(S, sigma_E, d, Lambda, sigma_B, t, Rec, r)
Dim d1, sigma, xi, H
d1 = (S + Lambda * d) * Exp(sigma_B ^ 2) / (Lambda * d)
sigma = (sigma_E * S) / (S + Lambda * d)
xi = sigma_B ^ 2 / sigma ^ 2
H = Exp(r * xi) * (CG_G(t + xi, d1, r, sigma) - CG_G(xi, d1, r, sigma))

CG_CDS = (r * (1 - Rec) * (1 - CG_PS(S, sigma_S, d, Lambda, sigma_B,
  0#) _ + H)) / CG_PS(S, sigma_E, d, Lambda, sigma_B, 0#) - _
CG_PS(S, sigma_E, d, Lambda, sigma_B, t) * Exp(-r * t) - H)
End Function
```

Using observed CDS spreads we can now use Solver in combination with the CG_CDS function, e.g., to find the implied debt-per-share ratio or any other parameter of interest.

[17] Note the difference between R and Λ. The former refers to the expected recovery of a specific part of the firm's liabilities, e.g., a bond, whereas the expected value of the random variable Λ gives the expected average recovery over all assets of the firm.

[18] For more details on CDS spreads and the procedure underlying the deviation of this equation, see Chapter 10.

NOTES AND LITERATURE

Assumptions

The Merton model, like any model, simplifies the reality to make things tractable. Important assumptions in Merton (1974) are: no transactions cost; no bankruptcy cost; no taxes; unrestricted borrowing and lending at the risk-free interest rate; no short selling restrictions; no uncertainty about liabilities; log-normally distributed assets. Many extensions to Merton (1974) have been proposed and tested, and the design and practical application of structural models is still high on the agenda in credit risk research.

Literature

The seminal paper is Merton, R.C., 1974, On the pricing of corporate debt. The risk structure of interest rates, *Journal of Finance* 29, 449–470.

The iterative method is used, for example, in Vassalou, M. and Xing, Y., 2004, Default risk in equity returns, *Journal of Finance* 59, 831–868. Our multi-year analysis follows Delianedis, G. and Geske, R., 2001, The components of corporate credit spreads. Default, recovery, tax, jumps, liquidity, and market factors, *Working paper*, UCLA. The approach behind Moody's KMV EDFs is described in Kealhofer, S., 2003, Quantifying credit risk I: Default prediction, *Financial Analysts Journal* 59(1), 30–44.

The CreditGrades model is extensively described in Finger, C., *et al.*, 2002, CreditGrades. Technical document, `Riskmetrics.com` (accessed August 9, 2010). The extensions with respect to implied volatility and implied leverage are based on Hull, J., Nelken, I. and White, A., 2005, Merton's model, credit risk and volatility skews, *Journal of Credit Risk* 1, 3–28 and Stamicar, R. and Finger, C., 2005, Incorporating equity derivatives into the CreditGrades model, `Riskmetrics.com` (accessed August 9, 2010). An exact solution to the CreditGrades survival probability is derived by Kiesel, R. and Veraart, L., 2008, A note on the survival probability in CreditGrades, *Journal of Credit Risk* 4(2), 65–74. The adjustments for financials are discussed by Veraart, L., 2004, Asset-based estimates for default probabilities for commercial banks, mimeo, University of Ulm.

3 Transition Matrices

A credit rating system uses a limited number of rating grades to rank borrowers according to their default probability. Ratings are assigned by rating agencies such as Fitch, Moody's and Standard & Poor's, but also by financial institutions. Rating assignments can be based on a qualitative process or on default probabilities estimated with a scoring model (see Chapter 1), a structural model (see Chapter 2) or other means. To translate default probability estimates into ratings, one defines a set of rating grade boundaries, e.g., rules that borrowers are assigned to grade AAA if their probability of default is lower than 0.02%, to grade AA if their probability of default is between 0.02% and 0.05% and so on.

In this chapter, we introduce methods for answering questions such as: 'With what probability will the credit risk rating of a borrower decrease by a given degree?' In credit risk lingo, we show how to estimate probabilities of rating transition or rating migration. They are usually presented in transition matrices.

Consider a rating system with two rating classes A and B, and a default category D. The transition matrix for this rating system is a table listing the probabilities that a borrower rated A at the start of a period has rating A, B or D at the end of the period; analogously for B-rated companies. Table 3.1 illustrates the transition matrix for this simple rating system.

Row headers give the rating at the beginning of the time period, column headers the rating at the end of period. The period length is often set to one year, but other choices are possible as well. The default category does not have a row of its own because it is treated as an absorbing category, i.e., probabilities of migrating from D to A and B are set to zero. A borrower that moves from B to D and back to B within the period will still be counted as a defaulter. If we counted such an instance as 'stay within B', the transition matrix would understate the danger of experiencing losses from default.

Transition matrices serve as an input to many credit risk analyses, e.g., in the measurement of credit portfolio risk (see Chapter 7). They are usually estimated from observed historical rating transitions. For agency ratings, there is practically no alternative to using historical transitions because agencies do not associate their grades with probabilities of default or transition. For a rating system based on a quantitative model, one could try to derive transition probabilities within the model – but this is not common.

In this chapter, we discuss two estimation procedures built on historical transitions: the cohort approach and the hazard approach. The *cohort approach* is the traditional technique, which estimates transition probabilities through historical transition frequencies. Though widely established, the cohort approach does not make full use of the available data. The estimates are not affected by the timing and sequencing of transitions within a year. One consequence hereof is that transition rates to low grades are often zero for high-quality issuers. Such events are so rare that they are seldom observed empirically. Still, there is indirect evidence that they can nevertheless happen. What one does observe is that high-grade issuers are downgraded within a year, say to BBB, and that BBB issuers can default within a few months. An approach that circumvents such problems and makes efficient use of the data would be to estimate transition rates using a *hazard rate approach*, similar to survival studies in medical science. After

Table 3.1 Structure of a transition matrix

Rating at start of period		Rating at end of period: A	B	D
	A	probability of staying in A	probability of migrating from A to B	probability of default from A
	B	probability of migrating from B to A	probability of staying in B	probability of default from B

presenting this approach, we show how to determine confidence intervals for the estimated transition probabilities.

COHORT APPROACH

A cohort comprises all obligors holding a given rating at the start of a given period. In the cohort approach, the transition matrix is filled with empirical transition frequencies that are computed as follows.

Let $N_{i,t}$ denote the number of obligors in category i at the beginning of period t ($N_{i,t}$ is therefore the size of the cohort i,t). Let $N_{ij,t}$ denote the number of obligors from the cohort i,t that have obtained grade j at the end of period t. The transition frequencies in period t are computed as

$$\hat{p}_{ij,t} = \frac{N_{ij,t}}{N_{i,t}} \tag{3.1}$$

Usually, a transition matrix is estimated with data from several periods. A common way of averaging the period transition frequencies is the obligor-weighted average, which uses the number of obligors in a cohort as weights:

$$\hat{p}_{ij} = \frac{\sum_t N_{i,t}\hat{p}_{ij,t}}{\sum_t N_{i,t}} \tag{3.2}$$

Inserting (3.1) into (3.2) leads to

$$\hat{p}_{ij} = \frac{\sum_t N_{i,t}\frac{N_{ij,t}}{N_{i,t}}}{\sum_t N_{i,t}} = \frac{\sum_t N_{ij,t}}{\sum_t N_{i,t}} = \frac{Ni_j}{N_i} \tag{3.3}$$

Therefore, the obligor-weighted average can be directly obtained by dividing the overall sum of transitions from i to j by the overall number of obligors that were in grade i at the start of the considered periods.

Table 3.2 A rating data set

	A	B	C	D	E	F	G	H
1	Id	Date	Rating Symbol	Rating Number		NR	0	0
2	1	30-May-00	CCC+	7	=VLOOKUP(C2,F$1:H$23,3,0)	AAA	1	1
3	1	31-Dec-00	B-	6	*(can be copied into D3:D4001)*	AA+	2	2
4	2	21-May-03	B	6		AA	3	2
5	3	30-Dec-99	BB-	5		AA-	4	2
6	3	30-Oct-00	B+	6		A+	5	3
7	3	30-Dec-01	BB	5		A	6	3
8	4	30-Dec-01	BB-	5		A-	7	3
9	4	30-May-02	B-	6		BBB+	8	4
10	5	24-May-00	AA-	2		BBB	9	4
11	5	30-May-01	A+	3		BBB-	10	4
12	5	30-Oct-01	AA-	2		BB+	11	5
13	6	30-Dec-99	BBB+	4		BB	12	5
14	6	30-Dec-01	BBB	4		BB-	13	5
15	7	30-Dec-02	BBB	4		B+	14	6
16	7	23-Jun-03	BB+	5		B	15	6
17	7	30-Dec-03	B+	6		B-	16	6
18	7	21-May-04	BB-	5		CCC+	17	7
19	8	30-Dec-02	A-	3		CCC	18	7
20	9	21-May-00	AA	2		CCC-	19	7
21	9	30-Dec-00	NR	0		CC	20	7
22	10	30-Dec-04	BB	5		C	21	7
23	11	30-Dec-99	B	6		D	22	8
...	...	...	...	...				
4001	1,829	30-Aug-00	A-	3				

The periodicity can be chosen by the analyst. In the following, we use calendar-year periods. A possible alternative with the same period length would be to use overlapping 12-month periods.

Let us now apply the cohort approach. A typical way of storing rating data is shown in Table 3.2. The first column contains an obligor identifier; the second column gives the date of the rating action and the third the rating that was assigned. In our hypothetical data set, we use the Standard & Poor's rating scale from AAA to C. A rating withdrawal is coded as NR (not rated).

For computations, it is convenient to convert the rating classes to numbers. We do this in column D using the VLOOKUP function. In the range F1:H23, we have two different conversion schemes. In column G, the rating symbol is mapped into 22 rating classes, maintaining the fineness of modified rating scale (+/flat/–) used in column C. In column H, the ratings are mapped into eight letter-grade classes. We will use the latter mapping in this chapter. It is obtained by entering =VLOOKUP(C2,F$1:H$23,3,0) in cell D2 and filling it down to the end of the data set. (To map the ratings into the 22-number scheme change the third argument

Table 3.3 Rating at year-end for id 1

Year-end	Grade
2000	7
2001	7
2002	6
...	...
Final year in data set	6

in the VLOOKUP function to two: =VLOOKUP(C2,F$1:H$23,2,0). Note that lower rating numbers correspond to better ratings, and that a rating withdrawal is assigned the (arbitrary) value zero.

To understand how the data should be analysed in the cohort approach, let us single out an obligor and determine the cohorts to which it belongs. With calendar-year cohorts, the first obligor (id 1) in Table 3.2 belongs to the cohorts shown in Table 3.3, formed at the end of the stated year.

The rating actions are 'stay in the same rating' with the exception of year 2002, where we record a transition from 7 to 6.

We will implement the cohort approach in a user-defined function. The output conforms to the way in which rating agencies publish transition matrices: transition from default and not-rated are not shown while transitions to not-rated are shown in the right-most column.

The function assumes that the data is sorted according to obligors and rating dates (ascending), as the data in Table 3.2 already is. The opening lines of our function COHORT() with the definition of the variables read:

```
Function cohort(id, dat, rat, _
      Optional classes As Integer, Optional ystart, Optional yend)
If IsMissing(ystart) Then ystart = _
                              Year(Application.WorksheetFunction.min(dat))
If IsMissing(yend) Then yend = _
                              Year(Application.WorksheetFunction.Max(dat)) -
1
If classes = 0 Then classes = Application.WorksheetFunction.Max(rat)
```

The input of the obligor identifier, the rating date and the rating itself are sufficient for our function. However, we add three optional variables. The first two are `ystart` and `yend`, which restrict the computation to cohorts formed at the end of year `ystart`, and to transitions occurring until the end of year `yend`. If these two optional parameters are not specified, we estimate the transition matrix from the year-end following the first rating action to the year-end preceding the last rating action. The third optional parameter is `classes`. Here, the number of rating grades can be supplied. Our function assumes that the highest rating number marks the default category, whereas rating withdrawals carry a zero as rating number. You can easily achieve this coding by the VLOOKUP function described above. When the input of the `classes` variable is omitted, we estimate the number of rating categories from the data.

Next, we declare variables:

```
Dim obs As Long, k As Long, kn As Long, i As Integer, j As Integer, _
     t As Integer
Dim Ni() As Long, Nij() As Long, pij() As Double, newrat As Integer
ReDim Nij(1 To classes - 1, 0 To classes), Ni(1 To classes)
obs = id.Rows.count
```

k is a counter for the observations; kn will be used to find the rating from the next year-end. `i`, `j`, `t`, `Ni`, `Nij` and `pij` are used as in Equation (3.3). `newrat` is an auxiliary variable that will contain the rating from the next year-end.

The `Ni` and `Nij` are determined in the following `For k = 1 to obs` loop:

```
For k = 1 To obs
'Earliest cohort to which observation can belong is from year:
     t = Application.Max(ystart, Year(dat(k)))

     'Loop through cohorts to which observation k can belong
     Do While t < yend
        'Is there another rating from the same year?
        If id(k + 1) = id(k, 1) And Year(dat(k + 1)) <= t _
                                  And k <> obs Then Exit Do
        'Is the issuer in default or not rated?
        If rat(k) = classes Or rat(k) = 0 Then Exit Do

        'Add to number of issuers in cohort
        Ni(rat(k)) = Ni(rat(k)) + 1

        'Determine rating from end of next year (=y+1)
        'rating stayed constant
        If id(k + 1) <> id(k) Or Year(dat(k + 1)) > t + 1 Or k = obs Then
            newrat = rat(k)
        'rating changed
        Else
           kn = k + 1
           Do While Year(dat(kn + 1)) = Year(dat(kn)) And _
                                                  id(kn + 1) =
id(kn)
                If rat(kn) = classes Then Exit Do 'Default is
absorbing!
                kn = kn + 1
           Loop
           newrat = rat(kn)
        End If

        'Add to number of transitions
        Nij(rat(k), newrat) = Nij(rat(k), newrat) + 1
```

```
        'Exit if observation k cannot belong to cohort of y+1
        If newrat <> rat(k) Then Exit Do
        t = t + 1
    Loop
Next k
```

With a `Do While` loop, we find the cohorts to which observation `k` belongs. To decide whether it belongs to a certain cohort, we check whether the current rating information is the latest in the current year *t*. If there is a migration during the current period, we exit the `Do While` loop and continue with the next observation. If not, we first check whether the issuer is in default or not rated; in these two cases we exit the `Do While` loop because we do not compute transitions for these two categories.

If observation `k` has passed these checks, we increase the `Ni` count by one and determine the associated rating from the end of the year *t*. We can quickly determine whether there was not any rating action before the end of year *t*; if there was, we again use a `Do While` loop to find the rating prevailing at the end of year *t*. We then increase the `Nij` count by 1. Before moving on to the next year within the `Do While` loop, we close it if we know that the current observation cannot belong to next year's cohort.

Next, we calculate the transition frequencies `pij=Nij/Ni`. Following convention, we also set the NR category to be the right-most column of the transition matrix:

```
ReDim pij(1 To classes - 1, 1 To classes + 1)

'Compute transition frequencies pij=Nij/Ni
For i = 1 To classes - 1
    For j = 1 To classes
        If Ni(i) > 0 Then pij(i, j) = Nij(i, j) / Ni(i)
    Next j
Next i

'NR category to the end
For i = 1 To classes - 1
    If Ni(i) > 0 Then pij(i, classes + 1) = Nij(i, 0) / Ni(i)
Next i

cohort = pij

End Function
```

There are eight rating grades in our example. The transition matrix therefore is a 7×9 dimensional matrix. It has only seven rows because we do not return the frequencies for the default and the not-rated category; it has nine columns because the not-rated category is not included in the eight classes.

To apply the function COHORT() to the example data from Table 3.2, select a range of 7×9 cells, enter

$$= \text{COHORT}\,(\text{A2:A4001, B2:B4001, C2:C4001})$$

and press [ctrl]+[shift]+[enter]. The result is the one shown in Table 3.4.

Table 3.4 One-year transition matrix with the cohort approach

	A	B	C	D	E	F	G	H	I	J	K	L	M	N
1	id	Date	Rat		**Transition matrix**									
2	1	30-May-00	7			1	2	3	4	5	6	7	8	NR
3	1	31-Dec-00	6		1	90.63%	1.04%	0.00%	0.00%	1.04%	0.00%	0.00%	0.00%	7.29%
4	2	21-May-03	6		2	1.53%	85.38%	8.64%	0.14%	0.00%	0.14%	0.00%	0.00%	4.18%
5	3	30-Dec-99	5		3	0.14%	2.99%	86.60%	5.69%	0.35%	0.14%	0.00%	0.07%	4.03%
6	3	30-Oct-00	6		4	0.00%	0.00%	3.75%	85.08%	6.09%	1.02%	0.08%	0.31%	3.67%
7	3	30-Dec-01	5		5	0.00%	0.00%	0.66%	7.57%	71.38%	10.69%	1.64%	0.99%	7.07%
8	4	30-Dec-01	5		6	0.00%	0.19%	0.38%	0.77%	7.31%	75.38%	8.08%	1.73%	6.15%
9	4	30-May-02	6		7	0.00%	0.00%	0.00%	0.00%	1.64%	7.10%	61.20%	10.38%	19.67%
10	5	24-May-00	2											
11	5	30-May-01	3			{=COHORT(A2:A4001,B2:B4001,C2:C4001)}								
12	5	30-Oct-01	2			*(applies to F3:N9)*								
...	...	...	...											
4001	1829	30-Aug-00	3											

The matrix mirrors two empirical findings common to the matrices published by rating agencies. First, on-diagonal entries are the highest; they are in the range of 61% to over 90%. This means that the rating system is relatively stable. Second, default frequencies for the best two rating classes are zero. Since one cannot rule out the possibility of an obligor defaulting, we would expect the true default probability of the best grades to be nonzero albeit very small. But with a very small default probability, the default events are so rare that it is typical to observe no defaults. For a rating class with 100 obligors and a default probability of 0.01%, for example, the expected number of defaults over 20 years is 0.2.

An NR-adjusted version of the transition matrix (3.2) would remove the NR column and adjust the other table entries such that they again sum up to 100%. One way for achieving this to exclude the obligors who had their rating withdrawn from the cohort. To perform such an adjustment, we do not need the original rating data; a matrix like the one in Table 3.4 suffices. See Chapter 4 for details.[1]

MULTI-PERIOD TRANSITIONS

If we want to estimate probabilities for transitions over a horizon of maybe three years instead of one, we can do this in much the same way as in the previous section. Just define the period length to be three years instead of one, and modify the function COHORT() accordingly.

Alternatively, we can convert a transition matrix that was estimated for a given period length – like one year in the previous section – into a multi-period matrix without analyzing the original data again. For doing so, we have to assume that transitions are independent across the years. Then, a T-period transition matrix can be obtained by multiplying the one-period matrix with itself $(T-1)$ times. Let P_T denote the transition matrix over T periods, then

$$P_T = P_1^T = \underbrace{P_1 P_1 \dots P_1}_{T\ times} \tag{3.4}$$

[1] Of course there are other possibilities to adjust the NR ratings, for example loading the NR probabilities into the diagonal elements.

Table 3.5 Two-year transition matrix based on Table 3.4

	A	B	C	D	E	F	G	H	I	J
1	**Extended matrix from Table 3.4**									
2		1	2	3	4	5	6	7	8	NR
3	1	90.63%	1.04%	0.00%	0.00%	1.04%	0.00%	0.00%	0.00%	7.29%
4	2	1.53%	85.38%	8.64%	0.14%	0.00%	0.14%	0.00%	0.00%	4.18%
5	3	0.14%	2.99%	86.60%	5.69%	0.35%	0.14%	0.00%	0.07%	4.03%
6	4	0.00%	0.00%	3.75%	85.08%	6.09%	1.02%	0.08%	0.31%	3.67%
7	5	0.00%	0.00%	0.66%	7.57%	71.38%	10.69%	1.64%	0.99%	7.07%
8	6	0.00%	0.19%	0.38%	0.77%	7.31%	75.38%	8.08%	1.73%	6.15%
9	7	0.00%	0.00%	0.00%	0.00%	1.64%	7.10%	61.20%	10.38%	19.67%
10	8	0.00%	0.00%	0.00%	0.00%	0.00%	0.00%	0.00%	100%	0.00%
11	NR	0.00%	0.00%	0.00%	0.00%	0.00%	0.00%	0.00%	0.00%	100%
12										
13										
14	**Two-year matrix**									
15		1	2	3	4	5	6	7	8	NR
16	1	82.14%	1.83%	0.10%	0.08%	1.69%	0.11%	0.02%	0.01%	14.02%
17	2	2.71%	73.16%	14.86%	0.73%	0.06%	0.24%	0.01%	0.01%	8.22%
18	3	0.29%	5.14%	75.47%	9.81%	0.91%	0.32%	0.02%	0.15%	7.89%
19	4	0.01%	0.11%	6.48%	73.07%	9.62%	2.29%	0.30%	0.67%	7.46%
20	5	0.00%	0.04%	1.36%	11.96%	52.22%	15.89%	3.05%	2.07%	13.41%
21	6	0.00%	0.32%	0.72%	1.81%	10.91%	58.19%	11.15%	3.95%	12.95%
22	7	0.00%	0.01%	0.04%	0.18%	2.69%	9.88%	38.06%	16.88%	32.27%
23	8	0.00%	0.00%	0.00%	0.00%	0.00%	0.00%	0.00%	100%	0.00%
24	NR	0.00%	0.00%	0.00%	0.00%	0.00%	0.00%	0.00%	0.00%	100%
25										
26		=MMULT(B3:J11,B3:J11)								
27		*(applies to B16:J24)*								

With this rule, we can also generate matrices over horizons that are longer than the time span covered by our rating data; for example, we can estimate a five-year transition matrix from two years of data.[2]

If we try to multiply the matrix in Table 3.5 with itself using the MMULT() command, we observe a problem. To multiply a matrix with itself, the matrix has to be symmetric, but our matrix has seven rows and nine columns. To fix this problem, we can add two rows for the default and not-rated category. For the default category, which we assumed to be absorbing, the natural way of filling the row is to put 0s off-diagonal and a 1 on-diagonal. For the NR category, we could have estimated the transition rates. In the previous section we did not include migrations to NR in our calculation. We could thus perform an NR-adjustment and

[2] Remember that we assume the transitions to be independent across years. This so-called 'Markovian' assumption contradicts empirical findings where rating transitions in one year are not found to be independent of the transition in the previous year. Therefore, this methodology should be used with caution.

work with the NR-adjusted matrix. Here, we refrain from doing so and assume that the NR status is absorbing as well. From a risk-management perspective, this can be an innocent assumption if lending relationships are (at least temporarily) terminated with a transition to NR.

In Table 3.5, we therefore extend the matrix from Table 3.4 by two rows having 0s off-diagonal and 1s on-diagonal, and compute a two-year matrix with the MMULT() command.

By repeated application of the MMULT command we can obtain any T-year matrix. To get a three-year matrix, for example, we would type

= MMULT (MMULT (B3:J11,B3:J11),B3:J11)

Since this can get tedious for large T, we propose a user-defined function MPOWER(array1, power), which takes `array1` to the power of `power` (see the Appendix at the end of this chapter for details).

HAZARD RATE APPROACH

The cohort approach does not make full use of the available data. Specifically, the estimates of the cohort approach are not affected by the timing and sequencing of transitions *within* the period. As an example, consider obligor number 5 from Table 3.2. For this obligor, we have recorded the following rating actions:

Id	Date	Rating Symbol	Rating Number
5	24-May-00	AA–	2
5	30-May-01	A+	3
5	30-Oct-01	AA–	2

In the cohort approach, we would conclude that the rating remained stable over the year 2001 even though there were two rating changes in that year.

An alternative approach that captures within-period transitions is called the *duration* or *hazard rate approach*. In the following, we demonstrate its implementation without explaining the underlying Markov chain theory; the interested reader is referred to the literature stated at the end of this chapter.

We first estimate a so-called generator matrix Λ providing a general description of the transition behavior. The off-diagonal entries of Λ estimated over the time period $[t_{0,t}]$ are given as

$$\lambda_{ij} = \frac{N_{ij}}{\int_{t_0}^{t} Y_i(s)ds} \text{for } i \neq j \tag{3.5}$$

where N_{ij} is the observed number of transitions from i to j during the time period considered in the analysis, and $Y_i(s)$ is the number of firms rated i at time s. The denominator therefore contains the number of 'obligor-years' spent in rating class i. Note the similarity to the cohort approach. In both cases, we divide the number of transitions by a measure of how many obligors are at risk of experiencing the transition. In the cohort approach, we count the obligors at discrete points in time (the cohort formation dates); in the hazard approach we count the obligors at any point in time.

The on-diagonal entries are constructed as the negative value of the sum of the λ_{ij} per row:

$$\lambda_{ij} = -\sum_{i \neq j} \lambda_{ij} \tag{3.6}$$

How would the history of obligor 5 shown above affect the generator matrix? It migrated from the second rating class to the third and back to the second. This adds a value of 1 both to $N_{2,3}$ and $N_{3,2}$.[3] The contribution to the denominator is as follows (assuming t_0 to precede 24-May-00): the first spell in rating class 2 adds roughly one year to the denominator of $\lambda_{2,j}$; the time spent in class 3 adds half a year to the denominator of $\lambda_{3,j}$; and the second time spent in class 2 adds the difference between t and 30-Oct-01, again to $\lambda_{2,j}$.

Form Markov chain mechanics, a T-year transition matrix $P(T)$ is derived from the generator matrix as follows:

$$P(T) = \exp(\Lambda T) = \sum_{k=0}^{\infty} \frac{\Lambda^k T^k}{k!} \tag{3.7}$$

where ΛT is the generator matrix multiplied by the scalar T and exp() is the matrix exponential function. If we want a one-year matrix, we simply evaluate exp(Λ), but generating matrices for other horizons is just as easy.

For the calculation of the generator matrix, we supply the user-defined function GENERATOR(). It assumes that the data is sorted according to obligors and dates (ascending). The arguments are the same as for the function COHORT() from above:

```
Function GENERATOR(id, dat, rat, _
  Optional classes As Integer, Optional ystart, Optional yend)
```

Again, we assign default values from the data set to unspecified optional parameters. In contrast to the COHORT() function where the knowledge of the year was sufficient, daily information is used here to define the start and end date. If `ystart` and `yend` are only specified as calendar years, we set the start and end day to the respective year-end:

```
Dim k As Long, i As Long, j As Long, dmin As Date, dmax As Date, _
    obs As Long

If classes = 0 Then classes = Application.WorksheetFunction.Max(rat)
obs = Application.WorksheetFunction.count(id)
dmin = Application.WorksheetFunction.min(dat)
dmax = Application.WorksheetFunction.Max(dat)
If IsMissing(ystart) = False Then
   dmin = ystart
   If Len(ystart) = 4 Then dmin = DateSerial(ystart, 12, 31)
```

[3] When referring to actual numbers we separate the classes in the subscripts by commas, e.g., we write $N_{2,3}$ instead of N_{23}.

```
End If

If IsMissing(yend) = False Then
   dmax = yend
   If Len(yend) = 4 Then dmax = DateSerial(yend, 12, 31)
End If

Dim spell() As Double, nlambda() As Double, dlambda() As Double, _
    lambda() As Double, spell_k As Double, dat_k As Date
ReDim nlambda(0 To classes, 0 To classes), dlambda(0 To classes)
```

As in the cohort function, `k` is the observation counter, while `i` and `j` are used as in Equation (3.5). `nlambda` is the numerator of the λ_{ij} and `dlambda` its denominator. `dat_k` and `spell_k` are auxiliary variables containing the migration date of the kth observation and the length of time that observation `k` spends in its grade.

Now we can enter the core of the function, a `For k=1 to obs-1` loop:

```
For k = 1 To obs - 1

dat_k = dat(k)
'Truncate
 If dat_k < dmin Then dat_k = dmin
 If dat_k > dmax Then dat_k = dmax
 If dat(k + 1) < dmin Then GoTo mynext

 If id(k) = id(k + 1) And dat(k + 1) <= dmax Then
   spell_k = (dat(k + 1) - dat_k)
   nlambda(rat(k), rat(k + 1)) = nlambda(rat(k), rat(k + 1)) + 1
 Else
   spell_k = (dmax - dat_k)
End If
   dlambda(rat(k)) = dlambda(rat(k)) + spell_k / 365
mynext:
Next k
 'last obs
  If dmax > dat(obs) Then dlambda(rat(obs)) = dlambda(rat(obs)) + _
                                              (dmax - dat(obs)) / 365
```

The final observation is treated differently to avoid the index running out of range. Now we treat special cases: if the rating action happened before the time interval $[t_0, t]$ we raise its date to t_0; if it happened afterwards, we lower it to t. Also, we move to the next observation if the current one is followed by another rating action before t_0.

A transition `nlambda` is recorded whenever the next observation belongs to the same obligor and has a date smaller than t. To determine the length of the spell in days, we subtract the current date from the next observation's date or from t; the latter applies if the next observation has a date larger than t or belongs to another obligor. With the spell we calculate the denominator of the λ_{ij}. Since the `spell_k` is measured in days, we divide by 365 to translate it into obligor-years.

Having gone through all observations, the generator matrix can be obtained by calculating the off-diagonal λ_{ij}, summing them up in the variable `sumoffdiag` and setting the on-diagonal λ_{ii} equal to `-sumoffdiag`:

```
Dim sumoffdiag As Double
ReDim lambda(0 To classes + 1, 0 To classes + 1)
For i = 0 To classes
    sumoffdiag = 0
    If dlambda(i) > 0 Then
       For j = 0 To classes
           lambda(i, j) = nlambda(i, j) / dlambda(i)
           If i <> j Then sumoffdiag = sumoffdiag + lambda(i, j)
       Next j

    End If
lambda(i, i) = -sumoffdiag
Next i
```

Adding the absorbing default class, which consists of zeros, and putting the NR category to the right, we are finished:

```
'Absorbing default class
For j = 0 To classes + 1
    lambda(classes, j) = 0
Next j

'Shift NR category to the end of the matrix
Dim lambdatmp: ReDim lambdatmp(1 To classes + 1, 1 To classes + 1)
For i = 1 To classes + 1
    lambda(classes + 1, i) = lambda(0, i)
    lambda(i, classes + 1) = lambda(i, 0)
    For j = 1 To classes + 1
        lambdatmp(i, j) = lambda(i, j)
    Next j
Next i
lambdatmp(classes + 1, classes + 1) = lambda(0, 0)

GENERATOR = lambdatmp

End Function
```

Table 3.6 shows how to use the function on our example data. It is an array function whose output extends over several cells. We select a 9×9 range, enter

$$= \text{GENERATOR}(\text{A2:A4001}, \text{B2:B4001}, \text{C2:C4001})$$

and confirm by [ctrl]+[shift]+[enter].

Table 3.6 Estimating the generator matrix from the rating data

	A	B	C	D	E	F	G	H	I	J	K	L	M	N
1	id	Date	Rat		**Generator**									
2	1	30-May-00	7			1	2	3	4	5	6	7	8	NR
3	1	31-Dec-00	6		1	-0.072	0.014	0.007	0.000	0.000	0.000	0.000	0.000	0.051
4	2	21-May-03	6		2	0.013	-0.125	0.073	0.002	0.000	0.000	0.000	0.000	0.037
5	3	30-Dec-99	5		3	0.001	0.026	-0.123	0.054	0.002	0.001	0.000	0.000	0.038
6	3	30-Oct-00	6		4	0.000	0.000	0.039	-0.155	0.065	0.014	0.003	0.000	0.034
7	3	30-Dec-01	5		5	0.000	0.000	0.005	0.095	-0.316	0.140	0.017	0.002	0.057
8	4	30-Dec-01	5		6	0.000	0.001	0.001	0.009	0.095	-0.294	0.114	0.019	0.055
9	4	30-May-02	6		7	0.000	0.000	0.000	0.012	0.024	0.130	-0.517	0.130	0.220
10	5	24-May-00	2		8	0.000	0.000	0.000	0.000	0.000	0.000	0.000	0.000	0.000
11	5	30-May-01	3		NR	0.000	0.003	0.006	0.008	0.008	0.008	0.005	0.004	-0.041
12	5	30-Oct-01	2											
13	6	30-Dec-99	4			{=GENERATOR(A2:A4001,B2:B4001,C2:C4001)}								
14	6	30-Dec-01	4			*(applies to F3:N11)*								
15	7	30-Dec-02	4											
...	...	...	...											
4001	1829	30-Aug-00	3											

The one-year transition matrix based on this generator is given by applying the exponential function to the generator. Assume for a moment that we have just four categories including default and NR. The matrix exponential $\exp(\Lambda T)$ would then be of the form

$$\exp(\Delta T) = \begin{bmatrix} 1 & 0 & 0 & 0 \\ 0 & 1 & 0 & 0 \\ 0 & 0 & 1 & 0 \\ 0 & 0 & 0 & 1 \end{bmatrix} + T \begin{bmatrix} \lambda_{11} & \lambda_{12} & \lambda_{13} & \lambda_{14} \\ \lambda_{21} & \lambda_{22} & \lambda_{23} & \lambda_{24} \\ \lambda_{31} & \lambda_{32} & \lambda_{33} & \lambda_{34} \\ \lambda_{41} & \lambda_{42} & \lambda_{43} & \lambda_{44} \end{bmatrix} + \frac{T^2}{2!} \begin{bmatrix} \lambda_{11} & \lambda_{12} & \lambda_{13} & \lambda_{14} \\ \lambda_{21} & \lambda_{22} & \lambda_{23} & \lambda_{24} \\ \lambda_{31} & \lambda_{32} & \lambda_{33} & \lambda_{34} \\ \lambda_{41} & \lambda_{42} & \lambda_{43} & \lambda_{44} \end{bmatrix}^2 + \sum_{k=3}^{\infty} \frac{(\Delta T)^k}{k!} \tag{3.8}$$

We can evaluate the matrix exponential by truncating the infinite sum in (3.8) at some suitable point. This is implemented in the user-defined function MEXP() – as explained in the Appendix to this chapter. Since truncation may be numerically problematic, we also supply the user-defined function MEXPGENERATOR(), which is more reliable for the special case of generator matrices; this function is also discussed in the chapter Appendix.

Applying the MEXPGENERATOR() function to the generator of Table 3.6 leads to the result shown in Table 3.7. Again, we first select a 9 × 9 range, enter

= MEXPGENERATOR (F3:N11)

where F3:N11 is the range containing the generator matrix, and confirm by [ctrl]+[shift]+[enter].

Table 3.7 Obtaining a one-year transition matrix from the generator

	D	E	F	G	H	I	J	K	L	M	N
1		**Generator matrix**									
2			1	2	3	4	5	6	7	8	NR
3		1	-0.072	0.014	0.007	0.000	0.000	0.000	0.000	0.000	0.051
4		2	0.013	-0.125	0.073	0.002	0.000	0.000	0.000	0.000	0.037
5		3	0.001	0.026	-0.123	0.054	0.002	0.001	0.000	0.000	0.038
6		4	0.000	0.000	0.039	-0.155	0.065	0.014	0.003	0.000	0.034
7		5	0.000	0.000	0.005	0.095	-0.316	0.140	0.017	0.002	0.057
8		6	0.000	0.001	0.001	0.009	0.095	-0.294	0.114	0.019	0.055
9		7	0.000	0.000	0.000	0.012	0.024	0.130	-0.517	0.130	0.220
10		8	0.000	0.000	0.000	0.000	0.000	0.000	0.000	0.000	0.000
11		NR	0.000	0.003	0.006	0.008	0.008	0.008	0.005	0.004	-0.041
12											
13											
14											
15											
16		**1-year transition matrix**									
17			1	2	3	4	5	6	7	8	NR
18		1	93.02%	1.33%	0.72%	0.04%	0.02%	0.02%	0.01%	0.01%	4.83%
19		2	1.20%	88.34%	6.49%	0.37%	0.03%	0.02%	0.01%	0.01%	3.54%
20		3	0.11%	2.33%	88.65%	4.78%	0.32%	0.11%	0.02%	0.01%	3.68%
21		4	0.00%	0.05%	3.42%	86.00%	5.22%	1.52%	0.32%	0.05%	3.42%
22		5	0.00%	0.02%	0.57%	7.61%	73.68%	10.54%	1.72%	0.45%	5.41%
23		6	0.00%	0.13%	0.18%	1.13%	7.16%	75.55%	7.70%	2.24%	5.91%
24		7	0.00%	0.03%	0.09%	1.10%	2.14%	8.93%	60.19%	10.33%	17.18%
25		8	0.00%	0.00%	0.00%	0.00%	0.00%	0.00%	0.00%	100.00%	0.00%
26		NR	0.00%	0.28%	0.56%	0.79%	0.69%	0.72%	0.44%	0.44%	96.08%
27											
28			{=MEXPGENERATOR (F3:N11)}								
29			*(applies to F18:N26)*								
30											

To obtain a three-year matrix, for example, enter

$$= \text{MEXPGENERATOR (F3:N11*3)}$$

in the range F18:N26.

In contrast to the transition matrix estimated with the cohort approach, we have default probabilities of nonzero value for each rating category (the default probabilities are given in column M of Table 3.7). We see in the data that top-graded obligors are at risk of being downgraded to lower rating grades, which are then at risk of moving into default. Chaining the two moves together, we also get a nonzero probability of default for top-graded obligors.

One cannot conclude, though, that default probabilities estimated with the hazard approach are always higher than those from the cohort approach. In Table 3.7, the opposite is true for grades 3, 4, 5 and 7. What matters for the difference is the sequencing of rating transitions.

Consider a 'pass-through' grade to which many obligors migrate shortly before their default. One would expect the hazard default probability to be higher because the cohort approach fails to capture many of the short stays in the pass-through grade.

OBTAINING A GENERATOR MATRIX FROM A GIVEN TRANSITION MATRIX

We are not always in the lucky position of having detailed rating information from which we can estimate a generator. If the only information available is a transition matrix for a given horizon, can we obtain a generator? The answer is both a Yes and a No. It is possible, but not all transition matrices have a generator and for those that do, the generator may not be unique.[4]

To construct an approximate generator, we can make the assumption that there is only one transition per obligor and period. Let p_{ij} denote the entries of the transition matrix P, then the generator is given by

$$\begin{aligned} \lambda_{ii} &= \ln(p_{ii}) \\ \lambda_{ij} &= p_{ij}\frac{\lambda_{ii}}{(p_{ii}-1)}, \quad i \neq j \end{aligned} \tag{3.9}$$

We have implemented this conversion methodology in the user-defined function `transition2generator(array)` whose only argument is the array containing the transition matrix:

```
Function transition2generator(array1)

Dim P, n As Integer, i As Integer, j As Integer, lambda
P = array1
If UBound(P, 1) <> UBound(P, 2) Then End
n = UBound(P, 1)
ReDim lambda(1 To n, 1 To n)

'lii=log(pii)
For i = 1 To n
   lambda(i, i) = Log(P(i, i))
   For j = 1 To n
      If i <> j And P(i, i) < 1 Then
        lambda(i, j) = P(i, j) * lambda(i, i) / (P(i, i) - 1)
      End If
   Next j
Next i
transition2generator = lambda
End Function
```

In Table 3.8, we apply the function to the transition matrix of Table 3.7 and reconvert it to a transition matrix with the function MEXPGENERATOR().

[4] Conditions for a valid generator include the underlying Markov chain to be stochastically monotonic. See Israel, Rosenthal and Wei (2001) for an overview.

Table 3.8 Obtaining an approximate generator from a transition matrix

	A	B	C	D	E	F	G	H	I	J
1	**Transition matrix estimated with hazard approach**									
2		1	2	3	4	5	6	7	8	NR
3	1	93.02%	1.33%	0.72%	0.04%	0.02%	0.02%	0.01%	0.01%	4.83%
4	2	1.20%	88.34%	6.49%	0.37%	0.03%	0.02%	0.01%	0.01%	3.54%
5	3	0.11%	2.33%	88.65%	4.78%	0.32%	0.11%	0.02%	0.01%	3.68%
6	4	0.00%	0.05%	3.42%	86.00%	5.22%	1.52%	0.32%	0.05%	3.42%
7	5	0.00%	0.02%	0.57%	7.61%	73.68%	10.54%	1.72%	0.45%	5.41%
8	6	0.00%	0.13%	0.18%	1.13%	7.16%	75.55%	7.70%	2.24%	5.91%
9	7	0.00%	0.03%	0.09%	1.10%	2.14%	8.93%	60.19%	10.33%	17.18%
10	8	0.00%	0.00%	0.00%	0.00%	0.00%	0.00%	0.00%	100.00%	0.00%
11	NR	0.00%	0.28%	0.56%	0.79%	0.69%	0.72%	0.44%	0.44%	96.08%
12										
13										
14	**Approximate generator for transition matrix**									
15		1	2	3	4	5	6	7	8	NR
16	1	-0.07	0.01	0.01	0.00	0.00	0.00	0.00	0.00	0.05
17	2	0.01	-0.12	0.07	0.00	0.00	0.00	0.00	0.00	0.04
18	3	0.00	0.02	-0.12	0.05	0.00	0.00	0.00	0.00	0.04
19	4	0.00	0.00	0.04	-0.15	0.06	0.02	0.00	0.00	0.04
20	5	0.00	0.00	0.01	0.09	-0.31	0.12	0.02	0.01	0.06
21	6	0.00	0.00	0.00	0.01	0.08	-0.28	0.09	0.03	0.07
22	7	0.00	0.00	0.00	0.01	0.03	0.11	-0.51	0.13	0.22
23	8	0.00	0.00	0.00	0.00	0.00	0.00	0.00	0.00	0.00
24	NR	0.00	0.00	0.01	0.01	0.01	0.01	0.00	0.00	-0.04
25		{=transition2generator(B3:J11)}				*(applies to B16:J24)*				
26										
27	**Transition matrix from approximate generator**									
28		1	2	3	4	5	6	7	8	NR
29	1	93.03%	1.26%	0.74%	0.08%	0.04%	0.04%	0.02%	0.02%	4.78%
30	2	1.16%	88.43%	6.13%	0.51%	0.06%	0.04%	0.02%	0.02%	3.63%
31	3	0.12%	2.19%	88.82%	4.47%	0.42%	0.16%	0.04%	0.02%	3.76%
32	4	0.00%	0.09%	3.25%	86.31%	4.57%	1.62%	0.36%	0.11%	3.67%
33	5	0.00%	0.05%	0.71%	7.17%	74.30%	9.32%	1.74%	0.71%	6.01%
34	6	0.00%	0.14%	0.24%	1.42%	6.29%	76.32%	6.06%	2.74%	6.80%
35	7	0.00%	0.07%	0.17%	1.24%	2.25%	7.92%	60.59%	10.51%	17.25%
36	8	0.00%	0.00%	0.00%	0.00%	0.00%	0.00%	0.00%	100.00%	0.00%
37	NR	0.00%	0.27%	0.56%	0.78%	0.65%	0.69%	0.38%	0.47%	96.19%
38		{=MEXPGENERATOR(B16:J24)}				*(applies to B29:J37)*				
39										

Comparing this approximate generator to the transition matrix in Table 3.8, we see that both are similar but not identical. In our data, the assumption that there is only one transition per year is not fulfilled, leading to a discrepancy between the approximate generator and the one estimated with the detailed data.

CONFIDENCE INTERVALS WITH THE BINOMIAL DISTRIBUTION

In both the cohort and the hazard approach, entries of the transition matrix are estimates of transition probabilities. Like any estimate, they are affected by sampling error. If we see a value of 0.05% in some cell of the matrix, we cannot be sure that the transition probability is truly 0.05%. It could very well be lower or higher.

An intuitive way of quantifying sampling error is to provide confidence intervals for the estimates. In this section, we show how to use the binomial distribution for obtaining confidence bounds within the cohort approach. Bootstrapped confidence bounds for the hazard approach are demonstrated in the next section.

We focus on default probability estimates because these are the most relevant for risk management purposes. Transition probabilities to grades other than default can be examined in much the same way.

Let PD_i denote the true probability of default for rating class i. The estimated default probability according to Equation (3.3) is

$$\hat{p}_{ik} = \frac{N_{ik}}{N_i} \tag{3.10}$$

Now assume that defaults are independent across time and across obligors. Then, the number of defaults is binomially distributed with N_i successes and success probability PD_i, and we can easily derive confidence bounds. In practice, defaults are not necessarily independent (see Chapter 6). Nevertheless, it can be useful to have a quick (yet somehow dirty) way of obtaining confidence bounds.

If we are seeking a two-sided, $1-\alpha$ confidence interval where α is a value such as 5%, the lower bound PD_i^{min} must be such that the probability of observing N_i defaults or more is $\alpha/2$. PD_i^{min} therefore solves the condition

$$1 - \text{BINOM}\,(N_{ik} - 1, N_i, PD_i^{min}) = \alpha/2 \tag{3.11}$$

where BINOM(x, N, q) denotes the cumulative binomial distribution for observing x or less success out of N trials with success probability q.

The upper bound PD_i^{min} must be such that the probability of observing N_i or less defaults is $\alpha/2$:

$$\text{BINOM}(N_{ik}, N_i, PD_i^{max}) = \alpha/2 \tag{3.12}$$

To obtain the number of observations N_i, we can adjust our function COHORT() to COHORTN().[5] The changes are highlighted in the following code:

```
Function COHORTN(id, dat, rat, _
      Optional classes As Integer, Optional ystart, Optional yend)
...

ReDim pij(1 To classes - 1, 0 To classes + 1)

'Compute transition frequencies pij=Nij/Ni
For i = 1 To classes - 1
   pij(i, 0) = Ni(i)
   For j = 1 To classes
       If Ni(i) > 0 Then pij(i, j) = Nij(i, j) / Ni(i)
   Next j
Next i

...

COHORTN = pij

End Function
```

In Table 3.9, we construct the confidence sets. The transition matrix is computed in the range E2:M8 with the function COHORTN(); the table shows only the first and the last column of

Table 3.9 Confidence sets for the probability of default

	A	B	C	D	E	...	M	N	O	P	Q	R
1	Id	Date	Rat		Ni	...	p_{i8}		PD_i^{min}	PD_i^{max}	Eq. (3.11)	Eq. (3.12)
2	1	30-May-00	7	1	96	...	0.00%		0.00%	3.07%		
3	1	31-Dec-00	6	2	718	...	0.00%		0.00%	0.42%		
4	2	21-May-03	6	3	1440	...	0.07%		0.00%	0.39%	0.000%	0.000%
5	3	30-Dec-99	5	4	1280	...	0.31%		0.09%	0.80%	0.000%	0.000%
6	3	30-Oct-00	6	5	608	...	0.99%		0.36%	2.14%	0.000%	0.000%
7	3	30-Dec-01	5	6	520	...	1.73%		0.79%	3.26%	0.000%	0.000%
8	4	30-Dec-01	5	7	183	...	10.38%		6.37%	15.74%	0.000%	0.000%
9	4	30-May-02	6									
10	5	24-May-00	2						alpha:	5%		
11	5	30-May-01	3									
12	5	30-Oct-01	2									
13	6	30-Dec-99	4									
14	6	30-Dec-01	4									
15	7	30-Dec-02	4									
16	7	23-Jun-03	5									
17	7	30-Dec-03	6									
18	7	21-May-04	5									
19	8	30-Dec-02	3									
...	...	...	...									
4001	1829	30-Aug-00	3									

E2: {=COHORTN(A2:A4001,B2:B4001,C2:C4001)}
(applies to E2:M8, columns F-L are not shown)

Q4: =1-BINOMDIST(E4*M4-1,E4,O4,1)-P$10/2
(can be copied into Q2:Q8)

R4: =BINOMDIST(E4*M4,E4,P4,1)-$P$10/2
(can be copied into R2:R8)

Run the macro binomialconfidence to find the values in O2:P8.

[5] We could also add an additional optional argument to the function COHORT().

its output. Columns O and P are reserved for the confidence bounds. We leave them blank because we determine them with a macro. In columns Q and R we insert the conditions for the confidence sets according to Equations (3.11) to (3.12). In Excel, the binomial distribution function is available through BINOMDIST(x, N, q, 1) where the logical value 1 tells Excel to return the cumulative distribution rather than the density. Cell Q4, for example, reads:

$$= 1 - \text{BINOMDIST}\,(\text{E4*M4} - 1, \text{E4}, \text{O4}, 1) - \text{P\$10/2}$$

In the macro `binomialconfidence()`, we apply the Solver to set each cell within Q2:R11 to zero. (Make sure that a reference to the Solver is set in the VBA editor as described in Appendix A2.) The corresponding macro would be as follows:

```
Sub binomialconfidence()
Dim i As Long, target, change
SolverReset

For i = 2 To 8

    'PD non-zero?
    If Range("M" & i) > 0 Then
        'Lower Bound
        Range("O" & i) = Range("M" & i)
        target = "Q" & i
        change = "O" & i
        SolverOk SetCell:=target, MaxMinVal:=3, _
                  ValueOf:="0", bychange:=change
        SolverOptions AssumeNonNeg:=True
        SolverSolve UserFinish:=True
        'Upper Bound
        Range("P" & i) = Range("M" & i)
        target = "R" & i
        change = "P" & i
        SolverOk SetCell:=target, MaxMinVal:=3, _
                  ValueOf:="0", bychange:=change
        SolverOptions AssumeNonNeg:=True
        SolverSolve UserFinish:=True
    Else
        Range("O" & i) = 0
        Range("P" & i) = 1 - Range("P10") ^ (1 / Range("E" & i))
        Range("Q" & i & ":R" & i).Clear
    End If

Next i
End Sub
```

We start by declaring a counter i and resetting the Solver to its default parameters. We then loop through the seven rating grades contained in rows 2 to 8. First, start values for lower and upper bounds are set equal to the estimated PD from column M. We next define the cells that are handed to the Solver as target cell (`target`) and changing cell (`change`), and call the Solver.

We do not use the Solver if the estimated default probability is zero. In this case, the lower bound is obviously zero, because it cannot be negative. The upper bound can be obtained by solving the equation

$$(1 - \mathrm{PD}_i)^{N_i} = \alpha$$

The resulting confidence bounds are relatively wide. In most cases, they overlap with the ones of adjacent rating classes. What may seem surprising is that the upper bound for the best rating category 1 is higher than the ones for rating classes 2 to 5. The reason is that the number of observations in class 1 is relatively low (96), which increases (the length or the upper bound of) confidence intervals.

BOOTSTRAPPED CONFIDENCE INTERVALS FOR THE HAZARD APPROACH

Since it is not obvious how to apply the binomial distribution to estimates from the hazard approach (there is no direct counterpart to the N_i of the cohort approach), we employ bootstrap simulations. In a bootstrap analysis, one re-samples from the data used for estimation and re-estimates the statistics with the re-sampled data. Having done this many times, one can derive a distribution of the statistic of interest.

The steps of our bootstrap analysis are as follows:

1. Randomly draw with replacement an obligor's complete rating history. Repeat as many times as there are obligors in the original rating data set.
2. Calculate the generator Λ and transition matrix $\exp(\Lambda)$ for the sample generated in step 1.
3. Repeat steps 1–2 M times.
4. Determine percentiles of the transition probabilities from step 3.

The choice made in step 1 is not the only possible one. In a simple setting with N independent observations, one would re-sample N times with replacement to maintain the size of the original data set. Our rating data, by contrast, has several dimensions: the number of obligors, the number of rating actions, the number of obligor-years for which data is available, the calendar-time spanned by the first and last rating action, and several more. We could try to design the simulation such that the bootstrap sample closely resembles the original data in each dimension, but a perfect similarity would be infeasible. Among the one-dimensional bootstrap strategies, drawing obligors appears to be a natural one.

We implement the bootstrap in a user-defined function called BOOTCONF(). As with the COHORT() and GENERATOR() functions, arguments include the range containing the obligor identifier `id`, the migration date `dat` and the rating `rat`. Additionally, we include: a variable M for the number of repetitions; a variable `toclass` that selects the rating class to which we analyze transitions; and a final parameter that specifies the confidence level. To simulate a 95% confidence interval, set `confidence=0.05`.

The header together with some definitions reads

```
Function BOOTCONF(id, dat, rat, M As Long, toclass As Integer, _
                  Confidence)

If confidence < 0 Or confidence > 1 Then End

Dim i As Long, data() As Long, k As Long, obs As Long, jmax As Long, _
    j As Long, classes As Integer, bdmax As Date, bdmin As Date, _
    nobligor As Long, tmp
obs = id.Rows.count
classes = Application.WorksheetFunction.Max(rat)
```

Next we write the information on obligors into an array `data()`. We need one row for each obligor, but because we do not yet know the number of obligors, we reserve as many rows as there are observations in the data. In column one, we assign each obligor a new running id. In columns 2 and 3, we store the lines number from the original data in which the first and last observation belonging to this obligor is found:

```
'Input the obligor information into the array data
k = 1
ReDim data(1 To obs, 1 To 3)
jmax = 0
For i = 1 To obs
    If id(i) <> id(i + 1) Then
        data(k, 1) = id(i)
        data(k, 2) = i - j
        data(k, 3) = i
        k = k + 1
        If j + 1 > jmax Then jmax = j + 1
        j = 0
    Else
        j = j + 1
    End If
Next i

nobligor = k
```

The variable `jmax` contains the highest number of rating actions over all obligors, while `nobligor` contains the total number of different obligors. The number of observations in each simulation step is unknown but cannot exceed `jmax` times `nobligor`. This information will be used for dimensioning arrays.

We are now ready to start the simulation. In a `For i = 1 to M` loop, we perform the *M* repetitions, whose output (the transition probabilities) are stored in the array `dist`:

```
Dim bid(), bdat() As Date, brat(), brow, rand, bid_k, dist
ReDim dist(1 To M, 1 To classes + 1, 1 To classes + 1)
bdmin = Application.WorksheetFunction.Max(dat)
```

```
'Now we simulate
brow = 1: bid_k = 0
For i = 1 To M
    ReDim bid(1 To jmax * obs), bdat(1 To jmax * obs), _
          brat(1 To jmax * obs)
    For k = 1 To nobligor
        rand = Int((nobligor - 1) * Rnd + 1)
        bid_k = bid_k + 1
        For j = data(rand, 2) To data(rand, 3)
            bid(brow) = bid_k
            bdat(brow) = dat(j)
            brat(brow) = rat(j)
            If bdat(brow) < bdmin Then bdmin = bdat(brow)
            If bdat(brow) > bdmax Then bdmax = bdat(brow)
            brow = brow + 1
        Next j
    Next k
```

The variable `brow` counts the rows in the bootstrap data array. The variables `bid`, `bdat` and `brat` are bootstrapped ids, dates and ratings, respectively. `bmin` and `bdmax` are the minimum and maximum date in the bootstrap sample, respectively. As many times as they are obligors (`For k=1 to nobligor`), we draw a random obligor id `rand`, and then add the information from this obligor to the bootstrapped data set.

We then cut the empty rows in the bootstrap data using the `redim preserve` command, because our generator function cannot cope with empty entries:

```
'Cut unneeded observations
ReDim Preserve bid(1 To brow - 1), bdat(1 To brow - 1), _
               brat(1 To brow - 1)
```

Next, we calculate the generator Λ and the transition matrix $\exp(\Lambda)$ on this sample and save the result in the three-dimensional array `dist()`:

```
    'Calculate transition based on this sample
    tmp = mexpgenerator(GENERATOR(bid, bdat, brat, classes, bdmin, _
          bdmax))
    'Add calculated generator to distribution
    For j = 1 To classes + 1
        dist(i, j, toclass) = tmp(j, toclass)
    'To remember all classes, uncomment the three lines below:
        'For k = 1 To classes + 1
            'dist(i,j,k)=tmp(j,k)
        'Next k
    Next j
    brow = 1
Next i
```

Here, we only store the migration to the variable `toclass`. The whole transition matrix of each simulation step could be stored by adding a second `for` loop as shown in the code.

To obtain the confidence bands on this distribution, we convert the stored information into a one-dimensional array format, which can be analyzed with the worksheet function PERCENTILE:

```
'Now we obtain the percentiles
Dim percenti, upper, lower
ReDim percenti(1 To classes + 1, 1 To 2)
'Problem: PERCENTILE does not work with dist()
ReDim tmp(1 To M)
'only default categor
For j = 1 To classes + 1
    For k = 1 To M
        tmp(k) = dist(k, j, toclass)
    Next k
    percenti(j, 1) = Application.Percentile(tmp, confidence / 2)
    percenti(j, 2) = Application.Percentile(tmp, 1 - confidence / 2)
Next j

BOOTCONF = percenti

End Function
```

The function returns an array with two columns, where each row corresponds to a rating class and the columns contain the lower and upper confidence bounds. In Table 3.10, we apply

Table 3.10 Bootstrapped confidence bounds for default probabilities from the hazard approach

	A	B	C	D	E	F	G	H
1	Id	Date	Rat					
2	1	30-May-00	7					
3	1	31-Dec-00	6					
4	2	21-May-03	6			Lower	Upper	
5	3	30-Dec-99	5		1	0.00%	0.02%	
6	3	30-Oct-00	6		2	0.00%	0.01%	
7	3	30-Dec-01	5		3	0.00%	0.02%	
8	4	30-Dec-01	5		4	0.03%	0.07%	
9	4	30-May-02	6		5	0.20%	0.79%	
10	5	24-May-00	2		6	1.40%	3.18%	
11	5	30-May-01	3		7	7.21%	14.08%	
12	5	30-Oct-01	2		8	100.00%	100.00%	
13	6	30-Dec-99	4		NR	0.16%	0.76%	
14	6	30-Dec-01	4					
15	7	30-Dec-02						
16	7	23-Jun-03						
17	7	30-Dec-03						
18	7	21-May-04	5					
...								

{=BOOTCONF(A2:A4001,B2:B4001,C2:C4001,1000,8,0.05)}
(applies to F5:G15)

the function to our data set. We draw $M = 1{,}000$ bootstrap samples here and calculate the confidence for the probability of default (*toclass* = 8) with 5% confidence by entering

$$= \text{BOOTCONF}\,(\text{A2:A4001, B2:B4001, C2:C4001, 1000, 8, 0.05})$$

into the range F5:G15 and confirming by [ctrl]+[shift]+[enter]. Note that it takes some time for the function to return its output.

The smaller confidence bands for the top rating classes present a striking difference to the binomial confidence bounds obtained for the cohort estimates. The first rating class, for example, has a PD between 0.00% and 0.04% with 95% confidence. The intuition is that the hazard estimate of this grade's PD is not only based on the behavior of the few obligors within this grade but also on the behavior of obligors in other grades.

With slight modifications, the function BOOTCONF() could also be used for the cohort method. If we continue to re-sample issuers, however, the confidence bounds for rating grades with an estimated default probability of zero would be degenerate and equal to [0,0]. If there is no default in the original data, there will be no default in the bootstrap data.

NOTES AND LITERATURE

Jarrow, R.A., Lando, D. and Turnbull, S.M., 1997, A Markov chain model for valuing credit risk derivatives, *Journal of Derivatives*, 97–108 proposed the generator matrix when calculating rating transitions. For a detailed exposition of the cohort and the hazard approach, see Lando, D. and Skodeberg, T., 2002, Analyzing ratings transitions and rating drift with continuous observations, *Journal of Banking and Finance* 26, 423–444 or Lando, D., 2004, *Credit Risk Modelling*, Princeton University Press. More technical details can be found in Israel, R., Rosenthal, J. and Wei, J., 2001, Finding generators for Markov chains via empirical transitions matrices, with applications to credit ratings, *Mathematical Finance* 11, 245–265. The estimation of confidence bounds is discussed in Christensen, J., Hansen, E. and Lando, D., 2004, Confidence sets for continuous-time rating transition probabilities, *Journal of Banking and Finance* 28, 2575–2602 and Hanson, S. and Schuermann, T., 2006, Confidence intervals for probabilities of default, *Journal of Banking and Finance* 30, 2281–2301.

Empirical stylized facts present in transition matrices such as serial correlation are discussed by Altman, E. and Kao, D., 1992, Rating drift of high yield bonds, *Journal of Fixed Income*, 15–20. The dependence of migrations on the credit cycle is analyzed by Nickell, P., Perraudin, W. and Varotto, S., 2000, Stability of ratings transitions, *Journal of Banking and Finance* 24, 203–227.

APPENDIX

Matrix functions

In this chapter, we make use of the matrix exponential. Our user-defined function MEXP() makes heavy use of other matrix operations such as matrix multiplication, addition etc. Since Excel does not provide sufficiently flexible functions to perform these tasks, we provide some further user-defined matrix functions. To gain uniformity, the arguments of these functions are usually called array1 and array2. To avoid the referencing problem (see the troubleshooting in Appendix A1 for details), we pass all values by `ByVal`.

MSMULT(array1, array2) is identical to Excel's function MMULT if two arrays are provided. However, if you enter a scalar as first array (or point to a singular cell), our function returns the matrix in array2 multiplied by the scalar. MMULT, in contrast, returns an error. Our function performs both matrix by matrix and matrix by scalar multiplication:

```
Function MSMULT (ByVal array1, ByVal array2)
Dim output, i, j
If Application.WorksheetFunction.count(array1) = 1 Then
    array2 = array2
    ReDim output(1 To UBound(array2, 1), 1 To UBound(array2, 2))
    For i = 1 To UBound(array2, 1)
        For j = 1 To UBound(array2, 2)
            output(i, j) = array1 * array2(i, j)
        Next j
    Next i
    MSMULT = output
Else
    MSMULT = Application.WorksheetFunction.MMult(array1, array2)
End If
End Function
```

MADD(array1, array2) adds two matrices. If the input matrix array1 contains a number or a single cell, the function assumes that the first matrix consists entirely of entries with this value:

```
Function MADD(ByVal array1, ByVal array2)
Dim i, j, n1, n2
n1 = Application.WorksheetFunction.count(array1)
n2 = Application.WorksheetFunction.count(array2)
array1 = array1: array2 = array2

If n1 = 1 Then
    For i = 1 To UBound(array2, 1)
        For j = 1 To UBound(array2, 2)
            array2(i, j) = array2(i, j) + array1
        Next j
    Next i
Else
    For i = 1 To UBound(array2, 1)
        For j = 1 To UBound(array2, 2)
            array2(i, j) = array1(i, j) + array2(i, j)
        Next j
    Next i
End If
MADD = array2
End Function
```

MPOWER(array1, power) takes the matrix in array1 to the power supplied in the parameter power. This parameter is restricted to integers. If power is equal to zero, the function returns the identity matrix:

```
Function MPOWER(ByVal array1, power As Integer)
Dim i: MPOWER = array1

For i = 1 To power - 1
  MPOWER = Application.WorksheetFunction.MMult(mpower, array1)
Next i

If power = 0 Then MPOWER = mdiag(UBound(mpower, 1), 1)
End Function
```

MDIAG(m, d) returns a symmetric $m \times m$ matrix with on-diagonal entries of d and off-diagonal zeros. This is called a diagonal matrix and is equivalent to multiplying the identity matrix by the scalar D:

```
Function MDIAG(m As Integer, D As Double)
'Generate diag matrix with MxM and D as entries on diagonal

Dim i, j, output: ReDim output(1 To m, 1 To m)

For i = 1 To m
    For j = 1 To m
        output(i, j) = 0
    Next j
  output(i, i) = D
Next i

MDIAG = output
End Function
```

All these functions are provided in the Add-in and are useful in many other settings as well as the ones described here. We will now go into detail concerning the user-defined function MEXP(array1), which provides the exponential function of a matrix array1:

```
Function MEXP(array1)
'Calculate exp(matrix)
Dim error As Double, k As Long, calc, mpowerk, maddition
array1 = array1: mpowerk = array1
'Check symmetry
If UBound(array1, 1) <> UBound(array1, 2) Then End

'First and second entry (identity matrix + array1)
calc = madd(mdiag(UBound(array1, 1), 1), array1)
k = 2
error = 1
```

```
Do While (error > 10 ^ (-320) And k <= 170)
    mpowerk = msmult(mpowerk, array1)
    maddition = msmult(1 / Application.WorksheetFunction.Fact(k), _
      mpowerk)
    calc = madd(maddition, calc)
    k = k  + 1
    If k > 10 Then error = _
                    Application.WorksheetFunction.SumSq(maddition)
Loop
MEXP = calc
End Function
```

The function M EXP() directly implements Equation (3.8) and truncates the sum in the following way. For each step greater than ten ($k > 10$), we compute the sum of the squared elements of the kth summand. If this is smaller than 10^{-320}, i.e., equal to zero by Excel's precision, we stop the summation process. Each of the elements missed (all k greater than the stopping k) is smaller than the last addition. We furthermore stop the routine if $k > 170$ because Excel returns an #NUM! error for the factorial of $k > 170$. With some tricks we could go beyond these limits, but in most of our tests convergence was achieved in less than 150 steps.

In our application, however, we have to evaluate the matrix exponential of a special type of matrices: the generator matrix. On the diagonal, the generator matrix has negative values equal to minus the sum of the off-diagonal elements in the respective row (see Equation 3.6). Adding up large positive and negative numbers can lead to numerical problems, in turn rendering the truncated sum in MEXP() unreliable. To avoid such problems, we have programmed a function MEXPGENERATOR(), which adjusts the generator to contain only positive values. The idea is the following. We first find the maximal absolute on-diagonal element of array1 and denote this by $\lambda^{\max}$:

$$\lambda^{\max} = \max\{|\lambda_{ii}|\}$$

Then, we construct a diagonal matrix $D = \text{diag}(\lambda^{\max})$ with $\lambda^{\max}$ as entries, i.e., multiply the identity matrix by $\lambda^{\max}$. Here, D is shown for the case of a 4×4 matrix:

$$D = \begin{bmatrix} \lambda^{\max} & 0 & 0 & 0 \\ 0 & \lambda^{\max} & 0 & 0 \\ 0 & 0 & \lambda^{\max} & 0 \\ 0 & 0 & 0 & \lambda^{\max} \end{bmatrix}$$

The sum of the generator itself and the thus obtained diagonal matrix contains only positive entries. Let us call this matrix Λ^* with $\Lambda^* = \Lambda + D$. Since the identity matrix commutes with any other matrix, we obtain

$$\exp(\Lambda) = \exp(\Lambda^* - D) = \exp(\Lambda^*) \times \exp(-D) = \exp(-\lambda^{\max}) \times \exp(\Lambda^*)$$

We have therefore reduced our problem to that of the matrix exponential of Λ^* with only positive entries. The function reads

```
Function MEXPGENERATOR(array1)

'Calculate the matrix exponential

Dim n as long, i, D, lmax as double, tmp, Lstar
array1 = array1
n = UBound(array1)
lmax = 0
'Find maximal diagonal entry
For i = 1 To n
    If Abs(array1(i, i)) > lmax Then lmax = Abs(array1(i, i))
Next i
'Construct diagonal matrix with maximal entry and add this to the matrix
Lstar = madd(mdiag(n, lmax), array1)
'Now use the truncated sum method to obtain an estimate for Im+mymatrix
tmp = mexp(Lstar)
 'And finally:
MEXPGENERATOR = msmult(Exp(-1 * lmax), tmp)

End Function
```

In our tests, this function yielded the same result as MEXP(). However, we recommend using MEXPGENERATOR() for the matrix exponential of generator matrices.

4

Prediction of Default and Transition Rates

Default and transition rates are essential to pricing or risk management. Based on a forecast for next year's default rate, for example, a bank can set appropriate loan rates for short-term loans.

In Chapter 3, we showed how to estimate average transition rates based on data extending over several years. If such rates are used to estimate next year's transition rates, one would implicitly assume the next year to be a typical or average year. Although this may be an appropriate assumption in some situations, in others we may have good reason to believe that the following year should be relatively good or bad for credits. If the economy is just moving into a recession, for example, we should expect default rates to be relatively high.

In this chapter, we show how to use readily available information to predict default and transition rates for corporates rated by a major rating agency. The fact that default and transition rates can indeed be predicted might cast doubt on the efficiency of agency ratings. If there were good reasons to believe, say at the end of 2001, that the default rate of BB-rated issuers was to be relatively high in 2002, why did the agency not downgrade more BB-rated issuers? To understand this, it is crucial to know that agencies do not aim at assigning ratings in such a way that the one-year default probability of a rating category is constant across time. By contrast, ratings are meant to be *relative* assessments of credit quality. If overall economic conditions have deteriorated, affecting all borrowers in a similar way, the previous relative ordering would still be correct, even though the default probability of a given rating category may substantially deviate from its average in the past.

CANDIDATE VARIABLES FOR PREDICTION

In the examples studied in this chapter, we predict default and transition rates for calendar years, i.e., from the end of year t to the end of year $t+1$. Therefore, we need information that is already known at the end of year t. We consider four different predictive factors, each of which is captured by one empirical variable.

- *Macroeconomic conditions:* Liquidity and profits of corporates are affected by overall economic conditions. We could capture them by a measure of current activity, such as GDP growth over the preceding year. However, we can hope to do better if we use forecasts of future economic activity instead of current activity, and if we use a measure of activity that is closely associated with corporate conditions. We therefore use forecasts of one-year changes in corporate profits. To control for effects of inflation, we also deflate the forecasts. We denote this variable as PRF_t. It is defined as

$$PRF_t = \frac{1 + \text{forecasted change in corporate profits (in } t \text{ for } t, t+1)}{1 + \text{forecasted change in GDP deflator (in } t \text{ for } t, t+1)} - 1$$

The forecast data is taken from the Survey of Professional Forecasters, which is available on the Internet.[1]

- *Corporate bond spreads:* Yields of corporate bonds should be set such that the expected return from holding a bond is at least as large as the return from holding a risk-free government bond. Otherwise, there would be little incentive to buy risky corporate bonds. Roughly speaking, the expected return on a corporate bond is its yield minus the loss rate. The corporate bond spread, which is the difference between the yield of a corporate bond and a comparable government bond, should therefore vary with the loss rates expected by the market. We define the variable *SPR* as

$$SPR_t = \text{yield of corporate bonds (in } t) - \text{yield of US treasuries (in } t)$$

The corporate bonds used for computing the variable *SPR* should have a risk similar to the risk of the issuers whose transition rates are to be predicted. When predicting investment-grade default rates, for example, we use the yield of Baa-rated corporate bonds. The yield of US treasury bonds is taken from 10-year treasuries. The data is available from Econstats.[2]

- *Aging effect:* It has been documented in the literature that issuers who first entered the bond market three to four years ago are relatively likely to default. This empirical phenomenon is called the aging effect. There are several possible explanations, one being that the debt issue provides firms with cash – enough cash to survive for several years even if the business plan envisaged at the time of the bond issue did not work out. So if new issuers run into difficulties, liquidity problems will only appear with a certain delay. We define the variable *AGE* as the fraction of current issuers that had their first-time rating three to four years ago:[3]

$$AGE_t = \frac{\text{\#newly rated issuers (from } t-4 \text{ to } t-3)}{\text{\#rated issuers (in } t)}$$

The number of newly rated issuers and the overall number of issuers is taken from Standard and Poor's (S&P) (2006), Tables 19 and 20, respectively.

- *Average risk:* When analyzing average default rates of a group comprising several rating categories, we should take into account the fact that the composition of the group can change over time. Investment-grade issuers, for example, include issuers rated AAA, AA, A or BBB, and the percentage of BBB-rated issuers within this group has risen from 27% in 1981 to 46% in 2005. When predicting investment grade default rates, we capture differences in average risk by the percentage of current investment-grade issuers that are rated BBB

$$BBB_t = \frac{\text{\#BBB rated issuers (in } t)}{\text{\#Investment grade issuers (in } t)}$$

The necessary data can be taken from Standard and Poor's (2006), Table 24.

[1] `http://www.philadelphiafed.org/research-and-data/real-time-center/survey-of-professional-forecasters/` (accessed August 19, 2010).

[2] `www.econstats.com/`.

[3] Helwege and Kleiman (1997) also lag issuing activity by three years to define their aging variable.

PREDICTING INVESTMENT-GRADE DEFAULT RATES WITH LINEAR REGRESSION

Imagine that it is currently December 2005, and that we want to predict the investment-grade default rate for the year 2006. Having collected the variables just described, we could linearly combine the variables to produce a default rate forecast IDR^*:

$$IDR^*_{t,t+1} = b_1 + b_2 PRF_t + b_3 AGE_t + b_4 BBB_t + b_5 SPR_t, \quad t = 2005 \tag{4.1}$$

But from where do we get the *b*s? We could choose them based on the observed historical relationship between default rates and the four variables. To estimate this relationship, we can use the following regression equation for observed default rates *IDR*:

$$IDR_{t,t+1} = b_1 + b_2 PRF_t + b_3 AGE_t + b_4 BBB_t + b_5 SPR_t + u_t \quad t = 1984, \ldots, 2004 \tag{4.2}$$

where u_t is the default rate component that cannot be explained. The time span is determined by data availability. The data from Standard and Poor's starts in 1981, but we need to wait three years until the variable *AGE* can be computed for the first time. The investment-grade default rate can be collected from Standard and Poor's (2006), Table 1.

A straightforward way of estimating Equation (4.2) is linear regression (see Appendix A4). One can rightly point out that linear regression does not take into account that default rates are bounded between 0 and 1; default rate predictions coming out of the regression could easily be negative.[4] We nevertheless examine linear regression because it is a simple and widely used technique. In the next sections, we will compare its performance to a more sophisticated technique: the Poisson regression.[5]

In linear regression, the coefficients *b* are determined such that the sum of squared prediction errors is minimized. (To be precise, the prediction error for year *t* is given by $[IDR_{t,t+1} - (b_1 + b_2 PRF_t + b_3 AGE_t + b_4 BBB_t + b_5 SPR_t)]$.) Once we have estimates of the *b*s, we can apply them to current values of the four explanatory variables and get a prediction of the future default rate. In doing so, we assume that the error u_t is zero on average.

To perform a linear regression in Excel, we can use the command LINEST(*y's,x's,const,stats*), where *y's* denote the dependent variable (*IDR* in our case) and *x's* the explanatory variables (*PRF*, *AGE*, *BBB*, *SPR*). Const is a logical value that leads to inclusion of a constant (b_1) if set to 1. If the logical value stats is set to 1, the function LINEST returns several regression statistics, rather than just the estimated coefficients.[6]

LINEST returns an array and must be entered as an array function using [ctrl]+[shift]+[return]. If the explanatory variables in the sheet are ordered from 2 (leftmost) to *K* (rightmost) and a constant is included, the output is of the form shown in Table 4.1.

Note that the order of variables is reversed in the output. The coefficient of the rightmost variable in the data will appear leftmost in the output. SE(b_i) is the estimated standard error of coefficient b_i. R^2 is the coefficient of determination. It is the fraction of the variance of the dependent variable that is explained by the explanatory variables. RMSE is the standard

[4] They could also be larger than one but this is unlikely to occur if we examine investment grade default rates.

[5] Note that we should not use the LOGIT command developed in Chapter 1 because it requires the dependent variable to be either 0 or 1.

[6] For a more detailed description of tests and measures of goodness of fit, see Appendix A.4.

Table 4.1 Output of the LINEST function

b_K	...	b_3	b_2	b_1
SE(b_K)	...	SE(b_3)	SE(b_2)	SE(b_1)
R^2	RMSE	#NA	#NA	#NA
F-statistic	DF	#NA	#NA	#NA
MSS	RSS	#NA	#NA	#NA

deviation of the residuals u_t. The F-statistic tests the significance of the entire regression; *DF* is the degrees of freedom, which can be obtained as the number of observations used in the regression minus the number of independent variables (including the constant). MSS and RSS decompose the variation in the dependent variable into two parts: one that is explained (MSS = model sum of squares) and one that is not (RSS = residual sum of squares). R^2 is computed as 1 − RSS/(MSS + RSS).

The standard errors SE(b_i) can be used to construct a t-statistic for the hypothesis that a coefficient equals zero:

$$t_i = b_i/\mathrm{SE}(b_i)$$

which is referred to a t-distribution with *DF* degrees of freedom to determine the p-value of the test. In Excel, this can be done with the TDIST(*t*,*DF*,*tails*) function. It accepts only positive t-statistics. Since the t-distribution is symmetric, we can work around this limitation by inputting the absolute value of the statistic. Usually, one constructs a two-sided test, which can be specified by setting *tails* = 2.

Table 4.2 shows the data and some regression results. The default rate in the row headed by year t is the default rate in t. The values of the other variables are taken from the end of the year stated in the first column. All values are expressed in percent, and so 0.18 means that the default rate was 0.18%.

The results of estimating regression Equation (4.2) with LINEST are shown in the range H4:L7. For clarity, we shade the output of the LINEST function and label the columns and rows. Since the default rate to be explained is from the year following the observation of the x variables, the y range of the LINEST function is shifted one year into the future relative to the x range, which contains the explanatory variables.

The signs of the coefficients b meet our expectations. High spreads, a large fraction of risky BBB issuers and a large fraction of recently rated issuers should be associated with higher default rates, and therefore with positive bs. Higher profit expectations, on the other hand, should be coupled with lower default rates. Note that we cannot directly read something into the constant because it is not the average default rate.[7]

Examining the t-statistics and the associated p-values that are computed from the regression output, we see that profit forecasts (*PRF*) and the aging effect (*AGE*) are the most significant variables. Their p-values are below 7%, and so we can reject the hypothesis that the coefficients are zero with a significance level of 7% or better. Bond spreads (*SPR*) and the fraction of BBB-rated issuers (*BBB*) also seem to have some explanatory power, but with a lower significance.

[7] The constant in a linear regression is obtained as $\overline{y} - \sum_{i=2}^{K} b_i \overline{x}_i$ where $\overline{y}$ and $\overline{x}_i$ denote the mean of the dependent and the ith independent variable, respectively.

Table 4.2 Predicting investment-grade default rates with linear regression

	A	B	C	D	E	F	G	H	I	J	K	L	M
1	year	IDR	PRF	AGE	BBB	SPR							
2	1981	0.00	-7.3	#N/A	27.0	2.8			{=LINEST(B6:B26,C5:F25,1,1)}				
3	1982	0.18	5.5	#N/A	27.8	3.7	**Model 1**	SPR	BBB	AGE	PRF	CON	
4	1983	0.09	18.5	#N/A	25.7	2.0	Coeff	0.051	0.004	0.019	-0.016	-0.229	
5	1984	0.17	-0.1	3.6	23.3	1.8	SE(coeff)	0.033	0.003	0.009	0.004	0.098	
6	1985	0.00	4.3	6.3	22.6	2.4	R^2/RMSE	0.602	0.078	#NA	#NA	#NA	
7	1986	0.15	3.1	8.4	24.2	2.8	F/DF	6.050	16	#NA	#NA	#NA	
8	1987	0.00	-0.9	5.4	24.6	2.5	t-stat	1.536	1.325	1.993	-3.609	-2.336	=L4/L5!
9	1988	0.00	3.2	13.1	23.9	1.5	p-value	0.144	0.204	0.064	0.002	0.033	
10	1989	0.14	-4.2	7.8	24.2	1.9		=TDIST(ABS(H8),$I7,2)					
11	1990	0.14	-4.6	7.6	24.5	2.4							
12	1991	0.20	7.2	7.7	23.7	2.4			{=LINEST(B6:B26,C5:D25,1,1)}				
13	1992	0.00	8.2	5.4	25.5	2.1	**Model 2**	AGE	PRF	CON			
14	1993	0.00	5.9	5.3	26.4	1.9	Coeff	0.024	-0.013	-0.058			
15	1994	0.05	3.7	9.2	27.6	1.3	SE(coeff)	0.009	0.005	0.076			
16	1995	0.05	2.2	7.7	29.9	1.8	R^2/RMSE	0.439	0.088	#NA			
17	1996	0.00	0.1	7.7	31.9	1.5	F/DF	7.046	18	#NA			
18	1997	0.08	2.1	10.0	35.7	1.5	t-stat	2.655	-2.863	-0.761			
19	1998	0.15	-0.8	8.5	36.6	2.7	p-value	0.016	0.010	0.457			
20	1999	0.14	2.6	10.2	38.2	1.8							
21	2000	0.18	3.2	10.9	40.5	2.9	**F test for b(Spread)=b(BBB)=0 in Model 1**						
22	2001	0.20	-2.0	9.5	41.7	3.0	F	3.274	=(H6-H16)/(1-H6)*I7/2				
23	2002	0.46	8.7	8.7	44.2	3.6	p-value	0.064	=FDIST(H22,2,I7)				
24	2003	0.10	10.9	8.1	46.7	2.3	**Predictions for 2006 investment grade default rate**						
25	2004	0.00	9.6	10.3	47.0	1.9	Model 1	0.1048	=TREND(B6:B26,C5:F25,C26:F26)				
26	2005	0.03	3.2	6.7	45.8	1.9	Model 2	0.0602	=TREND(B6:B26,C5:D25,C26:D26)				

Note: IDR=investment-grade default rate; PRF=forecasted change in corporate profits; AGE=fraction of new issuers; BBB=fraction of BBB-rated issuers; SPR=spread on Baa bonds!

If some variables show only moderate or no contribution, it is interesting to examine how the results change if we drop these variables. This leads us to model 2. The remaining two variables *AGE* and *PRF* are now both significant on a level of 2% or better. The R^2 has decreased from 60% to 44%. To test whether this is a significant loss in explanatory power, we perform an F-test. If model 2 excludes J variables from model 1, then the F-statistic can be computed as

$$F = \frac{(R^2(\text{model 1}) - R^2(\text{model 2}))/J}{(1 - R^2(\text{model 1}))/DF} \tag{4.3}$$

It is distributed with (J, DF) degrees of freedom, where DF is the degrees of freedom of model 1. The p-value can be calculated with the function FDIST(F-value, J, DF).

The p-value of the F-test is 6.4%. So if we start with model 2 and include the two variables *SPR* and *BBB*, there is a probability of 6.4% that we do not add any explanatory power. There is no general rule for what to do in such a situation. Often, one applies stringent standards of statistical significance, e.g., variables should be significant at the 5% level or better in order to be included in a model. This could lead us to favor model 2. But such a procedure is somewhat ad hoc. If we choose model 2 instead of the more general model 1, we guard against inclusion of variables that are not truly significant; on the other hand, we are fairly likely to ignore some valuable information. In principle, both models could be justified on statistical grounds, and therefore we will examine the predictions of both models.

We could arrive at the prediction by multiplying each variable for the year 2005 with its associated coefficient as in Equation (4.1), and summing up (remembering not to forget the constant when doing so). The quicker alternative would be to use the Excel function

TREND(*known_y's*, *known_x's*, *new_x's*, *const*)

The *known_y's* and the *known_x's* are the same *y's* and *x's* that we used in the LINEST command. The *new_x's* are the x-variables from the end of year t that precedes the forecast horizon. We want to make a forecast for 2006, and so the *new_x's* are taken from 2005; the trend line is estimated using data from 1984 to 2005. If we set the logical value const = 1, we get the same effect as if we had not specified anything for const: the regression underlying TREND will include a constant.

Forecasts differ across the two models. Model 1 predicts a default rate of 0.1%, model 2 one of 0.06%. Looking at the x-values for the year 2005, the origin of difference is obvious. The profit forecast *PRF* is close to the average for the last 25 years, while the aging effect *AGE* is somewhat less present than in the past. Therefore, the default rate prediction based on model 2 should be below the average default rate, which is 0.1%. The fraction of BBB-rated issuers, having increased over the 1990s, is at a historically high level. Once we include the variable *BBB* as we do in model 1, the default rate forecast increases.

PREDICTING INVESTMENT-GRADE DEFAULT RATES WITH POISSON REGRESSION

We already mentioned a drawback of linear regression: default rate predictions could be negative. In addition, linear regression does not take into account that the realized default rate will vary less around the expected default probability if the number of issuers is large. To overcome these drawbacks, we can describe the data as being drawn from a probability distribution that has the desired properties: default rates should have a minimum of zero, and their variability should decrease with an increasing number of issuers. To determine the parameters of the distribution, we choose them in such a way that we maximize the probability of observing the data that we have actually observed – that is, we apply the maximum-likelihood-principle.[8]

What is an appropriate probability distribution for defaults? Default rates vary from year to year, but for a given year it might be a good approximation to assume that defaults are independent. This does not rule out, for example, a cluster of defaults during a recession. If the default probability of investment-grade issuers has increased from 0.1% to 0.4% during a recession, we would expect to see four times as many defaults as usual. Nevertheless, defaults could be independent in the sense that if one particular issuer defaults in a recession year, this does not *further* increase the default probability of another issuer.

With the independence assumption, the number of defaults observed in a given year follows a binomial distribution. One could base a maximum likelihood estimation on this distribution, but it is more convenient to use the Poisson distribution instead. If the number of issuers is large, and the default probability is small, the Poisson provides a very good approximation to the binomial.

The density function of the Poisson, which specifies the probability that the number of defaults is equal to some observed number D_t, is

$$\text{Prob}(\#\text{defaults}_t = D_t) = \frac{\exp(-\lambda_t)\lambda_t^{D_t}}{D_t!} \tag{4.4}$$

where $D_t!$ denotes the factorial of D_t, i.e., $D_t \times (D_t - 1) \times \ldots \times 1$. It can be shown that the expected number of defaults is λ_t.

In Excel, the density (4.4) can be computed with the function POISSON. For a given λ and a given N, the number of issuers that may default, we get Prob(#defaults=D) by using POISSON($D, \lambda{*}N$, 0). The binomial is also available in Excel (through the function BINOMDIST).

Table 4.3 compares the binomial and the Poisson densities for two different cases. The first one (columns B and C) is typical of investment-grade defaults. There are around 2500 investment-grade issuers, and the average default rate is around 0.1%. In the second case (columns D and E), we assume that there are just 20 issuers with a default rate of 40%. As can be seen from the tabulated densities as well as from the two charts, the Poisson and the binomial are almost identical for the first case, whereas they show big differences in the second.

Having established that the Poisson is a valid approximation to the binomial in our case, we can go on by modeling the variation of default rates across time. The standard way is to assume that the expected number of defaults varies in the following way with explanatory variables x:

$$\lambda_t = \exp\left[\beta_1 + \beta_2 x_{2t} + \beta_3 x_{3t} + \ldots + \beta_K x_{Kt}\right] \tag{4.5}$$

[8] For a more detailed discussion of the maximum likelihood method, see Appendix A.3.

Table 4.3 Comparison of binomial and Poisson density functions

	A	B	C	D	E	F	G	H	I
1	**Binomial and Poisson density functions compared**								
2		Binomial	Poisson	Binomial	Poisson				
3	# Issuers	2500	2500	20	20				
4	Def. prob	0.1%	0.1%	40.0%	40.0%				
5									
6	#Defaults	Densities->							
7	0	8.198%	8.208%	0.004%	0.034%				
8	1	20.516%	20.521%	0.049%	0.268%				
9	2	25.661%	25.652%	0.309%	1.073%				
10	3	21.388%	21.376%	1.235%	2.863%				
11	4	13.365%	13.360%	3.499%	5.725%				
12	5	6.678%	6.680%	7.465%	9.160%				
13	6	2.780%	2.783%	12.441%	12.214%				
14	7	0.991%	0.994%	16.588%	13.959%				
15	8	0.309%	0.311%	17.971%	13.959%				
16	9	0.086%	0.086%	15.974%	12.408%				
17	10	0.021%	0.022%	11.714%	9.926%				
18	11	0.005%	0.005%	7.099%	7.219%				
19	12	0.001%	0.001%	3.550%	4.813%				
20	13	0.000%	0.000%	1.456%	2.962%				
21	14	0.000%	0.000%	0.485%	1.692%				
22	15	0.000%	0.000%	0.129%	0.903%				
23	16	0.000%	0.000%	0.027%	0.451%				
24	17	0.000%	0.000%	0.004%	0.212%				
25	18	0.000%	0.000%	0.000%	0.094%				
26	19	0.000%	0.000%	0.000%	0.040%				
27	20	0.000%	0.000%	0.000%	0.016%				
28		B27: =BINOMDIST($A27,B$3,B$4,0)			E27: =POISSON($A27,E$4*E$3,0)				
29		*(can be copied into B7:B27 and D7:D27)*			*(can be copied into C7:C27 and E7:E27)*				

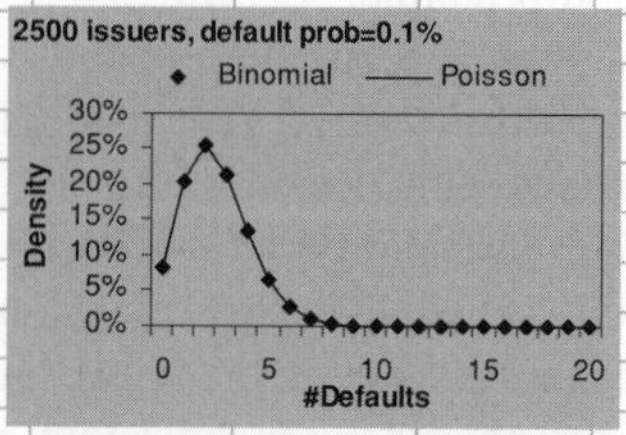

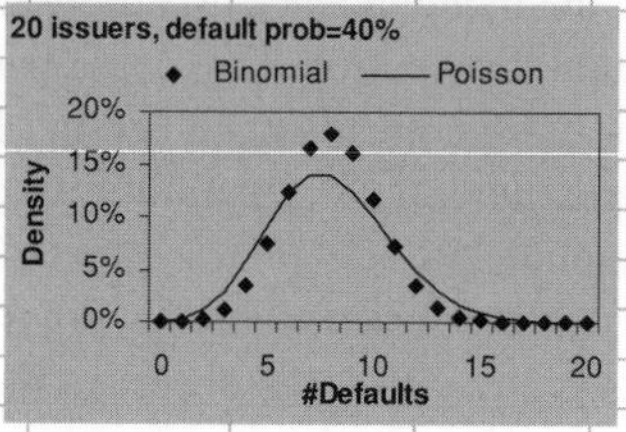

2500 issuers, default prob=0.1%
Binomial — Poisson
Density
#Defaults

20 issuers, default prob=40%
Binomial — Poisson
Density
#Defaults

The exponential function makes sure that the expected number of defaults is always non-negative. Equivalently, we can write

$$\ln \lambda_t = \beta_1 + \beta_2 x_{2t} + \beta_3 x_{3t} + \ldots + \beta_K x_{Kt} \tag{4.6}$$

In vector notation, with $\beta' = [\beta_1\ \beta_2\ \beta_3 \cdots \beta_K]$ and $x_t' = [1\ x_{2t}\ x_{3t} \cdots x_{Kt}]$, this can be reformulated as

$$\ln \lambda_t = \beta' x_t \tag{4.7}$$

The goal of the estimation is to determine the weights β that describe the impact of the variables on the default occurrence. To apply the maximum likelihood principle, we need the likelihood L, which is the probability of observing an entire sample. From the independence assumption and from (4.4), it is given by

$$\begin{aligned} L &= \text{Prob}(\#\text{defaults}_1 = D_1) \cdot \text{Prob}(\#\text{defaults}_2 = D_2) \cdot \ldots \cdot \text{Prob}(\#\text{defaults}_T = D_T) \\ &= \frac{\exp(-\lambda_1)\lambda_1^{D_1}}{D_1!} \frac{\exp(-\lambda_2)\lambda_2^{D_2}}{D_2!} \cdots \frac{\exp(-\lambda_T)\lambda_T^{D_T}}{D_T!} \end{aligned} \tag{4.8}$$

Table 4.4 Output of the user-defined function POIREG

β_1	β_2	.	β_K
SE(β_1)	SE(β_2)	.	SE(β_K)
$t_1 = \beta_1$ /SE(b_1)	$t_2 = \beta_2$ /SE(b_2)	.	$t_K = \beta_K$ /SE(b_K)
p-value(t_1)	p-value(t_2)	.	p-value(t_K)
Pseudo-R^2	ln Likelihood	#N/A	#N/A

Taking logarithms, we obtain

$$\ln L = \sum_{t=1}^{T} [-\lambda_t + D_t \ln \lambda_t - \ln D_t!] \tag{4.9}$$

Inserting (4.7), this can be written as

$$\ln L = \sum_{t=1}^{T} \left[-\lambda_t + D_t \beta' x_t - \ln D_t!\right] \tag{4.10}$$

We can use the Newton method described in Appendix A3 and already used in Chapter 1 to determine the vector β that maximizes this likelihood. A user-defined array function called POIREG(y's, x's) is available on the DVD and shown in the Appendix at the end of this chapter. Here, we do not want to go through the details of the function, but just present its output (see Table 4.4).

The function routinely adds a constant to the regression. In contrast to the LINEST function, the coefficients appear in the order the variables are entered. Also, we add t-statistics and p-values. As usual, we can compute t-statistics by dividing a coefficient estimate by its standard error, but irrespective of the number of observations, we refer the statistics to the standard normal distribution function.

For a nonlinear model such as the POISSON regression, we cannot compute an R^2 as we do in a linear regression. A Pseudo-R^2 that is often reported in the literature is defined by relating the log-likelihood of the model to the log-likelihood of a model that has just a constant in it:

$$\text{Pseudo-}R^2 = 1 - \frac{\ln L(\text{model})}{\ln L(\text{model with all } \beta \text{ except } \beta_1 \text{ set to } 0)}$$

Table 4.5 contains the data analysis with the Poisson approach. Note that the dependent variable is now the number of defaults D, and not the default rate. In addition to the variables that we used in the linear regression analysis, we therefore include *LNN*, the logarithm of the number of investment-grade issuers at the start of the year. It captures the effect that, for a given default probability which is modeled by the other variables, the expected number of defaults increases with the number of issuers. To see why we should enter the log issuers instead of the issuers, assume that the default probability PD is constant across time. The expected number of defaults is then PD*N, where N is the number of issuers at the start of the year. PD*N should equal λ, and here we check that it does. Entering the log issuers as a variable we get

$$\ln \lambda_t = \beta_0 + \beta_1 \ln(N_t) \tag{4.11}$$

Table 4.5 Predicting investment-grade default rates with Poisson regression

	A	B	C	D	E	F	G	H	I	J	K	L	M	N	O
1	Year	D	LNN	PRF	AGE	BBB	SPR								
2	1981	0	7.0	-7.3	#NA	27.0	2.8				{=POIREG(B6:B26,C5:G25)}				
3	1982	2	7.0	5.5	#NA	27.8	3.7		**Model 1**	CON	LNN	PRF	AGE	BBB	SPR
4	1983	1	7.1	18.5	#NA	25.7	2.0		Coeff	-14.10	1.46	-0.18	0.30	0.01	0.42
5	1984	2	7.1	-0.1	3.6	23.3	1.8		SE(coeff)	11.89	1.80	0.05	0.11	0.09	0.36
6	1985	0	7.2	4.3	6.3	22.6	2.4		t-stat	-1.19	0.81	-3.97	2.74	0.15	1.17
7	1986	2	7.2	3.1	8.4	24.2	2.8		p-value	0.12	0.21	0.00	0.00	0.44	0.12
8	1987	0	7.2	-0.9	5.4	24.6	2.5		Pseudo R²/lnL	0.49	-28.32	#NA	#NA	#NA	#NA
9	1988	0	7.2	3.2	13.1	23.9	1.5								
10	1989	2	7.3	-4.2	7.8	24.2	1.9				{=POIREG(B6:B26,C5:E25)}				
11	1990	2	7.3	-4.6	7.6	24.5	2.4		**Model 2**	CON	LNN	PRF	AGE		
12	1991	3	7.4	7.2	7.7	23.7	2.4		Coeff	-18.24	2.18	-0.20	0.29		
13	1992	0	7.5	8.2	5.4	25.5	2.1		SE(coeff)	4.21	0.55	0.04	0.11		
14	1993	0	7.6	5.9	5.3	26.4	1.9		t-stat	-4.33	3.98	-4.586	2.769		
15	1994	1	7.7	3.7	9.2	27.6	1.3		p-value	0.00	0.00	0.00	0.00		
16	1995	1	7.8	2.2	7.7	29.9	1.8		Pseudo R²/lnL	0.47	-29.77	#NA	#NA		
17	1996	0	7.8	0.1	7.7	31.9	1.5								
18	1997	2	7.9	2.1	10.0	35.7	1.5		**LR-test for b(SPR)=b(BBB)=0 in model 1**						
19	1998	4	7.9	-0.8	8.5	36.6	2.7		Chi-squared	2.918	=2*(K8-K16)				
20	1999	4	7.9	2.6	10.2	38.2	1.8		p-value	0.233	=CHIDIST(J19,2)				
21	2000	5	8.0	3.2	10.9	40.5	2.9								
22	2001	6	8.0	-2.0	9.5	41.7	3.0		**Predictions for 2006 investment grade default rate**						
23	2002	14	8.0	8.7	8.7	44.2	3.6		Model 1	0.051%	=EXP(J4+SUMPRODUCT(K4:O4, C26:G26)-C26)				
24	2003	3	8.0	10.9	8.1	46.7	2.3		Model 2	0.065%					
25	2004	0	8.1	9.6	10.3	47.0	1.9		Alternatively with function POITREND						
26	2005	1	8.1	3.2	6.7	45.8	1.9		Model 1	0.051%	=POITREND(B6:B26,C5:G25,C26: G26)/EXP(C26)				
27									Model 2	0.065%					

Note: D = number of investment grade defaulters; LNN = log number of issuers; PRF = forecasted change in corporate profits; AGE = fraction of new issuers; BBB = fraction of BBB-rated issuers; SPR=spread on Baa bonds

Estimating $\beta_0 = \ln(\text{PD})$ and $\beta_1 = 1$, we get

$$\ln \lambda_t = \ln(\text{PD}) + \ln(N_t) = \ln(\text{PD} \cdot N_t) \Leftrightarrow \lambda_t = \text{PD} \cdot N_t \tag{4.12}$$

As in the linear regression model, the profit forecast PFR and the aging variable AGE are highly significant in the more general model 1. (Their t-statistics are well above 1.96 in absolute terms.) The other variables show little significance. Excluding the spread and the fraction of BBB-rated issuers, we arrive at model 2; we do not exclude the number of issuers *LNN*, which is also insignificant, because we have seen that there is a good theoretical reason for including it. Looking at the results for model 2, one may wonder why *LNN* is significant in model 2, but not in model 1. The reason is that *LNN* is highly correlated with the fraction of BBB-rated issuers. If two correlated variables are included in one model as is done in model 1, the standard errors tend to increase.

As in the linear regression, there is an easy way to test whether model 2 is a sensible restriction of model 1. This time, we use a likelihood ratio test. In general, a likelihood ratio test has the following form:

$$\text{LR-statistic} = 2[\ln L(\text{general model}) - \ln L(\text{restricted model})] \tag{4.13}$$

where $\ln L$ denotes the log-likelihood. The more likelihood is lost by imposing the restriction, the larger the LR-statistic will be. Asymptotically, it is chi-squared distributed with degrees of freedom equal to the number of restrictions imposed. Here, there are two restrictions (the coefficients of two variables are set to zero).

In the table, the LR-statistic is computed from the output of the function POIREG. Its *p*-value can be calculated with the function CHIDIST(statistic, degrees of freedom). We obtain a value of 0.23, which means that if we add the two variables *SPR* and *BBB* to model 2, there is a probability of 23% that we do not add explanatory power.

Predictions of the default rate can be based on λ, which we get via (4.5). Dividing λ by the number of issuers N yields the expected default rate. To understand the formula in cell J23 of Table 4.5, note that the variable *LNN* is just $\ln(N)$ and

$$\begin{aligned} \lambda_t/N_t &= \exp\left[\beta_1 + \beta_2 x_{2t} + \beta_3 x_{3t} + \ldots + \beta_K x_{Kt}\right]/N_t \\ &= \exp\left[\beta_1 + \beta_2 x_{2t} + \beta_3 x_{3t} + \ldots + \beta_K x_{Kt} - \ln(N_t)\right] \end{aligned} \tag{4.14}$$

It is useful to have a function similar to TREND to make predictions. It can quickly be provided via a user-defined function. For your convenience, we show the relevant formulae below the code:

```
Function POITREND(y, x, xn)
Dim C As Integer, i As Integer
Dim poiregout As Variant, lnlambda As Double
C = x.Columns.Count
poiregout = POIREG(y, x)

lnlambda = poiregout(1, 1)
For i = 1 To C
    lnlambda = lnlambda + poiregout(1, 1 + i) * xn(i)
Next i

POITREND = Exp(lnlambda)
End Function
```

$$\begin{aligned} \ln\lambda_t &= \beta_1 + \beta_2 x_{2t} + \beta_3 x_{3t} + \ldots + \beta_K x_{Kt} \\ \lambda_t &= \exp\left[\ln\lambda_t\right] \end{aligned}$$

We programmed the function POITREND such that it returns the number of defaults, and not the default rate. The inputs are analogous to TREND. In the function, we start by determining C, the number of explanatory variables x excluding the constant. Note that there are $C+1=K$ coefficients because POIREG also includes a constant. Then, we call the function POIREG to get the βs and use a loop to compute `lnlambda`$=\ln\lambda=\beta' x$. The constant `poiregout(1,1)` is added to `lnlambda` before we enter the loop. The function then returns λ.

Compared to linear regression, the predictions made by model 1 and model 2 are relatively close. What may seem surprising is that Poisson model 2 predicts a higher default rate than does Poisson model 1. In the linear regression, this was reversed. Recall that the difference in linear regression results was due to excluding *BBB*, the fraction of BBB-rated issuers. In Poisson model 2, we also exclude *BBB*, but now we include *LNN*, the log number of issuers. Since *LNN* is highly correlated with *BBB*, *LNN* contains much of the information contained in *BBB*, and dropping *BBB* does not have a great effect on the forecast.

Linear or Poisson – which estimation method should we use? On conceptual grounds, the Poisson model is superior. However, this does not necessarily mean that it leads to better forecasts. To learn about the performance of the two models, we should conduct a backtest.

BACKTESTING THE PREDICTION MODELS

In a genuine backtest of a model, we employ the model for some time to make predictions in a certain setting and environment, and then examine the prediction errors that have arisen. So, after setting up a forecasting model, we would have to wait some time until we can learn something about its validity. In our case, in which we make one-year predictions, we would probably have to wait three years or more because we cannot learn too much from a single year. A work-around would be to perform something usually referred to as a backtest, albeit being sort of hypothetical: assuming that we had used the model over the last years, what prediction errors would we have gotten?

In performing such a test, we should make sure that when setting up a forecast for some year t in the past, we use only information that was available at the end of year $t-1$. In other words, the sample that we use for setting up the forecasting model should be kept separate from the sample used for validation. For this reason, backtests are also called out-of-sample tests.

With respect to some pieces of information, this requirement can be met fairly easily. If our forecast for year t is based on a regression, for example, we should estimate the coefficients with data available until $t-1$. With respect to other information, meeting the requirement may turn out to be much more difficult than expected at first. In the previous two sections, we looked at the entire sample when performing the regression analysis. This will probably affect our choice of regressions that we use in the backtest. One could avoid such a situation by keeping the data separated into two parts from the start. A sensible procedure might be to perform our previous regression analysis solely by looking at the years 1981–1995, holding out the years 1996–2005 for a backtest. But imagine that you had already seen another study that uses data until 2005. It would then be difficult to prevent this knowledge from having an influence on your modeling of the 1981–1995 data. Consciously or subconsciously, you may favor variables that you have seen perform well.

We take a pragmatic stance here. We are careful not to use obvious out-of-sample information, and try to prevent implicit knowledge from having an undue influence. For the data at hand, we decide to cut the sample into roughly two halves and use 1996–2005 for out-of-sample evaluation. The sample used for estimation always starts in 1981 and ends in the year before the respective forecast period. When making a forecast for the year 2000, for example, we use information from 1981 to 1999.

As before, predictions can be generated using the function TREND (for linear regressions) or the user-defined function POITREND (for Poisson regressions). The forecast error is the default rate in t minus the default rate prediction that was made for t at the end of year $t - 1$. In assessing the forecasts errors, we have to arrive at some assessment of their consequences. A common choice is to apply a quadratic loss function, meaning that we examine squared prediction errors. Why should we use a quadratic loss function in our case? A bank's profits will suffer both if it grants credit too easily and if it charges loan rates that are so high that attractive clients switch to competitors. Therefore, it seems appropriate to penalize a forecast model for both negative and positive errors, as is done with the quadratic loss function. The quadratic loss function also entails that making one big error (such as underestimating the investment-grade default rate by 0.2%) has bigger consequences than two errors that sum up to the same magnitude (such as underestimating the default rate by 0.1% over two years). For a bank, big errors can have drastic consequences because they could jeopardize their solvency and thus their very existence. Repeated smaller errors, on the other hand, can be more easily feathered by raising new equity capital or other measures.

Of course, one could just as well motivate other loss functions, e.g., by arguing that a bank loses more money by granting bad credits than by failing to make business with good credits. Our focus, however, is on the practical implementation of a backtest. Since the techniques employed in a backtest can be easily adapted to different loss functions, we proceed by assuming a standard quadratic loss function without going into a more detailed discussion here.

Even with an uncontroversial loss function it is often difficult to derive statements on whether observed losses are large, acceptable or small in absolute terms. A standard solution to this problem is to examine whether forecast errors are smaller than those from a simple alternative. In our case, a straightforward candidate for such benchmark forecasts is the prevailing average default rate. It is easily available, and it would be the optimal forecast if expected default rates did not vary over time.

In Table 4.6, we calculate squared out-of-sample prediction errors for the 10 years from 1996–2005. We do so for the prevailing mean as the benchmark model, and our forecast models 1 and 2, estimated with linear or Poisson regression. We cumulate the squared forecast errors – that is, we add the squared forecast error from 1997 to that from 1996, then add the squared forecast error from 1998 to the sum of the squared errors from 1997 and 1996, and so forth. In the spreadsheet, this can easily be done by adding the value of the previous cell to the current squared forecast error. Forecast errors are computed separately for all five forecasting models and then plotted in a chart.

Judging from the cumulative forecast error, each regression model outperforms the benchmark model. Within the regression models, Poisson leads to lower forecast errors than the linear regression. The difference between regression models and the benchmark is fairly large. Using linear regression reduces the cumulative squared prediction error by up to 38% (11.95/19.13 – 1); using Poisson regression reduces the error by up to 76% (4.44/19.13 – 1). From 2002 on, the more general models 1 perform better than models 2. This conforms to intuition: the more general a model, the more data is needed to get precise coefficient estimates. The overall difference between the two model specifications, however, is relatively small. Since it is difficult to assess which model we actually would have used over those 10 years, the fact that the choice of the model did not have such great an influence on the resulting prediction is certainly reassuring. (Recall the model selection problem that is inherent in such a backtest.)

Table 4.6 Backtesting: cumulative squared prediction errors of regression models compared to the ones of the trailing average

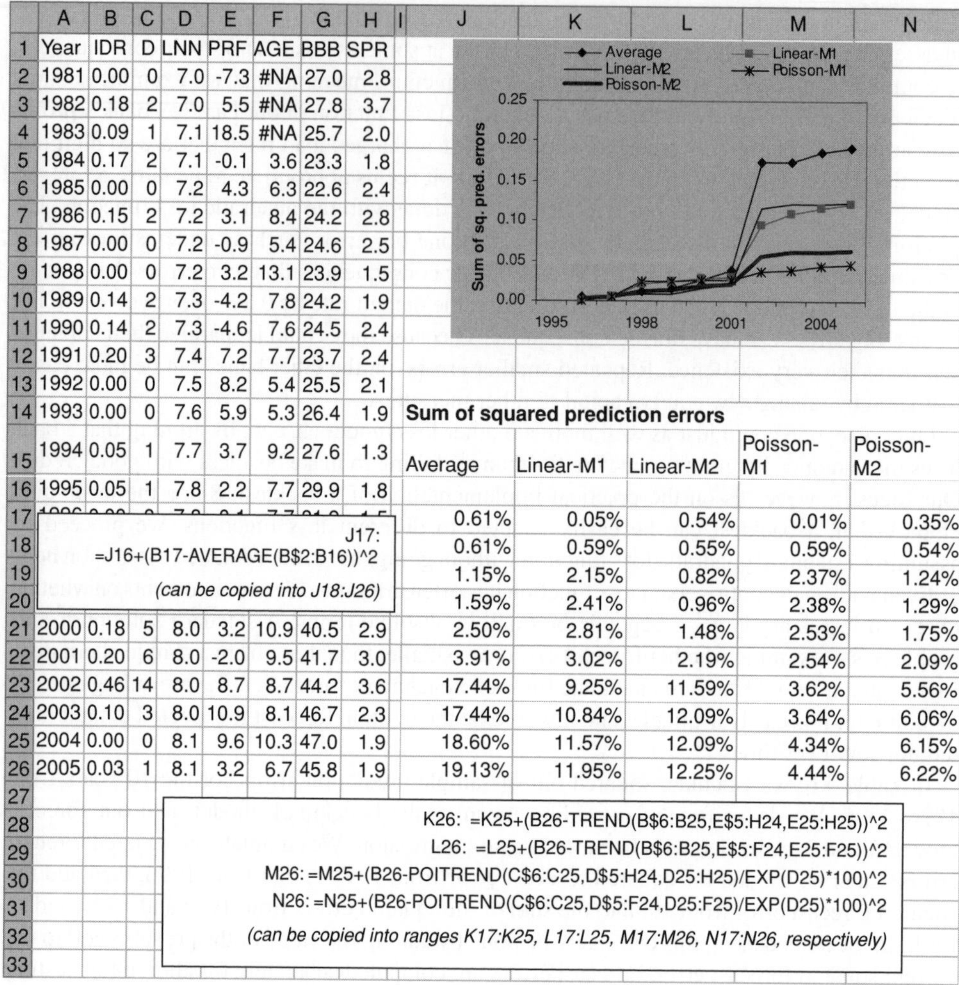

	A	B	C	D	E	F	G	H
1	Year	IDR	D	LNN	PRF	AGE	BBB	SPR
2	1981	0.00	0	7.0	-7.3	#NA	27.0	2.8
3	1982	0.18	2	7.0	5.5	#NA	27.8	3.7
4	1983	0.09	1	7.1	18.5	#NA	25.7	2.0
5	1984	0.17	2	7.1	-0.1	3.6	23.3	1.8
6	1985	0.00	0	7.2	4.3	6.3	22.6	2.4
7	1986	0.15	2	7.2	3.1	8.4	24.2	2.8
8	1987	0.00	0	7.2	-0.9	5.4	24.6	2.5
9	1988	0.00	0	7.2	3.2	13.1	23.9	1.5
10	1989	0.14	2	7.3	-4.2	7.8	24.2	1.9
11	1990	0.14	2	7.3	-4.6	7.6	24.5	2.4
12	1991	0.20	3	7.4	7.2	7.7	23.7	2.4
13	1992	0.00	0	7.5	8.2	5.4	25.5	2.1
14	1993	0.00	0	7.6	5.9	5.3	26.4	1.9
15	1994	0.05	1	7.7	3.7	9.2	27.6	1.3
16	1995	0.05	1	7.8	2.2	7.7	29.9	1.8
17	[illegible]							
18								
19								
20								
21	2000	0.18	5	8.0	3.2	10.9	40.5	2.9
22	2001	0.20	6	8.0	-2.0	9.5	41.7	3.0
23	2002	0.46	14	8.0	8.7	8.7	44.2	3.6
24	2003	0.10	3	8.0	10.9	8.1	46.7	2.3
25	2004	0.00	0	8.1	9.6	10.3	47.0	1.9
26	2005	0.03	1	8.1	3.2	6.7	45.8	1.9

J17: =J16+(B17-AVERAGE(B$2:B16))^2
(can be copied into J18:J26)

Sum of squared prediction errors

	J	K	L	M	N
15	Average	Linear-M1	Linear-M2	Poisson-M1	Poisson-M2
17	0.61%	0.05%	0.54%	0.01%	0.35%
18	0.61%	0.59%	0.55%	0.59%	0.54%
19	1.15%	2.15%	0.82%	2.37%	1.24%
20	1.59%	2.41%	0.96%	2.38%	1.29%
21	2.50%	2.81%	1.48%	2.53%	1.75%
22	3.91%	3.02%	2.19%	2.54%	2.09%
23	17.44%	9.25%	11.59%	3.62%	5.56%
24	17.44%	10.84%	12.09%	3.64%	6.06%
25	18.60%	11.57%	12.09%	4.34%	6.15%
26	19.13%	11.95%	12.25%	4.44%	6.22%

K26: =K25+(B26-TREND(B$6:B25,E$5:H24,E25:H25))^2
L26: =L25+(B26-TREND(B$6:B25,E$5:F24,E25:F25))^2
M26: =M25+(B26-POITREND(C$6:C25,D$5:H24,D25:H25)/EXP(D25)*100)^2
N26: =N25+(B26-POITREND(C$6:C25,D$5:F24,D25:F25)/EXP(D25)*100)^2
(can be copied into ranges K17:K25, L17:L25, M17:M26, N17:N26, respectively)

A closer look at the evolution of forecast errors reveals that differences in cumulated errors are largely due to the year 2002. Was 2002 just a lucky year for the regression models, which should not greatly affect our appraisal of the models? Logic suggests that it was not just pure luck. In 2002, the default rate strongly deviated from the historical average. It is exactly in such years that we would expect regression models to perform much better than the simple average. Surely you are curious how the models performed in the 2007–2009 crisis. The reason that we did not update the estimation is that Standard & Poor's no longer reports some of the information used in the analysis. In Box 4.1, however, we present an update of the analysis using data from Moody's. It shows that regression models continued to perform well.

Box 4.1 Extending the prediction model to the years 2006–2010.

The data used in the calculations of this chapter end in 2005. We did not update the estimation because the number of issuers per rating category and the number of new issuers is no longer publicly available through the S&P default studies. (Of course, it is possible to obtain such data from S&P or from data vendors.)

In order to examine the performance of the approach during the 2007–2009 financial crisis, we use data from Moody's. The default study for the year 2009 contains information on the number of issuers per year, which can be used to determine the fraction of issuers rated Baa (the Moody's symbol Baa corresponds to the S&P symbol BBB). The number of newly rated issuers is not reported by Moody's either. We therefore decide to approximate it as follows: number of firm's rated in $t - 3$ plus number of firms defaulted from $t - 4$ to $t - 3$ minus number of firm's rated in $t - 4$. Being an approximation, the resulting number can be negative. We therefore constrain it to be positive.

For both the linear regression and the Poisson regression framework, we select two models following the selection approach described in the body of this chapter. The main difference is that the number of issuers is not included in the Poisson analysis of the Moody's data. Contrary to expectations, the coefficient on this variable is negative, which is likely to be due to the high correlation with other variables.

The chart below summarizes the result of the backtesting exercise that was performed along the lines of the one presented in Table 4.6. As with the S&P data analyzed in Table 4.6, the prediction models outperform the simple average in the years 2001 and 2002. In 2008, the performance of the prediction models is mixed. Some add value, whereas others do not. In 2009, however, the prediction models again increase their advantage relative to forecasts based on the simple average.

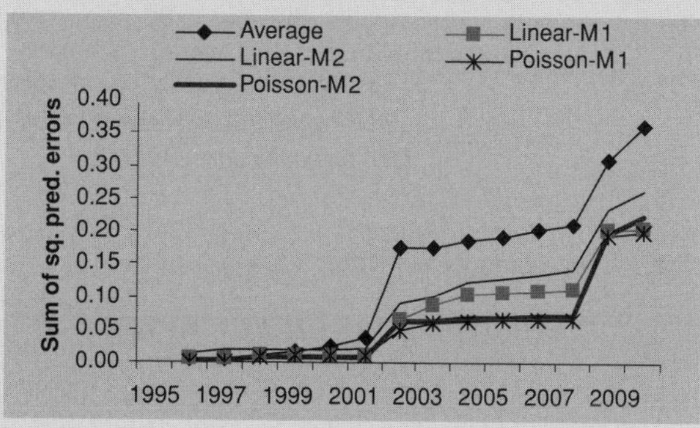

To learn more about the consistency of performance differentials, we count the number of years in which the simple average leads to lower annual squared forecast errors. As shown in Table 4.7, we can easily perform such calculations with the cumulative forecast errors we just examined.

By subtracting the previous cumulative error from the current cumulative one, we get the current year's error. We then compare the forecast error of a regression model to the one from

Table 4.7 Consistency of the outperformance of linear and Poisson models over the trailing average (extends Table 4.6)

	A	G	H	I	J	K	L	M	N	O
1	Year	BBB	SPR							
14	1993	26.4	1.9		**Sum of squared prediction errors**					
15	1994	27.6	1.3		Average	Linear-M1	Linear-M2	Poisson-M1	Poisson-M2	
16	1995	29.9	1.8							
17	1996	31.9	1.5		0.61%	0.05%	0.54%	0.01%	0.35%	
18	1997	35.7	1.5		0.61%	0.59%	0.55%	0.59%	0.54%	
19	1998	36.6	2.7		1.15%	2.15%	0.82%	2.37%	1.24%	
20	1999	38.2	1.8		1.59%	2.41%	0.96%	2.38%	1.29%	
21	2000	40.5	2.9		2.50%	2.81%	1.48%	2.53%	1.75%	
22	2001	41.7	3.0		3.91%	3.02%	2.19%	2.54%	2.09%	
23	2002	44.2	3.6		17.44%	9.25%	11.59%	3.62%	5.56%	
24	2003	46.7	2.3		17.44%	10.84%	12.09%	3.64%	6.06%	
25	2004	47.0	1.9		18.60%	11.57%	12.09%	4.34%	6.15%	
26	2005	45.8	1.9		19.13%	11.95%	12.25%	4.44%	6.22%	
27										
28					**Has the trailing average lower squared errors in year t? (yes=1)**					
29		K29: =(($J17-$J16)<(K17-K16))*1				0	0	0	0	
30		*(can be copied into K29:N38)*				1	1	1	1	
31						1	0	1	1	
32						0	0	0	0	
33						0	0	0	0	
34						0	0	0	0	
35						0	0	0	0	
36						1	1	1	1	
37						0	0	0	0	
38						0	0	0	0	
39					**p-values for sign test (H0: Average is better)**					
40						17.19%	5.47%	17.19%	17.19%	
41						=BINOMDIST(SUM(K29:K38),COUNT(K29:K38),0.5,1)				
42						*(can be copied into L40:N40)*				

the average. In cell K29, for example, we write

$$= ((\$J17 - \$J16) < (K17 - K16))^*1$$

The condition = ((\$J17 – \$J16) < (K17 – K16)) would return TRUE or FALSE. By multiplying this logical condition with 1, the output is 1 or 0, which can more easily be used as input to a function.

With so little data, visual inspection gives us a quick overview: the trailing average outperforms three models in three years out of 10; the linear regression model 2 is only outperformed in two years out of 10. Thus, regression models perform better in the majority of years.

We can also make a statement on the statistical significance of this consistency by performing a sign test. If the regression models were no better than the average, the number of years in which the average is superior would follow a binomial distribution with success probability 0.5. The fewer years we observe in which the average outperforms, the more confident can we be that a regression model is better.

The p-value of the sign test with the null hypothesis that the average is better can be computed through the function BINOMDIST(number of successes, trials, probability of success, cumulative). The number of successes can be obtained by summing over the range with 0s and 1s that mark the outperformance of the average; we know that the number of trials is 10 (years), but we can also calculate it using the function COUNT. The success probability is set to 0.5. The logical value cumulative is set to 1 such that the function returns the probability of obtaining the stated number of successes or less.

The resulting p-value is 17.19% in three out of four cases; it is 5.47% for the linear regression model 2. The lower the p-value, the higher the confidence with which we can reject the hypothesis that the trailing average is superior to the regression models. Thus, the test provides moderate statistical support for the conclusion that the regression models are consistent outperformers. In interpreting this result, we should not forget that the small sample size would make this a fairly likely outcome even if the regression models were truly superior.

PREDICTING TRANSITION MATRICES

The default rates we have analyzed in the previous sections are also recorded in transition matrices, together with transition rates. The latter are average frequencies with which ratings migrate from one rating to another. Like default rates, transition rates vary over time. This is evidenced in Table 4.8, which shows the average transition matrix over the years 1981–2005 as

Table 4.8 Transition matrices from Standard & Poor's (in %): average versus 2002

	A	B	C	D	E	F	G	H	I	J	K
1	**Global Average One-Year Transition Rates, 1981 to 2005 (%)***										
2	From/To		AAA	AA	A	BBB	BB	B	CCC/C	D	NR
3	AAA		88.20	7.67	0.49	0.09	0.06	0.00	0.00	0.00	3.49
4	AA		0.58	87.16	7.63	0.58	0.06	0.11	0.02	0.01	3.85
5	A		0.05	1.90	87.24	5.59	0.42	0.15	0.03	0.04	4.58
6	BBB		0.02	0.16	3.85	84.13	4.27	0.76	0.17	0.27	6.37
7	BB		0.03	0.04	0.25	5.26	75.74	7.36	0.90	1.12	9.29
8	B		0.00	0.05	0.19	0.31	5.52	72.67	4.21	5.38	11.67
9	CCC/C		0.00	0.00	0.28	0.41	1.24	10.92	47.06	27.02	13.06
10											
11	**Static Pool One-Year Transition Matrices (%)****										
12	2002 Static Pool										
13	From/To	Issuers	AAA	AA	A	BBB	BB	B	CCC/C	D	NR
14	AAA	132	81.06	11.36	0.00	0.76	0.00	0.00	0.00	0.00	6.82
15	AA	526	0.19	74.90	16.92	2.28	0.19	0.57	0.00	0.00	4.94
16	A	1120	0.00	0.54	83.13	10.54	0.80	0.18	0.09	0.09	4.64
17	BBB	1271	0.00	0.08	2.12	82.06	6.06	2.20	0.55	1.02	5.90
18	BB	802	0.12	0.00	0.37	3.24	77.68	7.61	1.37	2.74	6.86
19	B	754	0.00	0.00	0.00	0.27	4.64	68.30	9.15	8.09	9.55
20	CCC/C	170	0.00	0.00	0.59	0.00	1.18	7.65	34.12	44.12	12.35
21											
22	*Table 9 from Standard & Poor's (2006), Annual 2005 Global Corporate Default Study And Rating Transitions										
23	*Table 24 from Standard & Poor's (2006)										
24											

well as the 2002 transition matrix. Both matrices are from Standard and Poor's (2006, Tables 9 and 24), and are estimated with the cohort approach described in Chapter 3.

As seen above, default rates were very high in 2002. Looking at the transition matrix, it is evident that the downgrade frequencies were also relatively high. For example, 9.15% of the B-rated issuers from the start of 2002 ended up in the CCC category at the end of 2002. The long-run average transition rate from B to CCC was only 4.21%. The counterpart to this pronounced downward movement is that fewer ratings remained stable or were upgraded.

These observations suggest that ratings move somewhat in lockstep. In a bad year (such as 2002), many issuers default or experience downgrades, whereas few are upgraded. In the remainder of this chapter, we present a parsimonious model in which movements of the transition matrix are described by a single parameter. Once we have a forecast of this parameter, we can also forecast the entire transition matrix. Before introducing this framework, however, we have to deal with some irregularities of transition matrices.

ADJUSTING TRANSITION MATRICES

If an issuer rated at the start of the year is no longer rated at the end of the year, a standard transition matrix, like the one shown in Table 4.8, records a transition to the NR status, where NR denotes not-rated. (If it is known that such an issuer defaulted, however, one would record a default instead). There are various ways for producing transition matrices that do not contain this type of transition, and still have entries that sum up to 100%. One way is to exclude issuers whose rating was withdrawn from the analysis.

We use some formulae to clarify the procedure. Let N_i be the number of issuers with rating i at the start of the period; let $N_{i,j}$ be the number of issuers with rating i at the start of the period and rating j at the end of the period. The unadjusted transition rate from rating A to rating B, for example, would be calculated as $\text{TR}_{\text{A,B}} = N_{\text{A,B}}/N_{\text{A}}$. The unadjusted transition rate from A to NR would be $\text{TR}_{\text{A,NR}} = N_{\text{A,NR}}/N_{\text{A}}$. Removing the NR-category from the calculations leads to a NR-adjusted transition rate TR^{NR}:

$$\text{TR}^{\text{NR}}_{\text{A,B}} = \frac{N_{\text{A,B}}}{N_{\text{A}} - N_{\text{A,NR}}} = \frac{N_{\text{A,B}}}{N_{\text{A}} - \frac{N_{\text{A,NR}}}{N_{\text{A}}} N_{\text{A}}} = \frac{N_{\text{A,B}}}{N_{\text{A}} - \text{TR}_{\text{A,NR}} N_{\text{A}}}$$

$$= \frac{N_{\text{A,B}}}{N_{\text{A}}(1 - \text{TR}_{\text{A,NR}})} = \frac{\text{TR}_{\text{A,B}}}{(1 - \text{TR}_{\text{A,NR}})} \tag{4.15}$$

which means that we derive the NR-removed rates from the original transition rates by dividing each original transition rate from class i by one minus the transition rate from i to not-rated. In the following discussion, we will always use NR-removed matrices that have been constructed in this way.

There are two other simple ad hoc adjustments we routinely make: we set cells with zero entries to 0.001%; we adjust the on-diagonal cells containing the frequency with which the rating is maintained such that the sum over one row equals 100%. Note that, due to rounding in the figures that we take from S&P, a row sum of 100% is not guaranteed even before replacing zero entries by 0.001%. Rounding can lead to deviations from 100% that amount to 0.01% or more. These adjustments facilitate the ensuing calculations, but are not essential. We could just as well adjust some of the formulae in such a way that they can deal with values of 0 or above 1.

REPRESENTING TRANSITION MATRICES WITH A SINGLE PARAMETER

Consider the following two statements:

- The probability of a migration from A to B is 2.5%.
- The rating migrates from A to B whenever a standard normal variable ends up between 1.645 and 1.960.

Both statements are equivalent because the probability that a standard normal variable ends up between 1.645 and 1.960 is 2.5%. In Excel, this can be verified by =NORMSDIST(1.960)–NORMSDIST(1.645).

In fact, we can describe the entire transition matrix by the concept that transitions are driven by a standard normally distributed variable x – and do so without losing any information. Instead of describing transition behavior through transition rates, we can describe it through a set of thresholds: 1.645 and 1.960 would be a pair of thresholds that together describes a bin. Each bin triggers a certain specific transition whenever the variable x ends up in this bin.

But why try to find another representation of the same information? We can use it to shift the transition matrix into bad or good years. But before showing this, let us first define the bins.

We can illustrate the binning procedure for transitions from A as follows:

	AAA	AA	A	BBB	BB	B	CCC/C	D
A	0.052%	1.991%	91.427%	5.858%	0.440%	0.157%	0.031%	0.042%
Bin	$(\infty, 3.28]$	$[3.28, 2.04]$	$[2.04, -1.51]$	$[-1.51, -2.47]$	$[-2.47, -2.83]$	$[-2.83, -3.18]$	$[-3.18, -3.34]$	$[-3.34, -\infty]$

We can start to define the bins at any of the two extreme transitions, transitions to AAA or transitions to default. Let us unroll the computations from transitions to default. If the probability of a migration from A to D is 0.042%, we can define the D bin as [$\Phi^{-1}(0.00042)$, $-\infty$), where $\Phi^{-1}()$ denotes the inverse cumulative standard normal distribution function. The upper threshold for this D bin becomes the lower threshold for the CCC/C bin. The latter should be hit with a probability of 0.031%. This can be achieved by setting the upper threshold to $\Phi^{-1}(0.00042 + 0.00031) = -3.18$. We can continue in this way. Though we have eight bins, we need to compute just seven thresholds. Since the normal distribution is symmetric, another valid binning would result if we multiplied all threshold values from above by -1.

Table 4.9 shows how the binning is done in Excel. The inverse of the normal distribution function is available through NORMSINV(). Note that the argument is computed by summing the transition rates in the current row from the rightmost column to the current column. Division by 100 is necessary because the transition rates are stated in percent. Recall from above that we set cells with entry zero to 0.001%; also, we adjust the no-change rate such that the sum over one row equals 100%.

Table 4.10 graphically illustrates the results from Table 4.9. The chart shows the standard normal density and the thresholds for transitions from BB. The density can be computed using the function NORMDIST(*x*,*mean*,*standard_dev*,*cumulative*). We set the mean to 0 and the standard deviation to 1 in order to get the standard normal, and we set the logical value cumulative to 0 to get the density function. Some experimentation shows that eight values are

Table 4.9 Thresholds for representing transitions through a standard normal variable

	A	B	C	D	E	F	G	H	I
1	**Transition rates with NRs and zeroes removed (in %)**								
2	1981-2005								
3		AAA	AA	A	BBB	BB	B	CCC/C	D
4	AAA	91.386	7.947	0.508	0.093	0.062	0.001	0.001	0.001
5	AA	0.603	90.650	7.936	0.603	0.062	0.114	0.021	0.010
6	A	0.052	1.991	91.427	5.858	0.440	0.157	0.031	0.042
7	BBB	0.021	0.171	4.112	89.854	4.561	0.812	0.182	0.288
8	BB	0.033	0.044	0.276	5.799	83.508	8.114	0.992	1.235
9	B	0.001	0.001	0.215	0.351	6.249	82.326	4.766	6.091
10	CCC/C	0.001	0.001	0.322	0.472	1.426	12.560	54.139	31.079
11									
12	**Upper thresholds for bins**								
13		AAA	AA	A	BBB	BB	B	CCC/C	D
14	AAA		-1.36	-2.48	-2.95	-3.22	-4.01	-4.11	-4.26
15	AA		2.51	-1.36	-2.40	-2.87	-2.98	-3.42	-3.71
16	A		3.28	2.04	-1.51	-2.47	-2.83	-3.18	-3.34
17	BBB		3.52	2.89	1.72	-1.57	-2.23	-2.60	-2.76
18	BB		3.41	3.17	2.69	1.54	-1.26	-2.01	-2.25
19	B		4.26	4.11	2.85	2.53	1.49	-1.23	-1.55
20	CCC/C		4.26	4.11	2.72	2.41	2.01	1.05	-0.49
21			=NORMSINV(SUM(C10:$I10)/100)						
22			*(can be copied into C14:I20)*						

Table 4.10 Thresholds for representing transitions through a standard normal variable – graphical illustration for transitions from BB

	A	B	C	D	E	F	G	H	I	J
...	...	...	...	...	...	...	...	...	...	
10	CCC/C	0.001	0.001	0.322	0.472	1.426	12.560	54.139	31.079	
11										
12	**Upper thresholds for bins**									
13		AAA	AA	A					D	
14	AAA		-1.36					.11	-4.26	
15	AA		2.51					.42	-3.71	
16	A		3.28					.18	-3.34	
17	BBB		3.52					.60	-2.76	
18	BB		3.41					.01	-2.25	
19	B		4.26					.23	-1.55	
20	CCC/C		4.26	4.11	2.72	2.41	2.01	1.05	-0.49	
21										
22	**Chart for BB (scatterplot with two series: (x, density) and (thresholds, bar height))**									
23	x	-3.5	-2.5	-1.5	-0.5	0.5	1.5	2.5	3.5	
24	density	0.00	0.02	0.13	0.35	0.35	0.13	0.02	0.00	
25		=NORMDIST(B23,0,1,0) *(can be copied into C24:I24)*								
26	thresholds		3.41	3.17	2.69	1.54	-1.26	-2.01	-2.25	=I18
27	bar height		0.4	0.4	0.4	0.4	0.4	0.4	0.4	

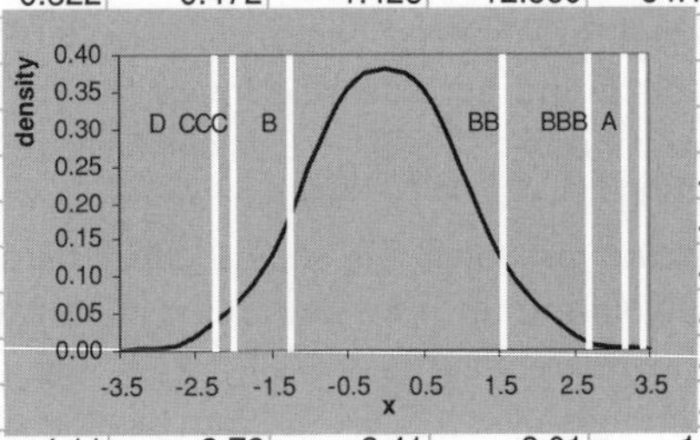

enough to get a nice curve provided that the *smoothed line* option is activated.[9] The chart type is *XY* (scatter).

We then add the thresholds to this chart. The thresholds themselves enter as x-values of a second series within the *XY* chart; the associated y-values are set to 0.4, the maximum value that we allow for the y-axis. Then, we need to use a little trick. Because one cannot directly choose bars in a scatter chart, we hide the symbols and the lines for this second series, but activate y-error bars for this series – with length 0.4.[10] Finally, we use a text box to label the thresholds.

SHIFTING THE TRANSITION MATRIX

Imagine that, in the chart from Table 4.10, the normal density is shifted to the left, i.e., assume that it has a negative mean rather than mean zero.

Figure 4.1 shows such a move to the left. The probability of a transition is the probability of ending up in the associated bin. This probability is equal to the area enclosed by the boundaries of the bin and the density function. Therefore, a shift to the left would increase the probabilities of downgrades as well as the probability of default. Importantly, we still have fully specified transition probabilities, albeit ones that are different from those we used for the threshold determination. Analogously, we could reduce the probabilities of downgrade and default by shifting the distribution to the right.

In Table 4.11, we compute the transition probabilities that result after a shift. The magnitude of the shift is called 'credit index' and specified in cell E23. A negative number means that the distribution function is shifted to the left, thus increasing the probabilities of downgrade and default.

The probability that a normal variable with mean m and standard deviation 1 ends up to the left of a threshold is given by $\Phi(threshold - m)$ = NORMSDIST($threshold - m$). To obtain the probability of ending up in a bin, we use this formula to obtain the probability of ending up below the upper threshold of the bin, and then subtract the probability of ending up below the lower threshold of the bin. We could compute the latter with the normal distribution, but

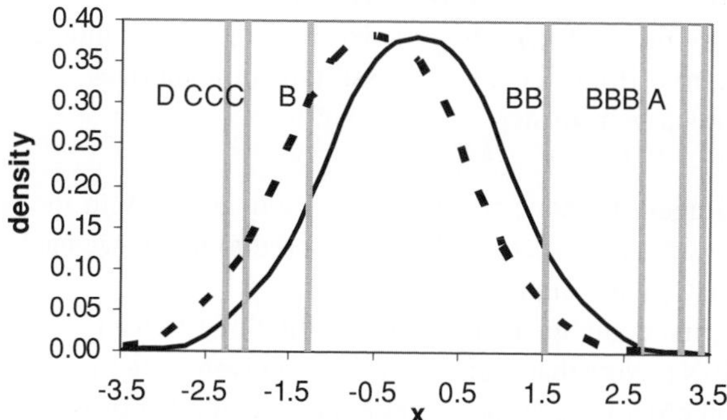

Figure 4.1 Shifting the distribution function to change transition probabilities

[9] To smooth a line chart: (i) double-click the data series you want to smooth; (ii) select the Patterns tab; (iii) select the Smoothed line check box.

[10] To show y-error bars: (i) Double-click the data series; (ii) select the Y Error Bars tab; (iii) specify the bars you want.

Table 4.11 Shifting transitions matrices with a credit index

	A	B	C	D	E	F	G	H	I	J
...	...	...	...	...	...	...	...	...	...	
10	CCC	0.001	0.001	0.322	0.472	1.426	12.560	54.139	31.079	
11										
12	**Thresholds**									
13		AAA	AA	A	BBB	BB	B	CCC	D	
14	AAA		-1.36	-2.47	-2.92	-3.15	-3.55	-4.11	-4.26	
15	AA		2.51	-1.36	-2.40	-2.87	-2.98	-3.42	-3.71	
16	A		3.28	2.04	-1.51	-2.47	-2.83	-3.18	-3.34	
17	BBB		3.52	2.89	1.72	-1.57	-2.23	-2.60	-2.76	
18	BB		3.41	3.17	2.69	1.54	-1.26	-2.01	-2.25	
19	B		4.26	4.11	2.85	2.53	1.49	-1.23	-1.55	
20	CCC		4.26	4.11	2.72	2.41	2.01	1.05	-0.49	
21										
22										
23	**Transitions with credit index set to:**				-0.25					
24		AAA	AA	A	BBB	BB	B	CCC	D	
25	AAA	86.756%	11.940%	0.958%	0.195%	0.143%	0.003%	0.003%	0.003%	
26	AA	0.289%	86.286%	11.862%	1.118%	0.125%	0.244%	0.049%	0.027%	
27	A	0.021%	1.066%	88.562%	9.039%	0.823%	0.321%	0.069%	0.100%	
28	BBB	0.008%	0.076%	2.378%	88.165%	6.997%	1.430%	0.343%	0.602%	
29	BB	0.013%	0.019%	0.130%	3.493%	80.777%	11.639%	1.633%	2.296%	
30	B	0.000%	0.000%	0.095%	0.175%	3.826%	79.651%	6.523%	9.728%	
31	CCC	0.000%	0.000%	0.147%	0.242%	0.802%	8.561%	49.872%	40.376%	
32		=1-SUM(C31:I31)		=NORMSDIST(D20-$E$23)-SUM(E31:$J31)						
33	*(formula for B31, can be copied*			*(formula for D31, can be copied into C25:I31)*						
34		*into B25:B31)*								

we can also sum over the cells in the same row that are located to the right of the bin we are in. For the AAA bins, we exploit the fact that transition probabilities sum up to 1.

The next steps in the analysis are as follows:

1. We find credit indices that best fit historically observed annual transition matrices.
2. Based on step 1, we build a forecasting model to predict credit indices.
3. We use the predictions from step 2 to forecast transition matrices.
4. We subject the forecasts from step 3 to a backtest.

The backtest will again be done for the years 1996–2005. With the requirements of the backtest in mind, we set up the sheet such that the credit indices we back out for a particular year use only information up to that year.

In Table 4.12, we first compute an average transition matrix using the years 1981 up to the year specified in cell N1. Note that transition rates are given in percent even though we do not state this explicitly in order to save space. Let $N_{i,t}$ be the number of issuers with rating i at the start of year t; let TR_{ij} be the transition rate from i to j in year t. The average transition rate from i to j that uses data until year T is an issuer weighted average of the annual transition rates:

$$TR_{ij}^{T} = \sum_{t=1981}^{T} N_{i,t} TR_{ij,t} \Big/ \sum_{t=1981}^{T} N_{i,t} \tag{4.16}$$

Table 4.12 Backing out credit indices that best fit annual transition matrices

	A	B	C	J	K	L	M	N	O	P	Q	R	S	T
1	1981					**Average up to**		2005	i.e. up to row		226	=MATCH(N1,A1:A500)+9		
2		#	AAA	D			AAA	AA	A	BBB	BB	B	CCC	D
3	AAA	87	0.89	0.00		AAA	0.91	0.08	0.01	0.00	0.00	0.00	0.00	0.00
4	AA	210	0.02	0.00		AA	0							
5	A	489	0.00	0.00		A	0							
6	BBB	271	0.00	0.00		BBB	0							
7	BB	215	0.00	0.00		BB	0							
8	B	81	0.00	0.02		B	0							
9	CCC	11	0.00	0.00		CCC	0.							
10	1982													
11		#	AAA	D		**Thresholds for average**								
12	AAA	86	0.93	0.00			AAA	AA	A	BBB	BB	B	CCC	D
13	AA	224	0.00	0.00		AAA		-1.36	-2.47	-2.96	-3.23	-4.01	-4.11	-4.26
14	A	476	0.00	0.00		AA		2.		.1	-2.88	-2.99	-3.44	-3.71
15	BBB	278	0.00	0.00		A		3.30	2.05	-1.51	-2.48	-2.83	-3.17	-3.33
16	BB	150	0.00	0.05		BBB		3.56	2.89	1.72	-1.57	-2.23	-2.59	-2.75
17	B	138	0.00	0.04		BB		3.37	3.13	2.69	1.54	-1.26	-2.01	-2.25
18	CCC	12	0.00	0.25		B		4.26	3.23	2.77	2.50	1.49	-1.23	-1.55
19	1983					CCC		4.26	4.11	2.73	2.41	2.00	1.03	-0.51
20		#	AAA	D										
21	AAA	96	0.81	0.00		**Matrix with credit index:**				0.39072				
22	AA	244	0.00	0.00			AAA	AA	A	BBB	BB	B	CCC	D
23	A	449	0.01	0.00		AAA	0.96	0.04	0.00	0.00	0.00	0.00	0.00	0.00
24	BBB	292	0.00	0.00		AA	0.02	0.		0	0.00	0.00	0.00	0.00
25	BB	156	0.00	0.01		A	0.00	0.05	0.92	0.03	0.00	0.00	0.00	0.00
26	B	136	0.00	0.05		BBB	0.00	0.01	0.08	0.88	0.02	0.00	0.00	0.00
27	CCC	15	0.00	0.07		BB	0.00	0.00	0.01	0.11	0.83	0.04	0.00	0.00
28	1984					B	0.00	0.00	0.01	0.01	0.12	0.81	0.03	0.03
29		#	AAA	D		CCC	0.00	0.00	0.01	0.01	0.03	0.21	0.55	0.19
30	AAA	109	0.72	0.00										
31	AA	292	0.02	0.00		**Matrix in year**		2005						
32	A	458	0.00	0.00			AAA	AA	A	BBB	BB	B	CCC	D
33	BBB	294	0.00	0.01		AAA	0.90	0.					00	0.00
34	BB	170	0.00	0.01		AA	0.00	0.94					00	0.00
35	B	167	0.00	0.04		A	0.00	0.02					0.00	0.00
36	C							0.00	0.06	0.90	0.03	0.00	0.00	0.00
37	1							0.00	0.00	0.06	0.86	0.08	0.00	0.00
38								0.00	0.00	0.01	0.10	0.83	0.04	0.02
39	A							0.00	0.00	0.01	0.01	0.31	0.57	0.11
40	A								**Sum of squared errors**					
41	A								0.032		= SUMXMY2(M33:T39,M23:T29)			
42	B								**Credit index**					
43	B								1981	0.17				
44	B								1982	0.00				
45	C								1983	0.16				
...	.	#	.	.	.	.			...	...				
67	AA	353	0.01	0.00					2005	0.39				

Off-diagonal (here for cell N3)
{=MAX(0.00001,SUM(IF(ROW($A$3:$A$500)<$Q$1,IF($A$3:$A$500=$L3,$B$3:$B$500*D$3:D$500,)))/SUM(IF(ROW($A$3:$A$500)<$Q$1,IF($A$3:$A$500=$L3,$B$3:$B$500,))))}
On-diagonal except for M3 (here for cell N4)
=1-SUM($M4:M4,O4:$T4)
For M3: =1-SUM(N3:$T3)

As in Table 4.7

As in Table 4.9

Array-function for entire matrix:
{= OFFSET(C3:J9,(N31-1981)*9,0)}

```
Sub creditindex()
Dim i As Integer
For i = 1981 To 2005
    Range("N1") = Application.Max(1995, i)
    Range("N31") = i
    SolverOk SetCell:="$O$41", MaxMinVal:=2, _
    ValueOf:="0", ByChange:="$P$21"
    SolverOptions Precision:=0.00001
    SolverSolve Userfinish:=True
    Range("O" & i - 1938) = i
    Range("P" & i - 1938) = (Range("P21"))
Next i

End Sub
```

For cell N3, for example, the formula used to compute (4.16) is

```
{=MAX(0.00001, SUM(IF(ROW($A$3:$A$500) < $Q$1,
IF($A$3:$A$500 = $L3, $B$3:$B$500*D$3:D$500, )))/
SUM(IF(ROW($A$3:$A$500) < $Q$1, IF($A$3:$A$500 = $L3, $B$3:$B$500, ))))}
```

The annual transition matrices in columns A to J extend until row 225. Applying the function to the wider range A3:A500 does not change the results and allows us to enter new data in subsequent years without changing the formula. The steps in the formula are as follows:

1. The maximum condition ensures that a transition rate is not smaller than 0.001%. (Recall that we decided to adjust matrices in this way.)
2. The function SUM applied to the product of the number of issuers and the transition rates yields the scalar product of the two, i.e., the numerator of formula (4.16). We use encapsulated IF-conditions to restrict the operations to those rows that (i) have the same initial rating as the rating for which we are computing the average and that (ii) belong to years smaller or equal to one specified in cell N1. To check condition (ii), we determine the number of the first row that belongs to the year following the one specified in N1. Since the year is stated before each annual transition matrix, we can use the function MATCH to identify where an annual matrix begins, and then add nine rows to get to the end of this matrix. This calculation is done in cell Q1, and we then check in the IF-condition that the row numbers are smaller than this value.
3. We compute the denominator in a fashion similar to the numerator.

The formula just described applies to all off-diagonal elements of the matrix. Diagonal elements are determined on the basis that transition probabilities add up to 1. Thresholds and the shifted matrix are determined as shown in Tables 4.9 and 4.11. The final matrix (in M33:T39) is the annual matrix for the year specified in cell N31. As the annual transition matrices are all equally spaced, we can quickly obtain them using the function OFFSET(*reference*, *rows*, *columns*, *height*, *width*). This function returns a reference to a range that is a specified number of *rows* and *columns* from a cell specified in the argument *reference*. Arguments *height* and *width* are optional and can be used to specify the size of the new range.

Now we can determine the credit index that brings the matrix M23:T29 as close as possible to the matrix in M33:T39. We make this operational by minimizing the sum of squared differences between matrix elements. This sum of squared errors is calculated in cell O41 using the function SUMXMY2(). Of course, other distance norms are also possible.

To minimize the distance, we use the Solver (see Appendix A2). The target cell to be minimized is O41; the changing cell is the credit index in P21. Since we have to determine a credit index for more than 20 years, we use a macro, called 'creditindex', shown in Table 4.12. It loops from 1981 to 2005. The easiest way to get the necessary commands for running the Solver is to record a macro, run the Solver analysis in a sheet, stop recording and edit the macro. One crucial element is to have *Userfinish:=True* at the end of the Solver procedure; otherwise, the macro would ask us to confirm the solution in each step of the loop. It is also useful to check for sufficient precision. Here, we use SolverOptions to set the precision to the default value of 0.00001 (the lower this value, the more precise the solution will be). Running the Solver within a macro requires a reference to the Solver in the VBA editor. This can be set by selecting 'Tools' from the VBA editor menu, and then 'References'.

Table 4.13 Predicting the credit index CINDEX with corporate profits and the aging effect

	A	B	C	D	E	F	G	H	I	J	K
1	year	CINDEX	PRF	AGE							
2	1981	0.17	-7.3	#NA							
3	1982	0.00	5.5	#NA							
4	1983	0.16	18.5	#NA							
5	1984	-0.07	-0.1	4.8							
6	1985	0.20	4.3	6.3				{=LINEST(B6:B26,C5:D25,1,1)}			
7	1986	0.00	3.1	8.6		**Model**	AGE	PRF	CONST		
8	1987	0.18	-0.9	6.6		coef	-0.031	0.021	0.286		
9	1988	0.03	3.2	14.4		SE(coef)	0.011	0.008	0.124		
10	1989	-0.13	-4.2	14.1		R²/RMSE	0.525	0.157	#NA		
11	1990	-0.13	-4.6	13.9		F/DF	9.963	18	#NA		
12	1991	-0.21	7.2	10.9		t-stat	-2.96	2.55	2.30		
13	1992	0.01	8.2	8.0		p-value	0.01	0.02	0.03		
14	1993	0.41	5.9	5.1							
15	1994	0.07	3.7	7.8							
16	1995	-0.01	2.2	9.2		**Out-of-sample forecasts**					
17	1996	0.29	0.1	12.1		0.033	=TREND(B$6:B16,C$5:D15,C16:D16)				
18	1997	0.20	2.1	11.4		-0.046					
19	1998	-0.22	-0.8	8.9		0.030					
20	1999	-0.12	2.6	11.9		0.022					
21	2000	-0.11	3.2	16.4		-0.004					
22	2001	-0.29	-2.0	16.1		-0.110					
23	2002	-0.35	8.7	12.9		-0.223					
24	2003	-0.05	10.9	10.0		-0.002					
25	2004	0.27	9.6	10.3		0.109					
26	2005	0.39	3.2	9.7		0.120					
27	2006					0.047					

The years that we use to derive the thresholds for year *t* are one of the following:

- 1981–1995 if the year *t* is smaller than 1996. Since we start our backtest in 1996, we can use information until 1995 to produce the first forecast, which is for 1996.
- 1981 to *t* if the year *t* is larger than 1995.

The macro writes the credit indices (and the years) into the range O43:P67.

Table 4.13 shows how to produce out-of-sample predictions based on the credit indices derived in Table 4.12. Since the credit index is a continuous variable that is potentially unbounded and can be negative or positive, there is no obvious reason why the linear regression model should be inappropriate. Issues involved in specifying the regression model are similar to those discussed in the prediction of default rates. Therefore, we choose to present just one model. The in-sample regression conducted with the LINEST command shows that corporate profit forecasts and the aging variable explain a significant part of the variation in the credit index. The out-of-sample forecasts are then generated using the function TREND. (We could insert the forecast for 2006 into cell E23 of Table 4.11 to get a forecast of the transition matrix for 2006.)

BACKTESTING THE TRANSITION FORECASTS

Now we can go back to the sheet built for Table 4.12 and perform the backtest; it is shown in Table 4.14. We first copy the out-of-sample forecasts for the credit index into the sheet. Starting in 1996, we then use the credit index forecast for year t to produce a transition matrix forecast for t, and compare it to the observed matrix in year t. The function HLOOKUP is used to fetch the credit index from the range L44:U45 for the year following the one specified in N1, and write it into cell P21.

Again, we use a quadratic loss function and benchmark the forecast errors against an average. The sum of squared differences between matrix elements is computed in cells N41 and N42 for the average and our forecast, respectively. The average is the average transition matrix based on years 1981 to $t-1$. We have to be careful to select the corresponding years. In contrast to Table 4.12, the year stated in N1 has to be one year less than the year stated in N31. The cumulative error analysis is performed by the macro 'backtest' that loops through years 1995 to 2004, corresponding to out-of-sample forecasts for the years 1996 to 2005. The errors are already cumulated within the macro and then written into cells L47:U49.

The resulting pattern in forecast errors is similar to the one in the default rate backtest. Up until 2001, it does not matter greatly in terms of squared errors whether one uses the average transition matrix or the forecasted one. Over the entire 10-year horizon, however, the forecast model leads to squared errors that are 20% lower ($=0.54/0.67-1$) than those associated with the simple average.

SCOPE OF APPLICATION

We have shown that default and transition rates can be predicted using readily available information. In line with the frequency of the data that we have used, analyses were performed on a calendar year basis. With the forecasting models that we estimated, however, we could directly produce forecasts for arbitrary 12-month-horizons, provided that the explanatory variables are available at the beginning of such a 12-month-horizon. With data on within-year or multi-year transitions, one could also implement forecasting models with a higher or lower frequency, respectively.

In this chapter, forecasts were made for transition rates of ratings produced by one of the major rating agencies. We could apply the methods to the prediction of transition rates of other rating systems. However, when analyzing transitions of a rating system in which ratings directly correspond to short-term default probabilities – e.g., a system based on logit scores (Chapter 1) – we should expect transition rates to be less predictable. As such ratings adjust more quickly to new information than agency ratings, there is less potential of finding information that predicts rating transitions.

Table 4.14 Backtesting forecasts of transition matrices (table construction as in Table 4.12)

	A	B	C	J	K	L	M	N	O	P	Q	R	S	T	U
1	1981					**Average up to**		2004	i.e. up to row		226				
2		#	AAA	D			AAA	AA	A	BBB	BB	B	CCC	D	
3	AAA	87	0.89	0.00		AAA	0.91	0.08	0.01	0.00	0.00	0.00	0.00	0.00	
4	AA	210	0.02	0.00		AA	0.01	0.91	0.08	0.01	0.00	0.00	0.00	0.00	
5	A	489	0.00	0.00		A	0.00	0.02	0.91	0.06	0.00	0.00	0.00	0.00	
6	BBB	271	0.00	0.00		BBB	0.00	0.00	0.04	0.90	0.05	0.01	0.00	0.00	
7	BB	215	0.00	0.00		BB	0.00	0.00	0.00	0.06	0.84	0.08	0.01	0.01	
8	B	81	0.00	0.02		B	0.00	0.00	0.00	0.00	0.06	0.82	0.05	0.06	
9	CCC	11	0.00	0.00		CCC	0.00	0.00	0.00	0.00	0.01	0.13	0.54	0.30	
10	1982														
11		#	AAA	D		**Thresholds for average**									
12	AAA	86	0.93	0.00			AAA	AA	A	BBB	BB	B	CCC	D	
13	AA	224	0.00	0.00		AAA		-1.36	-2.47	-2.96	-3.23	-4.01	-4.11	-4.26	
14	A	476	0.00	0.00		AA		2.51	-1.36	-2.41	-2.88	-2.99	-3.44	-3.71	
15	BBB	278	0.00	0.00		A		3.30	2.05	-1.51	-2.48	-2.83	-3.17	-3.33	
16	BB	150	0.00	0.05		BBB		3.56	2.89	1.72	-1.57	-2.23	-2.59	-2.75	
17	B	138	0.00	0.04		BB		3.37	3.13	2.69	1.54	-1.26	-2.01	-2.25	
18	CCC	12	0.00	0.25		B		4.26	3.23	2.77	2.50	1.49	-1.23	-1.55	
19	1983					CCC		4.26	4.11	2.73	2.41	2.00	1.03	-0.51	
20		#	AAA	D											
21	AAA	96	0.81	0.00		**Matrix with credit index:**				0.12	=HLOOKUP(N1+1,L44:U45,2,0)				
22	AA	244	0.00	0.00			AAA	AA	A	BBB	BB	B	CCC	D	
23	A	449	0.01	0.00		AAA	0.96	0.04							
24	BBB	292	0.00	0.00		AA	0.02	0.94							
25	BB	156	0.00	0.01		A	0.00	0.05							
26	B	136	0.00	0.05		BBB	0.00	0.01							
27	CCC	15	0.00	0.07		BB	0.00	0.00							
28	1984					B	0.00	0.00							
29		#	AAA	D		CCC	0.00	0.00							
30	AAA	109	0.72	0.00											
31	AA	292	0.02	0.00		**Matrix in year**		2005							
32	A	458	0.00	0.00			AAA	AA	A	BBB	BB	B	CCC	D	
33	BBB	294	0.00	0.01		AAA	0.90	0.09	0.01	0.00	0.00	0.00	0.00	0.00	
34	BB	170	0.00	0.01		AA	0.00	0.94	0.05	0.01	0.00	0.00	0.00	0.00	
35	B	167	0.00	0.04		A	0.00	0.02	0.94	0.05	0.00	0.00	0.00	0.00	
36	CCC	15	0.00	0.27		BBB	0.00	0.00	0.06	0.90	0.03	0.00	0.00	0.00	
37	1985					BB	0.00	0.00	0.00	0.06	0.86	0.08	0.00	0.00	
38		#	AAA	D		B	0.00	0.00	0.00	0.01	0.10	0.83	0.04	0.02	
39	AAA	92	0.92	0.00		CCC	0.00	0.00	0.00	0.01	0.01	0.31	0.57	0.11	
40	AA	321	0.00	0.00		**Squared errors**									
41	A	491	0.00	0.00		Average		0.097	=SUMXMY2(M33:T39,M3:T9)						
42	BBB	271	0.00	0.00		Forecast		0.069	=SUMXMY2(M33:T39,M23:T29)						
43	BB	193	0.00	0.02		**Credit index forecasts (from separate analysis, Table 4.13)**									
44	B	189	0.00	0.07		1996	1997	1998	1999	2000	2001	2002	2003	2004	2005
45	CCC	13	0.00	0.15		0.03	-0.05	0.03	0.02	0.00	-0.11	-0.22	0.00	0.11	0.12
46	1986					**Cumulated squared errors (via macro backtest)**									
47		#	AAA	D		1996	1997	1998	1999	2000	2001	2002	2003	2004	2005
48	AAA	107	0.93	0.00		0.08	0.12	0.24	0.27	0.29	0.38	0.49	0.50	0.57	0.67
49	AA	339	0.01	0.00		0.07	0.12	0.24	0.28	0.30	0.36	0.41	0.42	0.47	0.54
...															

```
Sub backtest()
Dim i As Integer
For i = 1995 To 2004
    Range("N1") = i
    Range("N31") = i + 1

    Cells(47, i - 1983) = i + 1
    Cells(48, i - 1983) = Cells(48, i - 1984) + Range("N41")
    Cells(49, i - 1983) = Cells(49, i - 1984) + Range("N42")
Next i
End Sub
```

NOTES AND LITERATURE

Default and transition rates are often serially correlated, which means that current rates can be predicted just by looking at lagged rates. This correlation can vanish once other variables are controlled for. In our multivariate regression models, lagged default rates or credit indices are not significant.

Default and transition data are reported by rating agencies, e.g., in Standard and Poor's, 2006, *Annual 2005 Global Corporate Default Study and Rating Transitions*.

Studies that propose and discuss forecasting models for default rates include Fons, J., 1991, *An Approach to Forecasting Default Rates*, Moody's Special Report; Helwege, J. and Kleiman, P., 1997, Understanding aggregate default rates of high yield bonds, *Journal of Fixed Income* 5, 79–88; Keenan, S., Sobehart, J. and Hamilton, D., 1999, *Predicting Default Rates: A Forecasting Model for Moody's Issuer-based Default Rates*, Moody's Special Comment.

The representation of transition matrices through a continuous state variable has been introduced into the credit literature by Gupton, G.M., Finger, C.C. and Bhatia, M. 1997, *CreditMetrics – Technical document*, New York.

Our approach of backing out a credit index from annual transition matrices has been inspired by Belkin, B., Suchower, S. and Forest, L.R. Jr., 1998, A one-parameter representation of credit risk and transition matrices, *CreditMetrics Monitor*, Third Quarter, 46–56 and Kim, J., 1999, *A way to condition the transition matrix on wind*, Working Paper, Riskmetrics Group.

APPENDIX

The following function returns estimates from a Poisson regression of `y` on *x*, where *x* is the argument `xraw` plus a column with 1s. The function assumes that the input data `y` and `xraw` are column vectors. The output is described in the main text of this chapter.

```
Function POIREG(y, xraw)

'count rows and columns of data
Dim i As Long, j As Integer
Dim N As Long, K As Integer
Dim x() As Double, lny() As Double, b() As Double
Dim x1b As Variant, yhat() As Double

N = xraw.Rows.Count
K = xraw.Columns.Count + 1

'Add constant to x matrix, initialize coeffs based on linear regression
ReDim x(1 To N, 1 To K)
ReDim lny(1 To N, 1 To 1)
ReDim b(1 To K, 1 To 1)

For i = 1 To N
    x(i, 1) = 1
    lny(i, 1) = Log(y(i, 1) + 0.01)
    For j = 2 To K
        x(i, j) = xraw(i, j - 1)
```

```
    Next j
Next i
Dim tmp
tmp = Application.WorksheetFunction.LinEst(lny, x, 0, 0)
For j = 1 To K
    b(j, 1) = tmp(K + 1 - j)
Next j


'Compute initial Predicted Values
ReDim yhat(1 To N, 1 To N)
x1b = Application.WorksheetFunction.MMult(x, b)
For i = 1 To N
    yhat(i, 1) = Exp(x1b(i, 1))
Next i

'Defining the variables used in the Newton procedure
Dim diff As Double, maxiter As Integer, crit As Double, iter As Integer
Dim g() As Double, x11() As Double
Dim g1 As Variant, g2 As Variant, hinv As Variant, hinvg As Variant


'Compute constant element of gradient
g1 = Application.WorksheetFunction.MMult( _
    Application.WorksheetFunction.Transpose(x), y)

'iterations

ReDim x11(1 To N, 1 To K)
ReDim g(1 To K, 1 To 1)
ReDim b1(1 To K, 1 To 1)
diff = 10
crit = 10 ^ -10
maxiter = 100

Do While diff > crit
    'Compute gradient
    g2 = Application.WorksheetFunction.MMult( _
        Application.WorksheetFunction.Transpose(x), yhat)
    For j = 1 To K
        g(j, 1) = g1(j, 1) - g2(j, 1)
    Next j

    'Compute Hessian
    For i = 1 To N
        For j = 1 To K
            x11(i, j) = x(i, j) * yhat(i, 1) ^ 0.5
```

```
        Next j
    Next i

    'update coefficient
    hinv = Application.WorksheetFunction.MInverse( _
           Application.WorksheetFunction.MMult _
           (Application.WorksheetFunction.Transpose(x11), x11))
    hinvg = Application.WorksheetFunction.MMult(hinv, g)
    For j = 1 To K
        b1(j, 1) = b(j, 1) + hinvg(j, 1)
    Next j

    'check convergence
    diff = Application.WorksheetFunction.SumXMY2(b, b1)

    If diff > crit Then
        x1b = Application.WorksheetFunction.MMult(x, b1)
        For i = 1 To N
            yhat(i, 1) = Exp(x1b(i, 1))
        Next i
        For j = 1 To K
            b(j, 1) = b1(j, 1)
        Next j

    ElseIf diff <= crit Then
        x1b = Application.WorksheetFunction.MMult(x, b)
    End If

    iter = iter + 1

    If iter > maxiter Then
        diff = 0
        b1(1, 1) = "no convergence"
    End If

Loop

'Compile output
Dim repoisson(), yq As Double, lnL As Double, lnlr As Double, lnfact As
Double
ReDim repoisson(1 To 5, 1 To K)
For j = 1 To K
    repoisson(1, j) = b(j, 1)
    repoisson(2, j) = hinv(j, j) ^ 0.5
    repoisson(3, j) = repoisson(1, j) / repoisson(2, j)
    repoisson(4, j) = (1 - Application.WorksheetFunction.NormSDist( _
                      Abs(repoisson(3, j))))*2
```

```
    repoisson(5, j) = "#NA"
Next j

yq = Application.WorksheetFunction.Average(y)
For i = 1 To N
    If y(i, 1) <= 170 Then
        lnfact = Log(Application.WorksheetFunction.Fact(y(i, 1)))
    Else 'use Stirling's approximation for factorial
        lnfact = (y(i, 1) + 0.5) * Log(y(i, 1)) - y(i, 1) _
               + 0.5 * Log(2 * Application.Pi())
    End If
    lnL = lnL - yhat(i, 1) + y(i, 1) * x1b(i, 1) - lnfact
    lnlr = lnlr - yq + Log(yq) * y(i, 1) - lnfact
Next i
repoisson(5, 1) = 1 - lnL / lnlr
repoisson(5, 2) = lnL


POIREG = repoisson

End Function
```

5

Prediction of Loss Given Default

The preceding chapters covered methods for estimating the probability of default. Although such estimates are crucial for assessing the risk incurred by lenders, they do not give a complete picture. Lenders also need to assess the magnitude of losses that arise in the event of default.

In the literature, loss magnitude is usually expressed as a percentage loss rate: the loss given default (LGD). If a lender has a claim of 100 but receives only 40, the LGD would be $(100 - 40)/100 = 60\%$. Alternatively, we can capture the same information through recovery rates. The recovery rate is obtained by $1 - \text{LGD}$. To complete the terminology, note that a lender's claim is usually called exposure at default (EAD).

Bankruptcy procedures can take years to resolve, a fact that creates measurement problems. In the above example, it would make a difference whether the lender receives 40 one month after default, two years after default or in several installments over the next two years. Two common ways of addressing this issue are the following:

- Determine the discounted value of cash flows that a lender receives until the end of the bankruptcy procedure and relate it to the claim.
- Take secondary market prices of debt instruments. A frequent choice is to take prices 30 days after the default event and relate them to the face value of the instrument.

The practical advantage of the second approach is that loss given default can be measured shortly after default and that we do not need to determine an appropriate discount rate. On the other hand, market prices will not be available for each instrument.

Since the focus of this book is on modeling techniques, we do not discuss the choice of measurement in detail. First we present variables that are useful for LGD prediction, and then we apply regression techniques to a hypothetical but representative data set.

CANDIDATE VARIABLES FOR PREDICTION

It is useful to classify the variables used for predicting LGD into four categories:

- instrument-related;
- firm-specific;
- macroeconomic;
- industry-specific.

In the next four sections, we present typical variables for each category that one could consider for LGD prediction.

Table 5.1 Average loss given default (LGD), 1987–2009

Debt type	Average LGD
Bank loans	0.262
Senior secured bonds	0.428
Senior unsecured bonds	0.570
Senior subordinated bonds	0.717
Subordinated bonds	0.806

Note: own calculations based on Standard & Poor's (2010), Table 29

Instrument-related variables

Debt instruments can differ in several aspects that are relevant for LGD estimation. In the event of default, not all borrowers are equal. Some are more senior than others, i.e., have priority of repayment in a liquidation or restructuring. Further, some debt instruments are secured, giving the debt holders the right to claim specific assets connected with the instrument. An example is a mortgage loan. In case of default, the bank has the right to seize the building and use the sale proceeds to (partially) recover the debt. There may also be differences between the LGD of bank loans and public bonds, e.g., because the quality of the security is typically higher for bank loans than for bonds. Average historical LGDs for different debt types are shown in Table 5.1. As is evident from the table, differences in seniority and security can have a large impact.

In a regression model, we can capture such average differences in two alternative ways:

- Create *one* variable that contains the historical average LGD of the respective debt type. For a senior secured bond, this variable would record the average LGD of senior secured bonds; for a subordinated bond, the same variable would record the average LGD of subordinated bonds, and so forth.
- Introduce dummy variables for debt types. The senior secured bond dummy, for example, would take the value 1 for senior secured bonds, and 0 otherwise.

In the second approach, we estimate average LGD differences across debt types with our data. Any differences not explained by other variables will be reflected in the regression coefficients of the dummy variables. With the first approach, we can bring in information from other sources. This can help to increase the precision of the estimates, in particular if the size of the data set at hand is small. In the application presented later, we will use the first approach. When using the dummy variable approach to model differences among K debt types, we would only include dummy variables for $K - 1$ debt types. The coefficients of the dummy variables then reflect how LGDs differ from the LGD of the type that is not represented in the regression. Readers interested in applying the dummy variable approach can consult the final section of Chapter 8, where the dummy variable approach is detailed for another regression model, but the issues involved in using dummy variables are the same.

Modeling average differences across debt types is typically not sufficient to capture the effects of seniority and security. Consider a firm whose outstanding debt consists only of subordinated bonds. In this case, the subordinated bonds are the most senior bonds. We can capture such effects by ordering the claims according to their seniority and security as in

Table 5.1. We can summarize the priority standing of an instrument in different ways. For instance, we could define it through

$$\frac{\text{Face value of debt with higher priority} - \text{Face value of debt with lower priority}}{\text{Total face value of debt}}$$

The higher this measure, the higher is the expected LGD.

Firm-specific variables

The overall losses incurred by creditors will equal the value of liabilities minus the value of the firm's assets after bankruptcy costs. We can therefore hope to increase predictive accuracy if we find variables that contain information about the post-default asset value or bankruptcy costs. Below, we list variables that have been considered in the literature:

- *Tangibility.* For several reasons, tangible assets (usually defined as property, plant and equipment) could on average lead to lower LGD. For instance, they can be used to generate revenue during restructuring, or they may tend to lose less in value than intangible assets. A standard definition would be

$$\frac{\text{Property, Plant, Equipment}}{\text{Total assets}}.$$

- *Market-to-book ratio.* For firms with traded equity, the market-to-book ratio, which is often referred to as Tobin's Q, is usually computed as

$$\frac{\text{Market value of equity} + \text{book value of liabilities}}{\text{Total assets}}$$

  where total assets is book value of assets. The higher the ratio, the higher is the market's valuation of the firm's assets. If the valuation continues to be relatively high after default, the LGD will be relatively low. On the other hand, firms with a high market-to-book ratio are typically growth firms, which are valued highly because they promise high profits in the future. As such promises can dissipate quickly in the case of default, a high market-to-book ratio could also indicate high LGDs.
- *Leverage.* This can, for example, be measured through

$$\frac{\text{Total debt}}{\text{Total assets}}$$

  and is usually expected to be positively correlated with the LGD. One possible reason for such a relationship is that debt structure is typically more complex for highly-levered firms. This can complicate bankruptcy procedures, leading to larger bankruptcy costs and a higher LGD.

Macroeconomic variables

Macroeconomic conditions can be useful for predicting LGD because they can help to estimate the value of the assets in case of a default. In many cases, we would use figures for the country in which the borrower is domiciled or generating the largest part of its income. In other cases, regional or global aggregates can be more suitable.

Variables that could be considered include the following:

- *Capacity utilization.* If capacity utilization is low, demand for a firm's assets will tend to be low because competitors do not need additional production capacities. This depresses prices and leads to a high LGD.
- *GDP growth.* The explanation is similar to capacity utilization. A negative economic environment is expected to go along with high LGD. One could use the most recent growth figures or professional forecasts such as the ones studied in Chapter 4.
- *Corporate bond spreads.* Generally, the value of an asset is obtained as the present value of cash flows that can be generated with the assets. *Ceteris paribus*, the asset value will therefore fall with increasing discount rates. To capture variation in discount rates we can use a yield spread, for instance defined through –

    yield of US corporate bonds – yield of US treasuries

  The higher the spread, the higher is the expected LGD.

- *Default rates.* High default rates indicate a negative economic environment. The mechanisms leading to high LGDs would therefore be similar to the ones described above. Default rates may measure the relevant valuation factors in a more specific way. High default rates imply a high supply of defaulted debt, which tends to depress prices of such debt. In a practical application, one can use either the trailing default rate (e.g., computed over the previous 12 months) or default rate forecasts from models such as those presented in Chapter 4.

Industry variables

We can augment or replace the variables suggested above by variables defined on the level of the industry to which the firm under analysis belongs. Here, we give some examples why this could be useful:

- *Capacity utilization.* At a given point in time, the economic environment can differ substantially between industries. Using industry capacity utilization instead of (or in addition to) economy-wide capacity utilization can help to better capture the economic environment that is relevant for the valuation of a bankrupt firm's assets.
- *Market-to-book ratio.* If a firm does not have traded equity, we cannot compute the firm-specific market-to-book ratio. In such cases, we can use the average market-to-book ratio of traded firms in an industry. Including the industry ratio can be useful even if the firm-specific market-to-book ratio is observable. One reason is that market valuations can be noisy. An industry average is less affected by firm-specific fluctuations, and can therefore help to capture the information contained in market valuations.

CREATING A DATA SET

In this section, we show how to prepare a data set in which LGD values are associated with explanatory variables. The data are hypothetical but representative. In the example, we consider data on an annual frequency. They cover the years 2007–2009. The firm-specific data contain information on the default year, the borrower's id and its industry affiliation, the debt type, the LGD, and the leverage in the year prior to default. The data are assumed to contain only information on the LGD of defaulted bonds. Specifically, it contains four different types: senior secured; senior unsecured; senior subordinated; and subordinated.

We show how to create the following variables:

- A variable containing the historical average LGD of the respective debt type, computed with data ending in the year before the default. Defining the variable in this way (rather than taking the average across all years) has the advantage that we do not have to redefine the variable when we proceed to an out-of-sample analysis.
- A variable containing the industry default rate in the year before the default.

In a practical application, one would typically use more variables. For the sake of brevity, we only include three (the two mentioned above plus the leverage). For most variables, the data preparation techniques introduced here will be sufficient.

Table 5.2 shows the data. The historical LGD averages are contained in the range J3:M6. To align LGD observations with the LGD average, we use the function VLOOKUP. For the

Table 5.2 Building the data set

	J	K	L	M
1	**Mean LGD for data until year**			
2		2006	2007	2008
3	Sr. Sec.	0.457	0.482	0.365
4	Sr. Unsec.	0.626	0.636	0.538
5	Sr. Sub.	0.672	0.681	0.703
6	Sub.	0.685	0.711	0.712
7				
8	**Industry default rates (in %)**			
9		2006	2007	2008
10	Cap Ind	1.285	0.715	3.071
11	Cons G	0.967	0.651	3.783
12	Energy	0	0	1.835
13	Media	1.415	0.92	4.147
14	Retail	1.183	1.802	2.247
15	Tech	0.743	0.486	1.164
16	Transp	2.353	0	2.963

	A	B	C	D	E	F	G	H
1	**Year**	**ID**	**Industry**	**Type**	**LGD**	**LEV**	**LGD_A**	**I_DEF**
2	2007	1	Media	Sr. Unsec.	0.748	0.414	0.626	1.415
3	2007	1	Media	Sub.	0.990	0.414	0.685	1.415
4	2007	2	Retail	Sr. Sec.	0.066	0.230	0.457	1.183
5	2007	3	Transp	Sr. Unsec.	0.351	0.541	0.626	2.353
6	2007	3	Tr					353
7	2007	4	Te					43
8	2007	6	Tr					53
9	2007	7	R					83
10	2007	8	Tr					353
11	2007	9	Tech	Sr. Unsec.	0.046	0.314	0.626	0.743
12	2007	10	Energy	Sr. Sec.	0. 026	0.191	0.457	0
13	2007	11	Transp	Sr. Unsec.	0.760	0.491	0.626	2.353
14	2007	12	Media	Sr. Unsec.	0.758	0.911	0.626	1.415
15	2007	13	Retail	Sr. Unsec.	0.600	0.336	0.626	1.183
16	2007	14	Cons G	Sr. Sec.	0.374	0.415	0.457	0.967
17	2007	15	Retail	Sr. Unsec.	0.169	0.612	0.626	1.183
18	2007	16	Transp	Sr. Unsec.	0.284	0.694	0.626	2.353
19	2007	17	Media	Sr. Unsec.	0.747	0.937	0.626	1.415
20	2007	21	Transp	Sr. Sub.	0.686	0.801	0.672	2.353
21	2007	22	Energy	Sr. Sec.	0.050	0.366	0.457	0
22	2007	23	Retail	Sr. Sub.	0.664	0.177	0.672	1.183
...	...	...	...	...	...	...	...	...
318	2009	446	Cons G	Sr. Sec.	0.748	0.607	0.365	3.783

G2: =VLOOKUP(D2,J$3:M$6,A2-2005,0)
(can be copied into G2:G318)

H2: =VLOOKUP(C2,J$10:M$16,A2-2005,0)
(can be copied into H2:H318)

first observation (in G2), we type

=VLOOKUP(D2,J$3:M$6,A2-2005,0)

The lookup value is the debt type (D2). This value is looked up in the data range J3:M6. For a default that occurred in 2007, we need to extract the value from the second column of the data range. Using A2-2005 as column index number does the job for 2007 and for later years, too. Finally, we set the logical value to 0 to require an exact match between the debt type of the observation and the debt type in the range containing the historical averages. We use $ signs in the appropriate places such that the formula can be filled down.

Industry default rates can be aligned with the LGD data in much the same way. Type

=VLOOKUP(C2,J$10:M$16,A2-2005,0)

into cell H2 and fill it down to create the variable I_DEF, which contains the prior year's default rate in the industry to which the LGD observation belongs.

REGRESSION ANALYSIS OF LGD

We start by applying ordinary least squares (OLS) regression to the data created in the previous section. We estimate the following equation:

$$LGD_{ijt} = b_1 + b_2 LEV_{i,t-1} + b_3 LGD\_A_{j,t-1} + b_4 I\_DEF_{i,t-1} + u_{ij.t} \tag{5.1}$$

where LGD_{ijt} is the LGD on instrument j of firm i, observed in year t. $LGD\_A_{j,t-1}$ is the average LGD of instruments with the same type as j, computed with data ending in $t-1$. $I\_DEF_{i,t-1}$ is the default rate that was observed in year $t-1$ for the industry to which borrower i belongs. $LEV_{i,t-1}$ is firm is leverage in $t-1$.

Regression analysis has already been used in Chapter 4; additional information for interpreting OLS results is given in Appendix A4. We therefore refrain from general remarks on the use of OLS and directly address specific issues that arise when OLS is applied to a LGD equation such as (5.1).

As we study instrument-level data, one firm can contribute several observations to a data set. In our data, the firm with id 1, for instance, enters with LGD values for both senior unsecured and subordinated bonds. This is likely to lead to correlations in the error terms u. If the assets of a defaulted firm have lost significantly in value or if its bankruptcy costs are high, the instruments issued by the firm will have a relatively high LGD. If the reasons behind such a high loss rate are not adequately captured through our explanatory variables, the error terms will be correlated. Coming back to the firm with id 1, we would tend to underestimate the LGD of its senior unsecured bonds, but we would also tend to underestimate the LGD of its subordinated bonds.

In the presence of such correlations, OLS coefficient estimates are still reliable but the standard errors are no longer so. Depending on the nature of the correlation, OLS standard errors can be too low or too high, leading to inflated or deflated t-statistics. Fortunately, there is a fairly simple and robust way of estimating standard errors in such a situation. We do not

Table 5.3 Regression analysis of LGD (with cluster-robust standard errors; columns A, C and D are hidden)

	B	E	F	G	H	I	J	K	L	M
1	**ID**	**LGD**	**LEV**	**LGD_A**	**I_DEF**		I_DEF	LGD_A	LEV	const
2	1	0.748	0.414	0.626	1.415	Coeff	0.029	0.506	0.183	0.196
3	1	0.990	0.414	0.685	1.415	SE(coeff)	0.014	0.155	0.068	0.104
4	2	0.066	0.230	0.457	1.183	R²/RMSE	0.073	0.279	#NV	#NV
5	3	0.351	0.541	0.626	2.353					
6	3	0.258	0.541	0.457	2.353	t-stat	2.044	3.261	2.670	1.892
7	4	0.020	0.812	0.672	0.743		=J2/J3			
8	6	0.931	0.547	0.672	2.353					
9	7	0.341	0.710	0.672	1.183					
10	8	0.351	0.855	0.672	2.353					
11	9	0.046	0.314	0.626	0.743					
12	10	0.026	0.191	0.457	0					
...	...	...	...	...	...					
318	446	0.748	0.607	0.365	3.783					

J2: {=CLINEST(E2:E318,F2:H318,B2:B318)}
(applies to J2:M4)

need to specify the sign or magnitude of correlation that we expect; we only need to specify which observations are likely to have correlated errors, and which are not.

A set of observations with correlated errors is called a *cluster*. In the Appendix at the end of this chapter, we describe a user-defined function CLINEST(*y's*, *x's*, *cluster*). It implements an estimator of the coefficients' standard errors that is robust to correlation within clusters. Observations that share the same value in the input range *cluster* are assigned to one cluster. The function's output is organized in the same way as that of Excel's LINEST. The first row returns the OLS coefficient estimates in the same order as in LINEST. The second row returns the cluster-robust standard errors. The third row again returns the same values as LINEST.[1] In contrast to LINEST, CLINEST always includes a constant and always returns standard errors and other statistical information (if more than one row is selected before entering the function). Being an array function, CLINEST has to be entered with [ctrl]–[shift]–[enter]. Finally, note that CLINEST assumes that the data are arranged in columns and sorted according to the variable that defines the cluster. Of course, the function could be generalized so that it works with any data format.

In Table 5.3, the function CLINEST is used to estimate the regression equation (5.1). We use the firms' id values to define clusters.[2]

In the example data, estimated coefficients conform to expectations. The LGD increases with increasing leverage. The historical LGD average helps explain the observed LGDs; higher default rates in the year prior to default lead to higher LGDs. The slope coefficients are all significant on a level better than 5% because their *t*-statistics are all larger than 1.96. If we did not find other useful predictive variables we could therefore base our predictions on the estimated model.

A possible drawback of using OLS for LGD prediction is that OLS predictions can take values smaller than 0 or larger than 1. This does not mean that OLS is inappropriate. First, depending on how LGD is defined, LGD values need not be restricted to the interval [0, 1].

[1] CLINEST() does not report the *F*-statistic from OLS because it is also misleading in the presence of correlated errors.

[2] Since errors can also be correlated within an industry, it could also be appropriate to define a cluster through the set of observations that belong to one industry in a given year.

If LGD is based on a comparison of the post-default bond price with the bond's face value, LGD can be smaller than 0 because bonds can trade at prices above the face value. Second, violations of theoretical bounds may not matter greatly if they are small individually, or tend to cancel in a portfolio analysis.

Nevertheless, it is worthwhile to examine a method that explicitly uses information about the distribution of LGD. In the following, we sketch a procedure that has repeatedly been used in the literature. The idea is to transform the dependent variable LGD so that we can expect it to be normally distributed; then we run a regression on the transformed variable and derive predictions. In a final step, these predictions are re-transformed such that they again conform to the actual LGD distribution.

We start by identifying a probability distribution that is able to describe the observed empirical distribution of LGDs. For this purpose, the beta distribution is often used. In its standard form, it is a two-parameter distribution bounded between 0 and 1. The distribution is fully specified once we have determined its mean and standard deviation. The mean and variance of a beta-distributed variable Y are given by

$$E[Y] = \frac{a}{a+b} \tag{5.2}$$

$$\text{var}[Y] = \frac{ab}{(a+b)^2(a+b+1)} \tag{5.3}$$

where a and b are the two parameters of the distribution. Having determined estimates for the mean and the variance of observed LGDs, we can solve (5.2) and (5.3) to calibrate the parameters a and b:

$$a = \frac{E[Y]}{\text{var}(Y)}(E[Y](1 - E[Y]) - \text{var}[Y]) \tag{5.4}$$

$$b = \frac{1 - E[Y]}{\text{var}(Y)}(E[Y](1 - E[Y]) - \text{var}[Y]) \tag{5.5}$$

If the calibrated beta distribution provides a good description of the empirical LGD distribution, transforming the LGDs with the cumulative beta distribution function should result in a variable that is uniformly distributed on the unit interval. To get an intuition as to why this is so, consider the outcome of throwing a six-sided die. We observe values from 1 to 6. Transforming these values with the cumulative probability distribution function means that we transform 1 to 1/6 (the probability of observing 1 or less), 2 to 2/6 (the probability of observing 2 or less) and so forth. The transformed values will be spread out evenly across the unit interval.

Coming back to our LGD analysis, we would apply the cumulative beta distribution function to the observed LGD. In Excel, we can use the command

=BETADIST(LGD, a, b)

In a next step, we can create a variable that is (approximately) normally distributed. To do so, apply the inverse of the cumulative normal distribution function, which is available through NORMSINV(), to the beta-transformed LGD:

=NORMSINV(BETADIST(LGD, a, b))

Table 5.4 Regression analysis of transformed LGD (with cluster-robust standard errors, columns A, C and D are hidden)

	B	E	F	G	H	I	J	K	L	M	N
1	ID	LGD	LEV	LGD_A	I_DEF	T_LGD		I_DEF	LGD_A	LEV	const
2	1	0.748	0.414	0.626	1.415	0.080	Coeff	0.088	2.017	0.512	-1.685
3	1	0.990	0.414	0.685	1.415	1.495	SE(coeff)	0.047	0.526	0.226	0.346
4	2	0.066	0.230	0.457	1.183	-1.922	R²/RMSE	0.080	0.908	#N/A	#N/A
5	3	0.351	0.541	0.626	2.353	-0.861					
6	3	0.258	0.541	0.457	2.353	-1.107	t-stat	1.889	3.835	2.266	-4.871
7								=K2/K3			
8											
9								**Empirical LGD distribution**			
10								Mean	0.652	=AVERAGE(E2:E318)	
11								St. dev.	0.288	=STDEV(E2:E318)	
12											
13	11	0.760	0.491	0.626	2.353	0.114		**Calibrated beta distribution**			
14	12	0.758	0.911	0.626	1.415	0.109		a	1.130		
15	13	0.600	0.336	0.626	1.183	-0.286		b	0.604		
16	14	0.374	0.415	0.457	0.967	-0.804					
17	15	0.169	0.612	0.626	1.183	-1.398					
...	...	...	...	...	...						
318	446	0.748	0.607	0.365	3.783	0.082					

I2 =NORMSINV(BETADIST(E2,L$14,L$15))
(can be copied into I2:I318)

K2 {=CLINEST(I2:I318,F2:H318,B2:B318)}
(applies to K2:N4)

L14 =L10/L11^2*(L10*(1-L10)-L11^2)
L15 =(1-L10)/L11^2*(L10*(1-L10)-L11^2)

The logic is the same. By applying the distribution function to a set of observations, we create a variable that is uniformly distributed on the unit interval; by applying the inverse of a distribution function to a variable that is uniformly distributed on the unit interval, we create a variable that follows the chosen distribution function.

In Table 5.4, we show how to perform the transformation. In cells L10 and L11, we estimate the mean and standard deviation of the observed LGD values, respectively. Using formulae (5.4) and (5.5), we then determine the parameters of the beta distribution (in cells L14 and L15). In column I, we transform the LGD values, first by applying the beta distribution, then by applying the inverse normal distribution.

In the linear regression that is performed in the range K2:N4, the transformed LGD values serve as dependent variable. We use the same explanatory variables as before. The signs of the slope coefficients have not changed; their *t*-statistics show only moderate changes. Importantly, we cannot directly compare the size of the coefficients to those of the regression from Table 5.3. Through the transformation, the dependent variable is more dispersed than before, which explains the larger size of the coefficients. To compare regression results, we should examine predictions, and we do so in the next section.

BACKTESTING PREDICTIONS

To derive predictions from a linear regression, we can use the function TREND:

$$=\text{TREND}(known\_y's, known\_x's, new\_x's, const)$$

If we set the logical value *const* to 1 or if we do not specify it, the regression underlying TREND() will include a constant.

To derive appropriate predictions for the model with beta-transformed LGDs, we need to transform them back to LGD space. We would therefore use the function in the following way:

=BETAINV(NORMSDIST(TREND(*transformed LGD*, *known_x's*, *new_x's*, *const*)), *a*, *b*)

Note that we choose the inverse of the functions that we applied in the transformation of LGD. In the previous section, we transformed the LGD with the cumulative beta distribution. To undo it, we use the inverse of the cumulative beta distribution, available through BETAINV(). Similarly, we apply the cumulative normal distribution NORMSDIST() because we have used the inverse cumulative normal before.

To assess the quality of a prediction model, it is advisable to check how predictions performed out-of-sample. In order to do so, we generate predictions that only use information that was actually available at the time the prediction was made. In our example, the explanatory variables that we use would have been available at the time of prediction. In addition, we have to make sure that the coefficient estimates used for prediction are based on past data only. To make a prediction for 2008, we would run the regression using data that are available at the end of the year 2007, and derive a prediction. To make a prediction for 2009, we can also include data from 2008.

In Chapter 4, we also performed a backtest of regression-based predictions. There, we had one observation per year and using the TREND for generating out-of-sample predictions was straightforward. In the present example, things are a bit more complicated. Since the data contain more than one observation per year, the estimation sample often does not change when we move from one row of the data set to the next.

To solve the problem, we suggest the user-defined function OOSTREND(). It generates out-of-sample regression predictions, and has the following syntax:

=OOSTREND(*known_y's*, *known_x's*, *new_x's*, *year*, *startyear*)

The first three arguments are the same as in Excel's TREND() function. *Year* is a range that contains the observation dates. *startyear* is the first date for which an out-of-sample prediction is made, i.e., we run a regression with data from before *startyear*, and then use the estimated coefficients from this regression together with the new predictors (*new_x's*), to generate a prediction. Here is the code:

```
Function oostrend(y, x, xnew, year, startyear)
'Function assumes data organized in columns
Dim N As Long, K As Integer, Nreg As Long
N = y.Rows.Count
K = x.Columns.Count
Nreg = Application.CountIf(year, "<" & startyear)
Dim yreg(), xreg()
ReDim xreg(1 To Nreg, 1 To K)
ReDim yreg(1 To Nreg, 1 To 1)

Dim i As Long, j As Integer, ii As Long
For i = 1 To N
```

```
    If year(i) < startyear Then
        ii = ii + 1
        yreg(ii, 1) = y(i)
        For j = 1 To K
            xreg(ii, j) = x(i, j)
        Next j
    End If
Next i

oostrend = Application.Trend(yreg, xreg, xnew)

End Function
```

At the heart of the function is a for loop. We go through all observations but consider only those for which `year<startyear`. The values of these observations are written into the new regression variables `yreg` and `xreg`. At the end, we use the TREND() function to generate a prediction based on a regression of `yreg` on `xreg`. Of course, one could modify the function such that it is also possible to specify the beginning of the estimation sample. In the present version, the entire history is used for estimation, which is sensible if the data set is as small as the one considered here. In other situations, moving estimation samples (e.g., the previous 10 years) could be more appropriate. One possible drawback of using OOSTREND() is that the regression equation is estimated for each prediction that is made, which increases computing time. This should not be of major concern with LGD data, because the size of such data sets is typically rather low.

Table 5.5 uses OOSTREND() to generate out-of-sample predictions for the years 2008 and 2009. As described above, we re-transform the predictions if they are based on a regression

Table 5.5 Out-of-sample forecasts for standard regression and regression with transformed LGD

	A	E	F	G	H	I	J	K	L	M	N
1	**Year**	**LGD**	**LEV**	**LGD_A**	**I_DEF**	**T_LGD**					
...		...	...	...	...	...					
28	2007	0.458	0.493	0.626	0.743	-0.608					
29	2007	0.827	0.493	0.685	0.743	0.323	**Forecasts**			**Root Mean Squared Error**	
30	2007	0.481	0.707	0.672	1.415	-0.556	Simple	Transf.		Simple	Transf.
31	2008	0.477	0.832	0.681	1.802	-0.564	0.569	0.580		0.340	0.368
32	2008	0.771	0.238	0.636	0.920	0.148	0.408	0.360			
33	2008	0.082	0.296	0.482	0.000	-1.813	0.088	0.062			
34	J31: =oosTREND(E$2:E$318,F$2:H$318,F31:H31,A$2:A$318,A31)										
35	*(can be copied into J31:J318)*										
36											
37	K31: =BETAINV(NORMSDIST(oosTREND(I$2:I$318,F$2:H$318,F31:H31,A$2:A$318,A31)),L$14,L$15)										
38	*(can be copied into K31:K318, L14 and L15 contain the calibrated parameters of the beta distribution)*										
39											
40	M31: =(SUMXMY2($E31:$E318,J31:J318)/COUNT($E31:$E318))^0.5										
41	*(can be copied into M31:N31)*										
42	2008	0.975	0.708	0.711	1.802	1.195	0.611	0.644			
43	2008	0.267	0.711	0.636	0.486	-1.082	0.339	0.241			
...		...	...	...	...	...					
318	2008	0.748	0.607	0.365	3.783	0.082	0.307	0.219			

analysis of transformed LGDs. To assess the predictive accuracy, we determine a root mean squared error (RMSE). For M LGD predictions, the RMSE is defined as

$$\text{RMSE} = \sqrt{\frac{1}{M}\sum_{i=1}^{M}(LGD_i - LGD\_forecast_i)^2}$$

In the spreadsheet, we can determine the sum of squared prediction errors with the function SUMXMY2(y, x). The number of predictions M can be determined with the function COUNT().

For the example data, the beta transformation leads to a larger RMSE than the standard regression. When deciding which model to use in the future, we would probably opt for the simple regression approach without transformations.

NOTES AND LITERATURE

In the example data, observed LGD is strictly larger than 0 and strictly smaller than 1. When this does not hold in the data under analysis, the transformation with the standard beta distribution does not work. The beta distribution is flexible, though. One can introduce additional parameters for the minimum and maximum. See Gupton and Stein (2002) for an application in which the minimum LGD is set to −0.1. To deal with cases in which the boundaries are hit, adjust observed values by a very small amount.

Data on LGD (or recovery rates) are reported by rating agencies, e.g., in Standard and Poor's, 2010, 2009, *Annual Global Corporate Default Study and Rating Transitions*, or Moody's Investors Service, 2010, *Corporate Default and Recovery Rates*, 1920–2009.

Studies that apply regression analysis to LGD (or recovery rates) include Gupton, G. and Stein, R., 2002, *LossCalc: Model for Predicting Loss Given Default (LGD)*, Moody's KMV; Varna, P., 2004, *Determinants of Recovery Rates on Defaulted Bonds and Loans for North American Corporate Issuers: 1983–2003*, Moody's Investors Service; Acharya, V., Srinivasan, A. and Bharath, S., 2007, Does industry-wide distress affect defaulted firms? – Evidence from creditor recoveries. *Journal of Financial Economics* 85, 787–821.

Useful references for the cluster-robust estimator are Froot, K., 1989, Consistent covariance matrix estimation with cross-sectional dependence and heteroskedasticity in financial data. *Journal of Financial and Quantitative Analysis* 24, 333–355, and Rogers, W., 1993, Regression standard errors in clustered samples. *Stata Technical Bulletin* 13, 19–23.

APPENDIX

We first motivate the structure of the cluster-robust estimator. Assume that the correct regression relationship is as follows:

$$y_{ij} = \beta_1 + \beta_2 x_{ij2} + \beta_3 x_{ij3} + \ldots \beta_K x_{ijK} + \varepsilon_{ij}$$

where observations with the same i belong to the same cluster. Let the overall number of observations be denoted by N. It is more convenient to formulate the regression equation with vectors and matrices:

$$\mathbf{y} = \mathbf{X}\boldsymbol{\beta} + \boldsymbol{\varepsilon}$$

where $\mathbf{y}$ collects the values of the dependent variable in a $N \times 1$ column vector; $\mathbf{X}$ collects the values of the explanatory variables in a $N \times K$ matrix. The coefficient vector $\boldsymbol{\beta}$ is $K \times 1$, while ε is $N \times 1$.

Denote the vector containing the OLS coefficient estimates by $\mathbf{b} = (\mathbf{X}'\mathbf{X})^{-1}\mathbf{X}'\mathbf{y}$. One can show that the estimates are unbiased, i.e., $\mathrm{E}[\mathbf{b}] = \boldsymbol{\beta}$. For the variance of the coefficient estimates, it then follows that

$$\begin{aligned}
\mathrm{Var}(\mathbf{b}) &= \mathrm{E}[(\mathbf{b}-\boldsymbol{\beta})(\mathbf{b}-\boldsymbol{\beta})'] \\
&= \mathrm{E}[((\mathbf{X}'\mathbf{X})^{-1}\mathbf{X}'\mathbf{y}-\boldsymbol{\beta})((\mathbf{X}'\mathbf{X})^{-1}\mathbf{X}'\mathbf{y}-\boldsymbol{\beta})'] \\
&= \mathrm{E}[(\boldsymbol{\beta}+(\mathbf{X}'\mathbf{X})^{-1}\mathbf{X}'\varepsilon-\boldsymbol{\beta})(\boldsymbol{\beta}+(\mathbf{X}'\mathbf{X})^{-1}\mathbf{X}'\varepsilon-\boldsymbol{\beta})'] \\
&= \mathrm{E}[(\mathbf{X}'\mathbf{X})^{-1}\mathbf{X}'\varepsilon\varepsilon'\mathbf{X}(\mathbf{X}'\mathbf{X})^{-1}] \\
&= (\mathbf{X}'\mathbf{X})^{-1}\mathbf{X}'\mathrm{E}[\varepsilon\varepsilon']\mathbf{X}(\mathbf{X}'\mathbf{X})^{-1}
\end{aligned}$$

In standard OLS, one would assume that the covariance of error terms, which is $\mathrm{E}[\varepsilon\varepsilon']$, takes a simple form: all off-diagonal elements are zero (i.e., errors are independent) and elements on the diagonal take an identical value, σ^2. In situations such as the one examined in the paper, these assumptions are likely to be inappropriate. To consider possible solutions, take a look at the above equation: first note that we know the matrix $\mathbf{X}$. Therefore, can we estimate var($\mathbf{b}$) by estimating $\mathrm{E}[\varepsilon\varepsilon']$ and inputting it into the equation? Unfortunately, this is not feasible. The number of different elements in the covariance matrix $\mathrm{E}[\varepsilon\varepsilon']$ is $N(N+1)/2$, larger than the number of observations N, and so we cannot hope to estimate it in a meaningful way. However, we can hope to estimate

$$\mathbf{X}'\mathrm{E}[\varepsilon\varepsilon']\mathbf{X}$$

because it contains only $K(K+1)/2$ different elements, with K being the number of explanatory variables (including the constant). This is the intuition behind the cluster-robust estimator (and other robust estimators, too). Each cluster gives us an estimate of $\mathbf{X}'\mathrm{E}[\varepsilon\varepsilon']\mathbf{X}$, and by averaging across the clusters, we can hope to get a reliable estimator.

To implement this approach, we estimate the error terms through the regression residuals u_{ij}, obtained through $y_{ij} - (b_1 + b_2x_{ij2} + b_3x_{ij3} + \ldots b_Kx_{ijK})$. Collect the x-values pertaining to a cluster i in the matrix $\mathbf{X}_i$, and collect the residuals of cluster i in a vector $\boldsymbol{u}_i$. They look as follows:

$$\mathbf{X}_i = \begin{bmatrix} 1 & x_{i11} & \ldots & x_{i1K} \\ 1 & x_{i21} & \ldots & x_{i2K} \\ \ldots & \ldots & \ldots & \ldots \\ 1 & x_{iJ1} & \ldots & x_{iJK} \end{bmatrix}, u_i = \begin{bmatrix} u_{i1} \\ u_{i2} \\ \ldots \\ u_{ij} \end{bmatrix}$$

where J is the number of observations in cluster i, meaning that J can differ across the clusters. Determine

$$\Theta = \sum_{i=1}^{M} \mathbf{X}_i' u_i u_i' \mathbf{X}_i$$

where M is the number of clusters. The estimate of the variance-covariance matrix of coefficients is then given through

$$\frac{N-1}{N-K}\frac{M}{M-1}(X'X)^{-1}\Theta(X'X)^{-1}$$

where $(N-1)/(N-K) \times M/(M-1)$ is a small-sample adjustment commonly made.

Here is the VBA implementation:

```
Function clinest(yraw, xraw, cl)
'Function assumes data organized in columns, and sorted according to cl

Dim ij As Long, j As Integer
Dim N As Long, K As Integer
Dim x() As Double, b() As Double, y() As Double

'count rows and columns of data
N = xraw.Rows.Count
K = xraw.Columns.Count + 1

'Add constant to x matrix, define y
ReDim x(1 To N, 1 To K)
ReDim y(1 To N, 1 To 1)
ReDim b(1 To K, 1 To 1)
For ij = 1 To N
    y(ij, 1) = yraw(ij)
    x(ij, 1) = 1
    For j = 2 To K
        x(ij, j) = xraw(ij, j - 1)
    Next j
Next ij

'Determine regression coefficients
Dim regout
regout = Application.WorksheetFunction.LinEst(y, x, 0, 1)
For j = 1 To K
    b(j, 1) = regout(1, K + 1 - j)
Next j

'Determine regression residuals u
Dim fit
fit = Application.MMult(x, b)
Dim u() As Double
ReDim u(1 To N, 1 To 1)
For ij = 1 To N
    u(ij, 1) = y(ij, 1) - fit(ij, 1)
Next ij
```

```
'Covariance matrix estimation
Dim xuuxtmp(), xtmp(), utmp(), xuux(), M As Long, Jtmp As Long, _ jj As
  Integer
ReDim xuux(1 To K, 1 To K)
ij = 1
Do While ij <= N
    Jtmp = Application.CountIf(cl, "=" & cl(ij)) 'Size of cluster i
    ReDim xtmp(1 To Jtmp, 1 To K), utmp(1 To Jtmp, 1 To 1)
    M = M + 1
    For j = 1 To Jtmp
        utmp(j, 1) = u(ij, 1)
        For jj = 1 To K
            xtmp(j, jj) = x(ij, jj)
        Next jj
        ij = ij + 1
    Next j
    xuuxtmp = Application.MMult(Application.MMult _
             (Application.MMult(Application.Transpose(xtmp), utmp), _
              Application.Transpose(utmp)), xtmp)
    For j = 1 To K
        For jj = 1 To K
            xuux(j, jj) = xuux(j, jj) + xuuxtmp(j, jj)
        Next jj
    Next j
Loop

Dim xxinv(), var()
ReDim xxinv(1 To K, 1 To K), var(1 To K, 1 To K)

xxinv = Application.MInverse(Application.MMult(Application.Transpose(x), _
  x))
var = Application.MMult(Application.MMult(xxinv, xuux), xxinv)

Dim recl(), adjust As Double
adjust = (N - 1) / (N - K) * (M / (M - 1))
ReDim recl(1 To 3, 1 To K)
For j = 1 To K
    recl(1, K - j + 1) = b(j, 1)
    recl(2, K - j + 1) = (adjust * var(j, j)) ^ 0.5
    recl(3, j) = regout(3, j)
Next j
recl(3, 1) = Application. Correl(y, fit) ^ 2
clinest = recl
End Function
```

6
Modeling and Estimating Default Correlations with the Asset Value Approach

The previous chapters have focused on the measurement of individual default probabilities. For a financial institution that wants to assess the default risk of its loan portfolio, however, individual default probabilities are not enough. Consider the simplest case: a portfolio comprises only two borrowers, and the bank would like to know the probability that both borrowers default in the next period. This cannot be measured with the default probabilities alone. We could assume that the two borrowers are independent. The probability that both of them default would then equal the product of the two individual default probabilities. Default rates of firms, however, fluctuate with macroeconomic or industry-specific conditions, and so we should not rely on defaults being independent.

What we need to know in this case is the joint default probability. As we see in this chapter, this will lead us directly to the default correlation. We also examine a widely used way of modeling default correlations, the so-called *asset value approach*. We show how to estimate the relevant parameters based on historical default experience and how to assess the quality of the parameter estimates. The two estimation methods that we consider are the *method of moments* approach and the *maximum likelihood* approach.

DEFAULT CORRELATION, JOINT DEFAULT PROBABILITIES AND THE ASSET VALUE APPROACH

To formalize default correlation, we use the standard definition of the correlation coefficient of two random variables X_1 and X_2:

$$\rho_{X_1 X_2} = \frac{\text{cov}(X_1, X_2)}{\sigma(X_1)\sigma(X_2)} \tag{6.1}$$

where cov denotes the covariance, and σ the standard deviation. In our case, the random variable is a default indicator y_i that takes the value 1 if obligor i defaults and 0 otherwise. The default correlation we are searching is therefore

$$\rho_{ij} = \frac{\text{cov}(y_i, y_j)}{\sigma(y_i)\sigma(y_j)} \tag{6.2}$$

What can we say about the denominator of the correlation coefficient? Inserting our notation into the standard definition of variance leads us to

$$\sigma^2(y_i) = \text{Prob}(y_i = 1)(1 - \text{E}(y_i))^2 + \text{Prob}(y_i = 0)(0 - \text{E}(y_i))^2 \tag{6.3}$$

Denoting the default probability $\text{Prob}(y_i = 1)$ by p_i and exploiting the fact that $\text{Prob}(y_i = 1)$ is the same as $\text{E}(y_i)$ we get

$$\begin{aligned}\sigma^2(y_i) &= p_i(1-p_i)^2 + (1-p_i)(0-p_i)^2 = p_i(1-p_i)^2 + p_i^2(1-p_i) \\ &= p_i(1-p_i)\end{aligned} \tag{6.4}$$

which is the familiar result for the variance of a Bernoulli variable with success probability p_i.

To express the covariance in terms of default probabilities, we utilize the general result $\text{cov}(X_1, X_2) = \text{E}(X_1 X_2) - \text{E}(X_1)\text{E}(X_2)$. Applied to our case, this implies:

$$\text{cov}(y_i, y_j) = \text{E}(y_i y_j) - \text{E}(y_i)\text{E}(y_j) = p_{ij} - p_i p_j \tag{6.5}$$

where p_{ij} denotes the joint default probability $\text{Prob}(y_i = 1, y_j = 1)$. Thus, the default correlation is completely specified by the individual and the joint default probabilities:

$$\rho_{ij} = \frac{p_{ij} = p_i p_j}{\sqrt{p_i(1-p_i)p_j(1-p_j)}} \tag{6.6}$$

Even though the default correlation can be expressed with two intuitive measures – individual and joint default probabilities – it would be a daunting task to build a portfolio risk analysis on estimated pair-wise default correlations. In a portfolio with 1000 obligors, there are $(1000^2 - 1000)/2 = 499{,}500$ default correlations – far too much to specify.

In practical applications, one therefore imposes some simplifying structure that reduces the number of parameters to be estimated. Instead of directly imposing the structure on default correlations themselves, it is more convenient to first represent defaults as a function of continuous variables and then to impose structure on these variables. Let us name these variables A_i, $I = 1$ to N. The default indicator can then be represented as

$$\begin{aligned}&\textit{Default}_i \Leftrightarrow y_i = 1 \Leftrightarrow A_i \le d_i \\ &\textit{No default}_i \Leftrightarrow y_i = 0 \Leftrightarrow A_i > d_i\end{aligned} \tag{6.7}$$

where d_i is the critical value that marks the default of borrower i if the variable A_i falls below it. The joint default probability between two obligors then is

$$\text{Prob}(y_i = 1, y_j = 1) = \text{Prob}(A_i \le d_i, A_j \le d_j) \tag{6.8}$$

From an econometrician's perspective, the variables A are latent, i.e., unobservable variables that determine an observed, discrete outcome. In the credit risk literature, the latent variables are usually interpreted as the firms' asset values. This goes back to the option-theoretic approach of Merton (1974), in which a firm defaults if its asset value falls below a critical threshold associated with the value of liabilities (see Chapter 2).

In the following, the mechanics of the approach are described for the most simple but widely used case in which the asset values are assumed to be normally distributed with correlations that go back to a single common factor. Formally, borrower i's asset value A_i depends on the common factor Z and an idiosyncratic factor ε_i:

$$A_i = w_i Z + \sqrt{1 - w_i^2}\varepsilon_i, \quad \text{cov}(\varepsilon_i, \varepsilon_j) = 0, \quad i \neq j; \quad \text{cov}(Z, \varepsilon_i) = 0, \forall_i \tag{6.9}$$

where Z and ε_i are standard normal variables. By construction, A_i is also standard normal. The asset correlation is completely determined by the factor sensitivities w:

$$\begin{aligned} \rho_{ij}^{asset} &= \frac{\text{cov}(A_i, A_j)}{\sigma(A_i)\sigma(A_j)} = \frac{\text{cov}(w_i Z + \sqrt{1 - w_i^2}\varepsilon_i, w_j Z + \sqrt{1 - w_j^2}\varepsilon_j)}{1 \times 1} \\ &= \text{cov}(w_i Z, w_j Z) = w_i w_j \text{var}(Z) \\ &= w_i w_j \end{aligned} \tag{6.10}$$

Which default correlation follows? As seen above, we first need the default probability. This is given by

$$\text{Prob}(A_i \leq d_i) = p_i = \Phi(d_i) \tag{6.11}$$

where $\Phi(\cdot)$ denotes the cumulative standard normal distribution function. The joint default probability is

$$\text{Prob}(A_i \leq d_i, A_j \leq d_j) = p_{ij} = \Phi_2(d_i, d_j, \rho_{ij}^{asset}) \tag{6.12}$$

where $\Phi_2(\cdot,\cdot,\rho)$ denotes the bivariate standard normal distribution function with correlation ρ.

There are several ways of parameterizing the asset correlation model, i.e., choosing the ds and the ws. We can set the default triggers d such that they result in the default probabilities that we have estimated with a default prediction model like the logit model (Chapter 1), a structural model (Chapter 2) or from an analysis of default rates (Chapter 3).

To determine the factor sensitivities, we could go to the roots of the asset value approach and estimate correlations of borrowers' asset values. However, this brings in some potential for model error: even if default behavior can be described by some latent variable A, we do not know if this variable A behaves in the same manner as the asset values; also, we do not know if problems in estimating asset values impair the estimation of asset correlations.[1] Another approach that requires fewer assumptions is to choose the factor sensitivities such that they are in line with observed default behavior. This will be described in the following sections.

CALIBRATING THE ASSET VALUE APPROACH TO DEFAULT EXPERIENCE: THE METHOD OF MOMENTS

Assume that we have collected default information for a group of obligors over several years. Let D_t denote the number of obligors that defaulted in period t, and N_t the number of obligors that belonged to the group at the start of period t. We will assume that one period corresponds to one year. Data is observed over T years.

[1] Asset values are usually not traded, and so we have to estimate their market value with a structural model (see Chapter 2).

The essential information for our purpose is the default probability and the joint default probability. The average default probability can be estimated by averaging the annual default rates:

$$\hat{p} = \frac{1}{T}\sum_{t=1}^{T}\frac{D_t}{N_t} \tag{6.13}$$

In the absence of other information, we will assume that all obligors have the same default probability, i.e., we set $p_i = p_j = p$; our default threshold is then $d_i = d_j = d = \Phi^{-1}(p)$.

We can estimate the joint default probability in a similar way. In (6.13), we relate the number of observed defaults to the possible number of defaults; now we relate the number of observed joint defaults to the possible number of joint defaults. If there are D_t defaults, the number of pairs of defaulters that we can form follows from combinatorial analysis as[2]

$$\binom{D_t}{2} = \frac{D_t(D_t-1)}{2} \tag{6.14}$$

If all obligors defaulted, we would get the maximum number for pairs of defaulters, which is

$$\binom{N_t}{2} = \frac{N_t(N_t-1)}{2} \tag{6.15}$$

The joint default rate in year t is the number of default pairs (6.14) divided by the maximum number of default pairs (6.15):

$$\hat{p}_{2t} = \frac{\frac{D_t(D_t-1)}{2}}{\frac{N_t(N_t-1)}{2}} = \frac{D_t(D_t-1)}{N_t(N_t-1)} \tag{6.16}$$

Using the information from the T years, the estimator for the joint default probability takes the average from the observed annual joint default rates:

$$\hat{p}_2 = \frac{1}{T}\sum_{t=1}^{T}\hat{p}_{2t} = \frac{1}{T}\sum_{t=1}^{T}\frac{D_t(D_t-1)}{N_t(N_t-1)} \tag{6.17}$$

Again, we would assume that the joint default probability is equal for all borrowers.

The asset correlation follows suit. From (6.12) we know that

$$p_{ij} = \Phi_2(d_i, d_j, \rho_{ij}^{asset}) \tag{6.18}$$

We can estimate p_{ij} by (6.17) and d_i and d_j from (6.13). Equation (6.18) then turns into an equation with one unknown: the asset correlation. We cannot solve it analytically, but we can use numerical procedures to get a quick solution. Specifying the default thresholds and

[2] Recall that the binomial coefficient $\binom{n}{k}$, read as 'n choose k', yields the number of subsets with k elements that can be formed out of a set with n elements. It is given by $n!/(k!(n-k)!)$.

Table 6.1 The method of moments approach applied to investment grade defaults

	A	B	C	D	E	F	G	H
1	**Data**							
2	year t	# defaults (D_t)	# obligors (N_t)		$\frac{D_t(D_t-1)}{N_t(N_t-1)}$		**Estimated moments**	
3	1981	0	1064		0.0000%		Default probability	
4	1982	2	1093		0.0002%		0.114402%	
5	1983	1	1114		0.0000%		{=AVERAGE(B3:B31/C3:C31)}	
6	1984	2	1174		0.0001%		Joint default probability	
7	1985	0	1210		0.0000%		0.0002199%	
8	1986	2	1327		0.0001%		=AVERAGE(E3:E31)	
9	1987	0	1324		0.0000%			
10	1988	0	1337		0.0000%		**Asset value representation**	
11	1989	2	1381		0.0001%		Default threshold	
12	1990	2	1426		0.0001%		-3.050048588	
13	1991	2	1465		0.0001%		=NORMSINV(G4)	
14	1992	0	1617		0.0000%		Asset correlation	
15	1993	0	1769		0.0000%		0.048832133	
16	1994	1	1853		0.0000%		Joint default probability	
17	1995	1	2061		0.0000%		0.0002199%	
18	1996	0	2263		0.0000%		=BIVNOR(G12,G12,G15)	
19	1997	2	2512		0.0000%			
20	1998	4	2791		0.0002%			
21	1999	5	2893		0.0002%			
22	2000	7	2958		0.0005%		Goal Seek	
23	2001	8	3035		0.0006%		Set cell: G17	
24	2002	13	3149		0.0016%		To value: 0.000002199	
25	2003	3	3068		0.0001%		By changing cell: G15	
26	2004	1	3181		0.0000%		OK Cancel	
27	2005	1	3290		0.0000%			
28	2006	0	3312		0.0000%			
29	2007	0	3393		0.0000%			
30	2008	14	3398		0.0016%			
31	2009	11	3445		0.0009%			
32					=(B31*(B31-1))/(C31*(C31-1))			

the asset correlation in this way is an application of the method of moments. In this method, one calibrates unknown parameters such that the model results match empirical estimates of moments. The two moments used here are $E(y_i) = p_i$ and $E(y_i y_j) = p_{ij}$.

The application of the method of moments approach to investment grade default data from Standard & Poor's is illustrated in Table 6.1. The annual default counts (D_t) are in column B, the number of issuers at the start of year (N_t) in column C. In column E, we compute the annual joint default rates according to (6.16).

The two moments are estimated in G4 and G7, respectively. G4 implements (6.13) with the array function {=AVERAGE(B3:B31/C3:C31)}. G7 implements (6.17) by averaging over the annual joint default rates in E3:E31. The default threshold in G12 is obtained by applying the inverse cumulative normal to the default probability estimated in G4. In G15, we reserve a cell for the asset correlation that we want to determine, and in G17 we compute the joint default probability (6.18) for the threshold and the asset correlation that we have in G12 and G15. For this, we need a function that evaluates a bivariate standard normal distribution function. It is not available in Excel, but we can, for example, use the function BIVNOR written by Erik Heitfield and Michael Gordy, which is available on the Internet.[3]

We can now use the Goal Seek (or the Solver) functionality of Excel to determine the asset correlation G15 such that the estimated joint default rate G7 equals the joint default probability G17 implied by our asset value model. The Goal Seek window is shown in the table. Note that we have to make sure that Goal Seek applies sufficient precision in solving the problem. To that end, we can choose a very small value in menu Tools→Calculation→Maximum change (Excel 2003) or Microsoft Office Button (Excel 2007)/File Ribbon (Excel 2010)→Excel Options→Formulas→Maximum Change. Of course, we could also write =(G7−G17) in some cell and then use Goal Seek or the Solver to set it to zero by changing G15. In this way, we would avoid the small rounding errors associated with typing the value for the joint default rate into Goal Seek.

If there are several groups of obligors (e.g., investment grade and speculative grade issuers) and we want to calibrate the asset value model for both, we could do it separately for the individual groups. There is a drawback to this, however. Estimating the parameters for groups of issuers separately means that we assume that the defaults are independent across groups, which they are not: the correlation of investment and speculative default rates over the years 1981–2009 is 62%. In principle, one could generalize the method of moments procedure in such a way that it could also deal with correlated groups. But there is another approach that is not only more flexible but also makes better use of the available information. It is the maximum likelihood approach used repeatedly in this book, which we discuss in the next section.

ESTIMATING ASSET CORRELATION WITH MAXIMUM LIKELIHOOD

Applied to the asset value approach, the maximum likelihood principle says the following: Determine default probabilities and factor sensitivities such that the probability (=likelihood) of observing the historical default data is maximized (see Appendix A3 for a general introduction to maximum likelihood).

We first need to describe default behavior through an appropriate distribution function. To derive this distribution function, let us start with the concept of a conditional default probability. Here, it is the default probability conditional on Z, i.e., the default probability $p_i(Z)$ that is associated with a given factor realization Z. Formally, we write

$$p_i(Z) = \text{Prob}(A_i \leq \Phi^{-1}(p_i)|Z) \tag{6.19}$$

[3] http://mgordy.tripod.com/software/bivnorf.zip (accessed August 19, 2010). We are grateful to Erik Heitfield and Michael Gordy for the permission to use their function.

Inserting our factor model (6.9) in (6.19) and rearranging yields

$$p_i(Z) = \text{Prob}\left(w_i Z + \sqrt{1-w_i^2}\varepsilon_i \le \Phi^{-1}(p_i)\right)$$
$$= \text{Prob}\left(\varepsilon_i \le \frac{\Phi^{-1}(p_i) - w_i Z}{\sqrt{1-w_i^2}}\right)$$
$$= \Phi\left[\frac{\Phi^{-1}(p_i) - w_i Z}{\sqrt{1-w_i^2}}\right] \tag{6.20}$$

If the factor realization is 'bad' (e.g., -2), the conditional default probability is relatively high, and there will be many defaults. The crucial insight for the following is that once we know Z, the default of borrower i provides no information on the likely default of another borrower. To understand this, note that once we have fixed the value of Z, the randomness in (6.20) is entirely due to ε_i – but we have assumed that ε_i and ε_j are independent for $i \neq j$.

Conditional on a factor realization, defaults are thus independent; knowing whether borrower i has defaulted or not does not help us predict whether borrower j defaults or not. Each default variable y_i can then be seen as a 0–1 random variable with success probability $p_i(Z)$. If the conditional default probability is uniform across issuers at $p(Z)$, the total number of defaults D follows a binomial distribution with success probability $p(Z)$ and N trials.

Recall that the binomial density for x successes out of n trials with success probability q is $\binom{n}{x} q^x(1-q)^{n-x}$. Applying this formula to our problem leads to the following likelihood for the number of defaults within sector k in a given year t:

$$L_{kt} = \int_{-\infty}^{\infty} \binom{N_{kt}}{D_{kt}} p_k(Z)^{D_{kt}}(1-p_k(Z))^{N_{kt}-D_{kt}} d\Phi(Z) \tag{6.21}$$

We integrate over the factor Z because we do not know which factor has materialized. If we have default data for sector k that spreads over T years, we assume that defaults are independent across time and arrive at the following likelihood:

$$L_k = \prod_{t=1}^{T} \int_{-\infty}^{\infty} \binom{N_{kt}}{D_{kt}} p_k(Z)^{D_{kt}}(1-p_k(Z))^{N_{kt}-D_{kt}} d\Phi(Z) \tag{6.22}$$

If we were to apply the maximum likelihood approach to the data of just one sector – e.g., the investment grade defaults that we examined in the previous section – we would maximize Equation (6.22) to obtain the parameters p_k and w_k. (Recall that p_k and w_k are contained in $p_k(Z)$, because $p_k(Z)$ is given by Equation (6.20).)

If there are more sectors $k = 1, \ldots, K$, we have to model the joint distribution of defaults. Surely we want to allow for dependence. The simplest way is to assume that there is only one systematic factor that affects each sector. For a single year t, the likelihood can be written as

$$L_t = \int_{-\infty}^{\infty} \prod_{k=1}^{K} \left(\binom{N_{kt}}{D_{kt}} p_k(Z)^{D_{kt}} (1 - p_k(Z))^{N_{kt}-D_{kt}} \right) d\Phi(Z) \tag{6.23}$$

For T years, this leads to

$$L = \prod_{t=1}^{T} \int_{-\infty}^{\infty} \prod_{k=1}^{K} \left(\binom{N_{kt}}{D_{kt}} p_k(Z)^{D_{kt}} (1 - p_k(Z))^{N_{kt}-D_{kt}} \right) d\Phi(Z) \tag{6.24}$$

Unfortunately, likelihoods such as (6.24) are difficult to maximize. A common procedure – setting the first derivatives of the likelihood to zero – is not feasible. What we need are numerical techniques for evaluating the integrals in the likelihood. Here, we suggest using the Gauss-Hermite procedure. It approximates the integral with a weighted sum. The integral is evaluated at a discrete number of points, the abscissas; these values are then weighted with a specific weighting function. To integrate over a function $f(x)$, Gauss-Hermite uses

$$\int_{-\infty}^{\infty} f(x)dx \approx \sum_{i=1}^{n} w(x_i) \exp(x_i^2) f(x_i) \tag{6.25}$$

For the sake of brevity, we do not discuss the details of how the abscissas x_i and the weights $w(x_i)$ are obtained in the Gauss-Hermite procedure.[4] The higher the order n, i.e., the higher the number of abscissas in the discrete sum, the more precise is the estimated integral. We will use Gauss-Hermite with order $n = 32$. A simulation study (see the 'Notes and literature' section at the end of the chapter) suggests that this choice provides sufficient accuracy. The abscissas as well as the weights are shown in Table 6.2.[5] As we will integrate over the standard normal distribution, the function $f(x)$ in (6.25) will always be of the form $g(x)\phi(x)$, where $\phi()$ is the density of the standard normal distribution function, which is available through the Excel function NORMDIST(x,0,1,0). To avoid repeated, time-consuming evaluations of $\phi()$, we can compute $w(x)\exp(x^2)\phi(x)$ and weight $g(x)$ with this expression.

Table 6.2 also contains a simple application. Assume that you want to evaluate the expectation of exp(x), where x is standard normally distributed. From the properties of lognormal distributions we know that the exact solution is E[exp(x)] $= \exp(\mu + \sigma^2/2)$, with $\mu = 0$ and $\sigma^2 = 1$ in our case. To determine E[exp(x)] with Gauss-Hermite, evaluate the function exp(x) for each abscissa and form the weighted sum, where the total weights are given by $w(x)\exp(x^2)\phi(x)$. In cell H8 this is done with the function SUMPRODUCT(). The exact solution and our approximation obtained with Gauss-Hermite are very close.

In Table 6.3, we use the numbers from Table 6.2 to apply the maximum likelihood approach to investment grade defaults. We thus need to determine Equation (6.22) for $k =$ I (investment

[4] The abscissas for a chosen order n are the roots of the nth Hermite polynomial. The Hermite polynomials are given by $H_0 = 1$, $H_1 = 2x$, $H_{n+1} = 2xH_n - 2nH_{n-1}$.

[5] The abscissas and weights were obtained in VBA using the procedure described in Vetterling *et al.*, 2002, *Numerical Recipes in C++: The Art of Scientific Computing*, Cambridge University Press.

Table 6.2 Gauss-Hermite integration

	A	B	C	D	E	F	G	H
1	x	w(x)exp(x²)ϕ(x)	w(x)exp(x²)ϕ(x)		Example: Evaluate E[exp(x)] if x is N(0,1)			
2	7.12581391	0.82456652	3.0974E-12		1243.660			
3	6.40949815	0.64095049	3.0688E-10		607.589			
4	5.81222595	0.56174902	1.0346E-08		334.363			
5	5.27555099	0.51503728	1.8588E-07		195.498			
6	4.7771				118.767		E[exp(x)]	
7	4.3055				74.110		Exact	1.64872127070
8	3.8537				47.170		Gauss-Hermite	1.64872127067
9	3.4171				30.483			
10	2.9924				19.935		H7: =EXP(0+1^2/2)	
11	2.57724954	0.41120613	0.00592422		13.161		H8: =SUMPRODUCT(E2:E33,C2:C33)	
12	2.16949918	0.40455706	0.01534042		8.754			
13	1.76765411	0.39935484	0.03340185		5.857			
14	1.37037641	0.39539394	0.06168115		3.937			
15	0.97650046	0.39253186	0.09721282		2.655			
...	...	...	...		...			
33	-7.12581391	0.82456652	3.0974E-12		0.001			

C2: =B2*NORMDIST(A2,0,1,0)
(can be copied into C2:C33)

E2: =EXP(A2)
(can be copied into E2:E33)

grade) and maximize it. As usual, we maximize the log-likelihood. It is given by

$$\ln L_k = \sum_{t=1}^{T} \ln \int_{-\infty}^{\infty} \binom{N_{kt}}{D_{kt}} p_k(Z)^{D_{kt}} (1 - p_k(Z))^{N_{kt}-D_{kt}} d\Phi(Z) \tag{6.26}$$

Figure 6.1 serves to clarify the correspondence between calculations in the sheet and in the likelihood formula.

The data, N_t and D_{kt}, are shown in columns B and C of Table 6.3. The 32 abscissas for the Gauss-Hermite procedure are in G2:AL2; the integration weights can be found in G3:AL3. For each Z, we use Equation (6.20) to determine $p_k(Z)$ in G6:AL6. The binomial probabilities for a given Z and a given year are in G10:AL38. In E10:E38, we compute the weighted sum of the binomial densities, which corresponds to integration over Z, and take logs. We then obtain the overall likelihood (in B6) by summing over the annual likelihoods.

Having determined the log-likelihood for the given data and given parameters specified in cells B2 (default probability) and B3 (factor sensitivity), we can apply the Solver to maximize it. In doing so, we choose the following Solver options: precision is set to 0.000001; we tick *Assume non-negative* (as both default probability and factor sensitivity are non-negative), and we tick *Automatic-scaling*. Before starting the Solver, we choose sensible values for p and w, e.g., the method of moments estimators from Table 6.1; these starting values are written into cells B2 and B3, respectively, before calling the Solver.

Before examining the results, let us look at the likelihoods. Why, for example, is the column G likelihood in the year 2002 (3.2E-56) much lower than in the year 2006, where it is close to one? The factor value for this column is $Z = 7.13$ (in G2), and so it is a column for an extremely good year. Now 2002 was a very bad year with a default rate of 0.41%, and 2006 was a very good year with a zero default rate. If we assume that the year was very good as we

Table 6.3 The maximum likelihood approach applied to investment grade defaults

	A	B	C	D	E	F	G	H	.	AL
1	**To be estimated**				**32-order approximation for Z (Gauss-Hermite)**				.	
2	p_l	0.1215%				Z	7.1258	6.4095	.	-7.1258
3	w_l	27.64%			w(Z)exp(Z²)φ(Z)		3.097E-12	3.069E-10	.	3.097E-12
4										
5	**log Likelihood**				**Calculations for likelihood**					
6	$\ln L_l$	-60.270				$p_l(Z)$	0.00001%	0.00003%	.	13.45575%
7		=SUM(E10:E38)								
8	**Data**									
9	T	N_{lt}	D_{lt}		$\ln L_{lt}$					
10	1981	1064	0		-0.85		1.0E+00	1.0E+00	.	1.7E-67
11					96		5.6E-09	5.0E-08	.	3.6E-65
12					33					E-68
13	1984	1174	2		-1.93					E-70
14	1985	1210	0		-0.93					E-76
15	1986	1327	2		-1.89		8.3E-09	7.3E-08	.	1.1E-79
16	1987	1324	0		-0.99		1.0E+00	1.0E+00	.	8.0E-84
17	1988	1337	0							84
18	1989	1381	2							83
19	1990	1426	2							86
20	1991	1465	2							88
21	1992	1617	0							02
22	1993	1769	0							12
23	1994	1853	1							14
24	1995	2061	1							27
25	1996	2263	0							43
26	1997	2512	2							53
27	1998	2791	4							66
28	1999	2893	5							71
29	2000	2958	7							71
30	2001	3035	8							74
31	2002	3149	13		-4.76		3.2E-56	4.5E-50	.	3.4E-173
32	2003	3068	3		-2.16		4.4E-12	1.2E-10	.	5.1E-186
33	2004	3181	1		-1.70		3.1E-04	9.2E-04	.	1.1E-197
34	2005	3290	1		-1.72		3.2E-04	9.5E-04	.	1.7E-204
35	2006	3312	0		-1.80		1.0E+00	1.0E+00		1.4E-208
36	2007	3393	0		-1.83		1.0E+00	1.0E+00		1.1E-213
37	2008	3398	14		-4.84		2.0E-60	8.5E-54		8.0E-187
38	2009	3445	11		-4.18		1.5E-46	2.3E-41		1.6E-194

G6: =NORMSDIST((NORMSINV($B$2)-$B$3*G$2)/(1-$B$3^2)^0.5)
(can be copied into H6:AA6)

E10: =LN(SUMPRODUCT(G10:AL10,G$3:AL$3))
(can be copied into E10:E38)

G10: =COMBIN($B10,$C10)*G$6^$C10*(1-G$6)^($B10-$C10)
(can be copied into G10:AL38)

Solver Parameters
Set Target Cell: $B$6
Equal To: Max / Min / Value of: 0
By Changing Cells: $B$2:$B$3
Subject to the Constraints:
Solve | Close | Guess | Options | Add | Change | Delete | Reset All | Help

do in column G, we can do a much better job of explaining the 2006 experience. In column AL, it is the other way around.

Comparing the results of the maximum likelihood (ML) approach from Table 6.3 to the method of moments (MM) estimator from Table 6.1, we see that with ML, the default probability and the asset correlation are somewhat higher (see the following table):

	MM (%)	ML (%)
Default probability p	0.114	0.121
Factor sensitivity w	22.098	27.645
Asset correlation w^2	4.883	7.642

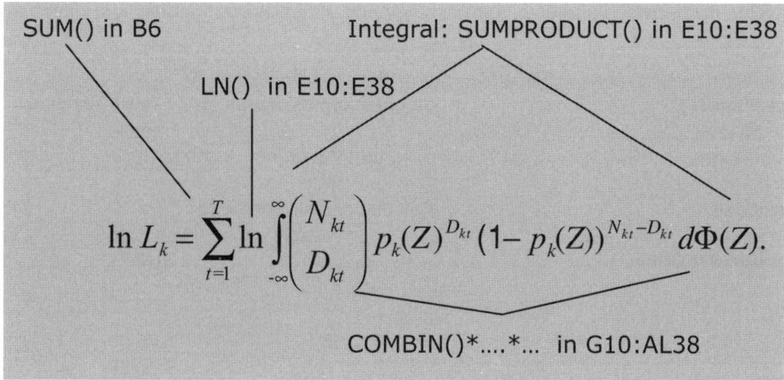

Figure 6.1 How the likelihood is calculated in Table 6.3

We can use likelihood ratio tests to test hypotheses such as 'the default correlation is 20%'.[6] We would write 0.2^0.5 = 0.4472 into B3 and then maximize the likelihood solely by varying the default probability in B2. Doing so, we get a log-likelihood of −62.85. The LR statistic is

$$\text{LR} = 2(-60.27 + 62.85) = 5.16$$

where −60.27 is the likelihood from Table 6.3. The p-value of this test is CHIDIST(5.16,1) = 2.3%, and so we could reject the hypothesis at a significance level better than 5%.

One motivation for the ML procedure was that it allows estimation of correlations with data from several segments. Next, we give examples of such calculations for data on both investment grade and speculative grade defaults. In doing so, we allow that the two sectors have different factor sensitivities.

Building on Table 6.3, we need to change little to get to Table 6.4. We have to allow for different default probabilities and factor sensitivities, which we do in cells B2:B3 and E2:E3, respectively. We insert the speculative grade data in D10:E38, shifting the likelihood calculations two columns to the right. In I7:AN7 we compute the conditional default probabilities of speculative issuers analogously to the approach we used for investment grade issuers. In doing so, we have to be careful to refer to the right parameters. The conditional default rate of investment grade issuers depends on the default probability in B2 and the factor sensitivity in E2, while the conditional default rate of speculative grade issuers depends on B3 and E3.

Then, we only have to change the calculation of the binomial densities in the range I10:AN38. Since we assume that both grades are driven by the same factor, we evaluate the joint probability of observing investment and speculative grade defaults for a given Z. The joint probability of independent events (recall what we said about conditional independence) is the product of individual probabilities, and so we multiply binomial densities of investment and speculative defaults for a given Z. In cell I10, for example, we could write:

```
=COMBIN($B10,$C10)*I$6^$C10*(1-I$6)^($B10-$C10)
*COMBIN($D10,$E10)*I$7^$E10*(1-I$7)^($D10-$E10)
```

[6] See Appendix A4 for more details on likelihood ratio tests.

Table 6.4 The maximum likelihood approach applied to investment grade and speculative grade defaults

	A	B	C	D	E	F	G	H	I	...	AN
1	**To be estimated**						**32-order approximation for Z (Gauss-Hermite)**				
2	p_I	0.137%		w_I	26.68%			Z	7.1258	...	-7.1258
3	p_S	4.45%		w_S	32.71%		w(Z)exp(Z²)φ(Z)		3.097E-12	...	3.097E-12
4											
5	**log Likelihood**						**Calculations for likelihood**				
6	lnL	-185.7244						$p_I(Z)$	0.00002%	...	12.83131%
7		=SUM(G10:G38)						$p_S(Z)$	0.00099%	...	74.74909%
8	**Data**										
9	t	N_{It}	D_{It}	N_{St}	D_{St}		lnL_t				
10	1981	1064	0	321	2		-3.63		5.0E-06	...	2.1E-250
11									9.8E-58	...	3.1E-232
12									9.8E-36	...	2.4E-245
13									2.4E-46	...	7.6E-259
14									1.4E-59	...	4.8E-283
15									2.1E-109	...	0.0E+00
16									3.6E-59	...	0.0E+00
17									1.5E-93	...	0.0E+00
18									4.8E-123	...	0.0E+00
19									3.5E-205	...	0.0E+00
20	1991	1465	2	589	65		-8.71		7.6E-246	...	0.0E+00
21	1992	1617	0	526	32		-7.00		1.3E-109	...	0.0E+00
22	1993	1769	0	56							
23	1994	1853	1	71							
24	1995	2061	1	82							
25	1996	2263	0	89							
26	1997	2512	2	100							
27	1998	2791	4	132							
28	1999	2893	5	166							
29	2000	2958	7	178							
30	2001	3035	8	178							
31	2002	3149	13	171							
32	2003	3068	3	180							
33	2004	3181	1	192							
34	2005	3290	1	211							
35	2006	3312	0	225							
36	2007	3393	0	2397	21		-5.93		1.4E-54		0.0E+00
37	2008	3398	14	2528	88		-16.70		0.0E+00		0.0E+00
38	2009	3445	11	2415	223		-8.48		0.0E+00		0.0E+00

E10: =LN(SUMPRODUCT(I10:AC10,I$3:AN$3))
(can be copied into E10:E38)

*I6: =NORMSDIST((NORMSINV($B2)-$E$2*I$2)/(1-$E$2^2)^0.5)*
(can be copied to I6:AN7)
I10: =EXP(lncombin($B10,$C10)+LN(I$6)*$C10+LN(1-I$6)*($B10-$C10)+lncombin($D10,$E10)+LN(I$7)*$E10+LN(1-I$7)*($D10-$E10))
(can be copied to I10:AN38)

Solver Parameters

Set Target Cell: $B$6
Equal To: Max / Min / Value of: 0
By Changing Cells: $B$2:$B$3,$E$2:$E$3
Subject to the Constraints:
Solve | Close | Guess | Options | Add | Change | Delete | Reset All | Help

There is a small complication. The speculative grade data contains combinations of N (number of issuers) and D (number of defaults) for which the Excel function COMBIN(N,D) yields error values because the result is larger than the largest number displayed by Excel. We can work around this difficulty by doing the calculations for logarithms, and by using an approximation for the factorial that is then used to calculate the binomial coefficient. Specifically, we suggest the following user-defined function that returns the logarithm of the binomial coefficient based on Stirling's approximation of the factorial:

```
Function lncombin(n, k)
'lfn is the log of n!, lfk is log of k!, lfnk is log of (n-k)!
Dim lfn As Double, lfk As Double, lfnk As Double
```

```
If IsError(Application.Combin(n, k)) = False Then 'Use Excel's Combin
    lncombin = Log(Application.Combin(n, k))
Else 'Use Stirling's approximation for factorial
    If k = 0 Then
        lncombin = 0
    Else
        lfn = (n + 0.5) * Log(n) - n + 0.5 * Log(2 * Application.Pi())
        lfk = (k + 0.5) * Log(k) - k + 0.5 * Log(2 * Application.Pi())
        lfnk = ((n - k) + 0.5) * Log(n - k) - (n - k) _
                  + 0.5 * Log(2 * Application.Pi())
        lncombin = lfn - lfk - lfnk
    End If
End If

End Function
```

Table 6.4 shows how we use this function to determine the probability in cell I10.

Compared to the previous ML estimates, the default probability is higher, while the asset correlation is lower:

	MM (%)	ML (%)	ML (joint with spec grade) (%)
Default probability p	0.114	0.121	0.137
Factor sensitivity w	22.098	27.645	26.681
Asset correlation w^2	4.883	7.642	7.119

To come to an intuitive explanation for this result, note that we observe a few years with high investment grade default rates. There are two reasons why we can expect to see high default rates: a high default probability or a high asset correlation. If high investment grade defaults are not perfectly coupled with high speculative grade default rates, the joint use of the data could favor the default probability explanation, providing one reason why we can observe the shift in the parameter estimates.

We could also test the hypothesis that the two factor sensitivities are the same. We write '=E2' into cell E3 and let the Solver maximize over B2, B3 and E2. Again, we use a likelihood ratio test. Its p-value is 0.16, which means that the evidence against uniform sensitivities is relatively weak.

The change in results from Table 6.3 to Table 6.4 exemplifies the importance of making efficient use of data. Speculative grade defaults can be useful not only for estimating investment grade correlations, but also for estimating investment grade default probabilities. When choosing between different estimators, however, we should be aware of the possibility that estimators that appear desirable with respect to some criteria might perform poorly with respect to others. In particular, we should be aware of small sample problems. Many estimators have good properties if the number of observations is large, but if the sample is small they can be beset by low precision or biases, i.e., produce estimates that are on average too low or too high. When estimating default correlations, we are typically dealing with small samples: the relevant dimension for estimating correlations is not the number of borrowers but rather the number of years. With the Standard & Poor's data, we have just 29 of them. Many financial institutions wishing to estimate correlations with their own data will have less. So having a tool to help assess problems arising in small samples is a good idea. In the next section, we present such a tool: Monte Carlo studies.

EXPLORING THE RELIABILITY OF ESTIMATORS WITH A MONTE CARLO STUDY

Consider the following setting: having estimated parameters with empirical data, you want to examine the properties of the estimates. A Monte Carlo study would then be structured as follows:

1. Specify a probability distribution that is a good description of the empirical data you work with.
2. Randomly draw a hypothetical data set from the distribution specified in step 1.
3. Determine the estimators to be studied for the simulated data from step 2.
4. Repeat steps 2 to 3 sufficiently often and analyze the estimates.

In our illustration of a Monte Carlo study, we build on Table 6.3, leading to Table 6.5. We assume that there exists (and is available to us) data on investment grade defaults over 29 years. The number of issuers at the start of each year are the actual ones taken from the history. Defaults are generated (step 1) according to a one-factor asset value model with the parameters estimated in Table 6.3: $p_{\mathrm{I}} = 0.12\%$ (investment grade default probability), $w = 0.28$ (factor sensitivity). We study the maximum likelihood estimator, which is determined as in Table 6.3, and the method of moments estimator. To obtain the latter, we follow the procedure from the second section of this chapter.

The Monte Carlo study is conducted by running the macro MCstudy() on Table 6.5. Note first the changes that were made in the table relative to Table 6.3. We add the method of moments estimator for the default probability in C2, and the method of moments estimator for the factor sensitivity in F2. We add a column with annual joint default rates in E10:E38, shifting the likelihood calculations two columns to the right. In F3, we calculate the squared difference between the estimated joint default probability (6.17) and the theoretical one (6.18). We multiply this difference with a large number (10^{10}) because when we later set it to zero by varying F2, we want to make sure that the numerical routine we apply stops only when the difference is in the very near proximity of zero.

The macro (see Table 6.5) starts by setting the parameters: default thresholds d depend on the chosen default probability $p_{\mathrm{I}} = 0.12\%$. Factor sensitivity is set to $w = 0.28$. We then loop through the trials of the Monte Carlo simulation. To start, we simulate defaults. Defaults are drawn from a binomial with success probability equal to the conditional default probability. The latter depends on the factor realization Z, which is drawn from a standard normal distribution. To draw random numbers, we use the inverse distribution method: if a variable follows the distribution function $F(x)$, we can draw realizations by drawing a variable y that is uniformly distributed on the unit interval, and then apply the inverse of F. For a draw y^* we then receive the draw $x^* = F^{-1}(y^*)$. In VBA, a uniform random number is generated by RND(). The inverse of the standard normal and the binomial are given by calling the worksheet functions NORMSINV() and CRITBINOM(), respectively.

Table 6.5 A Monte Carlo study of method of moments (MM) and maximum likelihood estimators (ML) for default probability p and factor sensitivity w

	A	B	C	D	E	F	G	H	I	.	AN
1		ML	MM		ML	MM	**32-order approximation for Z (Gauss-Hermite)**				
2	p_l	0.000942	0.00095	w	0.200	0.160		Z	7.1258	.	-7.1258
3						2.1176E-12	$w(x)\exp(x^2)\phi(x)$		3.09743E-12	.	3.09743E-12
4											
5	**log Likelihood**						**Calculations for likelihood**				
6	lnL	-54.18	0					$p_l(Z)$	0.00019%	.	4.28904%
7			=SUM(G10:G34)								
8	**Data**										
9	t	N_{lt}	D_{lt}								
10	1981	1064	0		0.0000%		-0.81		1.0E+00	.	5.5E-21
11	1982								E+00	.	1.6E-21
12	1983								E-09	.	1.3E-17
13	1984								E-09	.	1.1E-18
14	1985								E-03	.	5.0E-22
15	1986								E+00	.	5.4E-26
16	1987								E-06	.	1.1E-22
17	1988								E-03	.	2.1E-24
18	1989								E-03	.	3.2E-25
19	1990								E+00	.	7.1E-28
20	1991								E-06	.	2.8E-25
21	1992								E-12	.	1.9E-25
22	1993								E-09	.	1.7E-29
23	1994								E-06	.	1.8E-32
24	1995								E-03	.	5.3E-38
25	1996								E+00	.	8.2E-44
26	1997								E-03	.	1.7E-46
27	1998								E-01	.	7.3E-54
28	1999								E-03	.	1.1E-53
29	2000								E-11	.	6.2E-50
30	2001								E-08	.	6.9E-53
31	2002								E-05	.	1.1E-56
32	2003								E-01	.	3.9E-59
33	2004								E-01	.	2.7E-61
34	2005								E-03	.	3.4E-61
35	2006								E-08	.	4.8E-58
36	2007								E-23	.	1.8E-52
37	2008								E-29	.	3.7E-50
38	2009								E-11	.	6.1E-59
39											
40											
41											
42											
43											
44	pl	0.0015	0.0015	w	0.3135	0.2614					
45	pl	0.0013	0.0013	w	0.2158	0.2041					
46	pl	0.0017	0.0017	w	0.3452	0.3588					

C2: {=AVERAGE(C10:C38/B10:B38)}
F3: =(bivnor(NORMSINV(C2),NORMSINV(C2),F2^2)-AVERAGE(E10:E38))*10^10

```
Sub MCstudy()
Dim i As Long, j As Integer, dl, w, z, pl_z

Application.ScreenUpdating = False
Application.Calculation = xlCalculationAutomatic
Application.MaxChange = 0.00000000001

'set parameters for asset value model
dl = Application.WorksheetFunction.NormSInv(0.0012)
w = 0.28

'Loop through simulation trials
For i = 1 To 1000
  Application.StatusBar = i

  'Simulate defaults (Binomial with conditional default prob)
  For j = 10 To 38
    z = Application.WorksheetFunction.NormSInv(Rnd())
    pl_z = Application.WorksheetFunction.NormSDist((dl - w * z) / (1 - w ^ 2) ^ 0.5)
    Cells(j, 3) = Application.WorksheetFunction.CritBinom(Cells(j, 2), pl_z, Rnd())
  Next j

  'Method of moments (MM) estimator of correlation
  Range("F2") = 0.5
  Range("F3").GoalSeek Goal:=0, ChangingCell:=Range("F2")

  'Maximum Likelihood estimator of default probability and correlation
  'Initial values from MM
  Range("B2:B3") = (Range("C2:C3"))
  Range("E2") = 0.5
  If IsError(Range("F3")) = False Then
    If Range("F3") < 0.0000001 Then Range("E2") = Range("F2")
  End If
  'Likelihood maximization with Solver
  SolverReset
  SolverOk SetCell:="$B$6", MaxMinVal:=1, ValueOf:="0", ByChange:="$B$2,$E$2"
  SolverOptions Precision:=0.000001, Scaling:=True, AssumeNonNeg:=True
  SolverSolve Userfinish:=True

  'Write estimates into sheet
  Range(Cells(43 + i, 1), Cells(43 + i, 6)) = (Range("A2:F2"))
  Cells(43 + i, 7) = (Range("F3"))
Next i
End Sub
```

The method of moments estimates for default probabilities are automatically calculated in the sheet. To obtain the MM estimate for the correlation, we use the Goal seek functionality to set cell F3 equal to zero; our starting value is $w = 0.5$. We use the MM estimates as starting values for the ML estimation. However, if the MM estimator for the factor sensitivity did not converge, we use $w = 0.5$. (The MM is classified as nonconvergent if it yields an error value for the squared difference in F3, or if this difference is larger than 0.0000001). We then call the Solver to maximize the likelihood in cell B6 with the same options that we used in Table 6.3.

Finally, we insert the estimates for investment grade default probability and for the factor sensitivity into the sheet (starting in row 44). We conduct $M = 1000$ Monte Carlo trials and get the following results:[7]

	p_{ML} (%)	p_{MM} (%)	w_{ML} (%)	w_{MM} (%)
Average	0.120	0.120	26.79	24.66
RMSE	0.029	0.029	6.62	6.92

RMSE is root mean squared error. For the ML estimator w_{ML} of the factor sensitivity $w = 0.28$, for example, it is defined as

$$\text{RMSE}_w = \sqrt{\frac{1}{M}\sum_{i=1}^{M}(w_{ML} - 0.28)^2}$$

Regarding default probabilities, there is little difference between the two estimators. They both appear to be unbiased, and they both have a similar precision (as measured by RMSE). This is not the same for the factor sensitivity, however. Both are downward biased, i.e., their average value is below the true value of 0.28, but the downward bias is more pronounced for the MM estimator. The Monte Carlo study would thus prefer the ML procedure if we believe that the data we work with is similar to the one we simulated. However, since we have found the ML estimate of the factor sensitivity to be biased by roughly one percentage point, we could adjust our estimates accordingly. If ML leads to a factor sensitivity estimate of 0.27, for example, we could work with one of 0.28 instead.

The magnitude of the RMSE values suggests that there may be considerable uncertainty about the true values. If the true factor sensitivity is 0.28, we may well obtain an estimate of 0.171 with the data at hand, even though we use 29 years of data (0.171 is 0.28 minus 1.645 times the RMSE, yielding an estimate of the 5th percentile based on the normal distribution). Note that the RMSE is not driven by the bias but by the dispersion in the estimates. The standard deviation of the ML estimate, which is not affected by the bias, is 6.51%, little less than the RMSE of 6.62%.

In practical applications, ignoring parameter uncertainty may lead to an underestimation of risk. In Chapter 7, we will therefore discuss how to take uncertainty about parameters into account when estimating portfolio credit risk.

[7] We ignored those trials where either of the two estimators did not converge.

CONCLUDING REMARKS

The model of default correlation presented in this chapter can be generalized in many ways. We can increase the number of factors, turn the factor sensitivities into random variables, or let the asset values follow non-normal distributions.

The sheer number of modeling alternatives might call into question our trust in the simple model we have examined here. Most definitely, model set up is an important issue at hand. Should the model be wrong in some way, however, we can still hope for the estimation procedure to pick the parameters in such a way that even a flawed model might explain the data satisfactorily well. Hamerle and Rösch (2005), for example, have shown that the consequences of choosing a normal asset value distribution instead of a Student t-distribution are largely offset in the estimation of the factor sensitivity. If we assume a normal distribution when the true one is t, the default correlation for a *given* factor sensitivity is underestimated; but when we falsely use the normality assumption in estimating the factor sensitivity from default data, we tend to overestimate the factor sensitivity, neutralizing the error from the distributional assumption.

NOTES AND LITERATURE

To assess the reliability of our estimation procedure, we exactly replicated a Monte Carlo study by Gordy and Heitfield (2002), in which they examined the behavior of the ML estimator for a data set with three sectors that are driven by a single common factor, the factor sensitivity being uniform at 30%:

	ML estimate of factor sensitivity Gordy and Heitfield, Table 4(b), MLE3	Method of this chapter
Average	28.49%	28.53%
RMSE	6.39%	6.38%

The differences between the results are small and within the bounds of simulation error.

The asset value approach goes back to Vasicek, O., 1987, *Probability of loss on loan portfolio*. White paper, KMV, and Gupton, G.M., Finger, C.C. and Bhatia, M., 1997, *CreditMetrics – Technical Document*, J.P. Morgan.

The method of moment approach was suggested by Gordy, M., 2000, A comparative anatomy of credit risk models, *Journal of Banking and Finance* 24, 119–149. In this chapter, we use the estimator suggested in Frey, R. and McNeil, A.J., 2003, Dependent defaults in models of portfolio credit risk, *Journal of Risk* 6, 59–92.

On the maximum likelihood approach, see Gordy, M. and Heitfield, E., 2002, *Estimating default correlations from short panels of credit rating performance data*, Working paper, Federal Reserve.

For a discussion of the importance of distributional assumptions, see Hamerle, A. and Rösch, D., 2005, Misspecified copulas in credit risk models: How good is Gaussian? *Journal of Risk* 8, 41–58. The full reference details for Merton (1974) are: Merton, R.C., 1974, On the pricing of corporate debt: The risk structure of interest rates, *Journal of Finance* 29(2), 449–470.

7
Measuring Credit Portfolio Risk with the Asset Value Approach

A credit portfolio risk model produces a probability distribution of losses that can arise from holding a portfolio of credit risky instruments. A financial institution can use such models to answer questions such as: 'What is the probability that losses on my loan portfolio exceed 100m over a horizon of one year?'

The *annus mirabilis* of portfolio credit risk models is 1997, which saw the publication of three different approaches; a fourth approach was developed at about the same time.[1]

Even though extant models are similar in underlying structure, it is beyond the scope of this chapter to provide thorough implementations of each. Accordingly, we cover just one approach – the asset value or latent variable approach exemplified by CreditMetrics. In this approach, the portfolio loss distribution is obtained through a Monte Carlo simulation. Computing time is thus an important implementation issue. To keep focused on this issue, we start with a simplified framework in which we just consider losses from default (but not from changes in market value). We then show how to speed up simulations, and conclude with some generalizations.

A DEFAULT-MODE MODEL IMPLEMENTED IN THE SPREADSHEET

We can split portfolio credit risk modeling into four main steps. In the following, we describe those steps for a general model and for a specific approach – a default-mode model in which we consider only losses from default:

1. *Specify probabilities of individual credit events.* Default mode: specify only probabilities of default (PDs) because other events (changes in credit quality) are ignored in the modeling.
2. *Specify value effects of individual credit events.* Default mode: specify the loss given default (LGD), which is the percentage of exposure at default (EAD) that is lost in the case of default.
3. *Specify correlations of individual credit events and value effects.* Default mode: specify default correlations and (possibly) correlations of LGDs.
4. Based on steps 1 to 3, obtain the portfolio value distribution (via simulations or analytically).

In previous chapters, we explored different ways of obtaining default probabilities: logit scores, structural models or historical default rates per rating category. We could use any of the three approaches (as well as others) to determine PDs as required in step 1. LGD can be

[1] These models are CreditMetrics (Gupton, Finger and Bhatia, 1997), CreditRisk+ (CSFB, 1997), CreditPortfolioView (Wilson, 1997a,b) and KMV PortfolioManager.

measured in similar ways. We can use historical averages of LGDs or multivariate prediction models to obtain LGD estimates (see Chapter 5).

In step 3, we choose to employ the asset value approach detailed in Chapter 6. It models default correlations by linking defaults to a continuous variable: the asset value A. Borrower i defaults if its asset value falls below some threshold d_i chosen to match the specified PD_i:

$$\begin{aligned} \text{Default}_i &\Leftrightarrow A_i \leq d_i \\ \text{No default}_i &\Leftrightarrow A_i \leq d_i \end{aligned} \tag{7.1}$$

If the asset values are assumed to be standard normally distributed, we would set $d_i = \Phi^{-1}(\text{PD}_i)$, where Φ denotes the cumulative standard normal distribution function.

Correlation in asset values can be modeled through factor models. We start with a simple one containing just one systematic factor Z:

$$\begin{gathered} A_i = w_i Z + \sqrt{1 - w_i^2}\varepsilon_i,\ \text{cov}(\varepsilon_i, \varepsilon_j) = 0, i \neq j; \text{cov}(Z, \varepsilon_i) = 0, \forall i \\ Z \sim N(0,1),\ \varepsilon_i \sim N(0,1), \forall i \end{gathered} \tag{7.2}$$

In words, we assume that: systematic (Z) and idiosyncratic (ε) shocks are independent; idiosyncratic shocks deserve their name because they are independent across firms; shocks are standard normally distributed.

In the asset value approach, the standard way of obtaining the portfolio distribution (step 4) is to run a Monte Carlo simulation. It has the following structure:

1. Randomly draw asset values for each obligor in the portfolio (which we will do here according to (7.2)).
2. For each obligor, check whether it defaulted according to (7.1); if yes, determine the individual loss $\text{LGD}_i \times \text{EAD}_i$.
3. Aggregate the individual losses into a portfolio loss.
4. Repeat steps 1 to 3 sufficiently often to arrive at a distribution of credit portfolio losses.

In the following, we implement such a simulation in an Excel spreadsheet. We assume that we have estimates of the PD_i, LGD_i, EAD_i and asset correlations. We use a one-factor model with normally distributed asset values, and so correlations are fully specified once we have specified the factor sensitivities w_i.

Table 7.1 shows these parameters for a portfolio of 100 loans. Loan-specific PDs, LGDs, EADs and factor sensitivities w are contained in B10:E109. Simulation steps 1 to 3 are also implemented in the sheet. For each loan, we first determine its default threshold d_i by applying the function NORMSINV() to PD_i (column G) before drawing a factor realization in J10. RAND() gives a uniform random number between 0 and 1. With the inversion method, we can transform it into a standard normal variable by applying the inverse of the standard normal. J10 thus reads =NORMSINV(RAND()). Next, we determine the individual scenario asset value according to formula (7.2). In doing so, we refer to the factor sensitivities and the factor, and generate a loan-specific random variable ε_i. H10, for example, reads

```
= E10*J$10 + (1 – E10^2)^0.5*NORMSINV(RAND())
```

Table 7.1 Simulating a default-mode model – spreadsheet implementation

	A	B	C	D	E	F	G	H	I	J	K
1	**Simulation specifications**						**Simulated loss distribution**				
2							Confidence	Percentile			
3	# trials		1000				90%	350	=PERCENTILE(K$10:K$65536,G3)		
4							95%	400	*(can be copied into H4:H6)*		
5							99%	600			
6							99.90%	850			
7											
8	**Portfolio**						**Monte Carlo Simulation**				
9	Loan	PD	LGD	EAD	W		Default threshold d	Asset value A	Loss (per loan)	Factor Z	Saved portfolio losses
10	1	1%	50%	100	0.3		-2.33	0.81	0	0.85	0
11	2	1%	50%	100	0.3		-2.33	-1.81	0	Portfolio loss	200
12	3	1%	50%	100	0.3		-2.33	-2.08	0	50	100
13	4										100
14	5										250
15	6										300
16	7										50
17	8										250
18	9										50
19	10										100
20	11	1%	50%	100	0.3		-2.33	-1.89	0		250
21	12	1%	50%	100	0.3		-2.33	0.53	0		100
22	13	1%	50%								0
23	14	1%	50%								150
24	15	1%	50%								50
25	16	1%	50%								200
26	17	1%	50%								50
27	18	1%	50%								100
...	...	...	...								...
103	94	5%	50%								150
104	95	5%	50%								100
105	96	5%	50%								150
106	97	5%	50%								0
107	98	5%	50%								650
108	99	5%	50%								300
109	100	5%	50%								50
...											...
1009											50

G10: =NORMSINV(B10)
H10: =E10*J$10+(1-E10^2)^0.5*NORMSINV(RAND())
I10: =C10*D10*(H10<G10)
(can be copied into G11:I109)

J10: =NORMSINV(RAND())
J12: =SUM(I10:I65536)

```
Sub simsheet()
Dim M As Long, i As Long
Application.ScreenUpdating = False
Application.Calculation = xlCalculationAutomatic

'Clear output and formulae from previous runs
Range("K10:K65536").Clear
Range("H3:H6").Clear

M = Range("c3")

'Conduct trials
For i = 1 To M
    Application.StatusBar = Int(i / M * 100) & "%"
    'Write loss of trial i into sheet
     Range("K" & i + 9) = Range("J12")
Next i

'Fill in formula for analysis of loss data
Range("H3") = "=PERCENTILE(K$10:K$65536,G3)"
Range("H3:H6").FillDown

End Sub
```

With the asset values and the default threshold in hand, we can decide whether a loan defaulted in the scenario or not. If it defaulted, the associated loss is LGD × EAD. Generally speaking, the individual scenario can be written as

$$= \text{LGD} \times \text{EAD} \times (1 \text{ if default, } 0 \text{ otherwise})$$

Cell I10, for example, reads

$$= \text{C10*D10*(H10} < \text{G10)}$$

In cell J12, we then sum up the individual loan losses to obtain the portfolio loss in the scenario. But we have not yet completed the Monte Carlo simulation. To derive an estimate of the loss distribution, we need many scenarios, not just one. Within the sheet, we could press F9 to produce another random scenario, but it is more convenient to employ a macro. We propose the macro `simsheet`, which is also shown in Table 7.1.

At the heart of the macro lies a 'for' loop. As many times as specified in cell C3 in the sheet, we let Excel compute a new scenario in the sheet and have our macro save the resulting portfolio loss in column K. We do not need to tell Excel to compute a new scenario because we made sure that the Automatic-Calculation-Option (to be found via Tools→Options→Calculation in Excel 2003; via Office Button (Excel 2007)/File Ribbon (Excel 2010)→Excel Options→Formulas) is activated. When we change something in the sheet – and there is a change once we write the result into column K – the sheet is recalculated, including a new draw of random numbers.

The motivation for the other statements is as follows. Without

```
Application.Screenupdating=False
```

computing time would increase because Excel would update the displayed screen content in the course of each trial. We also clear output from previous runs (to make sure that we do not mix old and new results) and clear the formulae that analyze the loss distribution (Excel would recalculate them whenever the macro writes a new scenario, requiring additional computing time). At the end of the macro, we write the formulae back into cells H3:H6. They return percentiles of the loss distribution for the confidence levels specified in cells G3:G6. Finally,

```
Application.StatusBar = Int(i / M * 100) & "%"
```

keeps us informed about simulation progress.

The portfolio examined in Table 7.1 contains only 100 obligors, which is representative of a corporate bond fund, but certainly not representative of a bank's loan portfolio. Even with such a low number, the simulation is not done in a wink. If we increased the number of obligors to, say, 5000, or increased the number of simulations to 20,000 to make the simulation results more precise (we come back to this issue in a later section), the simulation time would be unacceptably long.

The implementation in the worksheet thus mainly serves our purpose of introducing the simulation methodology. In the following sections, we explore faster and more efficient ways of implementing such a simulation in Excel.

VBA IMPLEMENTATION OF A DEFAULT-MODE MODEL

In the simulation of Table 7.1, two very time-consuming elements are

- drawing random numbers through NORMSINV(RAND());
- writing simulation output into the sheet.

To gain an idea of the time that these two elements consume, start with an empty sheet and fill =NORMSINV(RAND()) into the range A1:F50000. It takes several seconds until the numbers are determined and filled in.

In the following, we therefore propose an alternative implementation which uses another algorithm to produce standard normal numbers and also moves all computations to VBA.

To generate random normal numbers, we use the polar method algorithm:

1. Generate two uniform random variables U_1 and U_2; compute $V_1 = 2U_1 - 1$, $V_2 = 2U_2 - 1$.
2. Repeat step 1 until $W = V_1^2 + V_2^2 < 1$.
3. $Z_1 = V_1\sqrt{-2\ln(W)/W}$ and $Z_2 = V_2\sqrt{-2\ln(W)/W}$ are standard normal variables.

Thus, one application of the polar method produces two standard normal variables. An implementation of this algorithm is our function NRND():

```
Function NRND() As Double
Dim W As Double, z As Double
Static NRND2 As Double, take2 As Boolean

'Check whether a non-used variable is available
If take2 = True Then
      NRND = NRND2
      take2 = False
Else
      'Polar method
      Do
             NRND = 2 * Rnd - 1
             NRND2 = 2 * Rnd - 1
             W = NRND * NRND + NRND2 * NRND2
      Loop Until W < 1
      z = Sqr(-2 * Log(W) / W)
      NRND = NRND * z
      NRND2 = NRND2 * z
      take2 = True
End If
End Function
```

The do loop and the following calculations (until `NRND2=NRND2*z`) implement the polar method described above. In addition, we exploit the fact that the algorithm produces two random variables. If the function is called for the first time, it returns the first random variable NRND. But we store the second random variable in NRND2. This variable is declared to be static, and so it will be available after the function has returned NRND. Through `If take2 = True`, we check whether such a non-used variable is available. If this is indeed the case, we do not enter the polar method algorithm but immediately return the random number that was stored in a previous run of the function.

Let us ponder another issue before building the simulation macro. In Table 7.1, we wrote the simulated loss scenarios into the sheet and applied the worksheet function PERCENTILE to it. In the macro to be written, we will record the loss scenarios in a VBA array. Once we increase the number beyond the maximum number of rows within a sheet, we run into two problems (at least in Excel 2003): first, saving the losses in the sheet is not convenient because we would need more than one column; second, the function PERCENTILE does not work for arrays longer than the maximum number of rows in the spreadsheet. Our strategy will be as follows. To compute percentiles, we sort the array containing the loss function; the α percentile of this ascendingly-sorted array with M elements is taken to be the element with index $\alpha(M+1)$, rounded to the nearest integer. We then write the percentiles determined in VBA back into the sheet.

As there is no sorting functionality in VBA, we provide one through a macro SORT(). It implements the following Quicksort algorithm:[2]

1. Partition the data into two subsets by selecting a partitioning element.
2. Simultaneously move from the left and from the right towards the partitioning element. Compare elements on the left to those on the right and swap them when you find a pair with the left one larger than the partitioning element while the right one is smaller.
3. Refer the sorted subsets created by steps 1 and 2 to step 1.

Here is the implementation, in which the partitioning element is the one in the middle of the (sub)sets:

```
Sub SORT(x(), Optional lower, Optional upper)
Dim a, p1, p2, tmp
If IsMissing(lower) Then lower = LBound(x)
If IsMissing(upper) Then upper = UBound(x)

'Determine partitioning element
a = x((lower + upper) / 2)
p1 = lower: p2 = upper

Do
        Do While (x(p1) < a): p1 = p1 + 1: Loop
        Do While (x(p2) > a): p2 = p2 - 1: Loop
        If p1 <= p2 Then
                'exchange elements
                tmp = x(p1): x(p1) = x(p2): x(p2) = tmp
                p1 = p1 + 1: p2 = p2 - 1
        End If
Loop Until (p1 > p2)
'Recursively sort subarrays
If lower < p2 Then: SORT x, lower, p2
If p1 < upper Then: SORT x, p1, upper
End Sub
```

With NRND() and SORT() at hand, we can build a macro that performs the Monte Carlo simulation. We use the same portfolio as in Table 7.1. As shown in Table 7.2, we use the spreadsheet only for collecting the input parameters and for displaying the results of the

[2] There are other sorting algorithms as well as variants of the Quicksort implemented here. We refrain from a discussion and instead refer readers concerned about efficiency and reliability to the literature, e.g., Vetterling *et al.*, 2002, *Numerical Recipes in C++: The art of scientific computing*, Cambridge University Press.

Table 7.2 Simulating a default-mode model – VBA implementation

	A	B	C	D	E	F	G	H	I
1	**Simulation specifications**						**Simulation results**		
2							Confidence	Loss percentile	
3	# trials		100000				90%	350	
4							95%	400	
5							99%	600	
6							99.90%	850	
7							99.95%	950	
8	**Portfolio**								
9	Loan	PD	LGD	EAD	w				
10	1	1%	50%	100	0.3		Run macro simVBA to simulate and return the loss percentiles		
11	2	1%	50%	100	0.3				
12	3	1%	50%	100	0.3				
...	...	...	...	...	...				
109	100	5%	50%	100	0.3				

Monte Carlo simulation. All calculations are performed through the macro simVBA, with the structure of this macro as follows.

After declaring variables, we read the number of simulations M (in cell C3) and the number of loans N (count the entries in B10:B65536) from the sheet. We then write the loan characteristics contained in columns B to E into arrays. We do not store the PD_i but instead the default thresholds $d_i = \Phi^{-1}(PD_i)$, because the latter are needed in the simulation and the PD_i themselves are not. The other input parameters written into arrays are LGD_i, EAD_i and the factor sensitivities w_i. We also create an array w2 containing $\sqrt{1-w_i^2}$. This transformation of the factor sensitivity will be used again and again in the course of the simulation (see Equation (7.2)).

The Monte Carlo trials are conducted with a `For j=1 to M` loop. In one single trial j, we first draw a factor, then determine the loss for an individual loan i and add it to the portfolio loss. Once we have done this for all loans, we store the trial's portfolio loss (named `loss_j`) in an array (named `loss`).

Having conducted M trials, we use the SORT macro to sort the array loss. For the percentile levels stated in the sheet (in the range H3:H7), we infer the loss percentiles and write them into the sheet.

```
Sub simVBA()

Dim M As Long, N As Long, i As Long, j As Long
M = Range("c3")  'Number of simulations
N = Application.Count(Range("B10:B65536"))   'Number of loans

Dim d(), LGD() As Double, EAD() As Double, w() As Double, w2() As Double
Dim loss(), factor As Double, loss_j As Double

ReDim d(1 To N), LGD(1 To N), EAD(1 To N), w(1 To N), w2(1 To N), _
      loss(1 To M)
```

```
'Write loan characteristics into arrays
For i = 1 To N
    d(i) = Application.NormSInv(Range("B" & i + 9))
    LGD(i) = Range("C" & i + 9)
    EAD(i) = Range("D" & i + 9)
    w(i) = Range("E" & i + 9)
    w2(i) = ((1 - w(i) * w(i))) ^ 0.5
Next i

'Conduct M Monte Carlo trials
For j = 1 To M
    factor = NRND()
    'Compute portfolio loss for one trial
    loss_j = 0
    For i = 1 To N
        If w(i) * factor + w2(i) * NRND() < d(i) Then
            loss_j = loss_j + LGD(i) * EAD(i)
        End If
    Next i
    loss(j) = loss_j
Next j

SORT loss
For i = 3 To 7
    Range("H" & i) = loss(Int((M+1) * Range("G" & i)))
Next i

End Sub
```

On the two-year-old laptop we are using at the time of writing, 50,000 trials take less than 5 seconds for the small portfolio with 100 obligors. With 5000 obligors and 50,000 trials, simulation time is 2 minutes and 21 seconds.

We reported the simulation time for 50,000 trials because we should not expect to get precise results if we choose considerably less. Note that looking at the overall number of trials and considering it to be 'large' can give a false sense of precision. The precision with which a percentile is estimated will be related to the expected number of simulations that are above the percentile. For the 99.95th percentile, this would be 5 if the number of trials were 10,000. Intuitively, relying on five observations is likely to be problematic.

Before we delve deeper into the relation between the number of trials and the precision of the estimates, we first consider two variations on the approach that we followed in the macro simVBA. Both variations aim at providing higher precision with fewer trials.

IMPORTANCE SAMPLING

Simulating portfolio losses in the way we did in the previous section produces a lot of more or less irrelevant trials. Risk managers are mainly concerned with extreme events, e.g., what is happening beyond the 99th percentile. However, the bulk of trials will have much smaller portfolio losses; and the distribution of losses below the target percentile level does not matter for the calculation of the percentile.

The idea of importance sampling is to adjust the simulation procedure such that we produce more trials that are important for the users of the simulation output. Since we are concerned with large losses, let us first state how such large losses can come about. Recall that default occurs if the asset value A_i drops below the default threshold, and that we modeled A_i as $w_i Z + \sqrt{1 - w_i^2}\varepsilon_i$. So there are two situations in which the number of defaults is large (they can, of course, come about at the same time):

- the factor realization Z is negative (think of the economy moving into a recession);
- the average ε_i is negative (think of many firms having individual bad luck).

The larger the number of obligors in a portfolio, and the more even the exposures distributed across obligors, the more important will be the first effect relative to the second.[3] This is due to diversification: some obligors will be lucky ($\varepsilon_i > 0$), some will not ($\varepsilon_i < 0$), and so good and bad luck tend to offset each other in the portfolio.

In the following, we therefore concentrate on how to adjust the distribution of the factor such that we have more relevant scenarios. Remember that we drew the factor from a standard normal distribution. To tilt our simulation towards scenarios with large losses, we can instead sample the factor from a normal distribution with mean $\mu < 0$, leaving the standard deviation at 1. When doing so, we have to take into account that our simulation results will be biased. When modeling correlations through the one-factor model (7.2), we assumed the factor to have a mean of zero, but now we work with a mean different from zero. There is a quick way of correcting this bias, however.

Before importance sampling, the probability of observing a trial j is just $1/M$, where M is the chosen number of trials. With importance sampling, we get the trial's probability by multiplying $1/M$ with the likelihood ratio:

$$\frac{\phi(Z_j)}{\phi(Z_j - \mu)} \tag{7.3}$$

where ϕ denotes the standard normal density, Z_j is the factor drawn in trial j, and μ is the mean of Z assumed in the importance sampling. Consider the case $Z_j = -2$ and $\mu = -1$. With $\mu = -1$, a realization of $Z_j = -2$ has a probability that is higher than the one we assumed in the modeling, and so we have to downweigh the scenario. Since the ratio (7.3) is 0.22 for these example values, this is what we achieve when applying the likelihood ratio (7.3).

When implementing importance sampling, it is useful to note that

$$\frac{\phi(Z_j)}{\phi(Z_j - \mu)} = \frac{(2\pi)^{-1/2}\exp(-Z_j^2/2)}{(2\pi)^{-1/2}\exp(-(Z_j - \mu)^2/2)} = \exp(-\mu Z_j + \mu^2/2) \tag{7.4}$$

The probability of observing the loss of trial j is therefore

$$\text{Prob}_j = \exp(-\mu Z_j + \mu^2/2)/M \tag{7.5}$$

[3] The magnitude of the asset correlation also plays a role.

Once we have a vector of simulated losses and a vector of associated likelihood ratios, we can proceed as follows. To start, sort the two vectors according to the magnitude of losses. Then, starting from the largest loss, cumulate the trial probabilities (7.5). Determine the α percentile as the maximum loss that has a cumulated probability larger than $(1 - \alpha)$.

Before implementing the importance sampling scheme through the macro simVBAis, we adjust Table 7.2 such that we can enter in cell C4 a mean μ for the factor. The changes to the previous macro simVBA are shaded in the following code:

```
Sub simVBAis()

Dim M As Long, N As Long, i As Long, j As Long, shift As Double
M = Range("c3")  'Number of simulations
N = Application.Count(Range("B10:B65536"))    'Number of loans
shift = Range("C4")  'Mean of factor in importance sampling

Dim d(), LGD() As Double, EAD() As Double, w() As Double, w2() As Double
Dim loss(), factor As Double, loss_j As Double, prob()

ReDim d(1 To N), LGD(1 To N), EAD(1 To N), w(1 To N), w2(1 To N), _
       loss(1 To M)
ReDim prob(1 To M)

'Write loan characteristics into arrays
For i = 1 To N
    d(i) = Application.NormSInv(Range("B" & i + 9))
    LGD(i) = Range("C" & i + 9)
    EAD(i) = Range("D" & i + 9)
    w(i) = Range("E" & i + 9)
    w2(i) = ((1 - w(i) * w(i))) ^ 0.5
Next i

'Conduct M Monte Carlo trials
For j = 1 To M
    factor = NRND() + shift
    prob(j) = Exp(-shift * factor + shift ^ 2 / 2) / M

    'Compute portfolio loss for one trial
    loss_j = 0
    For i = 1 To N
        If w(i) * factor + w2(i) * NRND() < d(i) Then
            loss_j = loss_j + LGD(i) * EAD(i)
        End If
    Next i
    loss(j) = loss_j
Next j

SORT2 loss, prob
'cumulate probabilities
For j = M - 1 To 1 Step -1
```

```
    prob(j) = prob(j + 1) + prob(j)
Next j

j = M
For i = 7 To 3 Step -1
    Do
        j = j - 1
    Loop Until prob(j) > 1 - Range("G" & i)
    Range("H" & i) = loss(j)
Next i

End Sub
```

Since we have to sort both the array `loss` and the array `prob` by `loss`, we need to adjust our SORT macro from the previous section such that it can sort two vectors. This is done in the macro SORT2(1st array, 2nd array, optional lower bound, optional upper bound), which sorts the two arrays according to the first one:

```
Sub SORT2(x(), x2(), Optional lower, Optional upper)
Dim a, P1, P2, tmp
If IsMissing(lower) Then lower = LBound(x)
If IsMissing(upper) Then upper = UBound(x)

'Determine partioning element
a = x((lower + upper) / 2)
P1 = lower: P2 = upper
Do
Do While (x(P1) < a): P1 = P1 + 1: Loop
Do While (x(P2) > a): P2 = P2 - 1: Loop
If P1 <= P2 Then
'exchange elements
tmp = x(P1): x(P1) = x(P2): x(P2) = tmp
tmp = x2(P1): x2(P1) = x2(P2): x2(P2) = tmp
P1 = P1 + 1: P2 = P2 - 1
End If
Loop Until (P1 > P2)
'Recursively sort subarrays
If lower < P2 Then: SORT2 x, x2, lower, P2
If P1 < upper Then: SORT2 x, x2, P1, upper
End Sub
```

The optimal choice of the shift will depend on the percentiles in which we are interested.[4] The more extreme the percentiles, the more extreme will be the optimal shift. A rule of thumb is to shift the mean to a value that is somewhat less extreme than the percentiles of the loss distribution in which one is interested. In the example calculations of this chapter, we consider a mean of $\mu = -1.5$. Under a standard normal, -1.5 is exceeded with a probability of 93.3%,

[4] See Glasserman and Li (2005) for an approach that determines the optimal shifting factor.

and so this is less extreme than the percentiles above 95% on which risk managers usually focus.

Before we examine the efficiency gain from importance sampling, let us examine another variant of standard Monte Carlo simulation.

QUASI MONTE CARLO

Due to the randomness inherent in a simulation trial, the properties of a set of simulated numbers will deviate from the distribution from which they were drawn. If we draw 10,000 factor realizations from the standard normal distribution, for example, we will typically not observe that exactly $100 = 0.01 \times 10{,}000$ factor values are below -2.326 $(=\Phi^{-1}(0.01))$. As a result, the simulated loss distribution will deviate from the true one. This problem grows larger if the number of trials becomes smaller.

A possible way of alleviating this problem is to employ quasi Monte Carlo numbers. They follow a deterministic rule[5] that is meant to produce simulated distributions very close to the specified theoretical distribution, even for small sets of random numbers. The concept is best understood by looking at an example. The Halton sequence (here with base 2) leads to the following quasi random numbers that are uniformly distributed on the unit interval:

$$\frac{1}{2}, \frac{1}{4}, \frac{3}{4}, \frac{1}{8}, \frac{5}{8}, \frac{3}{8}, \frac{7}{8}, \frac{1}{16}, \frac{9}{16}, \ldots$$

When in need of M random numbers, we would take the first M numbers of this sequence.

The Halton sequence fills the unit interval with an ever increasing fineness. This is illustrated in Figure 7.1, which shows how Halton numbers (with base 2) and a randomly chosen set of 100 uniform random numbers are distributed on the unit interval. Note that the random sample exhibits more clustering, and larger gaps between clusters.

Two things are worth noting. First, we can apply the inversion method to get standard normal numbers from the Halton numbers (which we need in our credit portfolio simulation). Second, we can produce different Halton sequences. The Halton sequence with base 3 (above we used base 2) would be

$$\frac{1}{3}, \frac{2}{3}, \frac{1}{9}, \frac{4}{9}, \frac{7}{9}, \frac{2}{9}, \ldots$$

A function for determining Halton numbers requires little code. To draw the jth element of a Halton sequence with base b, start by writing the index j as a number in the numerical system with base b. Consider index $j = 4$ for base 2. Its representation in the binary system is

$$4 = (1,0,0)_2 = 1 \cdot 2^2 + 0 \cdot 2^1 + 0 \cdot 2^0 =: (d_2\, d_1\, d_0)_2$$

[5] The random numbers produced by computers are also deterministic (which is why they are often called pseudo-random numbers); they are, however, not designed to have minimum deviation from the specified distribution.

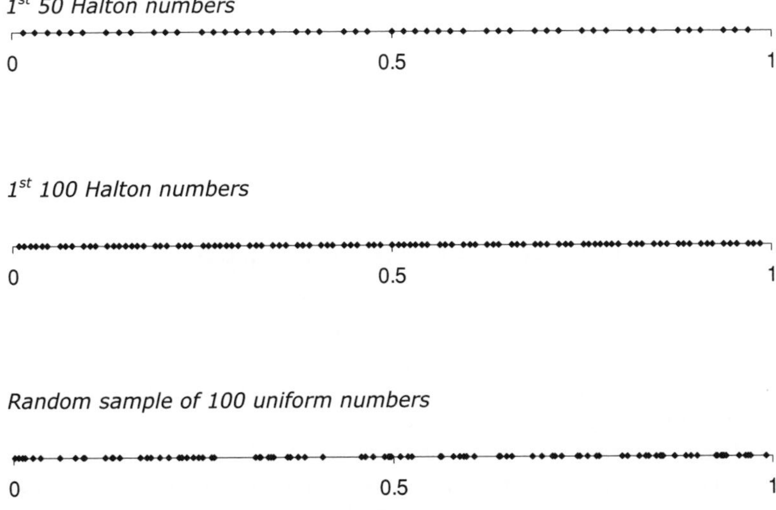

Figure 7.1 Halton numbers and a randomly chosen set of 100 uniform numbers

where the d_is are the binary digits. Now reverse the digits and put the radix point in front of the sequence:

$$(.d_0\, d_1\, d_2)_2 = \frac{0}{2^1} + \frac{0}{2^2} + \frac{1}{2^3} = \frac{1}{8}$$

to get the 4th Halton number for base 2. In the same way, we can determine the Halton number for any index j and base b.

We generate Halton numbers with the following function:

```
Function HALTON(j, base)

Dim i As Long, invbase As Double, digit As Long
invbase = 1 / base
i = j

Do While i > 0
  digit = i Mod base
  HALTON = HALTON + digit * invbase
  i = (i - digit) / base
  invbase = invbase / base
Loop

End Function
```

Having entered the do loop, we start by determining the digit d_0 through `i Mod base`, and apply the base inversion. We then loop to d_1 and so forth.

A straightforward application of quasi Monte Carlo is to draw the factor values in our importance sampling scheme from a Halton sequence. There is little we have to adjust. Just write

```
factor = Application.WorksheetFunction.NormSInv(HALTON(j, 2)) + shift
```

instead of `factor = NRND() + shift` in macro simVBAis. We have made this change in the macro simVBAisqmc.

ASSESSING SIMULATION ERROR

We now want to examine the question of how many simulations are sufficient to obtain a desired level of accuracy. Additionally, we want to determine whether modifications such as importance sampling or quasi Monte Carlo lead to significant improvements relative to standard Monte Carlo.

One way of providing answers to these questions is to conduct a simulation study (by which we mean a simulation study to examine several ways of doing Monte Carlo simulations). To assess the accuracy of a specific simulation method, follow this structure:

1. Determine the portfolio loss distribution with a large number of trials (e.g., 1,000,000) that is judged to yield sufficient accuracy.
2. Determine the portfolio loss distribution with the method under scrutiny, and a specified number of trials (e.g., 10,000). Compare the differences with respect to the results from step 1.
3. Repeat step 2 sufficiently often to get a precise estimate of the average differences.

We apply such a study to a portfolio that is more representative of a banking portfolio than the small portfolio we examined so far; the new portfolio contains 5000 obligors. The distribution of borrowers across probabilities of default (PD) is presented in Table 7.3.

The *mean* loan size is set to 1 for each grade. N_j, the number of loans contained in grade j, is then 5000 × portfolio weight$_j$. Lumpiness in exposures is modeled as follows. Within rating grade j, EAD_{ij}, the exposure of loan i is determined through

$$EAD_{ij} = i^4 N_j \Big/ \sum_{i=1}^{N_j} i^4$$

Table 7.3 Structure of example portfolio

Grade	PD (%)	Portfolio weight (%)
1	0.01	4%
2	0.05	7
3	0.10	15
4	0.20	25
5	1.00	40
6	5.00	8
7	20.0	1

Table 7.4 Testing simulation accuracy

	A	B	C	D	E	F	G	H	I	J
1	**Simulation specifications**						**Simulation results**			
2							Confidence	Loss percentile		
3	# trials		10000				90%	52.9		
4							95%	65.6		
5							99%	94.6		
6							99.90%	117.8		
7							99.95%	117.8		
8	**Portfolio**									
9	Loan	PD	LGD	EAD	w		**Saved simulation results (1000000 trials)**			
10	1	0.01%	50%	4.9381	0.3		Confidence	Loss percentile		
11	2	0.01%	50%	4.8400	0.3		90%	52.5		
12	3	0.01%	50%	4.7435	0.3		95%	66.0		
13	4	0.01%	50%	4.6484	0.3		99%	99.2		
14	5	0.01%	50%	4.5547	0.3		99.90%	151.2		
15	6	0.01%	50%	4.4625	0.3		99.95%	167.4		
16	7	0.01%	50%	4.3716	0.3					
17	8	0.01%	50%	4.2822	0.3		**Mean absolute errors for various #trials**			
18	9	0.01%	50%	4.1941	0.3			1000	5000	10000
19	10				3		90%	1.5	0.5	0.4
20	11				3		95%	2.2	1.0	0.7
21	12				3		99%	5.9	2.6	2.0
22	13				3		99.90%	15.4	11.4	7.2
23	14				3		99.95%	23.3	15.3	9.2
24	15				3					
...	...	...	...	...	...					
5009	5000	20.00%	50%	7.6E-07	0.3					

Run macro accuracy to determine mean absolute errors relative to the values in H11:H15

This rule is meant to produce a portfolio structure that is representative for commercial bank loan portfolios.[6]

We start by using the simple VBA macro simVBA to determine the loss percentiles. The number of trials is chosen to be 1,000,000 – this is step 1 from the simulation structure outlined above. In Table 7.4, we show how to do steps 2 and 3 for the standard Monte Carlo simulation method. We thus build on Table 7.2. In the range G11:H15, we have stored the results from running the macro simVBA with 1,000,000 trials before running the following macro accuracy:

```
Sub accuracy()
Dim i As Integer, j As Integer, jmax As Integer, a As Integer, abserr()
As Double

'Number of repetitions
jmax = 50
```

[6] See Gordy, M., 2003, A risk-factor model foundation for ratings-based bank capital rules, *Journal of Financial Intermediation* 12, 199–232.

```
'Loop for three settings differing in #trials
For i = 1 To 3
    Range("C3") = Cells(18, i + 7) 'get #trials from H18:J18
    ReDim abserr(1 To 5)

    'jmax Monte Carlo simulations for a specific setting
    For j = 1 To jmax
        simVBA
        'Analyze 5 different percentiles
        For a = 1 To 5
            abserr(a) = abserr(a) + Abs(Range("H" & a + 2) - _
Range("H" &
10 + a))
        Next a
    Next j
    'Write result in sheet
    For a = 1 To 5
        Cells(18 + a, 7 + i) = abserr(a) / jmax
    Next a
Next i
End Sub
```

The macro computes the mean absolute error (MAE), i.e., it returns the average absolute difference between simulated percentiles of the model under scrutiny and the percentiles obtained with 1,000,000 trials. Obtaining a precise estimate of a mean is much easier than obtaining a precise estimate of an extreme percentile. `jmax`, which specifies how often our model under scrutiny is compared to the one with 1,000,000 trials, can thus be set to a relatively low number (here we choose 50).

We examine the accuracy of the following simulation techniques with the number of trials set to 1000, 5000, or 10,000:

- standard Monte Carlo (run simVBA);
- importance sampling (IS, run simVBAis);
- importance sampling combined with Halton numbers (IS-QMC, run simVBAisqmc).

Figure 7.2 shows the MAEs in estimating the 95% and 99.9% percentiles, respectively.

Evidently, importance sampling leads to a dramatic improvement of simulation accuracy. For a given number of trials, the MAE is much lower than the one of standard Monte Carlo. Combining importance sampling with quasi Monte Carlo leads to a further improvement. With 5000 trials, for example, it results in an absolute error of 0.9 when estimating the 99.9th percentile (=151.2). In percentage terms, this is an error of less than 1%.

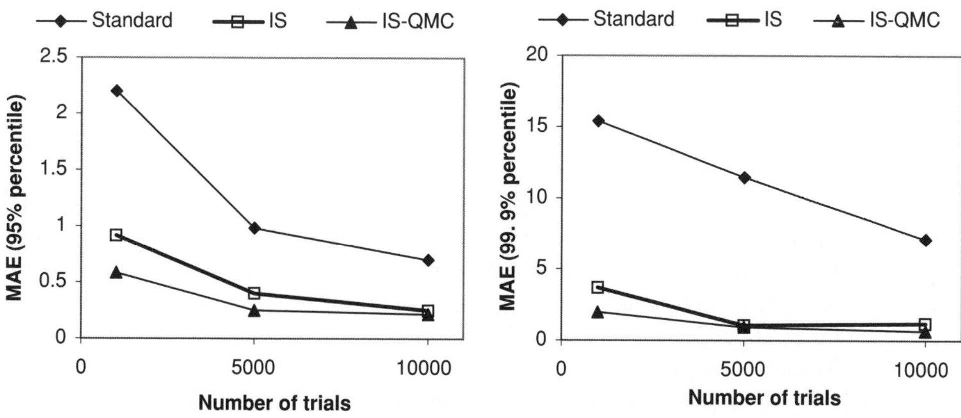

Figure 7.2 Mean absolute simulation errors (MAE)

EXPLOITING PORTFOLIO STRUCTURE IN THE VBA PROGRAM

All three variants of Monte Carlo simulation that we considered check the following condition to find out whether borrower i is in default or not:

```
w(i) * factor + w2(i) * NRND() < d(i)
```

This is the condition in which the asset value of borrower i ends up below the default point of borrower i. In our general notation, it can be written as (insert Equation (7.2) into (7.1)):

$$w_i Z + \sqrt{1 - w_i^2}\varepsilon_i \leq d_i \tag{7.6}$$

Rearranging (7.6), we obtain an equivalent condition:

$$\varepsilon_i \leq \frac{d_i - w_i Z}{\sqrt{1 - w_i^2}} \tag{7.7}$$

Now apply the cumulative normal Φ to both sides of (7.7):

$$\Phi(\varepsilon_i) \leq \Phi\left(\frac{d_i - w_i Z}{\sqrt{1 - w_i^2}}\right) \tag{7.8}$$

Since ε_i is a standard normal variable, $\Phi(\varepsilon_i)$ is uniformly distributed on the unit interval (this is the reversal of the inversion method that we repeatedly use to produce random variables). Instead of (7.6), we could thus also check:

$$u_i \leq \Phi\left(\frac{d_i - w_i Z}{\sqrt{1 - w_i^2}}\right) \tag{7.9}$$

where u_i is a uniform random variable. In the macro, (7.9) can be coded as

```
RND() < Application.Worksheetfunction.NormSDist _
          ((d(i) - w(i) * factor) / w2(i))
```

On the left-hand side, we now need just a uniform random variable RND(), which requires less time than the standard normal NRND(). On the right-hand side, however, we have to evaluate the cumulative standard normal. A little experimentation tells us that one evaluation of the cumulative normally costs more time than the time saved by using RND() instead of NRND(). But we may not have to evaluate the right-hand side as many times as we evaluate the left-hand side. The right-hand is identical for borrowers with the same default point d (i.e., the same PD) and the same factor sensitivity w. In our example portfolio, there are seven rating grades, each with uniform PD and uniform factor sensitivity. In one trial of the Monte Carlo simulations, we thus would need only seven evaluations of the standard normal. By contrast, we can exploit the advantage of RND() over NRND 5000 times (=the number of loans).

Many financial portfolios resemble our example portfolio in the fact that borrowers are grouped into rating categories with uniform PDs; the use of uniform factor sensitivities is also common. It is thus worthwhile exploring the potential savings from building the macro on condition (7.9) instead of condition (7.6). Here is an adapted version of the macro simVBA (changes are highlighted):

```
Sub simVBAgroups()

Dim M As Long, N As Long, i As Long, j As Long
M = Range("c3")   'Number of simulations
N = Application.Count(Range("B10:B65536"))    'Number of loans

Dim d() As Double, LGD() As Double, EAD() As Double, w() As Double, _
w2() As Double
Dim loss(), factor As Double, loss_j As Double, group() As Long , _
crit as Double

ReDim d(0 To N), LGD(1 To N), EAD(1 To N), w(0 To N), w2(1 To N), _
      loss(1 To M)
ReDim group(0 To N)

'Write loan characteristics into arrays
group(0) = 0
For i = 1 To N
    d(i) = Application.NormSInv(Range("B" & i + 9))
    LGD(i) = Range("C" & i + 9)
    EAD(i) = Range("D" & i + 9)
    w(i) = Range("E" & i + 9)
    w2(i) = ((1 - w(i) * w(i))) ^ 0.5
    If d(i) = d(i - 1) And w(i) = w(i - 1) Then
        group(i) = group(i - 1)
```

```
    Else
        group(i) = group(i - 1) + 1
    End If
Next i

'Conduct M Monte Carlo trials
For j = 1 To M
    factor = NRND()
    'Compute portfolio loss for one trial
    loss_j = 0

       For i = 1 To N
         If group(i) > group(i - 1) Then
             crit = Application.WorksheetFunction.NormSDist _
                    ((d(i) - w(i) * factor) / w2(i))
         End If
         If Rnd() < crit Then
             loss_j = loss_j + LGD(i) * EAD(i)
         End If
    Next i
    loss(j) = loss_j

Next j

SORT loss
For i = 3 To 7
    Range("H" & i) = loss(Int((M+1) * Range("G" & i)))
Next i

End Sub
```

We identify subsets with uniform PD and uniform factor sensitivity w through the array `group`; in doing so, it is assumed that the loan data is sorted by PD and w. Note that we changed the lower bound of the arrays `d` and `w` from 1 to 0. With this little trick, the index is not out of range if we compare, say, `w(i)` to `w(i-1)` for a value of `i` equal to 1. In the `For i=1 to N` loop containing the calculations for one Monte Carlo trial, we use an `If` statement to check whether the right-hand side of (7.9), which is denoted by `crit`, has to be evaluated or not.

If we run simVBAgroups on the example portfolio with 50,000 trials, we need 31 seconds. The macro simVBA, by contrast, requires 2 minutes and 21 seconds for the same problem. For portfolios with homogeneous subsets, one should thus consider an implementation along the lines of simVBAgroups.

Another variation also has the potential to further speed up calculations. As described in Chapter 6, individual defaults are independent conditional on the factor realization. The number of defaults within groups with uniform PD and uniform factor sensitivity thus follows a binomial distribution. We could exploit this by drawing the number of defaults from a binomial distribution instead of separately drawing each individual default. In general though, knowing the number of defaults is not sufficient to determine the portfolio loss as exposure size and LGD typically differ across loans. Allocating the simulated aggregate default occurrences to individual loans then requires additional computing time. In cases where not only PDs and factor sensitivities but also exposures and LGDs are uniform within subsets, one should consider the binomial distribution for drawing defaults.

DEALING WITH PARAMETER UNCERTAINTY

To determine portfolio credit risk, we need to estimate the parameters of our model, i.e., default probabilities, default correlations and loss given default in the case of a default-mode model. Inevitably, we will incur some errors when estimating the parameters. Analysis in Chapter 6, for example, has demonstrated the uncertainty associated with estimates of default probabilities and factor sensitivities in an asset value model.

Risk managers should be aware that uncertainty in parameter estimates can be relevant even if the estimates are correct on average. The reason is that credit risk may be nonlinearly related to our parameters. The following example illustrates the effects of parameter uncertainty. Take the portfolio from Table 7.4. There we assumed that the factor sensitivity w is 0.3. Now assume that we do not really know the true value of w. It could be 0.3, but it could also be 0.2 or 0.4. Let us use the macro simVBAis with 50,000 trials to determine the 99th and 99.9th percentiles:

	$w = 0.2$	$w = 0.3$	$w = 0.4$
99th loss percentile	69.84	99.20	137.37
99.9th loss percentile	94.40	151.20	235.78

When we increase the factor sensitivity from 0.3 to 0.4, the 99.9th percentile increases by 85.58 (=235.78 − 151.20); when we lower the factor sensitivity to 0.2 the 99.9th percentile decreases by only 56.80 (= 151.20 − 94.40). Using the middle value of 151.20 would lead to an underestimation of risk because we would ignore that an underestimation of the factor sensitivity has a larger impact than a symmetrical overestimation.

There is a simple solution to estimating portfolio risk correctly. We treat the parameter uncertainty as an additional risk factor in our simulations. Similar to the way in which we draw a random number to decide whether the factor realization is benign or not, we draw a random number to decide whether the factor sensitivity or any other parameter is benign or not. In the terminology of statistics, we implement a Bayesian approach to deal with parameter uncertainty.

We will illustrate the procedure for the example portfolio from Table 7.4. For the sake of presentation, we limit our analysis to the case in which we model only uncertainty in the factor sensitivity. We follow a parametric approach. We assume that our estimates are normally distributed around the correct value, which is motivated by the asymptotic distribution of maximum likelihood estimates.[7] Once we have specified the mean and the standard error we can draw realizations of the parameters within our simulation. In some situations, standard errors can be directly derived (see Appendix A4). In others, we may resort to simulations. For the data used in Chapter 6, for example, simulations showed that the estimates are dispersed around the true value with a standard deviation of around 6%.

[7] If the assumption is likely to lead to undesirable consequences, e.g., negative default probabilities, we could use other distributions instead of the normal.

Table 7.5 Incorporating parameter uncertainty

	A	B	C	D	E	F	G	H	I	J
1	**Simulation specifications**						**Simulation results**			
2							Confidence	Loss percentile		
3	# trials		50000				90%	51.663		
4	factor mean (for IS)		-1.5				95%	65.474		
5							99%	103.059		
6							99.90%	173.302		
7							99.95%	200.505		
8	**Portfolio**									
9	Loan	PD	LGD	EAD	w	σ(w)				
10	1	0.01%	50%	4.9381	0.3	0.06	Run macro simVBAisError to determine loss percentiles			
11	2	0.01%	50%	4.8400	0.3	0.06				
12	3	0.01%	50%	4.7435	0.3	0.06				
13	4	0.01%	50%	4.6484	0.3	0.06				
14	5	0.01%	50%	4.5547	0.3	0.06				
15	6	0.01%	50%	4.4625	0.3	0.06				
...	...	...	...	...	...	...				
5009	5000	20.00%	50%	7.6E-07	0.3	0.06				

In order to specify the uncertainty for the factor sensitivity, we add another column in which we specify the standard error of the estimate, $\sigma(w)$. This is shown in Table 7.5. In the implementation, we assume that errors in the factor sensitivity are perfectly correlated. This is a sensible assumption given that we assume uniform factor sensitivities both during estimation and in portfolio modeling. We then adapt the importance sampling macro SimVBAis such that it takes estimation error in factor sensitivities into account.

Of course, we need to declare any new variables that we use. Apart from that, the following highlighted changes are necessary:

```
...

'Write loan characteristics into arrays
For i = 1 To N
    d(i) = Application.NormSInv(Range("B" & i + 9))
    LGD(i) = Range("C" & i + 9)
    EAD(i) = Range("D" & i + 9)
    w(i) = Range("E" & i + 9)
    s(i) = Range("F" & i + 9)

Next i

'Conduct M Monte Carlo trials
For j = 1 To M
    factor = NRND() + shift
    wrand = NRND()
    prob(j) = Exp(-shift * factor + shift ^ 2 / 2) / M
```

```
    'Compute portfolio loss for one trial
    loss_j = 0
    For i = 1 To N
        werror = w(i) + s(i) * wrand
        If werror * factor + ((1 - werror ^ 2)) ^ 0.5 * NRND() < d(i)
Then
            loss_j = loss_j + LGD(i) * EAD(i)
        End If
    Next i
    loss(j) = loss_j
Next j
...
```

We write the assumed standard error into the variable `s()`. For one trial `j`, we generate a standard normal random variable `wrand`. By adjusting factor sensitivities through `w(i) + s(i) * wrand`, we introduce an estimation error that is perfectly correlated across obligors, and whose size is determined by the standard error assumed in the sheet. We modify the condition through which we check default such that the factor sensitivities `werror` are used, and we are done. Since we have introduced an additional risk factor, we should again check whether the number of trials that we use is adequate. Such a check can be performed similar to the one performed in the previous section.

With the assumed estimation error, the 99.9th percentile is around 15% larger than the one obtained with the standard approach, in which estimation error is ignored. This shows that the effects of parameter uncertainty can be substantial.

Note that the procedure we have implemented differs from a typical stress scenario analysis. In such an analysis, one determines risk under specific, adverse parameter constellations. The risk figures determined in Table 7.5, by contrast, are obtained by averaging over all possible parameter constellations. Provided that the impact of estimation error is significant, they should be used instead of naïve estimates that ignore parameter uncertainty.

Extending the analysis to the case in which several parameters are subject to estimation error is straightforward. In the estimation setup from Chapter 6, for example, the simulation analysis also leads to estimates of the precision of default probability estimates; in addition, we can determine how simulated estimates of the default probability and simulated estimates of the factor sensitivity are correlated. In the portfolio risk model, we would then draw correlated realizations of default probabilities and factor sensitivities.[8]

EXTENSIONS

First extension: Multi-factor model

The one-factor model that we used is widely used in practice and seems adequate for many portfolios. In some situations, however, dependence may be richer than what can be described through a one-factor model. In an international portfolio, for example, it may be necessary to allow within-country correlations to be larger than across-country correlations.

[8] In Excel, we can draw correlated random numbers using the Cholesky matrix. See Chapter 11 for an application of the Cholesky matrix.

In a model with K factors, the asset value of obligor i is modeled as

$$A_i = \sum_{k=1}^{K} w_{ik} Z_k + \sqrt{1 - \left(\sum_{k=1}^{K} w_{ik}^2 \right)} \varepsilon_i \tag{7.10}$$

In addition to the assumptions that we made above (see Equation (7.2)), we also assume the factors Z_k to be independent.

To implement such a model, we first need to specify as many factor sensitivities as there are factors. In Table 7.2, we could record them to the right of column E.

In the VBA program, we would draw not just one factor, but K factors, and we would adjust the scenarios for individual asset values according to (7.10).

When performing importance sampling of the factors, we can shift each factor and then apply the following likelihood ratio to correct the probability weight of a trial j:

$$\exp(-\boldsymbol{\mu}'\mathbf{Z}^{(j)} + \boldsymbol{\mu}'\boldsymbol{\mu}/2) \tag{7.11}$$

where the vector $\boldsymbol{\mu}$ collects the means of the factors ($\boldsymbol{\mu}'$ is the transpose of $\boldsymbol{\mu}$) and the vector $\mathbf{Z}^{(j)}$ collects the realized factor values for trial j.

When using the Halton sequence to generate quasi-random numbers, we would use different prime numbers as bases of the sequences from which we draw the K factors. There is a caveat. We need independent factor realizations but Halton sequences exhibit dependencies when the number of dimensions (here K) is large. Therefore, care should be taken when the number of factors K is larger than five.

Second extension: *t*-distributed asset values

Following industry practice, we have assumed that asset values are normally distributed. Equivalently, we could say that we modeled default correlation through a normal or Gaussian copula.[9] For a given correlation assumption, other distributional assumptions (i.e., other copulas) can imply different portfolio loss distributions. In the following, we therefore show how to implement an alternative often considered: the multivariate t-distribution.

A multivariate t-distribution with df degrees of freedom is obtained when multivariate standard normal variables X_i are divided by a chi-squared variable Y with df degrees of freedom:

$$t_i = X_i / \sqrt{Y/df}; \; X_i \sim N(0,1), \; Y \sim \chi^2(df) \tag{7.12}$$

Applied to our case, implementation steps are as follows: we determine the X_i according to the one-factor model (7.2) and then divide by $\sqrt{Y/df}$ to get t-distributed asset values. For small df, this can dramatically increase default correlations. To see why this is so, recall that default occurs once the asset value (here represented by t_i) falls below some threshold. Consider what happens if Y/df is found to be smaller than 1. As each X_i is divided by the same $\sqrt{Y/df}$,

[9] A copula is a multivariate distribution with the property that its marginal distributions are standard uniform. It can be used to describe the dependence between random variables.

this makes the asset values of all obligors more extreme, thus increasing the probability of observing many defaults.

Our previous approach requires little adaptation. As before, we use the factor model (7.2) to generate correlated standard normal asset values. To transform them into t-distributed variables, we just add a step in which the simulated asset values are divided by a chi-squared random variable. We also have to adjust the default points $d_{i;}$; instead of using the inverse of the standard normal, we apply the inverse of a t-distribution with df degrees of freedom. The Excel function TINV(α, df) returns the critical t-value for a two-sided test at significance α. TINV(0.05, 1000), for example, returns 1.96. To get a d_i such that Prob($t < d_i$) = PD$_i$ we apply –TINV(PD$_i$*2, df). A chi-squared variable can be drawn with the inversion method: =CHIINV(RAND(), df).

We implement the t-copula in the macro simVBAt, highlighting the changes that we make relative to the macro simVBA (the degrees of freedom are stated in cell C4 of the spreadsheet; `tadjust` is $\sqrt{Y/df}$):

```
Sub simVBAt()

Dim M As Long, N As Long, i As Long, j As Long, df As Long
M = Range("c3")  'Number of simulations
N = Application.Count(Range("B10:B65536"))    'Number of loans
df = Range("C4")

Dim d(), LGD() As Double, EAD() As Double, w() As Double, w2() As Double
Dim loss(), factor As Double, loss_j As Double, tadjust As Double

ReDim d(1 To N), LGD(1 To N), EAD(1 To N), w(1 To N), w2(1 To N), _
       loss(1 To M)

'Write loan characteristics into arrays
For i = 1 To N
    d(i) = -Application.WorksheetFunction.TInv(Range("B" & i + 9) * 2, _
           df)
    LGD(i) = Range("C" & i + 9)
    EAD(i) = Range("D" & i + 9)
    w(i) = Range("E" & i + 9)
    w2(i) = ((1 - w(i) * w(i))) ^ 0.5
Next i
'Conduct M Monte Carlo trials
For j = 1 To M
    factor = nrnd()
    tadjust = (Application.WorksheetFunction.ChiInv(Rnd, df) / df) ^ 0.5
    'Compute portfolio loss for one trial
    loss_j = 0
    For i = 1 To N
        If (w(i) * factor + w2(i) * nrnd()) / tadjust < d(i) Then
            loss_j = loss_j + LGD(i) * EAD(i)
        End If
    Next i
```

Table 7.6 Characteristics of loss given default (LGD)

Asset class	Mean LGD	Standard deviation of LGD
Bank Debt	0.225	0.309
Senior Secured Bonds	0.380	0.333
Senior Unsecured Bonds	0.574	0.348
Senior Subordinated Bonds	0.697	0.333
Subordinated Bonds	0.708	0.342
Junior Subordinated Bonds	0.809	0.306

Note: Own calculations based on Standard & Poor's (2006), Table 17

```
    loss(j) = loss_j
Next j

Sort loss
For i = 3 To 7
    Range("h" & i) = loss(Int((M+1) * Range("g" & i)))
Next i
End Sub
```

Third extension: Random LGDs

So far, we have assumed loss given default (LGD) to be equal to the values we specified in the spreadsheet. Effectively, this means that we have perfect foresight of future LGD's, which clearly is not the case.

A look at empirical data (Table 7.6) on LGDs may serve to clarify the issue.

If we fix an instrument's LGD at the mean observed in the same asset class (e.g., bank debt), we capture only variation across asset classes. We do not capture the substantial variation within asset classes that manifests itself in the high standard deviations of empirical LGDs. To model this risk, we can assume that LGDs follow some parametric distribution, the parameters of which are calibrated to the observed data.

A good candidate for this choice is the beta distribution. It is a two-parameter distribution bounded between 0 and 1 that is fully specified once we have determined its mean and standard deviation.

The density of the beta distribution is

$$\beta(a, b, x) = \frac{\Gamma(a+b)}{\Gamma(a)\Gamma(b)} x^{a-1}(1-x)^{b-1}, \quad 0 < x < 1 \tag{7.13}$$

where Γ denotes the Gamma function. The expectation and variance of a beta-distributed variable Y are given by

$$E[Y] = \frac{a}{a+b} \tag{7.14}$$

$$\text{var}[Y] = \frac{ab}{(a+b)^2(a+b+1)} \tag{7.15}$$

Having determined estimates for the expectation and the variance, we can solve (7.14) and (7.15) to calibrate the parameters a and b:

$$a = \frac{E[Y]}{\mathrm{var}(Y)}(E[Y](1 - E[Y]) - \mathrm{var}[Y]) \tag{7.16}$$

$$b = \frac{1 - E[Y]}{\mathrm{var}(Y)}(E[Y](1 - E[Y]) - \mathrm{var}[Y]) \tag{7.17}$$

In credit portfolio modeling, we would calibrate a and b to our estimates of the LGD's mean and variance; these estimates can be based on empirical data, as shown above. If a default occurs within a Monte Carlo simulation, we would then draw a random variable that follows a beta distribution with the specified a and b. In Excel, this can be done with the inversion method. In the spreadsheet, we can use

$$= \mathrm{BETAINV}(\mathrm{RAND}(), a, b)$$

to draw a variable distributed beta with parameters a and b. In VBA, we can call BETAINV through

```
application.worksheetfunction.BETAINV().
```

Table 7.7 exemplifies the calculations for the asset class bank debt. In cells B6 and B7 we use (7.16) and (7.17) to calibrate the parameters of the beta distribution to the empirical mean and standard deviation of bank debt LGDs.

For illustrational purposes, we also plot the density associated with the chosen values. Excel does not provide a function for the Gamma function itself, but there is a function GAMMALN(x) that returns the logarithm of $\Gamma(x)$, which allows us to compute the density (7.13).

At first sight, the shape of the density may appear somewhat odd but it conforms nicely to the empirical frequency distribution of bank debt LGDs as shown, for example, in Gupton, Finger and Bhatia (1997, Chart 7.1).

With the approach just described, we can capture specific LGD risk, i.e., the risk that the LGD of a specific issuer deviates from the mean LGD in its asset class. There is, however, evidence that LGD varies systematically with the business cycle. In periods of high default rates, LGDs tend to be high, and vice versa. This is exemplified in Table 7.8, which plots the annual average LGDs of senior secured bonds against the average bond default rate.[10] The chart is a *xy* (scatter) chart. To add a trend line and the R^2 of the associated linear regression,[11] select the data series, right-click the mouse and choose *Add Trendline*; then select *Linear* on the Type tab and *Display R-squared value on chart* on the Options tab (Excel 2003); starting with Excel 2007, you get an overview of all trendline options after having chosen *Add Trendline.* The R^2 between default rates and LGDs is 0.4463; the correlation between the two is thus $0.4463^{0.5} = 0.6680$.

In the Monte Carlo simulation, we could incorporate systematic LGD risk by making the parameters of the LGD distribution depend on the factor realization Z. We refrain from detailing such an approach here and refer the interested reader to the literature.[12]

[10] Data are taken from Moody's (2006), Exhibit 29 and Exhibit 30.

[11] See Appendix A4 for details on regressions and R^2.

[12] For example, Giese, G., 2005, The impact of PD/LGD correlations on credit risk capital. *RISK*. April, 79–84.

Table 7.7 Calibrating a beta distribution to the historical mean and standard deviation of LGDs

	A	B	C	D	E	F	G
1	**LGD data**						
2		Mean	Standard deviation				
3	Bank debt	0.225	0.309				
4							
5	**Calibrated beta distribution**						
6	a	0.186	=B3/C3^2*(B3*(1-B3)-C3^2)				
7	b	0.640	=(1-B3)/C3^2*(B3*(1-B3)-C3^2)				
8							
9	LGD	Density					
10	0.01	6.958	=EXP(GAMMALN(B$6+B$7)-GAMMALN(B$6)-GAMMALN(B$7))*A10^(B$6-1)*(1-A10)^(B$7-1)				
11	0.05	1.905	*(can be copied into B11:B30)*				
12	0.1	1.105					
13	0.15	0.811					
14	0.2	0.656					
15	0.25	0.560					
16	0.3	0.494					
17	0.35	0.448					
18	0.4	0.414					
19	0.45	0.388					
20	0.5	0.368					
21	0.55	0.354					
22	0.6	0.344					
23	0.65	0.338					
24	0.7	0.336					
25	0.75	0.340					
26	0.8	0.349					
27	0.85	0.369					
28	0.9	0.407					
29	0.95	0.500					
30	0.99	0.862					

Fourth extension: Other risk measures

Measuring credit portfolio risk through percentiles is intuitive, and very widespread in the financial industry. The commonly used term is Value at Risk (VaR): VaR(α), the VaR at confidence α, is the α percentile of the loss distribution.[13]

However, we should be aware that a percentile does not tell us anything about the distribution of losses beyond the percentile. Also, the use of percentiles can have additional drawbacks. When combining two portfolios, for example, the VaR of the new portfolio could exceed the sum of the two individual VaRs – something that runs against the logic of diversification.

[13] Value at Risk is sometimes also defined as the percentile of the portfolio loss distribution minus the expected portfolio loss.

Table 7.8 Evidence for systematic risk in LGDs

	A	B	C	D	E	F	G
1	**Corporate default rates and LGD of senior unsecured bonds**						
2	Year	Default rate	LGD				
3	1982	1.04%	64.21%				
4	1983	0.97%	47.28%				
5	1984	0.93%	50.59%				
6	1985	0.95%	39.84%				
7	1986	1.86%	48.90%				
8	19						
9	19						
10	19						
11	19						
12	19						
13	19						
14	19						
15	19						
16	19						
17	19						
18	19						
19	19						
20	19						
21	20						
22	20						
23	20						
24	2003	1.80%	58.13%				
25	2004	0.86%	47.91%				
26	2005	0.68%	45.12%				
27	2006	0.66%	44.98%				
28	2007	0.37%	46.75%				
29	2008	2.02%	66.20%				

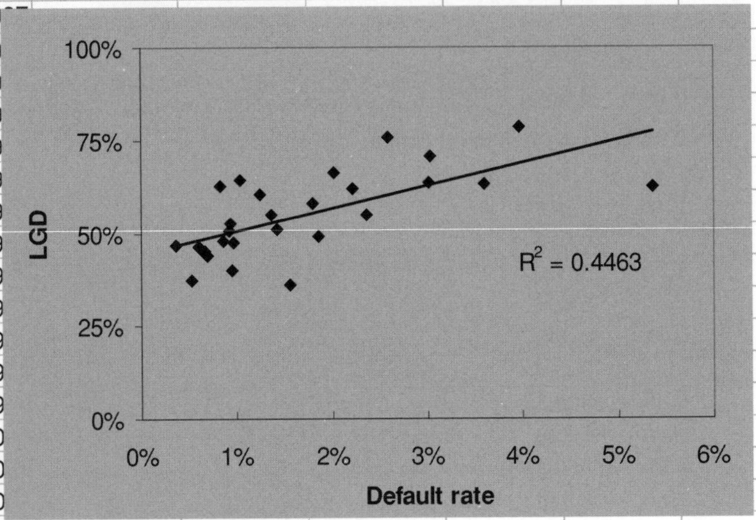

An often-considered alternative to VaR is expected shortfall (ES, also called expected tail loss, or conditional value at risk). It is the expected loss conditional on the portfolio loss being larger than the VaR for a chosen confidence α:

$$\mathrm{ES} = \mathrm{E}[\mathrm{loss}|\mathrm{loss} \geq \mathrm{VaR}(\alpha)] \tag{7.18}$$

With M simulated loss scenarios, the expected shortfall can be computed as (j denotes one portfolio scenario):

$$\mathrm{ES} = \frac{\sum_{j=1}^{M} \mathrm{Prob}(j)\mathrm{loss}(j)\mathrm{I}\{\mathrm{loss}(j) \geq \mathrm{Var}(\alpha)\}}{\mathrm{Prob}(\mathrm{loss} \geq \mathrm{VaR}(\alpha))} \tag{7.19}$$

where I{loss(j) $\geq$ VaR(α)} takes the value 1 if loss(j) is larger than the α VaR and 0 otherwise. In the following, we show how to change the importance sampling macro such that it produces expected shortfall figures. After the line `SORT2 loss, prob` we replace the code in simVBAis as follows:

```
Dim cwloss
ReDim cwloss(1 To M)

'cumulate probability-weighted losses and probabilities
For j = M - 1 To 1 Step -1
    cwloss(j) = cwloss(j + 1) + loss(j) * prob(j)
    prob(j) = prob(j + 1) + prob(j)
Next j

j = M
For i = 7 To 3 Step -1
    Do
        j = j - 1
    Loop Until prob(j) > 1 - Range("G" & i)
    Range("H" & i) = loss(j)  'Value at Risk
    Range("I" & i) = cwloss(j) / prob(j)   'Expected Shortfall
Next i
```

We first introduce the variable `cwloss`, which cumulates `loss(j)*prob(j)`, starting with the biggest loss. We do not evaluate the indicator variable in (7.19) because we can achieve the same result by restricting the summation to those losses that are above the VaR. This restriction is imposed in the second loop. As before, we return results for the five specified confidence levels, starting with the highest confidence level. Finally, we divide by the cumulated probability contained in the array Prob(j), which corresponds to dividing by Prob(loss $\geq$ VaR(α)) in (7.19).

Table 7.9 shows the results for the example portfolio.

Fifth extension: Multi-state modeling

In a multi-state model, we do not constrain the possible credit events to just two, default or no default; we also model changes in credit quality along with their effects on the market value of the instruments in the portfolio (this is why multi-state models are also called mark-to-market models).

A straightforward way of modeling changes in credit quality is to assign borrowers to certain rating categories and allow transitions from one category to another. The implementation can follow the simulation-based asset-value approach used throughout this chapter. In addition to default probabilities, we then have to specify transition probabilities (see Chapter 3), i.e., probabilities of migrating from one rating category to another. To determine the value associated with some scenario rating, we can use assumptions about rating-specific yield spreads.

We do not spell out here a complete implementation of a multi-state model, but instead just comment on one technicality that has to be solved in the course of the Monte Carlo simulation:

Table 7.9 Expected shortfall with importance sampling

	A	B	C	D	E	F	G	H	I	J
1	**Simulation specifications**						**Simulation results**			
2							Confidence	Loss percentile	Expected Shortfall	
3	# trials		10000				90%	52.8	72.7	
4	factor shift		-1.5				95%	66.4	86.5	
5							99%	98.4	120.9	
6							99.90%	150.7	175.9	
7							99.95%	168.2	192.8	
8	**Portfolio**									
9	Loan	PD	LGD	EAD	w					
10	1	0.01%	50%	4.9381	0.3		Run macro simVBAises to produce the output in H3:I7			
11	2	0.01%	50%	4.8400	0.3					
12	3	0.01%	50%	4.7435	0.3					
...	...	...	...	...	...					
5009	5000	20.00%	50%	7.6E-07	0.3					

how to find the scenario rating associated with a scenario asset value.[14] Assume that we have seven rating categories, and that we collect transition probabilities in the matrix shown in Table 7.10. We now have to define thresholds that allow us to associate a rating with the asset value that we draw in the course of the simulation. Note that we will have a set of thresholds for each initial rating. For the sake of presentation, we refrain from indexing the initial rating in the following; the description is thus to be read as pertaining to one specific initial rating.

As before, we determine the default threshold d by taking the inverse standard normal of the default probability. Next, we define $d(7)$, the threshold for rating category seven. We record a transition to category 7 if the asset value A_i ends up between $d(7)$ and d. We then have:

$$\text{Prob(Transition to 7)} = \text{Prob}(d(7) > A_i \geq d) = \Phi[d(7)] - \Phi[d] \tag{7.20}$$

We can solve for $d(7)$ to get

$$d(7) = \Phi^{-1}[\text{Prob(Transition to 7)} + \Phi(d)] \tag{7.21}$$

In general, thresholds for transitions to grade k are determined as follows: apply the inverse cumulative normal to the cumulative probability of moving into grade k or a lower grade (including default).

In the spreadsheet, this can be implemented as shown in Table 7.10. For the best rating, the rule leads to $\Phi^{-1}(1)$, which is infinity; accordingly, Excel would return an error value. For the rating look-up that we will do in the following, it is convenient to replace infinity by a large number, say 100,000.

Looking up the new rating comprises two steps:

1. Select the appropriate row in the threshold matrix. If an obligor has current rating 3, for example, the relevant thresholds are in the row headed by 3.
2. Find the column in which the threshold first exceeds the scenario asset value.

[14] In Chapter 4, we also represented transitions by means of a standard normal variable. Some practical problems that arise in this context are discussed in Chapter 4.

Table 7.10 From scenario asset values to scenario ratings

	A	B	C	D	E	F	G	H	I
1	**Transition probabilities (in %)**								
2					To				
3	From	1	2	3	4	5	6	7	D
4	1	91.386	7.947	0.508	0.093	0.062	0.001	0.001	0.001
5	2	0.603	90.650	7.936	0.604	0.062	0.114	0.020	0.010
6	3	0.052	1.991	90.427	6.858	0.440	0.157	0.032	0.041
7	4	0.021	0.171	4.112	89.854	4.561	0.812	0.182	0.288
8	5	0.033	0.044	0.276	5.799	83.508	8.114	0.992	1.235
9	6	0.001	0.001	0.215	0.351	6.249	82.326	4.766	6.091
10	7	0.001	0.001	0.322	0.472	1.426	13.560	54.139	30.079
11									
12	**Transition thresholds**								
13		1	2	3	4	5	6	7	D
14	1	100000	-1.36	-2.48	-2.95	-3.22	-4.01	-4.11	-4.26
15	2	100000	2.51	-1.36	-2.40	-2.87	-2.98	-3.43	-3.71
16	3	100000	3.28	2.04	-1.44	-2.47	-2.83	-3.18	-3.35
17	4	100000	3.52	2.89	1.72	-1.57	-2.23	-2.60	-2.76
18	5	100000	3.41	3.17	2.69	1.54	-1.26	-2.01	-2.25
19	6	100000	4.26	4.11	2.85	2.53	1.49	-1.23	-1.55
20	7	100000	4.26	4.11	2.72	2.41	2.01	1.00	-0.52
21		=100000	C20: =NORMSINV(SUM(C10:$I10)/100)						
22			*(can be copied into C14:I20)*						
23									
24	**How to associate a scenario asset value A_i with a rating**								
25		Current rating	Asset value A_i	Scenario rating					
26		5	2.61	4	=MATCH(C26,OFFSET(B$13:I$13,B26,0),-1)				

Step 2 can be done with the function MATCH (*lookup_value,lookup_array,match_type*). Our *look-up_value* is the asset value; the *lookup_array* is the threshold matrix; *match_type* is set to –1 because this tells MATCH to find the smallest value that is greater than or equal to *lookup_value*. MATCH then returns the position of this value within the *lookup_array*; according to the way we have set up the matrix, this position number is already the rating number that we are looking for.

To select the appropriate row, we use the function OFFSET to shift the *lookup_array* according to the current rating.

NOTES AND LITERATURE

Although we focused on efficient simulation techniques, we have not exploited all possible ways of improvement. For example, we have not shown how to do importance sampling on individual defaults (see Glasserman and Li, 2005).

The pathbreaking industry credit portfolio models are described in the following: CSFP, 1997, *CreditRisk+: A Credit Risk Management Framework*, Credit Suisse Financial Products; Gupton, G.M., Finger, C.C. and Bhatia, M., 1997, *CreditMetrics – Technical Document*, RiskMetrics Group; Kealhofer S. and Bohn, J., 2003, *Portfolio management of default risk*, KMV White Paper; Wilson, T., 1997a, Portfolio credit risk I. *Risk*, 10(9), 111–117; and Wilson, T., 1997b, Portfolio credit risk II. *Risk*, 10(9), 56–61.

For an overview and analysis of different modeling approaches, see Crouhy, M., Galai, D. and Mark, R., 2000, A comparative analysis of current credit risk models, *Journal of Banking and Finance* 24, 59–117; Gordy, M., 2000, A comparative anatomy of credit risk models, *Journal of Banking and Finance* 24, 119–149; and Frey, R. and McNeil, A., 2003, Dependent defaults in models of portfolio credit risk, *Journal of Risk* 6, 59–92.

Importance sampling techniques are discussed in Glasserman, P., and Li, J., 2005, Importance sampling for portfolio credit risk, *Management Science* 51, 1643–1656. Details on (quasi) random number generation can be found in many textbooks, e.g., Seydel R., 2003, *Tools for Computational Finance*, second edition, Springer.

The Bayesian approach for dealing with parameter uncertainty is used in Löffler, G., 2003, The effects of estimation error on portfolio credit risk, *Journal of Banking and Finance* 27, 1427–1453, and Tarashev, N., 2010, Measuring portfolio credit risk correctly: Why parameter uncertainty matters, *Journal of Banking and Finance*, 34, 2065–2076.

8

Validation of Rating Systems

Having set up a rating system, it is natural that one wants to assess its quality. There are two dimensions along which ratings are commonly assessed: discrimination and calibration. In checking discrimination, we ask: *How well does a rating system rank borrowers according to their true probability of default (PD)?* When examining calibration we ask: *How well do estimated PDs match true PDs?*

The following example illustrates that the two dimensions capture different aspects of rating quality:

Borrower	Rating of system 1 (associated PD)	PD of System 2 (%)	True PD (%)
B1	A (1%)	2.01	1.5
B2	B (5%)	2.00	2.0
B3	C (20%)	1.99	2.5

Rating system 1 might represent an agency rating system, with A being the best rating. An agency rating itself is not a PD but can be associated with PDs based on average historical default rates per rating class (see Chapter 3). Rating system 2 might be based on a statistical credit scoring model (see Chapter 1) which directly produces PD estimates. The rank ordering of system 1 is perfect, but the PDs differ dramatically from the true ones. By contrast, the average PD of rating system 2 exactly matches the average true PD, and individual deviations from the average PD are small. However, it does not discriminate at all because the system's PDs are inversely related to the true PDs.

The literature has proposed various methods that test for discrimination, calibration or both. There are several reasons why one would want to test for only one aspect of rating quality even though this cannot give a complete picture. Here are just two possible reasons. First, some rating systems do not produce default probabilities, and so it is not possible to test calibration without imposing default probability estimates. Second, some uses of ratings do not necessarily require default probabilities, for example, when banks use ratings solely to decide whether a client receives a loan or not.

In this chapter, we introduce methods for evaluating discriminatory power (cumulative accuracy profiles and receiver operating characteristics), both discrimination and calibration (Brier score) or just calibration (Binomial test and a test allowing for default correlation). Contrary to what was assumed in the example given above, true default probabilities cannot be observed in practice. The presented evaluation methods therefore rest on a comparison of predicted default risk with actual, observed default occurrence. We conclude with a discussion on how to structure the validation of a rating system and how to check for missing information.

CUMULATIVE ACCURACY PROFILE AND ACCURACY RATIOS

The cumulative accuracy profile (CAP) provides a way of visualizing discriminatory power. The key idea is the following: if a rating system discriminates well, defaults should occur mainly among borrowers with a bad rating.

To graph a CAP, one needs historical data on ratings and default behavior. The latter would, for example, record whether a borrower defaulted in the year subsequent to having received a certain rating. Observations belonging to a rating category that contains borrowers already in default would be excluded.

The CAP is constructed by plotting the fraction of all defaults that occurred among borrowers rated *x* or worse against the fraction of all borrowers that are rated *x* or worse. In Table 8.1, we look at a simple example to understand this definition.

We start with the worst rating C, asking 'what is the fraction of all defaults that we cover when we include all borrowers rated C (or worse, but there is no worse rating)?' Forty percent of all observations are rated C, the three defaults that occurred among C-rated borrowers making up 75% of all defaults. This gives us the first point of the curve (0.4, 0.75). Similarly, 70% of all observations are rated B or worse, while borrowers with a rating of B or worse cover 100% of all defaulters. This yields the second point (0.7, 1.0). The final point is always (1, 1) because if we look at all observations (here rating A or worse) we will, by construction, include all observations and all defaults. We then let the profile start at the origin (0, 0) and connect the data points.

An accuracy ratio condenses the information contained in CAP curves into a single number. It can be obtained by relating the area under the CAP but above the diagonal to the maximum

Table 8.1 Illustration of the cumulative accuracy profile (CAP)

	A	B	C	D	E	F
1	Rating and default data				CAP points	
2	Obser-vation	Rating (A is best)	Default (Yes=1)		Observations included (x-axis)	Defaults included (y-axis)
3	1	A	0		0.40	0.75
4	2	A	0		0.70	1.00
5	3	A	0		1.00	1.00
6	4	B	1			
7	5	B	0			
8	6	B	0			
9	7	C	1			
10	8	C	1			
11	9	C	1			
12	10	C	0			
13						
14						
15						
16						
17						

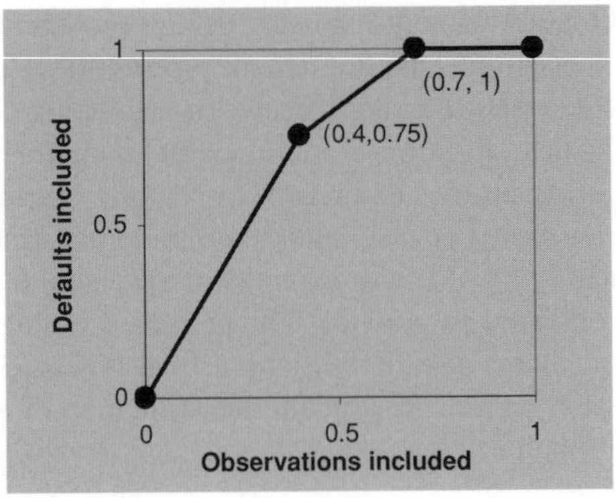

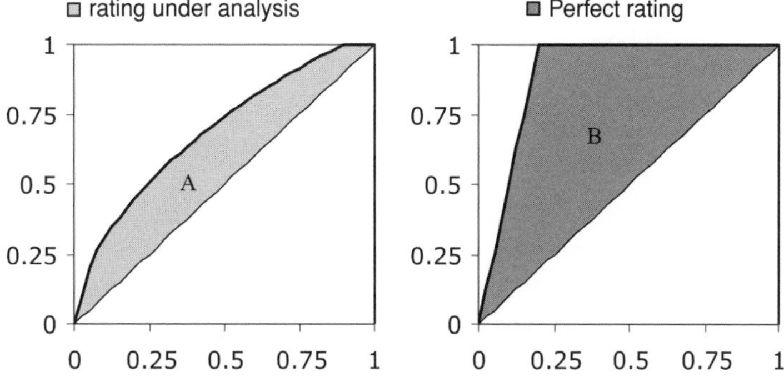

Figure 8.1 Computation of accuracy ratio as *A/B*

area the CAP can enclose above the diagonal. Thus, the maximum accuracy ratio is 1. One restricts the analysis to the area above the diagonal because the latter gives the expected CAP curve of an uninformative rating system which does not discriminate at all between low and high risks. To note why this is so, just read a diagonal CAP curve as follows: for every fraction of all borrowers that you pick, you get the same fraction of all defaults. Thus, the rank ordering of the rating does not contain any information about the rank ordering according to default risk. The maximum area under the CAP curve, by contrast, will be obtained if the lowest rating category contains all defaulters, and only those.

Figure 8.1 demonstrates the calculation of accuracy ratios: we compute the accuracy ratio as *A/B*, where A is the area pertaining to the rating system under analysis, and B is the one pertaining to the 'perfect' rating system.

Theoretically, accuracy ratios can lie in the range of [–1, 1]. For a rating system to have any value, the accuracy ratio should be above zero, because otherwise one should replace it with a system that assigns ratings by chance. If a rating system perfectly ranks debtors according to their true default probability, it will nevertheless fail to achieve an accuracy ratio of 1 except for some rare situations. To see why this is so, imagine a portfolio consisting of two groups of borrowers, one with a default probability of 5% and the other with a default probability of 0.1%. If one correctly assigns debtors to these two groups, the worst rating category with default probability of 5% will contain many non-defaulters, while the better category may contain some defaulters. Both are features that the 'perfect' rating system does not have. When making a probabilistic forecast, the best one can hope to achieve in practice is to get the probabilities right; one cannot foresee what will actually happen. If you throw two dice, you should expect a forecaster to know that the probability of a 1 is one-sixth for each dice. You should not expect the forecaster to know which of the dice will return a 1 and which not.

The video on the CD shows you how to construct a CAP in a spreadsheet using only standard Excel functions. Although this way of doing the analysis is very illustrative without taking too much time, it involves several steps that have to be repeated whenever analyzing a new data set.

We therefore present a user-defined Excel function that automates the analysis. It produces the points of the CAP curve and computes the accuracy ratio. Assume that you arranged data on ratings and defaults as above, i.e., into two arrays. Also sort the data from the worst rating category to the best. The function refers to these data arrays as `ratings` and `defaults`, respectively. It reads as follows:

```
Function CAP(ratings, defaults)
'Function written for data sorted from worst rating to best

Dim N As Long, K As Long, numdef As Long, a As Integer, i As Long
Dim xi As Double, yi As Double, xy(), area As Double

N = Application.WorksheetFunction.Count(defaults)
numdef = Application.WorksheetFunction.Sum(defaults)

'Determine number of rating categories K
K = 1
For i = 2 To N
  If ratings(i) <> ratings(i - 1) Then K = K + 1
Next i
ReDim xy(1 To K + 2, 1 To 2)

'First row of function reserved for accuracy ratio, 2nd is origin (0,0),
'so start with row a=3
a = 3

For i = 1 To N

  'Cumulative fraction of observations(xi) and defaults(yi)
  xi = xi + 1 / N
  yi = yi + defaults(i) / numdef

  'Determine CAP points and area below CAP
  If ratings(i) <> ratings(i + IIf(i = N, 0, 1)) Or i = N Then
    xy(a, 1) = xi
    xy(a, 2) = yi
      area = area + (xy(a, 1) - xy(a - 1, 1)) * (xy(a - 1, 2) _
                 + xy(a, 2)) / 2  a = a + 1
  End If
Next i

'Accuracy ratio
xy(1, 1) = (area - 0.5) / ((1 - numdef / N / 2) - 0.5)
xy(1, 2) = "(Accrat)"
CAP = xy

End Function
```

After defining the function and its input, we determine the number of observations `N` by counting the rows of the input range; we determine the number of defaults `numdef` by summing over the default indicator variable; and we loop through the data to determine the

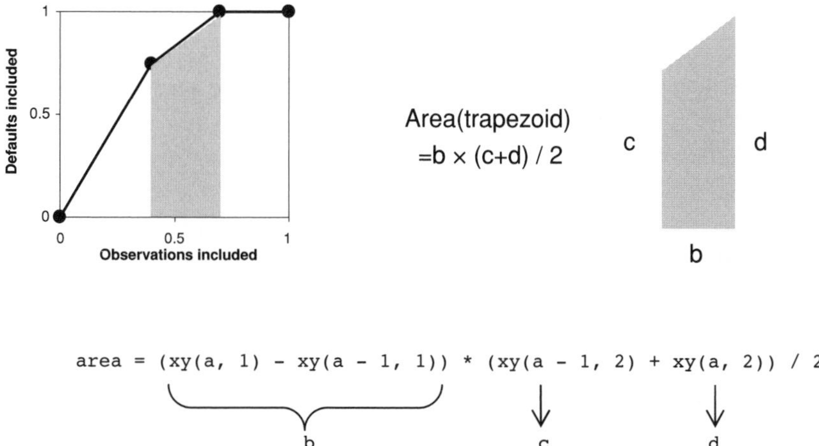

Figure 8.2 How segments of the area under the CAP are determined in VBA

number of rating grades K. With this information at hand, we can define the vector for the CAP coordinates (xy). It has two columns (for the x-axis and the y-axis) and $K + 2$ rows (one for the accuracy ratio, one for the origin and one for each rating grade).

Moving from one observation to the next (`For i=1 To N`), we determine the fraction of all observations included at a given i (`xi`) and the fraction of defaults included (`yi`). The values are recorded in the array `xy` only when the rating category changes; in checking this condition, the last observation is treated differently to prevent the subscript i from going out of range (`i+1` would give `N+1` for `i=N`). Whenever we update `xy`, we also update the area under the curve by adding the area under the CAP that is included by the current and the previous point.

The area under the CAP in between two points can be handled as a trapezoid (some areas are in fact triangles or rectangles, but the trapezoid formula is nonetheless valid). We compute the area of a segment as shown in Figure 8.2 (note that `xy(a,1)` contains the x-value of the CAP for rating category a, while `xy(a,2)` contains the y-value for category a).

The function CAP is an array function. Its output extends over two columns and over as many rows as there are ratings plus 2. The accuracy ratio is returned in the first row. Like any array function, CAP has to be entered using [ctrl]+[shift]+[enter]. Table 8.2 shows the result of applying the function to the example data.

RECEIVER OPERATING CHARACTERISTIC (ROC)

An analytic tool that is closely related to the CAP is the Receiver Operating Characteristic (ROC). The ROC can be obtained by plotting the fraction of defaulters ranked x or worse against the fraction of non-defaulters ranked x or worse. The two graphs thus differ in the definition of the x-axis. A common summary statistic of a ROC analysis is the area under the ROC curve (AUC). Reflecting the fact that the CAP is very similar to the ROC, there is an exact linear relationship between the accuracy ratio and the area under the curve:

$$\text{Accuracy ratio} = 2 \times \text{Area under curve} - 1$$

Table 8.2 The function CAP applied to the example data

	A	B	C	D	E	F
1	**Rating and default data**				**CAP and accuracy ratio**	
2	Obser-vation	Rating (A is best)	Default (Yes=1)			
3	7	C	1		0.7083	(Accrat)
4	8	C	1		0	0
5	9	C	1		0.4	0.75
6	10	C	0		0.7	1
7	4	B	1		1	1.00
8	5	B	0			
9	6	B	0		E3: {=CAP(B3:B12,C3:C12)}	
10	1	A	0		*(applies to E3:F7)*	
11	2	A	0			
12	3	A	0			
13						

The choice between CAP and ROC is therefore largely a matter of taste. Both convey the same information in a slightly different fashion. Our function CAP requires only a few changes to be turned into a function ROC that returns the coordinates of the ROC along with the area under curve (changes are shaded):

```
Function ROC(ratings, defaults)
'Function written for data sorted from worst rating to best

Dim N As Long, K As Long, numdef As Long, a As Integer, i As Long
Dim xi As Double, yi As Double, xy(), area As Double

N = Application.WorksheetFunction.Count(defaults)
numdef = Application.WorksheetFunction.Sum(defaults)

'Determine number of rating categories K
K = 1
For i = 2 To N
    If ratings(i) <> ratings(i - 1) Then K = K + 1
Next i
ReDim xy(1 To K + 2, 1 To 2)

'First row of function reserved for AUC, 2nd is origin (0,0),
'so start with row a=3
a = 3

For i = 1 To N

    'Cumulative fraction of non-defaulters(xi) and defaulters(yi)
    xi = xi + IIf(defaults(i) = 0, 1, 0) / (N - numdef)
    yi = yi + defaults(i) / numdef
```

Table 8.3 The function ROC applied to the example data

	A	B	C	D	E	F
1	**Rating and default data**				**ROC and area under curve**	
2	Obser- vation	Rating (A is best)	Default (Yes=1)			
3	7	C	1		0.8542	(AUC)
4	8	C	1		0	0
5	9	C	1		0.1667	0.75
6	10	C	0		0.5	1
7	4	B	1		1	1.00
8	5	B	0			
9	6	B	0		E3: {=ROC(B3:B12,C3:C12)}	
10	1	A	0		*(applies to E3:F7)*	
11	2	A	0			
12	3	A	0			
13						

```
    'Determine ROC points and area below ROC
    If ratings(i) <> ratings(i + IIf(i = N, 0, 1)) Or i = N Then
       xy(a, 1) = xi
       xy(a, 2) = yi
       area = area + (xy(a, 1) - xy(a - 1, 1)) * (xy(a - 1, 2) _
         + xy(a, 2)) / 2
       a = a + 1
    End If
Next i

'Area under curve
xy(1, 1) = area
xy(1, 2) = "(AUC)"
ROC = xy

End Function
```

In Table 8.3, the ROC function is applied to our example data.

BOOTSTRAPPING CONFIDENCE INTERVALS FOR THE ACCURACY RATIO

CAPs and ROCs, accuracy ratios and AUC are only estimates of a rating system's discriminatory power, based on the data we have. Their standard errors and associated confidence intervals can be determined analytically.[1] Alternatively, we can employ bootstrap simulations, which is the route we will follow here. The core idea of bootstrapping is to re-sample from the

[1] See Basel Committee on Banking Supervision (2005).

data used for estimation and re-estimate the statistics with this new, re-sampled data. Having done this many times, we can derive a distribution of the statistic of interest.

Here, we show how to estimate a confidence interval for the accuracy ratio through bootstrapping. The structure of this bootstrap is as follows:

1. From the N observations on ratings and default, draw N times with replacement (draw pairs of ratings and defaults, to be precise).
2. Compute the accuracy ratio with the data re-sampled in step 1.
3. Repeat steps 1. to 2. M times.
4. To construct a 1–α confidence interval for the accuracy ratio, determine the $\alpha/2$ and the 1–$\alpha/2$ percentile of the bootstrapped accuracy ratios.

We conduct the bootstrap simulation in a function – alternatively, we could also use a macro. The function requires rating and default data, the number of bootstrap trials to be conducted (M) and the desired confidence α for the confidence interval. Similar to the function CAP, the data have to be sorted from the worst rating to the best.

After declaring variables and inferring the number of observations N, we use a 'for' loop to assign numbers to the rating categories, stored in the array `ratnum`. The first (i.e., worst) rating receives the number 1. This array will allow us to sort bootstrapped data from worst to best.

To draw an observation randomly from the data, we draw `bootindex`, an integer number between 1 and N. Note that `Rnd()` returns a random variable between 0 and 1, and so `Int(Rnd()*N+1)` returns an integer random variable between 1 and N. From the observation with array index equal to `bootindex`, we take the rating and the default information and write them into our bootstrap arrays. Once we have N elements in the bootstrap arrays, we sort them, use the CAP function to determine the accuracy ratio and store the accuracy ratio in the array `bootar`. Sorting is done with the macro SORT2 introduced in Chapter 7. Having gone through M bootstrap trials, we compute the percentiles of the bootstrapped accuracy ratios. Here is the entire code:

```
Function BOOTCAP(ratings, defaults, M, alpha)
Dim ratnum(), bootindex, bootratings(), bootdefaults(), bootar(),
  bootout()
Dim N As Long, i As Long, j As Long, defnum As Long
Dim bootar_tmp, a
N = Application.WorksheetFunction.Count(defaults)

ReDim ratnum(1 To N), bootratings(1 To N), bootdefaults(1 To N)
ReDim bootar(1 To M), bootout(1 To 2)

'Assign numbers to rating categories (1 is best)
ratnum(1) = 1
For i = 2 To N
  ratnum(i) = IIf(ratings(i) = ratings(i - 1),
              ratnum(i - 1), _ ratnum(i - 1) + 1)
Next i
```

```
'Do M bootstrap trials
For j = 1 To M
  'Draw observations for trial j
  For i = 1 To N
     bootindex = Int(Rnd() * N + 1)
     bootratings(i) = ratnum(bootindex)
     bootdefaults(i) = defaults(bootindex)
  Next i

  'Compute accuracy ratio
  If Application.WorksheetFunction.Sum(bootdefaults) > 0 Then
     SORT2 bootratings, bootdefaults
     bootar_tmp = CAP(bootratings, bootdefaults)
     bootar(j) = bootar_tmp(1, 1)
  Else: j = j - 1
  End If
Next j

bootout(1) = Application.WorksheetFunction.Percentile(bootar, alpha / 2)
bootout(2) = Application.WorksheetFunction.Percentile(bootar, _
             1 - alpha / 2)

BOOTCAP = bootout
End Function
```

The function is applied in Table 8.4. Note that we have moved from our previous example data to a larger data set. We take default data and estimated default probabilities from Chapter 1, Table 1.7. The accuracy ratio is 75.77%; the bootstrapped 95% confidence interval is [63.8%, 85.8%].

The large confidence intervals in Table 8.4 illustrate that one should be careful in interpreting changes in accuracy ratios over time. In 2008, for example, the accuracy ratio of Moody's

Table 8.4 Bootstrapped confidence intervals for the accuracy ratio

	A	B	C	D	E
1	**Data from scoring model**			**Accuracy ratio**	
2	PD	Default			
3	99.2%	1		0.7577	
4	86.9%	0		{=CAP(A3:A4002,B3:B4002)}	
5	84.4%	0			
6	67.8%	0		**95% confidence for accuracy ratio**	
7	56.3%	1		0.638	0.858
8	56.0%	1		{=BOOTCAP(A3:A4002,B3:B4002,1000,0.05)}	
9	51.0%	0			
...	...	...			
4002	0.0%	0			

corporate credit ratings was 69%, which compares to a 1983–2009 average of 85% (see Excel appendix to Moody's Investors Service, 2010). At first sight, it might seem obvious from the figures that rating performance during the subprime crisis revealed that the quality of corporate credit ratings was low.[2] A second look suggests some caution. In 2009, a year that was also heavily affected by the crisis, the accuracy ratio was 82%, much closer to the long run average. Further, a bootstrap analysis along the lines of Table 8.4 shows that the 95% confidence interval for the 2008 accuracy ratio based on the seven letter grades extends from 58% to 75%.[3] A considerable part of the 2008 drop in the accuracy ratio could therefore be due to random variation. When interpreting the numbers, we should also take into account that the bootstrap procedure described here assumes independent defaults. With a realistic assumption about default dependence, the expected variation in accuracy statistics becomes much larger. This is exemplified below in the section on calibration tests (page 192).

INTERPRETING CAPS AND ROCS

Typical accuracy ratios of rating systems used in practice lie between 50% and 90%, but apart from this, there is little that can be said about the accuracy ratio that a 'good' system should achieve. The reason is that the maximum attainable accuracy depends on the portfolio structure, in particular on the heterogeneity of a portfolio with respect to default probabilities.

The interpretation of CAP curves and accuracy ratios is easier if one examines the relative performance of different rating systems within the same data set. But even then, one should be careful in drawing conclusions. In Figure 8.3, we present an application of the CAP from Löffler (2004). The author used CAP curves to compare the default prediction power of Moody's credit ratings to the one of Moody's KMV EDFs. The latter are quantitative estimates

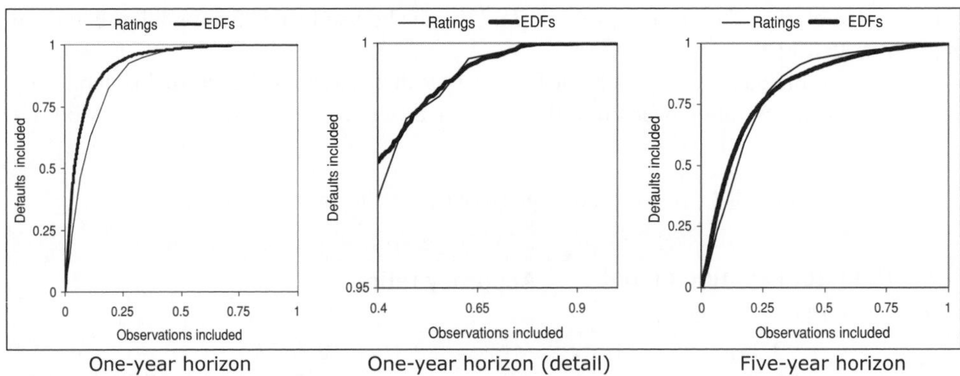

Figure 8.3 Cumulative accuracy profiles for ratings and EDFs
Source: Reprinted from Löffler, G., 2004, Ratings versus market-based measures of default risk in portfolio governance, *Journal of Banking and Finance*, 28, 2715–2746, with permission from Elsevier

[2] Structured finance ratings, which feature prominently in the recent discussion of rating quality, are discussed in Chapter 11.

[3] The necessary data is available in Moody's (2010, Exhibit 42). Note that the calculations presented here are based on letter grades, whereas the accuracy ratios reported by Moody's are based on modified grades. With letter grades, accuracy ratios are lower because the information contained in rating modifiers is not used.

of one-year default probabilities based on the structural approach to default risk (see Chapter 2). Figure 8.3 shows the profiles for one-year and five-year horizons. Horizon here refers to the definition of the default indicator variable. For a T-year horizon, this variable records whether a default occurred in the T years after the rating assignment.

Accuracy ratios are as follows:

	One-year horizon (%)	Five-year horizon (%)
Ratings	79.1	67.4
EDFs	86.2	67.8

Recall from the definition of the CAP that the more northwestern the curve, the better the corresponding rating system. On a one-year horizon, the EDF curve is mostly above the rating curve, and its accuracy ratio is larger. However, the two curves intersect repeatedly in the second half of the profile (see middle chart of Figure 8.3); this part of the data set more or less corresponds to issuers with investment grade ratings. The analysis thus does not allow an unambiguous conclusion about the superiority of EDFs. Among high-risk issuers, EDFs are superior at discriminating between defaulters and non-defaulters, but this does not hold true in the investment-grade domain. The differentiation is relevant, for instance for investors restricted to investing only in bonds with investment grade rating. For them, the second half of the profile is decisive.

The third chart, finally, shows that the prediction horizon can matter as well. On a five-year horizon, differences between accuracy ratios are marginal. The two curves intersect earlier, and the rating curve then stays above the EDF curve. When applying analytic tools like the CAP, one should therefore check whether the chosen horizon matches the horizon of the agent for which the analysis is done.

BRIER SCORE

CAPs and ROCs test discrimination; a measure that tests both discrimination and calibration is the Brier score. It translates the common principle of examining squared forecast errors to probability forecasts. An example of a probability forecast would be 'the probability of rain showers for next day is 60%'. Applied to ratings, the Brier score is defined as

$$\text{Brier Score} = \frac{1}{N}\sum_{i=1}^{N}(d_i - PD_i)^2 \tag{8.1}$$

where i indexes the N observations, d_i is an indicator variable that takes the value 1 if borrower i defaulted (0 otherwise), and PD_i is the estimated probability of default of borrower i. To compute the Brier score, we then need probabilities of default, which we do not need for CAPs and ROCs. The Brier score lies between 0 and 1; better default probability forecasts are associated with lower score values.

Table 8.5 shows how to compute the Brier score for an example data set. To calculate the sum of squared differences in (8.1), we can make use of the function SUMXMY2(*matrix1*,

Table 8.5 The Brier score for example data

	A	B	C	D	E	F
1	**Rating and default data**					
2	i	PD	Default		Brier score	
3	1	0.001	0		0.35068	
4	2	0.001	0		=SUMXMY2(B3:B12,C3:C12)/COUNT(B3:B12)	
5	3	0.001	0			
6	4	0.02	1		0.35068	
7	5	0.02	0		=Brier(B3:B12,C3:C12)	
8	6	0.02	0			
9	7	0.08	1			
10	8	0.08	1			
11	9	0.08	1			
12	10	0.08	0			
13						

matrix2). We then only have to divide by the number of observations, which we can determine through the function COUNT().

Of course, we can also create a user-defined function. This could, for example, read

```
Function BRIER(ratings, defaults)
BRIER = (Application.WorksheetFunction.SumXMY2(ratings, defaults)) / _
        (Application.Worksheetfunction.Count(ratings))
End Function
```

TESTING THE CALIBRATION OF RATING-SPECIFIC DEFAULT PROBABILITIES

In many rating systems used by financial institutions, obligors are grouped into rating categories. The default probability of a rating category can then be estimated in different ways. One can use the historical default rate experience of obligors in a given rating grade (see Chapter 3); one can map one's own rating into categories of rating agencies and use their published default rates, or one can average individual default probability estimates of obligors in the grade (e.g., estimates obtained through scoring – see Chapter 1).

Regardless of the way in which a default probability for a rating grade was estimated, we may want to test whether it is in line with observed default rates. From the perspective of risk management and supervisors, it is often crucial to detect whether default probability estimates are too low. In the following, we will thus present one-sided tests for underestimation of default probabilities; they can easily be extended to two-sided tests. In addition, the tests are conducted separately for each observation period (normally one year), and separately for each grade.

Let us start with the simplified assumption that defaults are independent (and so default correlation is zero). The number of defaults (D_{kt}) in a given year t and grade k then follows a binomial distribution. The number of trials is N_{kt}, the number of obligors in grade k at the start of the year t; the success probability is PD_{kt}, the default probability estimated at the start of year t. At a significance level of α (e.g., $\alpha = 1\%$), we can reject the hypothesis that the default probability is not underestimated if

$$1 - BINOM\,(D_{kt} - 1,\ N_{kt}, PD_{kt}) \leq \alpha \tag{8.2}$$

where BINOM(x, N, q) denotes the binomial probability of observing x successes out of N trials with success probability q. If condition (8.2) is true, we need to assume an unlikely scenario to explain the actual default count D_{kt} (or a higher one). This would lead us to conclude that the PD has underestimated the true default probability.

For large N, the binomial distribution converges to the normal, and so we can also use a normal approximation to (8.2). If defaults follow a binomial distribution with default probability PD_{kt}, the default count D_{kt} has a standard deviation of $\sqrt{PD_{kt}(1 - PD_{kt})N_{kt}}$; the default count's mean is $PD_{kt}N_{kt}$. Mean and standard deviation of the approximating normal are set accordingly. Instead of (8.2) we can thus examine

$$1 - \Phi\left(\frac{(D_{kt} - 0.5 - PD_{kt}N_{kt})}{\sqrt{PD_{kt}(1 - PD_{kt})N_{kt}}}\right) \leq \alpha \tag{8.3}$$

where Φ denotes the cumulative standard normal distribution.

To adjust the test for the presence of default correlations, we can use the one-factor asset value model introduced in Chapter 6. There, we had modeled default correlation through correlations in asset values and had assumed that the latter can be fully captured by just one factor Z. In such a model, there are two possible reasons why the observed default rate in year t is larger than the underlying default probability:

- many obligors happened to have had individual 'bad luck';
- year t was generally a bad year for all credits.

In the binomial test and its normal approximation, we allowed for only the first reason. We would like to allow for the two reasons at the same time. As it turns out, this is possible (for example with techniques used in Chapter 6), but complex to achieve. So let us consider only the second explanation in judging whether a PD is too low. The logic is as follows. We judge that a PD underestimated the default probability if we have to assume that the year was so extremely bad that it seems unlikely to be the right explanation.

Technically, ignoring individual bad luck means assuming that the default rate in year t is identical to the default probability in year t. The crucial thing to note is that the latter can vary. In the one-factor model (see Chapter 6), the probability of default in year t, p_{kt}, depends on the factor realization Z_t (as well as on the average default probability p_k and the asset correlation ρ):

$$p_{kt} = \Phi\left[\frac{\Phi^{-1}(p_k) - \sqrt{\rho}Z_t}{\sqrt{1-\rho}}\right] \tag{8.4}$$

Setting the average default probability to our estimate PD$_{kt}$, and the default probability equal to the default rate in year t we get

$$D_{kt}/N_{kt} = \Phi\left[\frac{\Phi^{-1}(PD_{kt}) - \sqrt{\rho}Z_t}{\sqrt{1-\rho}}\right] \tag{8.5}$$

Solving this for the factor Z_t tells us what kind of year we need in order to bring the PD in line with the default rate:

$$Z_t = \frac{\Phi^{-1}(PD_{kt}) - \sqrt{1-\rho}\,\Phi^{-1}(D_{kt}/N_{kt})}{\sqrt{\rho}} \tag{8.6}$$

Note that a negative Z_t will push the default rate above the PD. In the one-factor model, Z_t is standard normally distributed, and so the probability of observing a year as bad as t or worse is $\Phi(Z_t)$. At significance level α, we thus reject the PD if

$$\Phi\left[\frac{\Phi^{-1}(PD_{kt}) - \sqrt{1-\rho}\,\Phi^{-1}(D_{kt}/N_{kt})}{\sqrt{\rho}} \le \alpha\right] \tag{8.7}$$

If (8.7) is true, the scenario Z_t that reconciles the default rate and the PD is too extreme by our standards of significance. Therefore, we conclude that the PD estimate was too low.

In Table 8.6, we implement the three tests for default data from Standard & Poor's (S&P). We go back to the year 2002 – a bad year for credits – and set the PD estimates for the year 2002 equal to the average default rates observed over the years 1981–2001. Subsequently, we test whether these PDs would have passed tests of being in line with the 2002 default rates.

To get the default count from the observed default rates, which are only available in two-decimal precision, we round the product of default rates and number of issuers. The asset correlation ρ is set to 7%, a value close to the ones we obtained in Table 6.4 of Chapter 6.

Table 8.6 Testing underestimation of default probabilities in the year 2002, using 1981–2001 default rates as PD estimates

	A	B	C	D	E	F	G	H	I
1	**Data**						**Tests (p-values)**		
2									ρ
3									7.0%
4		Default rates		Counts					
5		1981-2001	2002	N_{2002}	D_{2002}		Binomial	Normal	One factor
6	AAA	0.00%	0.00%	132	0		#NUM!	#DIV/0!	#NUM!
7	AA	0.01%	0.00%	526	0		#NUM!	99.2%	#NUM!
8	A	0.05%	0.09%	1120	1		42.9%	53.2%	14.5%
9	BBB	0.26%	1.02%	1271	13		0.0%	0.0%	1.7%
10	BB	1.22%	2.74%	802	22		0.0%	0.0%	6.6%
11	B	5.96%	8.09%	754	61		1.1%	0.8%	21.5%
12	CCC/C	24.72%	44.12%	170	75		0.0%	0.0%	2.0%
13									
14									
15									
16									
17									
18									
19									
20									

```
E12: =INT(C12*D12+0.5)
G12: =1-BINOMDIST(E12-1,D12,B12,1)
H12: =1-NORMSDIST((E12-0.5-B12*D12)/((B12*(1-B12))*D12)^0.5)
I12:  =NORMSDIST((NORMSINV(B12)-NORMSINV(C12)*(1-I$3)^0.5)/I$3^0.5)
(can be copied into (E6:I11)
```

We then type the left-hand sides of formulae (8.2), (8.3) and (8.7) into the sheet to obtain the p-values of the binomial test, its normal approximation and the test incorporating correlation, respectively. The Excel formulae are shown in Table 8.6.

With the binomial test, we would classify three rating-specific PDs as underestimating the true default rate at a significance of 1%; the number increases to four with the normal approximation. Once we assume an asset correlation of 7%, however, the significance levels rise as we allow for the possibility that the year under scrutiny was a bad year in general. Now we can no longer reject a PD at a significance of 1%; we could, however, reject two PDs at a significance of 5%. Note that the tests return error values if the realized default rate is zero. Obviously, one cannot find any evidence for underestimating a default probability if the realized default rate is at its minimum.

Decisions on significance levels are somewhat arbitrary. In a traffic lights approach, we choose two rather than one significance level. If the p-value of a test is below α_{red}, we assign an observation to the red zone, meaning that an underestimation of the default probability is very likely. If the p-value is above α_{red} but below α_{yellow}, we interpret the result as a warning that the PD might be an underestimate (yellow zone). Otherwise, we assign it to the green zone.

In Excel, it is easy to assign traffic light colors to p-values. Table 8.7 copies the contents of Table 8.6 and uses the conditional formatting functionality accessible through Format→Conditional Formatting (Excel 2003) or Home→Conditional Formatting (starting with Excel 2007). We choose $\alpha_{\text{red}} = 0.01$ and $\alpha_{\text{yellow}} = 0.05$. (The colors may be hard to discern as the book is printed black and white.)

VALIDATION STRATEGIES

We can distinguish two major uses of accuracy measures:

- a rating system is already in place, and we want to find out whether its quality is (still) adequate;
- we are about to decide which rating system to implement, and thus want to compare alternatives according to their accuracy.

In the first situation, we would regularly update the accuracy measures as new data come in. For a system introduced in December 2006, for example, we would compute accuracy measures for the year 2007, 2008 and so on as soon as the data become available. To increase the updating frequency, we can consider 12-month intervals rather than calendar year intervals, i.e., compute accuracy measures from January 2007 to December 2007, February 2007 to January 2008 and so on.

A nice way of visualizing the results is to plot the evolution of accuracy measures. When considering the accuracy ratio, for example, we can show how the accuracy ratio computed with 12 consecutive months of data evolves over time. In doing so, it is advisable to also provide confidence intervals (see the section on bootstrapping starting on page 187). If there is a decrease in the accuracy ratio, for example, confidence intervals help discern whether the decrease is likely to be due to chance or to a worsening of the rating system's discriminatory power.

Table 8.7 Assigning traffic light colors to the *p*-values of the tests from Table 8.6

	A	B	C	D	E	F	G	H	I
1	**Data**						**Tests (p-values)**		
2									ρ
3									7.0%
4		Default rates		Counts					
5		1981-2001	2002	N_{2002}	D_{2002}		Binomial	Normal	One factor
6	AAA	0.00%	0.00%	132	0		#NUM!	#DIV/0!	#NUM!
7	AA	0.01%	0.00%	526	0		#NUM!	99.2%	#NUM!
8	A	0.05%	0.09%	1120	1		42.9%	53.2%	14.5%
9	BBB	0.26%	1.02%	1271	13		0.0%	0.0%	1.7%
10	BB	1.22%	2.74%	802	22		0.0%	0.0%	6.6%
11	B	5.96%	8.09%	754	61		1.1%	0.8%	21.5%
12	CCC/C	24.72%	44.12%	170	75		0.0%	0.0%	2.0%

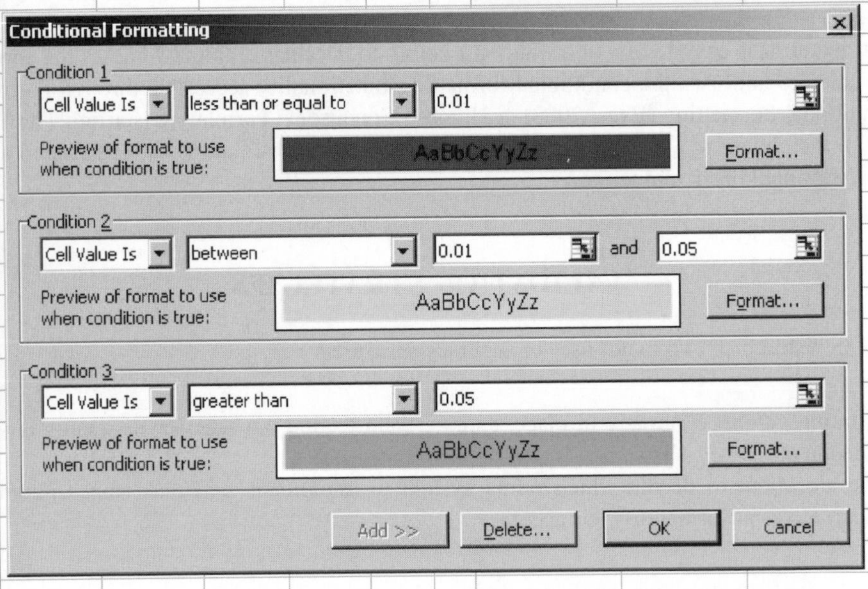

When developing a new rating system (the second bullet point above), one typically fits, tailors or calibrates a system to empirical data. In statistical scoring (Chapter 1), we choose variables, functional transformations and weights such that the resulting scoring model does a good job in predicting observed default behavior; when using structural models, we might base our choice of the model on how it discriminates defaults in the data at hand or alternatively calibrate features of the model to the data (see the approach taken by Moody's KMV described in Chapter 2).

Typically, a system's quality (discriminatory power or calibration) is higher for the default data we used to develop it than in the later, life application. To use model builders' jargon, the in-sample power is higher than the out-of-sample power, where sample refers to the development data. One reason for this loss in power is based on systematic changes in the relationships that we model. Another is that the past, by chance, contains patterns that are not representative. In both cases, we might end up fitting our system to peculiarities of past data that are unlikely to show up again. This danger of overfitting (or data mining) increases if we consider more variables, outlier treatments, functional relationships or model variants, and if the database is small.

To assess the extent to which a model's validity extends to the future, we can create a hypothetical future by separating the data that we have into a part that we use for developing the model, and a part that we use to validate it. Broadly, we can distinguish two ways of doing this (see Box 8.1). The first one, which we might call a walk-forward out-of-sample test (or backtest), mimics what we described above for a model already in use. If we are building a model in 2006 we can ask: assuming that we decided on the model in 2002, what would it have looked liked? And how would its performance have been in 2003, as, say, measured by the accuracy ratio? We then move one year forward, test a model that we would have used in 2003 on the data from 2004 and so forth. This gives as a series of accuracy measures, which we can compare across alternative rating models.

Box 8.1 Validation strategies for model design

Walk-forward out-of-sample test

1. Define a year *t* for the first test (here 2002).
2. Estimate rating system with complete data until year *t*-1.
3. Validate system with dotted white data from year *t*.
4. Set *t* = *t* + 1 and go back to step 2.
5. Analyze (e.g., average) the obtained accuracy measures.

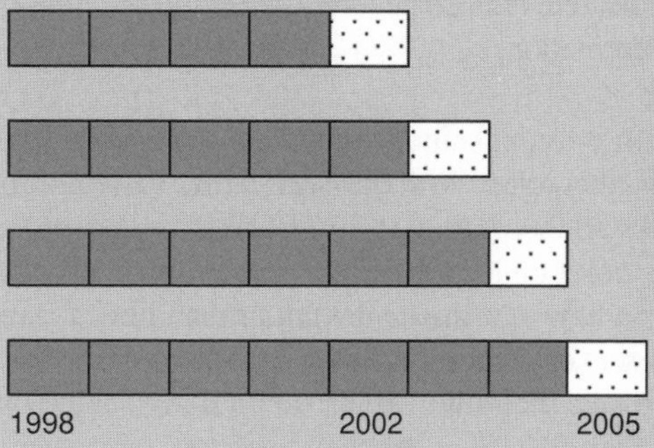

Cross-sectional validation

Estimate rating system with dark gray data; validate on dotted white data.

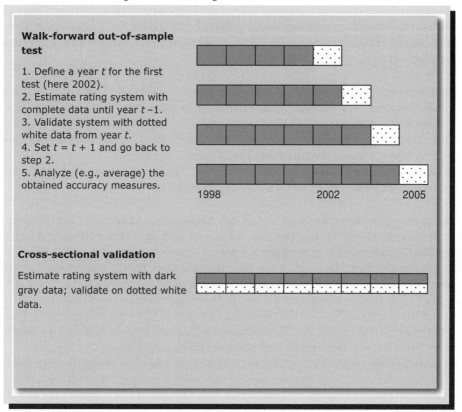

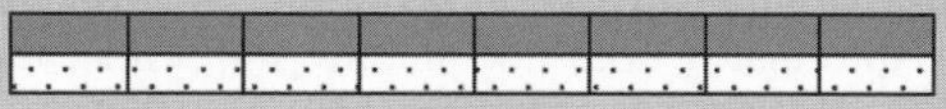

If our data encompasses only a few years, or if the number of defaults per year is very small, the walk-forward test may not be appropriate. We can then consider a cross-sectional validation. Instead of separating the data according to time, we separate it cross-sectionally. For instance, we could draw random numbers for each observation, and then assign observations with random numbers below the median to the development sample, while the others are assigned to the validation sample. Of course, we can consider splits other than 50–50, and we can repeat the exercise to make it less dependent on the particular split that resulted from drawing some random numbers.[4]

TESTING FOR MISSING INFORMATION

The validation measures presented above help to assess whether the performance of a rating system is adequate or not. They do not directly tell us how accuracy can be improved if we judge it to be insufficient. A good tool for uncovering improvement potential is the logit regression analysis introduced in Chapter 1. With the help of regressions, we can check whether rating information is sufficient to explain observed defaults. If we find that other variables explain defaults on top of ratings, we get an indication that these variables should receive higher weights in the rating process.

To implement this approach, we first need to decide how to represent the rating information in the regression analysis. If the rating system produces default probability estimates, we would enter the logit of the estimates (i.e., log(PD/(1 – PD)). If the rating information is given through discrete rating categories, we could consider one of the following three ways of coding rating information:

- Transform ratings into a numerical scale from 1 (best rating) to K, K being the number of rating categories. With the S&P rating system, for example, we would code the ratings as 1 = AAA, 2 = AA, . . . , 7 = CCC/C.
- Transform ratings into default probabilities associated with each rating category (see Chapter 3 on how to estimate default probabilities for rating categories).
- Represent each rating category by a dummy variable. The dummy variable AA, for example, would take the value 1 if the rating is AA, and 0 otherwise.

The dummy variable method requires only rating information and does not impose assumptions on the link between rating categories and default probabilities. For the second method, by contrast, default probability estimates are needed. The conversion of the first method may appear overly simplistic. However, it has been found to work well in many empirical applications. Note that it does not literally imply that the difference between AAA and AA is the same as the difference between BB and B. In a logit model, it would rather imply that there is a linear relationship between the logit of p (i.e., log(p/(1 – p)) and the rating. Due to the nonlinearity of the logistic transformation, the difference (in terms of default probability) between BB and B will therefore be larger than the difference between AAA and AA.

In the following, we sketch an example application in which we use the dummy variable method. Consider a rating system that assigns one out of seven possible grades to corporate borrowers; the grading employs the symbols used by S&P (AAA to C). Further, the objective of the analysis will be to test whether the rating system makes efficient use of the information

[4] A related procedure, K-fold testing, is described in Dwyer, D., Kocagil, A. and Stein, R., 2004, Moody's KMV RiskCalc v3.1. model. Moody's KMV.

Table 8.8 Checking for missing information through logit analysis

	A	B	C	D	E	F	G	H	I	J	K	L	M	N	O	P	Q	R	S	T	U
1	ID	Year	De-fault	Ra-ting	EBIT/ TA	AA	A	BBB	BB	B	C			CONST	EBIT/ TA	AA	A	BBB	BB	B	C
2	1	1999	0	BBB	0.043	0	0	1	0	0	0		b	-5.27	-21.56	0.08	0.65	0.94	1.95	2.32	3.08
3	1	2000	0	BBB	0.052	0	0	1	0	0	0		SE(b)	1.12	8.33	1.42	1.23	1.13	1.10	1.07	1.06
4	1	2001	0	BBB	0.027	0	0	1	0	0	0		t	-4.72	-2.59	0.06	0.53	0.83	1.77	2.15	2.89
5	1	2002	0	BB	0.030	0	0	0	1	0	0		p-value	0.00	0.01	0.95	0.60	0.40	0.08	0.03	0.00
6	1	2003	0	BB	0.032	0	0	0	1	0	0			=logit(C2:C4001,E2:K4001,1,1)							
7	1	2004	1	B	0.	F2: =IF ($D2=F$1,1,0)															
8	2	1999	0	BBB	0.	*(can be copied into F2:K4001)*															
	...	...	...	...																	
4001	830	2002	0	C	0.036	0	0	0	0	0	1										

contained in a firm's profitability as measured by earnings before interest and taxes (EBIT) over total assets (TA). Note that one can easily add more variables and thus test the incremental power of several variables in one regression.

Table 8.8 shows how the data might be organized. Along with information on ratings and profitability, the data contain an identification number for each firm, the year in which information on ratings and profitability was collected, and a default indicator. The latter takes the value 1 if a default occurred in the year following the year stated in column A, and 0 otherwise.

In the first step, we create the dummy variables in the columns to the right of the original data. As column headers, we use the rating symbols. If we include a constant in the regression analysis, we must not enter dummy variables for each rating grade. If we did so, the constant could be replicated by summing up the dummy variables.[5] Such a dependence between explanatory variables would lead to a breakdown of the regression procedure. With K rating categories, we enter dummy variables for $K - 1$ categories. Which category is left out does not affect the results. Here, we choose to represent rating categories AA to C through dummy variables. We therefore write the rating symbols for those categories into the range F2:K2. The dummy variables can be created through an application of the IF-function. In cell F3, we would write:

=IF($D3=F$2,1,0)

or, alternatively,

=($D3=F$2)*1

The formula can be copied to the right and down. Then we perform a logit regression in which the default indicator is the dependent variable. We employ the user-defined function LOGIT (see Chapter 1 for a detailed description). We select the cells N2:U5, type

=LOGIT(C2:C4001,E2:K4001,1,1)

---

[5] Consider the simple case with just two categories. If the rating belongs to category 1, the dummy variable for the first category takes the value 1, while the dummy variable for the second takes the value 0. Add them up and you obtain 1, which is the value through which the constant is represented in the vector of explanatory variables. If the rating belongs to the second category, we also get 1 if we add up the two dummy variables.

and enter it by [ctrl]+[shift]+[enter]. The first row of the output contains the regression coefficients. The next three rows contain their standard errors, t-statistics and p-values. The coefficient reported in the first column of the function's output is the constant; the next coefficients follow in the order of the variables.

Let us start by examining the coefficients of the dummy variables. Remember that we left out the dummy variable for the AAA category. The coefficient of the dummy of rating category i therefore indicates how the default probability of an i-rated borrower differs from the one of an AAA-rated borrower. A positive coefficient implies that belonging to rating category i increases the default probability relative to AAA. To understand this, recall from Chapter 1 that the default probability is positively related to the score, which is obtained through $\sum_{k=1}^{K} \hat{b}_k x_k$ ($\hat{b}_k$ being the estimated coefficient for variable k, which enters with a value of x_k). For an observation for which a dummy variable takes the value 1, the score increases if the variable's coefficient is positive.

Similarly, when we compare the coefficients of rating categories i and j, the average default probability of category i is larger than the one of category j when the coefficient of dummy variable i is larger than the one of dummy variable j.

Given that the credit quality should deteriorate monotonically when moving from AAA to C, we expect that the coefficients of the dummy variables are all positive, and that they increase when moving from AA to C. In the example data, this is indeed the case. Further, we would expect that the explanatory power of the rating variables is significant. Whereas the dummies for categories B and C are significant on a level better than 5%, the other dummies would be deemed to be insignificant based on conventional levels of significance. With a small data set such as the one here, this should not be taken as strong evidence that ratings better than B do not differentiate default risk. If the number of defaults is low, it is quite likely that we see such a pattern even if the ratings have discriminatory power.

Let us now turn to the main object of interest in the example analysis: the profitability variable. The coefficient on EBIT/TA is negative and significant on a 1% level; the sign conforms to expectations because a higher profitability should go along with a lower default probability. The results can be interpreted such that ratings did not fully capture the information that EBIT/TA contains about the likelihood of default.

To answer the question of whether the rating system should be redesigned in order to give a larger weight to EBIT/TA, we should not stop here. A regression such as the one performed in Table 8.8 is a backward-looking exercise. Finding that a variable would have helped to improve a forecast does not automatically imply that the architects of the rating system made an avoidable error in the past; nor does it guarantee that the system will work better in the future if EBIT/TA is given a larger weight. To better judge whether a change of the rating system can be expected to lead to an improvement, we should perform an out-of-sample analysis. For example, we could use logit regressions to build a new rating system with information that was actually available at the time the rating was assigned. Such an analysis could be performed through a walk-forward test as described in Box 8.1. For year t, run a logit regression that contains the same variables as in Table 8.8, but which uses only information available in t. The new rating can be based on the estimated regression score. This is repeated for all years. Then compare accuracy measures of the original rating system with those of the modified one. If the modified system would have significantly outperformed the existing one, we should consider modifying it.

NOTES AND LITERATURE

In the literature, the cumulative accuracy profile is also denoted as the Lorenz curve; an alternative expression for the accuracy ratio is Gini ratio or Gini coefficient.

For a summary on validation methods, see Sobehart, J.R., Keenan, S.C. and Stein, R.M., 2000, *Benchmarking Quantitative Default Risk Models: A Validation Methodology*, Moody's Investors Service, and Basel Committee on Banking Supervision, 2005, *Studies on the Validation of Internal Rating Systems*, Bank for International Settlements.

Validation strategies are discussed in Stein, R.M., 2002, *Benchmarking Default Prediction Models: Pitfalls and Remedies in Model Validation*, Moody's KMV.

In their annual default studies, rating agencies provide information on the accuracy of their ratings. See, for example, Moody's Investors Service, 2010, *Corporate Default and Recovery Rates 1920–2009*, or Standard & Poor's, 2010, *2009 Annual Global Corporate Default Study and Rating Transitions*.

9
Validation of Credit Portfolio Models

Portfolio credit risk models produce a probability distribution for portfolio credit losses (and gains, if it is a mark-to-market model). To validate the quality of a given model, we can examine whether observed losses are consistent with the model's predictions.

Some people argue that portfolio models are difficult or even impossible to validate empirically. Usually, such an opinion is justified by a comparison to market risk models. Market risk models produce loss forecasts for a portfolio (which might be the trading book of a bank) as well, but the underlying horizon is much shorter – often, it is restricted to a single day. A standard validation procedure is to check the frequency with which actual losses exceeded the Value at Risk (VaR). In a market risk setting, risk managers usually examine the 99% VaR, which is the loss that is predicted not to be exceeded with a probability 99%. Over one year containing roughly 250 trading days, the expected number of exceedances of the 99% VaR is $250 \times (1 - 0.99) = 2.5$, provided that the VaR forecasts are correct. When we observe the number of exceedances differing significantly from the expected number, we can conclude that the predictions were incorrect. Significance can be assessed with a simple binomial test.

Obviously, such a test is not very useful for the validation of credit portfolio models, which mostly have a one-year horizon. We would have to wait 250 years until we gain as many observations as we do after one year of tracking a market risk model. There is a way out, however. If we do not confine a test to the prediction of extreme events but rather test the overall fit of the predicted loss distribution, we make better use of information and possibly learn a significant amount about a model's validity with just 5 or 10 years of data.

There are many procedures for testing the quality of a distribution. Here, we introduce the Berkowitz test, which is a powerful test that has been examined both for credit risk and market risk models.

TESTING DISTRIBUTIONS WITH THE BERKOWITZ TEST

Let us begin with the information required. For each period (which usually has a length of one year), we need

- a loss figure (say 145 million USD);
- a forecast of the loss distribution made at the start of the period.

If our data span five years, the necessary information might look like Figure 9.1.

In the figure, the portfolio loss distribution is symbolized by a cumulative distribution for portfolio losses, $F(L)$. For a given loss L, it returns the probability $F(L)$ with which this loss is not exceeded. The portfolio model's prediction could also be summarized differently, and we will return to this later in the implementation of the test. Note that loss distributions can differ from year to year because of changes in portfolio composition or changes in the risk parameters of the portfolio constituents.

Year	2005	2006	2007	2008	2009
Loss	1.4	2.8	0.4	8.4	5.9
Prediction made at start of year					

Figure 9.1 Information required for the test

The basic idea behind the Berkowitz (2001) test is to evaluate the entire distribution. The test involves a double transformation of observed losses, with the two transformations as follows:

- *1st transformation:* replace L_t, the loss in t, by the predicted probability of observing this loss or a smaller one. We obtain this probability by inserting the loss L_t into the cumulative distribution function $F(L_t)$:

$$p_t = F(L_t) \tag{9.1}$$

- *2nd transformation:* transform p_t by applying $\Phi^{-1}(x)$, the inverse cumulative standard normal distribution function. Formally,

$$z_t = \Phi^{-1}(p_t) \tag{9.2}$$

The 1st transformation produces numbers between 0 and 1. If the predicted distribution is correct, we have even more information: the numbers should be uniformly distributed between 0 and 1. To see this, start by looking at the median of the distribution. If the model is correct, 50% of observed losses would be expected to end up below the median loss, which has $F(\text{median loss}) = 0.5$. Thus, the transformed variable p_t should be below 0.5 in 50% of all cases. We can go on in this way. The 25th percentile, which has $F(25\%\ \text{percentile}) = 0.25$, splits the first half into another pair of two halves, and again observations will be evenly spread on expectation. Similarly, we can conclude that there should be as many p_ts below 0.25 as there are p_ts above 0.75. We can use finer partitionings and still conclude that the p_t should be evenly spread across the intervals.

In principle, we could stop after the 1st transformation and test whether the p_ts are actually uniformly distributed between 0 and 1. However, tests based on normally distributed numbers are often more powerful. This is why the 2nd transformation is used. If the model summarized by $F(L)$ is correct, transformed losses z_t will be normally distributed with zero mean and unit variance. The intuition behind this is similar to the 1st transformation. If p_t is uniform between 0 and 1, 2.5% of all observations will be below 2.5%, for example. In consequence, 2.5% of all z_t will be below -1.96 ($=\Phi^{-1}(0.025)$) – but this is just what we expect for a standard normal variable.

Berkowitz (2001) suggested the restriction of the test to the hypothesis that z_t have zero mean and unit variance. We could additionally test whether they are normally distributed, but tests of normality tend not be very powerful if the number of observations is small, and so we do not lose much information if we do not test for this property on z_t as well.

A convenient and powerful way of testing the joint hypothesis of zero mean and unit variance is a likelihood ratio test. The likelihood is the probability that we observe given data with a given model. With a likelihood ratio test, we test whether imposing a restriction (here that the z_t have zero mean and unit variance) leads to a significant loss in the likelihood.

The test statistic is based on the log-likelihood function of the transformed series z_t. Since the z_t are normally distributed under the hypothesis that the model is correct, the likelihood is obtained through the normal density

$$\text{Likelihood} = \prod_{t=1}^{T} \frac{1}{\sqrt{2\pi\sigma^2}} \exp(-(z_t - \mu)^2/(2\sigma^2)) \tag{9.3}$$

That is, if we have T observations, we multiply the probabilities of observing individual observations z_t to get the likelihood to observing the set of T observations. This is correct if unexpected losses, which are captured here by $z_t - \mu$, are independent across time. Although this assumption may be violated in some situations, it should be fulfilled if the loss forecasts make efficient use of information. Note that this is not the same as assuming that losses themselves are independent across time. There is no need to abandon the concept of credit cycles as long as the notion of credit cycles relates to losses, not unexpected losses.

It is more convenient to work with $\ln L$, the logarithm of the likelihood (9.3):

$$\ln L = -\frac{T}{2}\ln 2\pi - \frac{T}{2}\ln \sigma^2 - \sum_{t=1}^{T} \frac{(z_t - \mu)^2}{2\sigma^2} \tag{9.4}$$

To evaluate the log-likelihood, we calculate the maximum likelihood (ML) estimators for the mean and variance of the transformed variable z_t (see Appendix A3 for details on maximum likelihood estimation):

$$\hat{\mu}_{ML} = \frac{1}{T}\sum_{t=1}^{T} z_t \tag{9.5}$$

$$\hat{\sigma}^2_{ML} = \frac{1}{T}\sum_{1}^{T} (z_t - \hat{\mu}_{ML}) \tag{9.6}$$

The likelihood ratio test is then structured to test the joint hypothesis that the z_t have zero mean and unit variance. It is given by

$$\lambda = 2\left[\ln L(\mu = \hat{\mu}_{ML}, \sigma^2 = \hat{\sigma}^2_{ML}) - \ln L(\mu = 0, \sigma^2 = 1)\right] \tag{9.7}$$

If imposing the hypothesis $\mu = 0$ and $\sigma^2 = 1$ leads to large loss in likelihood, λ will be large. Therefore, the larger λ is, the more evidence we have that the z_t do not have mean zero and unit variance. Under usual regularity conditions, the test statistic λ will be asymptotically distributed as a chi-squared variable with two degrees of freedom. Particularly in small samples, we cannot rely on this asymptotic property. Below, we will show how we can simulate the small sample distribution of the statistic. Until then, we will work with the asymptotic distribution.

Table 9.1 Example implementation of the Berkowitz test

	A	B	C	D	E	F	G
1	**Raw data**		**1st transform**	**2nd transform**		**Loss distribution**	
2	Year	Losses	p_t	z_t		L	F(L)
3	1	0	0.08%	-3.1543	C3: =VLOOKUP(B3,F$3:G$23,2,1)	0	0.08%
4	2	7	59.87%	0.2501	*(can be copied into C4:C7)*	1	0.66%
5	3	0	0.08%	-3.1543		2	2.77%
6	4	10	90.53%	1.3122	D3 =NORMSINV(C3)	3	7.81%
7	5	4	16.81%	-0.9615	*(can be copied into D4:D7)*	4	16.81%
8						5	29.62%
9	**Calculation of LR statistic λ**					6	44.71%
10						7	59.87%
11	T		5	=COUNT(B3:B7)		8	73.14%
12	ML estimate for σ^2		3.2185	=VARP(D3:D7)		9	83.41%
13						10	90.53%
14	terms		-5.422	=-C11/2*LN(C12)-DEVSQ(D3:D7)/(2*C12)		11	94.98%
15	for LR statistic		-11.304	=-SUMSQ(D3:D7)/2		12	97.53%
16						13	98.87%
17	LR statistic λ		11.764	=2*(C14-C15)		14	99.51%
18	p-value		0.003	=CHIDIST(C17,2)		15	99.80%
19						16	99.93%
20	*Recall:*					17	99.97%
21	$\ln L = -\frac{T}{2}\ln 2\pi - \frac{T}{2}\ln\sigma^2 - \sum_{t=1}^{T}\frac{(z_t-\mu)^2}{2\sigma^2}$					18	99.99%
22						19	99.997%
23	$\lambda = 2\left[\ln L(\mu=\hat{\mu}_{ML},\sigma^2=\hat{\sigma}^2_{ML}) - \ln L(\mu=0,\sigma^2=1)\right]$					20	99.999%

Example implementation of the Berkowitz test

Let us assume that we have five years of loss data. For the sake of exposition, also assume that

- the predicted loss distribution was the same for every year;
- the specification of the loss distribution is such that we can immediately determine the exact probability of each loss (we will relax this in the next section).

The data and the loss distribution are shown shaded in Table 9.1. The other cells contain calculations leading to the likelihood ratio statistic λ. The major steps are as follows.

For each loss, determine the associated cumulative probability of the predicted distribution (= 1st transformation). This can be achieved through the function VLOOKUP(). VLOOKUP(*lookup_value*, *table_array*, *col_index_num*, *range_lookup*) searches for *lookup_value* in the leftmost column of *table_array* and returns a value that is in the same row of *table_array* but in column *col_index_num*. Provided that the logical value *range_lookup* is set to 1, the function VLOOKUP() searches the largest value that is smaller than or equal to *lookup_value*. For taking the inverse of the standard normal distribution function (=2nd transformation), we can use the function NORMSINV().

Recalling the formula for the log-likelihood (9.4), we see that we need

- the number of observations: we determine them through the function COUNT applied to one column of the data;
- the maximum likelihood estimate of the variance of z_t: this can be obtained through the function VARP;

- the maximum likelihood estimate of the mean: we could determine it using the function AVERAGE, however, we will determine the log-likelihood with Excel functions that implicitly estimate the mean.

Examining the log-likelihood (9.4), we see that the first term $-T/2 \ln 2\pi$ is contained in both likelihoods (the one associated with the maximum likelihood estimates and the one with the hypothesis of zero mean and unit variance). Since we will subtract one likelihood from the other in the construction of the test statistic, we can dispose of this first term right away.

In row 14, we compute the second and third term of the log-likelihood that is associated with the ML estimates. In doing so, we use the T and the variance estimate of our data. To determine the sum of squared deviations $\Sigma(z_t - \mu)^2$, we can use the function DEVSQ(), which returns the sum of squared deviations from the mean. The corresponding calculations for the restricted likelihood (row 15) are simpler. The second term of the likelihood is zero as $\ln(1) = 0$. In the final term, $\Sigma(z_t - \mu)^2/\sigma^2$ simplifies to Σz_t^2 , as $\mu = 0$ and $\sigma^2 = 1$. Σz_t^2 can be evaluated using the function SUMSQ().

We can then directly compute the likelihood ratio statistic λ. Its associated asymptotic p-value can be obtained with the function CHIDIST.

In the example, the p-value is 0.3%. We could thus reject the hypothesis that the model is correct at a significance level of 0.3%, i.e., we can expect to err with a probability of 0.3% when rejecting the model. Looking at the data, it becomes evident why the test rejects the model. The loss series contains two years with zero losses, but the model's probability of observing a zero loss is just 0.08%. Therefore, two years with zero losses in a five-year period are an extremely unlikely event. Upon observing such an unlikely event, we reject the model.

REPRESENTING THE LOSS DISTRIBUTION

Information about the portfolio distribution can be represented in different ways. Simulation-based credit risk models will produce a long list of scenarios containing all the necessary information. This information can be processed into a cumulative distribution function.

Table 9.2 exemplifies these two types of expressing a loss distribution. Moving from the scenario representation to the cumulative distribution is straightforward. If the scenarios are sorted in ascending order, we can type

=COUNTIF(A$3:A$50002,"<="&B3)/COUNT(A$3:A$50002)

into cell C3 and copy the formula down. Note the little trick in COUNTIF that integrates a variable range into the condition. (A standard use of COUNTIF would be COUNTIF(B2:B5, ">55").)

In practical applications of the Berkowitz test, one notices that representing the loss distribution through a cumulative distribution is useful. One could apply the Berkowitz transformation directly to a list of scenarios, but the number of scenarios is quite often so large that they cannot conveniently be handled within the row constraint of an EXCEL spreadsheet (at least until Excel 2003, which has a maximum of 65,536 rows).[1]

[1] If scenarios are sorted ascending and saved in a range ('SCEN-RANGE'), the transformation $p_t = F(L_t)$ can be achieved, for example, through =MATCH(L_t, SCEN-RANGE,1)/COUNT(SCEN-RANGE).

Table 9.2 Different representations of the loss distribution

	A	B	C	D
1	Scenarios	Cumulative distribution		
2	(sorted)	L	F(L)=prob(loss ?L)	
3	0	0	2.70%	=COUNTIF(A$3:A$50002,"<=" &B3)/COUNT(A$3:A$50002)
4	0	1	12.92%	*(can be copied into C4:C23)*
5	0	2	31.40%	
6	0	3	53.25%	
7	0	4	72.37%	
...	...	...	...	
...	...	...	...	
22	0	19	100.00%	
23	0	20	100.00%	
...	...			
...	...			
50001	13			
50002	13			

The cumulative distribution should be specified with a large number of intervals. Otherwise, we lose too much information, possibly leading to biased tests. The 20 intervals shown in the example data were chosen for the sake of illustration and should not be viewed as a model implementation. The probability of the last value in the list should be very close to 100%.

In the calculations of the previous section, we chose losses and the loss distribution in such a way that losses did not lie within the intervals of the distribution. In practice, they will, and we have to find a way of dealing with this. A simple procedure would be to interpolate linearly the cumulative probabilities. If an interval ranges from 13 to 14 with associated probabilities of 30% and 30.5%, for example, we would assign a probability of 30.25% to a loss of 13.5. The interpolation as such is easy to do, but referring to the right values is somewhat of a complex task. One way of doing it is shown in Table 9.3.

We use two functions for associating a given loss with the lower and the upper end of an interval, respectively. VLOOKUP() with the logical value *range_lookup* set to 1 helps us identify the lower end of an interval. The function MATCH also finds the largest value that is less than or equal to the *lookup-value*. The difference to VLOOKUP is that MATCH returns the position of the *lookup-value* in the range instead of the value itself. Thus, the position of the upper end is the return value of MATCH plus 1. The associated probability can be identified with the function INDEX. If we use VLOOKUP and MATCH to interpolate the data linearly, the resulting equation is somewhat messy, but we reach our goal and the function can easily be copied from one cell to the next.

Note that realized losses could be outside of the range of losses for which loss probabilities are specified. This problem can be solved by adding a large value considered not to be surpassed and assigning a probability of one to it.[2] In Table 9.3, this is done in row 24. Note that there is a problem if the last probability of the original distribution (cell G23 in Table 9.3) already

[2] In a mark-to-market model, where profits can arise (corresponding to negative losses), one would proceed similarly at the lower end of the distribution.

Table 9.3 Assigning a probability to an observed loss

	A	B	C	D	E	F	G
1	**Raw data**		**1st transform**	**2nd transform**		**Loss distribution**	
2	Year	Losses	p_t	z_t		L	F(L)
3	1	0.5	0.37%	-2.6763		0	0.08%
4	2	5.8	41.69%	-0.2099		1	0.66%
5	3	12.1	97.66%	1.9888		2	2.77%
6	4	9.3	85.55%	1.0602		3	7.81%
7	5	4.5	23.21%	-0.7318		4	16.81%
8	C7: =VLOOKUP(B7,F\$3:G\$24,2,1)+ (B7-VLOOKUP(B7,F\$3:F\$24,1,1))/ (INDEX(F\$3:F\$24,MATCH(B7,F\$3:F\$24,1)+1)-VLOOKUP(B7,F\$3:F\$24,1,1))* ((INDEX(G\$3:G\$24,MATCH(B7,F\$3:F\$24, 1)+1)-VLOOKUP(B7,F\$3:G\$24,2,1)))					5	29.62%
…	*(can be copied into C3:C6; for C7 the resulting values are* = 16.81% + (4.5 – 4)/ (5 – 4)* (29.62%-16.81%)					…	…
23						20	99.999%
24						100000	100%

amounts to 100% and observed losses are even larger. Applying the inverse normal to a p_t of 100% yields an error. A simple fix to this problem is to set the next-to-last probability of the distribution (here, this would be the one in cell G23) to a value very close to 100%, e.g., 0.9999999999. Another problem could arise if zero losses occur but the predicted distribution assigns a probability of zero to losses of zero. A simple fix would be to set the probability to a very low number, e.g., 0.0000000001. Alternatively, we could use an IF-condition that signals a rejection of the model whenever an observed loss has probability zero within the model. With the typical time span T, the simple fix has the same effect because one loss that is assigned a very low probability such as 0.0000000001 suffices to reject the model.

SIMULATING THE CRITICAL CHI-SQUARE VALUE

Since the number of observations T will typically be small, we should be careful when using the asymptotic distribution of the likelihood ratio test. One way of achieving robust inference is to simulate critical values under the assumption that the model predictions are correct. We do this repeatedly and get a simulated distribution of the test statistic to which we can compare the statistic computed with actual data.

We need to make only a few changes to Table 9.1 to accomplish this; they are shown in Table 9.4. If the model is correct, the first transformation of losses p_t should be uniformly distributed between 0 and 1. Therefore, we can directly simulate the p_ts that follow a uniform distribution. The loss distribution and the actual losses are no longer needed.

We can directly insert the scenario generating function into the range C3:C7 by using the function RAND(), which returns random numbers distributed evenly across the interval (0, 1). The computation of the LR-statistic then follows Table 9.1

Table 9.4 Simulating critical values of the test statistic

	A	B	C	D	E	F	G
1			**1st transform**	**2nd transform**			
2	Year		p_t	z_t			
3	1		86.23%	1.0907	C3: =RAND()		
4	2		79.71%	0.8313	*(can be copied into C4:C7)*		
5	3		87.03%	1.1277			
6	4		95.02%	1.6467	D3 =NORMSINV(C3)		
7	5		32.64%	-0.4498	*(can be copied into D4:D7)*		
8							
9	**Calculation of LR statistic λ**						
10							
11	T		5	=COUNT(B3:B7)			
12	ML estimate for □ 2		3.2185	=VARP(D3:D7)			
13							
14	terms		-5.422	=-C11/2*LN(C12)-DEVSQ(D3:D7)/(2*C12)			
15	for LR statistic		-11.304	=-SUMSQ(D3:D7)/2			
16							
17	LR statistic □		11.764	=2*(C14-C15)			
18							
19							
20	**Simulated λs**		**Critical values based on simulated λs**				
21	2.6954		p-value	critical value			
22	0.8898		1%	11.317	=PERCENTILE(A$21:A$10020,1-C22)		
23	3.0749		5%	7.427	*(can be copied into D23:D24)*		
24	2.0273		10%	5.710			
...	...						
10020	0.4875						

In order to produce a sufficient amount of LR-statistics, we can use a macro. In each step of a loop, we write the LR-statistic to a cell in the worksheet. The macro might look as follows:

```
Sub simlr()
Application.ScreenUpdating = False
Application.Calculation = xlCalculationAutomatic
Dim i As Long
For i = 1 To 10000
    Application.StatusBar = i
    Range("A" & i + 20) = (Range("C17"))
Next i
End Sub
```

In the macro, we make sure that the option *Automatic calculation* (to be found via Tools→ Options→Calculation in Excel 2003; via Office Button→Excel Options→Formulas in Excel 2007) is activated. With this option activated, every change in the worksheet leads to a recalculation of the entire worksheet including new-drawn random variables. Since there is a change in each step of the loop – we write the LR-statistic into the sheet – random numbers are newly drawn in each step. If the option *Manual calculation* were chosen instead, we would have to insert a line with `calculate`, e.g., after `For i=1 to 10000`.

Once we have produced the list of simulated test statistics, we can use them to determine critical values of the test statistic. We reject a model if the statistic is above a certain set level. To obtain the critical value associated with a significance level of α, we determine the $(1 - \alpha)$ percentile of the data. This can be accomplished with the function PERCENTILE(Range, percentile value).

These critical values are then used as follows. If we want to conduct a test on the, say, 5% level, we would compare the λ statistic computed with actual losses to the simulated value of 7.427. If it is larger than this critical value, we can reject the model at a significance of 5% or better.

Note that the critical values do not have to be simulated again for each application. For a given number of observations T, we can use them to test different models on different data sets. As a reference, the following tabulation collects simulated critical values for various T and α (based on 50,000 simulations):

α	5 years	10 years	15 years	20 years	Asymptotic
0.1	5.70	5.09	4.90	4.78	4.61
0.05	7.42	6.60	6.35	6.24	5.99
0.01	11.32	10.21	9.78	9.62	9.21

There is a caveat to this, however. When simulating critical values in the way described above, we are implicitly assuming that both the true distribution of losses and the density forecast used for the transformation are continuous. Simulations show that discreteness of the distribution need not lead to major changes in critical values if the distribution is sufficiently smooth. For a typical, large bank portfolio with 5000 obligors, for example, there is almost no effect on critical values.[3] If there are concerns about effects of discreteness, the procedure proposed by Hamerle and Plank (2009) can be used.

TESTING MODELING DETAILS: BERKOWITZ ON SUBPORTFOLIOS

The test implemented above examines the model's prediction for the entire portfolio loss. It therefore serves to check whether modeling assumptions are correct on average. It might be useful, however, to check modeling details. If a model allows for differences in asset correlation across obligors, for example, one would like to know whether the chosen differences are consistent with the data.

Due to lack of historical loss data, we cannot hope to test the correctness of each individual assumption, but we might gain valuable insights by grouping obligors and checking whether the average difference in parameters between the groups can be validated. Consider the following example. A bank determines obligor-specific correlations in a one-factor model based on equity correlations or other information. With N obligors, there are up to N different correlation assumptions. We then group the obligors into two equal-sized portfolios: subportfolio 1 contains the obligors with the larger asset correlations; subportfolio 2 contains those with the

[3] We draw losses from a default-mode asset correlation model with 5000 obligors, uniform default probability of 1% and asset correlation of 5%. Each default leads to a loss of 1. For the Berkowitz transformation, the distribution is represented through 50,000 scenarios drawn from the distribution. With 10 years, the simulated critical value is 5.07 for $\alpha = 10\%$, very close to the value reported in the table.

lower asset correlations. We set up model predictions for the losses of these subportfolios and transform the observed subportfolio losses as we did above.

This gives us two series of transformed variables z_1 and z_2, with the subscript referring to one of the two subportfolios. Since the losses are expected to be correlated, we need to look at the joint likelihood. The appropriate distribution function is the bivariate normal, which has the following log-likelihood:

$$\ln L = -T\ \ln 2\pi - T\ \ln \sigma_1 - T\ \ln \sigma_2 - \frac{T}{2} \ln(1-\rho_{12}^2) - \frac{1}{2(1-\rho_{12}^2)} \sum_{t=1}^{T} \left[\left(\frac{z_{t1}-\mu_1}{\sigma_1}\right)^2 - 2\rho_{12}\left(\frac{z_{t1}-\mu_1}{\sigma_1}\right)\left(\frac{z_{t2}-\mu_2}{\sigma_2}\right) + \left(\frac{z_{t2}-\mu_2}{\sigma_2}\right)^2 \right] \tag{9.8}$$

where ρ_{12} is the correlation between z_1 and z_2, and μ_i and σ_i^2 denote the mean and variance of z_i, respectively. The likelihood ratio test examines the hypothesis $\mu_1 = 0, \mu_2 = 0, \sigma_1^2 = 1, \sigma_2^2 = 1$.

Before we implement the test, let us clarify the advantage of such an approach. A portfolio model might produce an aggregate forecast that is consistent with the data even if individual assumptions are far from being correct. For some obligors, asset correlations may be too high while being too low for others. If these errors average out over the entirety of the portfolio, a test based on the entire portfolio is unlikely to indicate a misspecification. A test based on grouped portfolios, however, could reveal the errors as they influence the prediction of subportfolio losses. An issue that needs to be answered in practical applications is the forming of the subportfolios. A good testing strategy is to form the subportfolios such that differences in predicted subportfolio risk are maximized. In many situations, such as the example sketched here, this is easy to achieve. Note that we are not restricted to performing the test on just two subportfolios (rather than three or more). For the sake of exposition, however, we will explain the procedure for the two-portfolio case.

To calculate the likelihood ratio statistic in the subportfolio setting, we first determine the maximum likelihood (ML) estimators for σ_t^2, which can be achieved by applying the same formula that we used above (9.6). The estimate for the correlation coefficient is given by

$$\hat{\rho}_{12} = \frac{1}{T} \frac{\sum_{t=1}^{T} (z_{t1}-\hat{\mu}_1)(z_{t2}-\hat{\mu}_2)}{\hat{\sigma}_1 \hat{\sigma}_2} \tag{9.9}$$

In the next step, we determine the likelihood under the restrictions $\mu_1 = 0, \mu_2 = 0, \sigma_1^2 = 1, \sigma_2^2 = 1$. The appropriate estimate for ρ_{12} is a restricted ML estimator. To determine the estimate, we can maximize the restricted log-likelihood, which we obtain by inputting $\mu_1 = 0, \mu_2 = 0, \sigma_1^2 = 1, \sigma_2^2 = 1$ into (9.8):

$$\ln L = -T \ln 2\pi - \frac{T}{2} \ln(1-\rho_{12}^2) - \frac{1}{2(1-\rho_{12}^2)} \sum_{t=1}^{T} (z_{t1}^2 - 2\rho_{12} z_{t1} z_{t2} + z_{t2}^2) \tag{9.10}$$

In Excel, we could use the Solver to find quickly the value of ρ_{12} that maximizes (9.10). For repeated applications of the test, however, it can be useful to define a function that returns the

Table 9.5 Implementation of a test based on two subportfolios

	A	B	C	D	E	F	G	H	I	J
1	**Raw data**			**1st transform**		**2nd transform**		**Loss distributions**		
2	Year	L_{t1}	L_{t2}	p_{t1}	p_{t2}	z_{t1}	z_{t2}	L	$F_1(L)$	$F_2(L)$
3	1	3	3	0.060	0.147	-1.557	-1.049	0	0.05%	0.23%
4	2	6	3	0.388	0.147	-0.284	-1.049	1	0.46%	1.62%
5	3	7	5	0.538	0.443	0.096	-0.143	2	2.02%	5.93%
6	4	14	19	0.992	1.000	2.412	4.515	3	5.98%	14.72%
7	5	11	10	0.930	0.960	1.478	1.749	4	13.47%	28.10%
8								5	24.74%	44.32%
9	**Calculation of LR statistic λ**							6	38.83%	60.63%
10	T		5	=COUNT(B3:B7)				7	53.82%	74.61%
11	ML for σ_1^2		1.9183	=VARP(F3:F7)				8	67.72%	85.04%
12	ML for σ_2^2		4.4855	=VARP(G3:G7)				9	79.12%	91.92%
13	ML for ρ_{12}		0.9316	=CORREL(F3:F7,G3:G7)				10	87.48%	95.99%
14	Restricted ML for ρ_{12}		0.6646	=RHOSEARCH(F3:F7,G3:G7)				11	93.02%	98.16%
15								12	96.38%	99.22%
16	Terms		-5.321	=-C10*LN(C11^0.5)-C10*LN(C12^0.5)-C10/2*LN(1-C13^2)-1/(2*(1-C13^2))*(DEVSQ(F3:F7)/C11-2*C13^2*C10+DEVSQ(G3:G7)/C12)				13	98.25%	99.69%
17	for LR statistic		-12.623	=-C10/2*LN(1-C14^2)-1/(2*(1-C14^2))*(SUMSQ(F3:F7)-2*C14*SUMPRODUCT(F3:F7,G3:G7)+SUMSQ(G3:G7))				14	99.21%	99.89%
18								15	99.66%	99.96%
19	LR statistic λ		14.603	=2*(C16-C17)				16	99.86%	99.99%
20	p(value)		0.006	=CHIDIST(C19,4)				17	99.95%	100.00%
21		$\ln L = -T\ln 2\pi - T\ln\sigma_1 - T\ln\sigma_2 - \frac{T}{2}\ln(1-\rho_{12}^2)$						18	99.98%	100.00%
22								19	99.99%	100.00%
23	*Recall:*	$-\frac{1}{2(1-\rho_{12}^2)}\sum_{t=1}^{T}\left[\left(\frac{z_{t1}-\mu_1}{\sigma_1}\right)^2 - 2\rho_{12}\left(\frac{z_{t1}-\mu_1}{\sigma_1}\right)\left(\frac{z_{t2}-\mu_2}{\sigma_2}\right)+\left(\frac{z_{t2}-\mu_2}{\sigma_2}\right)^2\right]$						20	100.00%	100.00%

restricted ML estimate of ρ_{12}. To this end, we can perform a simple line search across $(-1, 1)$, the possible values for ρ_{12}, and single out the one that maximizes the restricted log-likelihood.[4]

Table 9.5 shows an example implementation of the cross-sectional Berkowitz test. We observe losses on two subportfolios over five years. We start by transforming the raw subportfolio losses as we did above in Table 9.1. We then determine maximum likelihood estimates of variances and the correlation using VARP and CORREL, respectively.

The line search for the correlation is implemented in the following user-defined function:

```
Function RHOSEARCH(z1, z2)
Dim T As Long, sz1 As Variant, sz2 As Variant
Dim lmax As Double, lnL As Double, rmax As Double, r As Single

T = z1.Rows.Count
sz1 = Application.WorksheetFunction.SumSq(z1)
```

[4] One might think of applying the Newton method or other standard numerical routines here. The restricted likelihood function, however, can have more than one maximum which complicates the application of such routines.

```
sz2 = Application.WorksheetFunction.SumSq(z2)
lmax = -1 / 2 * (sz1 + sz2)

For r = -0.9999 To 0.9999 Step 0.0005
    lnL = -T / 2 * Log(1 - r ^ 2) - 1 / (2 * (1 - r ^ 2)) * _
        (sz1 - 2 * r * _
          Application.WorksheetFunction.SumProduct _
  (z1, z2) + sz2)
      If lnL > lmax Then
          rmax = r
          lmax = lnL
      End If
Next r
RHOSEARCH = rmax
End Function
```

We start the function by determining elements of the likelihood function that are independent of ρ_{12}. Specifically, we count the number of years and determine `sz1` $= \sum z_{t1}^2$ and `sz2` $= \sum z_{t2}^2$. Before starting the iteration, we determine a value to which the likelihood of the first iteration is compared; for simplicity, we take this to be the likelihood associated with $\rho_{12} = 0$. In steps of 0.0005, we then check all values for ρ_{12} within the interval $[-0.9999, 0.9999]$. If the likelihood in one iteration is larger than the previous maximum `lmax`, we write ρ_{12} of this iteration into `rmax`.

With the correlation estimates in hand, we can determine the likelihood ratio statistic similar to the way we did above. The squared deviations of the z_t from their mean are again calculated using DEVSQ; in the restricted likelihood, we use SUMSQ. To compute the covariance term in cell C16, we exploit the definition of the correlation estimator:

$$\hat{\rho}_{12} = \frac{1}{T}\sum \frac{(z_{t1} - \hat{\mu}_1)(z_{t2} - \hat{\mu}_2)}{\hat{\sigma}_1\hat{\sigma}_2} \Rightarrow \sum \left[-2\hat{\rho}_{12}\frac{(z_{t1} - \hat{\mu}_1)(z_{t2} - \hat{\mu}_2)}{\hat{\sigma}_1\hat{\sigma}_2} \right] = -2\hat{\rho}_{12}^2 T \qquad (9.11)$$

The covariance term in the restricted likelihood can be calculated with SUMPRODUCT. Finally, note that the likelihood ratio statistic λ is now referred to the chi-squared distribution with four degrees of freedom. Of course, we should check whether this provides a good approximation of the true distribution of the statistic. Since we estimate more parameters than in the previous test, the asymptotic distribution is likely to be less reliable. Again, we would deal with the problem by simulating the small-sample distribution of the test statistic. In doing so, we have to ascertain that the correlation structure across subportfolios is retained. We cannot simply draw independent uniform random numbers for the first transform p_{t1} and p_{t2}, because this would impose zero correlation. Instead, we would start by using our portfolio model to simulate losses for all obligors in the portfolio, then split the obligors into the two subportfolios, and insert the simulated subportfolio losses into the ranges B3:B7 and C3:C7, respectively.

ASSESSING POWER

Consider a situation in which a bank runs a Berkowitz test and finds that the model it used cannot be rejected. How sure can the bank be that the model is reliable? What the bank would like to know is called 'power' by statisticians. Power is the probability that we reject a hypothesis (here: 'the model is correct') if it is false.

Given that the number of observations available for a test is typically small, one could surmise that the power will also be small. But if the differences between the true model and the one we use are substantial, the power could be large even if we have only 5 or 10 years of data. As there is a lot of uncertainty in the industry about the correct modeling and parameterization of credit risk models, we are quite likely to encounter such a situation. In fact, simulation evidence shows that the Berkowitz test could resolve some of the questions debated by credit risk managers.[5]

If a bank uses model A, but considers one or several other models to be plausible rivals, one can use simulations to check the probability that model A is rejected if one of the rival models were true. Let us sketch the structure of such a simulation:

1. Randomly draw a loss history from model B, the rival model.
2. Use the data from step 1 to calculate the LR-statistic of model A, that is, the model actually in use.
3. Repeat steps 1 and 2 sufficiently often.
4. The power is then obtained as the relative frequency with which the LR-statistic is significant at a chosen confidence level.

Note that the power will increase if we use a less stringent significance level (say 10% instead of 5%).

The necessary computations (except those for step 1) have been discussed in the previous examples. Table 9.6 shows how to draw random losses from a given loss distribution if it is specified as a cumulative distribution.

Table 9.6 Drawing random losses from a given loss distribution

	A	B	C	D	E	F	G
1	**Simulated data**					**Loss distribution**	
2	Year	Random numbers	Random losses		B3: =RAND()	F(L)	L
3	1	0.1496	4.33		*(can be copied*	0.00%	0.0
4	2	0.4765	8.19		*into B4:B7)*	0.00%	0.2
5	3	0.6877	11.47			0.00%	0.4
6	4	0.3910	7.14			0.01%	0.6
7	5	0.0017	1.10			0.04%	0.8
8	C7: =VLOOKUP(B7,F$3:G$503,2,1)+ (B7-VLOOKUP(B7,F$3:F$503,1,1))/ (INDEX(F$3:F$503,MATCH(B7,F$3:F$503, 1)+1)-VLOOKUP(B7,F$3:F$503,1,1))* ((INDEX(G$3:G$503,MATCH(B7,F$3:F$503, 1)+1)-VLOOKUP(B7,F$3:G$503,2,1))) *(can be copied into C3:C6)*					0.11%	1.0
9						0.23%	1.2
...						...	...
502						99.9999%	99.8
503						100%	100

[5] See Frerichs and Löffler (2003).

We start by drawing a uniform random number (RAND) for each year. We take each of the random numbers to be a cumulative probability $F(L)$ and then use linear interpolation to find the loss associated with this number in the loss distribution. This is just the inverse of what we did in Table 9.3, and so the formula looks similar.

Drawing from a list of scenarios is simpler. If we have K scenarios sorted ascending within the range SCEN-RANGE, a random draw can be performed with

= INDEX(SCEN-RANGE, INT(RAND()*K) + 1)

RAND()*K produces random numbers that are uniformly distributed on the unit interval. We round them to the nearest integer using INT and add 1 to get integer values between 1 and K. Therefore, INT(RAND()*K)+1 corresponds to the drawing of one row out of the K rows of our scenario list. We then use the function INDEX to find the scenario-value in the row that was drawn.

SCOPE AND LIMITS OF THE TEST

The Berkowitz test provides a very flexible validation framework. It can be applied to any model independent of its structural form or of the sources of risk that are modeled.

As shown in this chapter, the test can be used to test the overall quality of the distribution as well as the validity of cross-sectional differences in parameter choices. Of course, there is a limit as to how far we can go into the cross-section. We could partition the portfolio into many subportfolios by using a multivariate normal distribution instead of the bivariate one. However, the number of the parameters in the likelihood function will grow very quickly with the number of subportfolios. With the usual 5–10 year history, we probably should not endeavor to form more than five subportfolios.[6]

A possible criticism is that risk managers and supervisory authorities are mainly concerned about the probability of extreme events, whereas the Berkowitz test is based on the entire range of the distribution. When responding to this criticism, three aspects seem to be important.

First, significant differences in the tails of the distribution often go along with significant changes in the rest of the distribution. This holds, for example, if we change parameter values (say the asset correlation) within a given modeling framework. If a model dramatically fails to predict extreme percentiles, it will also be severely wrong in the prediction of other percentiles, and the Berkowitz test is likely to detect these misspecifications.

Second, there are situations in which the model to be tested differs from the correct one mainly in the prediction of extreme percentiles. Using inappropriate distributional assumptions might lead to such a situation. In this case, there would be little hope of uncovering the model's deficiency. This, however, is not a problem of the Berkowitz test but a general one that cannot be healed by pinpointing the test at extreme realizations. Should model errors materialize mainly beyond the 99.9th percentile, even 50 or 250 years of data will typically not contain evidence against the model because only 1 out of 1000 years is expected to see a loss beyond the 99.9th percentile.

[6] An answer to the question of how many subportfolios we should form could be obtained via simulation studies.

Finally, one should not conclude that tests are worthless simply because they cannot uncover *some* model deficiencies. They might uncover others, which could be very valuable to risk managers.

NOTES AND LITERATURE

A general description of the Berkowitz test is given (together with applications to market risk models) in Berkowitz, J., 2001, Testing density forecasts with applications to risk management, *Journal of Business & Economic Statistics* 19, 465–474.

A simulation study of the properties of the Berkowitz test when applied to credit risk models is given in: Frerichs, H. and Löffler, G., 2003, Evaluating credit risk models using loss density forecasts, *Journal of Risk* 5, 1–23. Hamerle, A. and Plank, K., 2009, A note on the Berkowitz test with discrete distributions, *Journal of Risk Model Validation* 3, 3–10, suggest a modification to solve problems that may arise if the loss distribution is not continuous.

10

Credit Default Swaps and Risk-Neutral Default Probabilities

In this chapter, we discuss the most important instrument on the credit derivatives market: *the credit default swap* (CDS). A CDS is a bilateral contract that provides an insurance against the default of a particular issuer, known as the *reference entity*. The protection seller, who is short in the CDS (and thus long risk in the underlying), insures the protection buyer, who is long in the CDS, in the following way: in the case of a predefined credit event, the protection buyer has the right to sell bonds of the defaulted issuer to the protection seller – at their face value. The total volume covered by a CDS is called its *notional principal*. For single-name CDS, which we consider in this chapter, the credit event is the default of the issuer.

Of course, this insurance does not come for free. The buyer makes periodic payments (typically at the end of each quarter, half-year or year for which the insurance is bought) to the seller until the maturity of the CDS or the default. Upon default, settlement can take place either by physical delivery or in cash, depending on the terms agreed on in the contract. Physical delivery means that the buyer hands the bonds to the seller, who then pays their par value to the buyer. If cash settlement is specified in the contract, the protection seller pays the difference between the bonds' par value and some suitably defined market price.

Let us illustrate the structure of the CDS with an example: a five-year CDS contracted on January 1, 2010, with a notional principal of $100 million and IBM as reference entity.[1] The seller demands 30 basis points (bps) annually for the protection; this is the CDS spread. Flows between seller and buyer with physical settlement are illustrated in Figure 10.1.

In the case where IBM does not default until 2015, the buyer of the CDS pays $300,000 per year. Assuming that IBM defaults on June 1, 2011, the buyer hands over bonds with a total par value of $100 million to the seller and receives $100 million in turn. The buyer also has to pay the part of the annual fee accrued between January, 2011, and the default date on June 1, 2011. Typically, the accrued fee is proportioned linearly, meaning that the buyer would pay 5/12 of the annual fee as accrued fee in this example.

In this chapter, we show how to price such a CDS using the general risk-neutral valuation approach. We first introduce this approach and show how to use bond prices to infer its ingredients, in particular (risk-neutral) probabilities of default. The fact that we devote a lot of time to this concept explains why this chapter is called 'Credit default swaps and risk-neutral default probabilities', rather than just 'Credit default swaps'. We also show how to determine market values of CDS, how to convert spreads, and how to price forword CDS and swaptions.

[1] In our first edition we used General Motors (GM) as an example, but GM defaulted in June 2009.

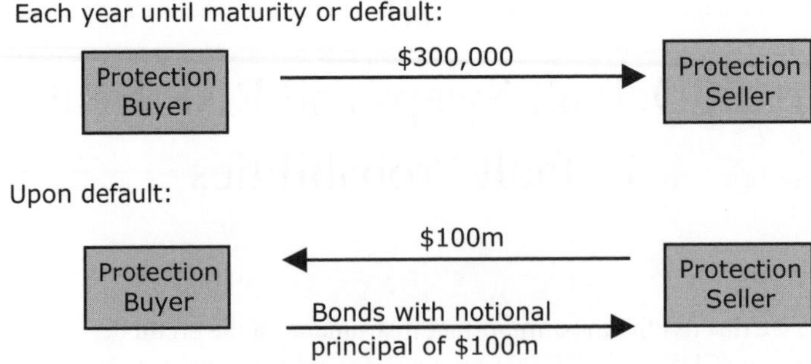

Figure 10.1 CDS structure

DESCRIBING THE TERM STRUCTURE OF DEFAULT: PDS CUMULATIVE, MARGINAL AND SEEN FROM TODAY

Since the standard maturity of a CDS is five years, we need more than a just a probability of default (PD) for the next year to describe the default risk relevant for a CDS. We have to describe the term structure of PDs, i.e., specify probabilities that default occurs at various dates in the future.

The term structure can be described in different ways. For our purpose, it is useful to specify a probability of default for each future period t as seen from today ($t = 0$). Let us denote this by PD_t^0, where the superscript zero indicates today's view.[2] Consider a pool of 100 issuers and suppose that you expect to see two defaults within the second year from today, then $\mathrm{PD}_2^0 = 2\%$. So PD_t^0 is the probability to default between January 1 of year t and December 1 of year t as expected today.

In other situations, PD term structures are more commonly expressed via cumulative PDs. Let us denote the cumulative PD over t years by $\mathrm{PD}_t^{\mathrm{C}}$. Suppose you expect a time-constant PD_t^0 of 2%, then the probability to default over two years, $\mathrm{PD}_2^{\mathrm{C}}$, is 4%. In more general terms, the relationship is

$$\mathrm{PD}_t^{\mathrm{C}} = \mathrm{PD}_{t-1}^{\mathrm{C}} + \mathrm{PD}_t^0 \tag{10.1}$$

The next and final concept is the marginal PD in year t, denoted by $\mathrm{PD}_t^{\mathrm{M}}$. It is the probability to default during year t conditional on having survived until the beginning of year t:

$$\mathrm{PD}_t^{\mathrm{M}} = \mathrm{PD}_t^0/(1 - \mathrm{PD}_{t-1}^{\mathrm{C}}) \tag{10.1a}$$

Note that the denominator of Equation (10.1a) is the survival probability over $t - 1$ years. Combining both equations, we obtain an expression for the cumulative PD in terms of the marginal PD:

$$\mathrm{PD}_t^{\mathrm{C}} = \mathrm{PD}_{t-1}^{\mathrm{C}} + \mathrm{PD}_t^{\mathrm{M}} \times (1 - \mathrm{PD}_{t-1}^{\mathrm{C}}) \tag{10.2}$$

[2] In the examples that follow, we set period length to one-year, but we could use any other periodicity.

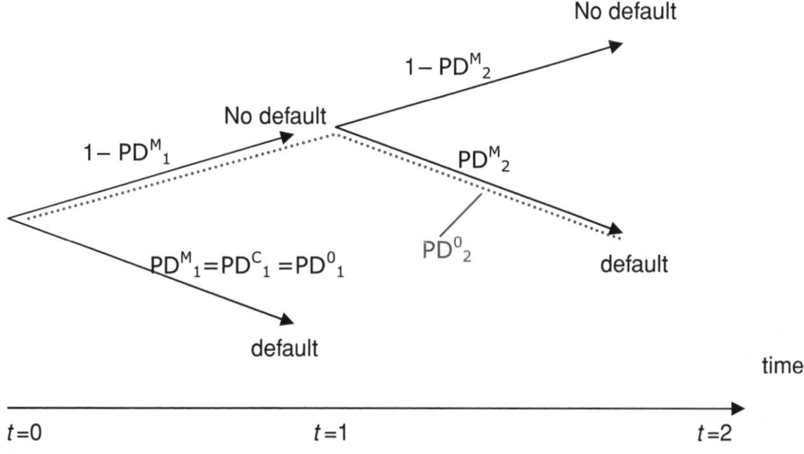

Figure 10.2 PD concepts: marginal (M), cumulative (C) and seen from today (0)

Here, we see that the t-year cumulative PD is composed of the previous year cumulative PD (PD^C_{t-1}) plus the marginal PD in that year (PD^M_t) times the cumulative survival probability over $t - 1$ years ($1 - PD^C_{t-1}$).

Comparing Equations (10.1) and (10.2), we see that the PD^0_t as seen from today is the marginal probability to default in year t (PD^M_t) times the probability to survive until year $t - 1(1 - PD^C_{t-1})$.

Finally, the marginal default probability in terms of the cumulative default probability is given via Equation (10.2a) as

$$PD^M_t = (PD^C_t - PD^C_{t-1})/(1 - PD^C_{t-1}) \tag{10.2a}$$

To clarify these three concepts and their relations to each other, consider Figure 10.2. PD^0_2, the probability of default in year 2 as seen from today, is the probability of following the dotted path from $t = 0$ to $t = 2$. The marginal probability in year 2 is the probability of taking the path to default from $t = 1$ to $t = 2$, conditional on having taken the upper path until $t = 1$.

FROM BOND PRICES TO RISK-NEUTRAL DEFAULT PROBABILITIES

Concepts and formulae

Intuitively, the higher the default risk of the reference entity, the higher the protection buyer's payment to the protection seller will be. But how do we obtain the probabilities of default (PDs) for pricing a CDS? In previous chapters, we already discussed several ways of obtaining PD estimates: the scoring model in Chapter 1 or the transition matrices in Chapter 3 are both based on historically observed defaults. If we use these PDs to price a CDS such that the seller is compensated for its expected loss in case of default, we would miss an important pricing component: we would fail to take into account that the seller might require a premium for taking this risk.

Instead, we can use bonds to back out risk-neutral probabilities. A risk-neutral PD is the probability of default in a hypothetical world in which investors are indifferent to risk, i.e., where they do not require an extra return for bearing risk. In such a world, the price of any asset can be obtained by discounting the asset's expected payoffs with the risk-free rate. Importantly, this price can be used to determine the appropriate price in a world like ours, which is populated by risk-averse investors. Why is this so? Risk aversion means that people assign higher weights to bad states than risk-neutral people; when translating the pricing to a risk-neutral world, this is captured by increasing the probabilities of bad states relative to the ones prevailing under risk aversion. Risk-neutral probabilities of default – expressing a bad state – can thus be expected to be higher than actual ones.

The most straightforward way of determining risk-neutral probabilities is to take market prices of corporate bonds or other default-risky instruments. If we know those prices and the risk-free rates of return, and if we assume the recovery rates to be constant over time and across different issues, the only unknowns in the risk-neutral pricing equation are the risk-neutral default probabilities.

Let us have a detailed look at the formula. A random cash flow CF_t received at time t has, at time $t = 0$, a price of $\mathrm{E}_0[\mathrm{CF}_t/(1 + r_t)^t]$, where $\mathrm{E}_0[\mathrm{CF}_t]$ is the risk-neutral expectation of CF_t as seen from today and r_t denotes the per annum risk-free spot rate from today to t. The spot rate is the interest rate that would be earned on a zero-coupon bond, i.e., a bond providing no coupons.[3] A bondholder receives cash flows at each coupon payment date and the principal at maturity. Generally, the price of bond today P_0 is then obtained as the sum of discounted cash flows as they are expected today:

$$P_0 = E_0\left[\sum_{t=1}^{r} \frac{\mathrm{CF}_t}{(1+r_t)^t}\right] \tag{10.3}$$

If the bond defaults at time $\tau < T$, the subsequent cash flows are zero, i.e., $\mathrm{CF}_i = 0,\ i \geq \tau$. When valuing a risk-*free* bond, we drop the expectations operator. To distinguish risky and risk-free bonds, we denote the price of the latter by B_0:[4]

$$B_0 = \sum_{t=1}^{T} \frac{\mathrm{CF}_t}{(1+r_t)^t} = \sum_{t=1}^{T} \frac{\mathrm{Coupon}_t}{(1+r_t)^t} + \frac{\mathrm{Principal}}{(1+r_T)^T} \tag{10.4}$$

For a corporate bond maturing in one year, we can easily express the expectation in Equation (10.3) in terms of a one-year default probability PD and a recovery rate. Consider a zero-coupon bond with principal 100 maturing in one year. There are two possible states of the world in one year: either the bond survives and the bondholder receives the principal, or the bond defaults and the bondholder receive 100 times the recovery rate, denoted by R. The second state's

[3] When using treasury bonds, which pay coupons, we cannot use their yield directly but have to convert it to a zero-coupon bond rate. This can be done, for example, with a recursive procedure or based on treasury STRIPS (Separate Trading of Registered Interest and Principal of Securities). Ready-to-use zero rates are available from many data providers.

[4] By assuming the interest rate to be deterministic, i.e., known at time $t = 0$, we abstract from the risk due to an unexpected change in interest rates. However, stochastic interest rate models could be implemented in the following analysis.

probability is the risk-neutral default probability PD_1^0. Today's price of the bond is thus

$$P_0 = \frac{100(1 - PD_1^0) + 100 \cdot R \cdot PD_1^0}{1+r} \tag{10.5}$$

Rearranging and using $B_0 = 100/(1 + r)$ for the price of a risk-free zero-coupon bond with the same principal as the corporate bond, we obtain

$$\begin{aligned} P_0 &= \frac{100}{1+r} - \frac{PD_1^0(100 - 100 \cdot R)}{1+r} \Leftrightarrow \\ B_0 - P_0 &= \frac{PD_1^0(100 - 100 \cdot R)}{1+r} \end{aligned} \tag{10.6}$$

In words, the difference between the price of a risk-free bond and a risky one (both having the same promised cash flows) is equal to the discounted expected loss from holding the risky rather than the risk-free bond; the loss associated with default is that one gets $100 \cdot R$ rather than 100, and this happens with probability PD.

Generally, the relationship 'difference between prices = present value of expected losses from default' also holds for (coupon) bonds with a maturity of more than one year. Note, however, that we abstract here from taxes, liquidity and other reasons which can also lead to a difference in the prices of risky and risk-free bonds. In the following, we will just consider the risk of default.

How can we express the relationship (10.6) in a general formula? At possible default dates τ, we assume that the bondholders have a claim C_τ on which they realize $C_\tau R$. This is compared to F_τ, the price of the risk-free bond that prevails at time τ. In our one-year example – assuming that default can occur only at maturity $t = 1$ – both C_1 and F_1 are 100, and we would write

$$B_0 - P_0 = \frac{PD_1^0(F_1 - C_1 \cdot R)}{1+r} \tag{10.7}$$

With more than one possible default date τ, the formula becomes

$$B_0 - P_0 = \sum_\tau \frac{PD_\tau^0(F_\tau - C_\tau \cdot R)}{(1+r_\tau)^\tau} \tag{10.8}$$

Let us consider the ingredients of formula (10.8), focusing on aspects relevant when using the formula to back out PDs from market prices of bonds:

- τ: in principle, default could occur on any date τ within the life of a bond. In practical applications, we may choose to simplify computations by assuming that default can only occur at discrete dates, e.g., once every quarter.[5]
- P_0: this is the observed market price of the corporate bond.

[5] Here, τ denotes dates on which a default can occur in our pricing framework. In some of the literature, τ contrarily denotes a default date.

- B_0: we determine B_0 by discounting the promised cash flows of the corporate bond with the risk-free spot rates, i.e., we apply formula (10.4).
- PD_τ^0: the probabilities PD_τ^0 are probabilities of default as seen from today, corresponding to the expectation E_0 in (10.3). The goal of the analysis is to solve (10.8) for PD_τ^0. If we have only one bond, we have only one equation of type (10.8), and so we can only solve it if we impose some structure on how PD_τ^0 evolves our time. The simplest structure is that it is constant. If we have more than one bond, we will assume that it is stepwise constant.
- F_τ: this is the price of the risk-free bond that is expected to prevail at date τ. The standard procedure is to determine this price with implied forward rates.[6]
- C_τ: this is the claim that bondholders have upon default. Some alternatives considered in the literature and in practice are

    - the principal (par value)
    - the principal plus accrued interest
    - the market price of a comparable risk-free bond
    - the market price of the bond before default

  The choice of one over the other can be motivated by, for example, bankruptcy regulations or ease of computation. The modeling presented in this chapter can easily accommodate various alternatives.
- R: this is the recovery rate, i.e., the percentage of the claim that bondholders receive in case of a default on average. Assumptions can be based on average historical recovery rates or multivariate prediction models.
- r: the spot rates. A common choice is spot rates derived from AAA-rated government bonds, such as treasury bills (T-bills) or treasury bonds (T-bonds) for the US. An alternative would be the LIBOR rate or swap rates. In this chapter, we will use risk-free rates based on US government bonds. The modeling, however, is general enough to accommodate other sources of risk-free rates.

Before moving on, we take notice of a reformulation of (10.8) that can simplify the implementation. One component of (10.8) is the forward price of the risk-free bond, which is then discounted with the risk-free rate. The way we construct forward prices, a discounted forward price from time τ is just today's present value of the payments from time τ onwards. We can thus avoid the explicit computation of forward rates and instead use

$$B_0 - P_0 = \sum_r PD_r^0 \left(B_o^r - \frac{C_r \cdot R}{(1+r_\tau)^\tau} \right) \tag{10.9}$$

where B_0^τ denotes today's present value of the payments to the risk-free bond that accrue after τ.

[6] Forward rates are rates for lending/borrowing contracts that start at some date a and last until date b. Forward rates f are derived from spot rates r via $f_{ab} = [(1+r_b)^b \times (1+r_a)^{-a}]^{(1/(b-a))} - 1$.

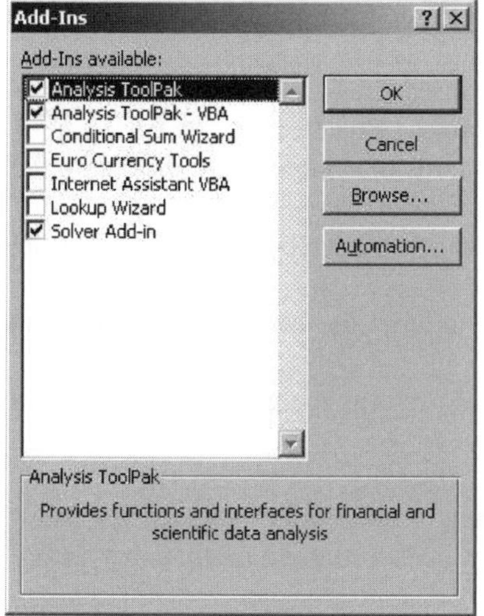

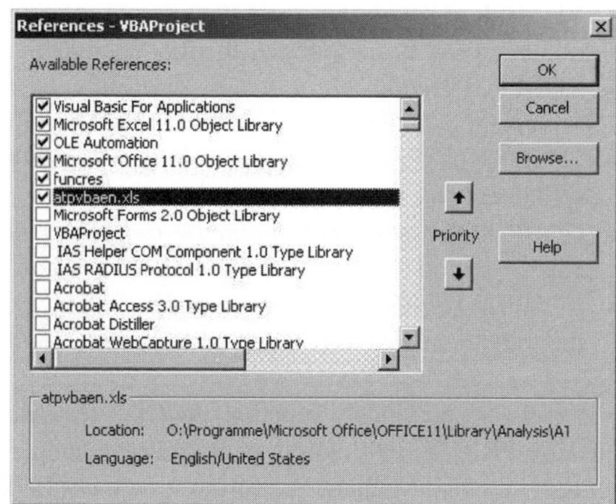

Figure 10.3 Installation of the Analysis Toolpak Add-in

Implementation

The challenges in implementing the approach outlined in the previous section are less conceptual than technical. When evaluating a bond pricing formula such as (10.4), for example, we have to deal with the fact that the time between today and the accrual of cash flows is typically fractions of years whose length need to be determined exactly. For such tasks, a host of functions is available through Excel's Add-in *Analysis Toolpak* (ATP). Before we look at some of them, make sure that the ATP is installed and available to VBA. To check the former in Excel versions prior to 2007, open the Add-in section of the Tools menu and check both items as shown in the left screenshot of Figure 10.3. If these items are not available in the list, you probably need to install ATP using Excel's setup routine (see, e.g., item 'Detect and Repair' in the help menu).

Now open the VBA editor by pressing [alt]+[F11]. In the editor's tools menu, you can find the item references. A window shown in the right screenshot of Figure 10.3 appears. Search the list for a reference called ATPVBAEN.xls, which stands for Analysis Toolpak Visual Basic for Application English. You can also try to locate the file manually by pressing the browse button.[7]

Starting with Excel 2007 the programs layout has changed. To install the Add-in you first press the Office-Button in the upper left of the program (Excel 2007) or choose the File-Ribbon (Excel 2010). Then press the Excel-Option button at the bottom right of the opened window. Now choose 'Add-in' from the menu on the left. In the right part of the window, at the very bottom choose 'Excel Add-ins' from the 'Manage' drop-down menu and press Go. Now the Add-in manager looks like the right screenshot of Figure 10.3. If you do not succeed refer to Help for more details.

[7] We experienced a different behavior of different Excel versions with respect to the use of the ATP functions in VBA. On our computers, versions starting with Excel 2007 seem to accept the functions only with the prefix "Application.Worksheetfunction", while versions prior to 2007 worked only without these prefixes. On the DVD we provide two different files for each chapter (xls for pre 2007, and xlsm for 2007 plus), which should help to solve any problems that may arise.

The ATP functions that we will use are as follows:

- YEARFRAC(*start_date*, *end_date*, *basis*) returns the difference between two dates as fraction of a year. Basis specifies the day-count convention (see Box 10.1)
- COUPPCD(*settlement*, *maturity*, *frequency*, *basis*) returns the coupon date preceding the settlement date. Frequency is the number of coupon payments per year.
- COUPNCD(*settlement*, *maturity*, *frequency*, *basis*) returns the next coupon date after the settlement date.
- COUPDAYS(*settlement*, *maturity*, *frequency*, *basis*) returns the number of days in the coupon period that contains the settlement date.
- COUPDAYSNC(*settlement*, *maturity*, *frequency*, *basis*) returns the number of days from the settlement date to the next coupon date.

Excel also provides a function PRICE() for calculating a bond price. We will not use it because PRICE() only works with constant rates, i.e., it does not allow r_ts that vary across maturity as we have them in a formula such as (10.4).

Box 10.1 Day-count convention and estimation

When dealing with interest rates, one has to be precise on the interest's definition. Excel's financial functions as well as our user-defined functions written for this purpose include the parameter basis. This parameter can take one of the following values, each defining a different day count basis. Omitting this parameter is equivalent to setting it to zero.

0 (or omitted) US (NASD) 30/360
1 Actual/Actual
2 Actual/360
3 Actual/365
4 European 30/360

Interest rates in the US and Europe (basis = 0 or basis = 4) are typically quoted assuming that each month has 30 days and a year has 360 days. Both cases differ in the way they deal with the 31st day of a month. In the European case, (basis = 4), dates on the 31st of a month are set back to the 30th of a month, whereas in the US case (basis = 0 or omitted), the end date is moved to the 1st of the next month if the starting date (of the interest period) is earlier than the 30th. LIBOR and EURIBOR rates are quoted according to the European case, whereas US treasuries and most of other US rates are quoted with basis equal to zero. The other three cases use the actual number of days within the current months (actual in the numerator) and/or within the current year (actual in the denominator).

Instead, we program a user-defined function that allows for a non-flat interest rate structure. In a preparatory step, we write a function INTSPOT(*spots*, *year*) that uses a term structure of interest rates as input and interpolates them according to the function argument *year*. The term structure is assumed to be contained in two columns, with the maturity in the first column (expressed in years), and the interest rate in the second. Table 10.1 shows an application of the function INTSPOT():

Table 10.1 The user-defined function INTSPOT()

	A	B	C	D	E	F
1	t	Spot Rate				
2	0.08	3.50%		5.25%		
3	0.25	4.00%		=INTSPOT(A2:B8,2.5)		
4	0.5	4.50%				
5	2	5.00%				
6	3	5.50%				
7	5	6.00%				
8	10	6.50%				
9						

Here is the code:

```
Function INTSPOT(spots, year)
'Interpolates spot rates to year

Dim i As Integer, spotnum As Integer
spotnum = spots.Rows.Count

If Application.WorksheetFunction.Count(spots) = 1 Then
'Single rate given
    INTSPOT = spots
Else    'Term structure given
    If year <= spots(1, 1) Then
        INTSPOT = spots(1, 2)
    ElseIf year >= spots(spotnum, 1) Then
        INTSPOT = spots(spotnum, 2)
    Else
        Do
            i = i + 1
        Loop Until spots(i, 1) > year
        INTSPOT = spots(i - 1, 2) + (spots(i, 2) - spots(i - 1, 2)) * _
                    (year - spots(i - 1, 1)) / _
                    (spots(i, 1) - spots(i - 1, 1))
    End If
End If

End Function
```

The core of the function is a `Do ... until` loop, which finds the first `t` in the interest range larger than the `t` specified as an argument. Having found this `t`, we linearly interpolate between this and the previous `t`. Before entering the loop, we deal with cases in which the input is a single rate rather than a term structure, or where the year specified as an argument is smaller than the minimum year in the range or larger than its maximum.

Now, we are ready to define the function MYPRICE() to price a bond according to Equation (10.4). We make it a bit more flexible, though, so that it allows us to specify the compounding frequency, i.e., the m in the following pricing formula:

$$B_0 = \sum_{t=1}^{T} \frac{\text{Coupon}_t}{(1+r_t/m)^{mt}} + \frac{\text{Principal}}{(1+r_T/m)^{mT}} \tag{10.10}$$

In addition, we include an optional argument `fromdate`. The function then returns the present value of cash flows accruing at or after `fromdate`:

$$B_0 = \sum_{t=fromdate}^{T} \frac{\text{Coupon}_t}{(1+r_t/m)^{mt}} + \frac{\text{Principal}}{(1+r_T/m)^{mT}} \tag{10.10a}$$

The syntax of the function is

MYPRICE(*settlement*, *maturity*, *coupon rate*, *spots*, *principal*, *frequency*, [*compound*], [*fromdate*], [*basis*])

where [*argument*] denotes an optional argument. Here is the code:

```
Function MYPRICE(settlement As Date, maturity As Date, rate, spots, _
    principal, freq As Integer, Optional compound As Integer, _
    Optional fromdate As Date, Optional basis As Integer)
'Determines present value of bond cash flows accruing after fromdate

Dim t As Date, y As Double

'Set default values and some error checking
If compound = 0 Then compound = freq
If fromdate = 0 Then fromdate = settlement
If fromdate > maturity Or settlement > maturity Then End

'Determine PV of payment at maturity
t = maturity
y = Yearfrac(settlement, maturity, basis)
MYPRICE = (notional + prinicpal * rate / freq) / _
            (1 + INTSPOT(spots, y) / compound) ^ (y * compound)

'Add PVs of coupon payments
t = Couppcd(t - 1, maturity, freq, basis)
Do While t > settlement And t >= fromdate
    y = Yearfrac(settlement, t, basis)
    MYPRICE = MYPRICE + rate / freq * principal / _
                (1 + INTSPOT(spots, y) / compound) ^ (y * compound)
    t = Couppcd(t - 1, maturity, freq, basis)
Loop

End Function
```

Table 10.2 Applying the function MYPRICE

	A	B	C	D	E	F	G
1		Coupon	Yield	Price		t	Spot rate
2	Corporate	7.125%	11.74%	78.38		0.08	5.56%
3	Risk-free	7.125%		108.18		0.25	5.64%
4						0.5	5.68%
5	Maturity	15-Jul-13				2	5.64%
6	Coupon freq.	2				3	5.62%
7						5	5.66%
8						10	5.76%
9	Settlement	15-Jul-06					
10							
11			D2: =MYPRICE(B9,B5,B2,C2,100,B6)				
12			D3: =MYPRICE(B9,B5,B3,F2:G8,100,B6)				

The function unravels the pricing equation (10.10a) from the maturity date. The difference between a payment date and today is computed through the ATP function YEARFRAC(). Coupon dates are found with the ATP function COUPCD(). If t is a coupon date, COUPCD(t, *maturity*, *basis*) returns t. So, we subtract 1 to find the previous dates in such cases, too. The application of the function is demonstrated in Table 10.2.

In the second row, we enter the characteristics of a corporate bond. It is a bond that was issued by General Motors. The coupon rate is located in cell B2. Maturity, coupon frequency and settlement date are located in cells B5, B6 and B9, respectively. In the table, we consider a case where we do not have the price of the bond itself, but its yield to maturity (in cells C2).[8] With the MYPRICE() function, however, we can find the price that matches the yield to maturity. In cell D3, we determine the price of a risk-free bond with the same payoff structure as the corporate bond. In doing so, we use the risk-free spot rates contained in F2:G8.

The difference between D3 and D2 is $B_0 - P_0$ of Equation (10.9). Accordingly, we have already made a step towards backing out a PD. Before moving on, however, we introduce another user-defined function. It returns the accrued interest, which we need if we define the bondholders' claim to be principal plus accrued interest. The function ACI() uses the ATP functions Coupdaysnc() and Coupdays():

```
Function ACI(settlement As Date, maturity As Date, rate, _
             freq As Integer, Optional basis As Integer)
'Calculates the accrued interest at settlement

If settlement < maturity Then
   ACI = 100 * rate / freq * (1 - Coupdaysnc(settlement,
maturity, freq, _
         -basis) / Coupdays(settlement, maturity, freq, basis))
End If

If ACI = 0 Or settlement = maturity Then ACI = 100 * rate / freq

End Function
```

[8] The yield to maturity is the constant r that sets the right-hand side of Equation (10.4) equal to an observed bond price.

One comment worth making is that in other modeling situations, one would set accrued interest to zero for a date that is a coupon date. Here, we set accrued interest equal to the coupon payment to be made at that date. The reason is the following: we use the function ACI() to determine accrued interest at default dates. If we set it to zero for default dates that are also coupon dates, we would assume that the borrower paid the full coupon on the date that it defaulted, which is not typically the case.

Now, consider again Equation (10.9)

$$B_0 - P_0 = \sum_{\tau} PD_{\tau}^{0}\left(B_o^{\tau} - \frac{C_\tau \cdot R}{(1+r_\tau)^{\tau}}\right)$$

We solve for the PD by assuming it to be constant across time. This directly leads to

$$PD^0 = \frac{B_0 - P_0}{\sum_{\tau}\left(B_o^{\tau} - \frac{C_\tau \cdot R}{(1+r_\tau)^{\tau}}\right)} \quad (10.11)$$

We now extend Table 10.2 to implement (10.11). In cell B7 of Table 10.3, we enter a recovery assumption, here 40%. From cell A15 on, we list the default dates τ that we consider. Prima facie, an obvious choice is the coupon dates of the bond we examine. They can be determined with the ATP function COUPNCD(). If a borrower has issued several bonds with different coupon dates, however, this choice becomes less obvious. Also, one might want to consider more default dates than can be modeled with COUPNCD(). For the sake of brevity, we nevertheless use the COUPNCD() function here. Since the settlement date in our example is a coupon date, this is equivalent to using time intervals of fixed length, starting at the settlement date. To fix the time interval length in cases where the settlement date is not a coupon date, we construct a hypothetical maturity date from the day and month of the settlement and the year following the actual maturity date. We could either write

= DATE(YEAR(B$5)+1,MONTH(B$9),DAY(B$9))

in any free cell and reference to that cell or use this formula directly in the COUPNCD() command. The default frequency per year is specified in cell B10 of Table 10.3. Note that the COUPNCD(function) allows only frequencies of 1, 2 and 4 per year. To develop the series of default dates, first we enter the settlement date in Cell A14. In the next cells A15, we write

= COUPNCD(A14,DATE(YEAR(B$5)+1,MONTH(B$9),DAY(B$9)),B$10,0)

which can be copied down to A42, where we reach the maturity date.

B_0^{τ}, the present value of the cash flows accruing at or after τ, is found with the MYPRICE () function. For the first date we enter

= MYPRICE(B$9,B$5,B$2,E$2:F$8,100,B$6,,A15)

and copy the formula down to B42.

In column C, we determine the accrued interest with our user-defined function ACI(). Column D contains the spot rate for the maturity corresponding to the default dates in column A. We use the interpolation routine INTSPOT() introduced above. In doing so, we convert the difference between a default date and the settlement date into a year fraction using the ATP

Table 10.3 Backing out risk-neutral probabilities of default from the market price of a corporate bond

	A	B	C	D	E	F	G
1		Coupon	Yield	Price		t	Spot rate
2	Corporate	7.125%	11.74%	78.38		0.08	5.56%
3	Risk-free	7.125%		108.18		0.25	5.64%
4						0.5	5.68%
5	Maturity	15-Jul-13				2	5.64%
6	Coupon freq.	2				3	5.62%
7	Recovery	40%				5	5.66%
8						10	5.76%
9	Settlement	15-Jul-06					
10	Default freq.	4					
11	PD^0 per period	1.97%	=(D3-D2)/SUMIF(A15:A1000,"<="&B5,E15:E1000)				
12	PD^0 p.a.	7.87%	=B10*B11				
13							
14	15-Jul-06	B_0^τ	Accrued Int.	Spot rate	Loss		
15	15-Oct-06	108.18	1.78	5.64%	68.03		
16	15-Jan-07	108.18	3.56	5.68%	67.89		
17	15-Apr-07	104.72	1.78	5.68%	65.66		
18	15-Jul-07						
19	15-Oct-07						
20	15-Jan-08						
21	15-Apr-08						
22	15-Jul-08						
23	15-Oct-08						
24	15-Jan-09						
25	15-Apr-09						
26	15-Jul-09						
27	15-Oct-09						
28	15-Jan-10						
29	15-Apr-10						
30	15-Jul-10						
31	15-Oct-10	[illegible]	[illegible]	[illegible]	[illegible]		
...	...	...	...	...	...		
42	15-Jul-13	69.88	3.56	5.70%	41.78		

A14: =B9

A15: =COUPNCD(A14,DATE(YEAR(B$5)+1,MONTH(B$9),DAY(B$9)),B$10,0)
B15: =MYPRICE(B$9,B$5,B$2,F$2:G$8,100,B$6,,A15)
C15: =ACI(A15,B$5,B$2,B$6,0)
D15: =INTSPOT(F$2:G$8,YEARFRAC(B$9,A15,0))
E15: =B15-(B$7*(100+C15))/(1+D15)^YEARFRAC(B$9,A15,0)
(can be filled down to row 42)

$$PD^0 = \frac{B_0 - P_0}{\sum_\tau \left(B_o^\tau - \frac{C_\tau \cdot R}{(1+r_\tau)^\tau} \right)}$$

function YEARFRAC(). Cell D15 reads

= INTSPOT(E$2:F$8, Yearfrac(B$9, A15,0))

In column E, we determine the loss amounts in case of default separately for each default date τ. The bondholders' claim is chosen to be principal plus accrued interest, but we could easily modify the formula to model other claim definitions. The formula in cell E15, which can be copied to E42, reads

= B15-(B$7*(100+C15))/(1+D15)^YEARFRAC(B$9, A15,0)

In B11, we evaluate Equation (10.11). We take the difference between B_0 and P_0 and divide by the sum of default losses. This gives the PD^0 for the assumed quarterly frequency. In B12, we can convert it into an annual PD by multiplying it by the frequency from B10.

The resulting PD^0 is 7.87% per year as seen from today. This appears to be in line with the rating of General Motors at the time of estimation, which was B– (note, of course, that default rates published for rating grades are estimates of actual PDs, not risk-neutral ones).

PRICING A CDS

With PD estimates in hand, we can go on to price the CDS. For doing so, we compare the expected payoffs of the protection buyer and seller. The CDS buyer pays a fee in regular intervals. Upon default, the buyer also pays the fee accrued since the previous payment date. In return, the buyer receives the difference between the par value and the recovery value of the defaulted bonds. As in the previous section, we work with risk-neutral probabilities of default.

We denote the life of the protection (in years) by T and the annual percentage CDS fee by s. If quarterly payments are contracted, for example, the protection buyer pays $s/4$ after each quarter of protection.

For the sake of exposition, we assume that the default dates considered are also CDS payment dates. We then do not have to model accrued fees.

With discrete payment and default dates τ, $\tau \leq \mathrm{T}$, the present value of the expected payments made by the protection buyer can be written as

$$\mathrm{E[fee]} = \mathrm{notional} \cdot s/freq \sum_{\tau} \left[\frac{1 - \sum\limits_{t=1}^{\tau-1} PD_t^0}{(1+r_\tau)^\tau} \right] \tag{10.12}$$

where *freq* is the frequency per year in which CDS payments are made. As in previous sections, PD_t^0 is the probability of default in t as seen from today. In Equation (10.12), we simply discount the payments and weigh them with the probability that they occur. The latter is the probability of survival until the start of period τ, which is given by $1 - \sum_{t=1}^{\tau-1} \mathrm{PD}_t^0$.

Let us take a look at the other side of the coin: the expected gain of the CDS buyer. Abstracting from details connected with physical or cash settlement, we express the gain as (1 – recovery rate) × claim. If we define the claim to be the principal plus accrued interest, we get

$$\mathrm{E[defaultpayments]} = \mathrm{notional} \sum_{\tau} (1 - R - A(\tau)R) \frac{PD_\tau^0}{(1+r_\tau)^\tau} \tag{10.13}$$

where $A(\tau)$ is the accrued interest as a percentage of the notional principal.

When two parties agree on the CDS spread s, they should settle on a value that sets Equations (10.12) and (10.13) to equal value. Otherwise, one party will gain (on expectation) at the expense of the other. To avoid arbitrage, the spread therefore has to follow through

$$\mathrm{E[fee]} \overset{!}{=} \mathrm{E[defaultpayment]} \Leftrightarrow s = \frac{\sum\limits_{\tau} (1 - R - A(\tau)R) \frac{PD_\tau^0}{(1+r_\tau)^\tau}}{\frac{1}{freq} \sum\limits_{\tau} \left[\frac{1 - \sum\limits_{t=1}^{\tau-1} PD_t^0}{(1+r_\tau)^\tau} \right]} \tag{10.14}$$

Table 10.4 Pricing a CDS

	A	B	C	D	E	F	G
1	Reference bond					t	Spot rate
2	Coupon	7.125%				0.0833	5.56%
3	Coupon freq.	2				0.25	5.64%
4	Maturity	15-Jul-13				1	5.68%
5	Recovery	40%				2	5.64%
6						3	5.62%
7	Compounding	2				5	5.66%
8						10	5.76%
9	Settlement	15-Jul-06					
10	Payment freq.	4					
11	CDS spread	5.64%	=SUM(F15:F34)/SUM(E15:E34)				
12							
13	Default dates	Accr. int. (%)	Spot rate	PD	Fees	Default payments	
14	15-Jul-06						
15	15-Oct-06	1.78%	5.64%	1.97%	24.17%	1.18%	
16	15-Jan-07	3.56%	5.68%	1.97%	23.83%	1.19%	
17	15-Apr-07	1.78%	5.68%	1.97%	23.50%	1.15%	
18	1						
19	15						
20	15						
21	15						
22	1						
23	15						
24	15						
25	15						
26	1						
27	15						
28	15						
29	15						
30	1						
31	15						
32	15						
33	15						
34	15-Jul-11	3.56%	5.66%	1.97%	18.54%	0.92%	

A14: =B9
D15: *from analysis in Table 9.3*

A15: =COUPNCD(A14,DATE(YEAR(B$4)+1,MONTH(B$9),DAY(B$9)),B$10,0)
B15: =ACI(A15,B$4,B$2,B$3,0)/100
C15: =INTSPOT(F$2:G$8,YEARFRAC(B$9,A15,0))
E15: =1/B$10*(1-SUM(D$14:D14))/(1+C15/B$7)^(B$7*YEARFRAC(B$9,A15))
F15: =(1-B$5-B15*B$5)*D15/(1+C15/B$7)^(B$7*YEARFRAC(B$9,A15))
(can be filled down to row 34)

$$s = \frac{\sum_{\tau}(1-R-A(\tau)R)\dfrac{PD^{0}{}_{\tau}}{(1+r_{\tau})^{\tau}}}{\dfrac{1}{freq}\sum_{\tau}\left[\dfrac{1-\sum_{t=0}^{\tau-1}PD_{t}^{0}}{(1+r_{\tau})^{\tau}}\right]}$$

In Table 10.4, we use this formula to price a five-year CDS. The default probabilities are taken from Table 10.2. Other characteristics of the reference entity that we require are the recovery rate, coupon rates and coupon payment dates of bonds. The latter are needed to determine the accrued interest in Equation (10.14). We take the data of the bond examined in Table 10.3.

In cell B7, we choose the compounding frequency for present value calculations. Default dates in A15:A34 are determined with the ATP function COUPNCD(), as in Table 10.2. The accrued interest in column B is computed with the user-defined ACI() function. Spot rates are interpolated in column C. In column D, we enter the quarterly probability of default from Table 10.3. We assumed it to be constant there, and so we make the same assumption here.

Column E contains the denominator of Equation (10.14). In E15, for example, we have τ = A15 = 15-Oct-06 and enter

= 1/B$10*(1-SUM(D$14:D14))/(1+C15/B$7)^(B$7*YEARFRAC(B$9,A15))

The expected payments to the buyer (numerator of (10.14)) are in column F:

= (1-B$5-B15*B$5)*D15/(1+C15/B$7)^(B$7*YEARFRAC(B$9,A15))

Both formulae can be filled down to row 34.

In B11, we sum the default payments and the fees, respectively, divide the former by the latter and get the CDS spread of 5.64%.

REFINING THE PD ESTIMATION

Having priced the CDS, we now present a generalization of the PD estimation conducted in Table 10.3. There, we had based the estimate of the PD term structure on one corporate bond. In practice, issuers often have several traded bonds outstanding. We can hope to increase the precision of the PD estimates if we make full use of the available bond price information.

Recall Equation (10.9), the basis for backing PDs out of bond prices:

$$B_0 - P_0 = \sum_{\tau} PD_{\tau}^{0}\left(B_{o}^{\tau} - \frac{C_{\tau} \cdot R}{(1+r_{\tau})^{\tau}}\right)$$

With one bond, we assumed the PD to be constant across maturities. With several bonds, we will assume that they are stepwise constant. Assume that we have three bonds, maturing at T_1, $T_2 > T_1$ and $T_3 > T_2$, respectively. From the first bond, we estimate the constant PD^0 from time zero (today) to time T_1. For default dates $\tau \leq T_1$, we insert this estimate into the equation as an input for bond 2, and back out the constant PD^0 between T_1 and T_2. Similarly, we proceed with the third bond.

If we want to estimate a PD structure over T years, we would take into account the bonds that mature before T as well as the one with the earliest maturity after T. Returning to our earlier IBM example, we select three IBM bonds. Their characteristics are entered in range A1:C4 of Table 10.5.

The next steps are the same as in Table 10.3. However, we compress the estimation procedure for one bond. We could do this by combining the formula contained in columns B to E of Table 10.3 into one column. For convenience, however, we write a user-defined function LOSS(), which returns the present value of the loss from default at a particular default date:

$$B_{\tau}^{0} - (C_{\tau} \times R/(1+r_{\tau})^{\tau})$$

The function reads as follows:

```
Function LOSS(settlement As Date, maturity As Date, rate, spots, _
         notional, freq As Integer, compound As Integer, _
         fromdate As Date, R As Double, Optional basis As Integer)
Dim price, A, y
```

Table 10.5 Estimating a PD structure with several corporate bonds

	A	B	C	D	E	F	G
1	Coupon	Maturity	Yield	B_0-P_0	PD	t	Spot
2	6.375%	1-May-08	11.65%	9.56	2.33%	0.08	5.56%
3	7.200%	15-Jan-11	10.99%	19.26	1.54%	0.25	5.64%
4	7.125%	15-Jul-13	11.74%	29.81	2.16%	0.50	5.68%
5						2	5.64%
6						3	5.62%
7	Coupon Freq	2	Settlement	15-Jul-06		5	5.66%
8	Recovery	40%	Default freq.	4		10	5.76%
9							
10		Bond 1		Bond 2		Bond 3	
11		Loss	PD^0	Loss	PD^0	Loss	
12	15-Oct-06	62.44	2.33%	65.92	2.33%	68.03	2.33%
13	15-Jan-07	59.24	2.33%	65.78	2.33%	67.89	2.33%
14	15-Apr-07	60.40	2.33%	63.52	2.33%	65.66	2.33%
15	15-J						2.33%
16	15-O						2.33%
17	15-Ja						2.33%
18	15-A						2.33%
19	15-J						1.54%
20	15-O						1.54%
21	15-Ja						1.54%
22	15-A						1.54%
23	15-J						1.54%
24	15-O						1.54%
25	15-Ja						1.54%
26	15-A						1.54%
27	15-J						1.54%
28	15-O						1.54%
29	15-Jan-11	0.00	0.00%	48.26	1.54%	50.64	1.54%
...	...	...	...	...	...	...	...
39	15-Jul-13	0.00	0.00%	0.00	0.00%	41.78	2.16%

D2:=MYPRICE(D$7,B2,A2,F$2:G$8,100,B$7)-MYPRICE(D$7,B2,A2,C2,100,B$7)
(can be copied into D3:D4)
E2: =D2/SUM(B12:B39)

E3: =(D3-SUMPRODUCT(C12:C39,D12:D39))/SUMIF(A12:A39,">"&B2,D12:D39)
E4: =(D4-SUMPRODUCT(E12:E51,F12:F51))/SUMIF(A12:A51,">"&B3,F12:F51)

A11: =D7

A12: =COUPNCD(A11,DATE(YEAR(B$4) +1,MONTH(D$7),DAY(D$7)),D$8,0)
B12: =LOSS(D$7,B$2,A$2,F$2:G$8,100,B$7,B$7,A12,B$8,0)
C12: =E$2*(B12>0)
D12: =LOSS(D$7,B$3,A$3,F$2:G$8,100,B$7,B$7,A12,B$8,0)
E12: =IF(A12<=B$2,E$2,E$3*(A12<=B$3))
F12: =LOSS(D$7,B$4,A$4,F$2:G$8,100,B$7,B$7,A12,B$8,0)
G12: =IF(A12<=B$3,E12,E$4*(A12<=B$4))
(can be filled down to row 39)

```
If fromdate <= maturity Then
    y = Yearfrac(settlement, fromdate, basis)
    price = MYPRICE(settlement, maturity, rate, spots, notional, _
            freq, compound, fromdate, basis)
    A = ACI(fromdate, maturity, rate, freq, basis)
    LOSS = price - R * (100 + A) / _
            (1 + INTSPOT(spots, y) / compound) ^ (compound * y)
Else
    LOSS = 0
End If

End Function
```

As stated before, we defined the claim C to be notional principal plus accrued interest. The major advantage of using such a function instead of performing the calculations in the worksheet is that we can quickly modify the claim definition or other aspects. In addition, we make the function return zero if the default date (`fromdate`) is outside the bond's maturity. This simplifies the calculations in the sheet because we can do operations across a full range of cells without controlling for the maturity of the bond.

The default dates in A12:A39 are again returned by the COUPNCD function described above. In B12, the first bond's expected loss for the date specified in A12 can be obtained by entering

= LOSS(D$7,B$2,A$2,F$2:G$8,100,B$7,B$7,A12,B$8,0)

Using the data from this first bond, we estimate a quarterly PD^0 of 2.33% in cell E2 by dividing $B_0 - P_0$ computed in cell D2 by the sum of the losses in B12:B39.

We go on and determine the LOSS() for bond three. In D12, for example, we type

= LOSS(D$7,B$3,A$3,F$2:G$8,100,B$7,B$7,A12,B$8,0)

The PD of the first bond is used in cell E3. The underlying formula is

$$B_0 - P_0 = PD^0(1) \sum_{\tau \leq T_1} \left(B_o^\tau - \frac{C_\tau \cdot R}{(1+r_\tau)^\tau} \right) + PD^0(2) \sum_{\tau > T_1} \left(B_o^\tau - \frac{C_\tau \cdot R}{(1+r_\tau)^\tau} \right) \tag{10.15}$$

where $PD^0(1)$ is the PD backed out from bond 1, and T_1 is the maturity of bond 1. We already know $PD^0(1)$, and so we can solve for $PD^0(2)$. We evaluate the first term on the right-hand side by writing $PD^0(1)$ into column C (with zeroes for dates in column A that are larger than T_1); then we use the function SUMPRODUCT(). The formula in cell E3 reads

= (D3-SUMPRODUCT(C12:C39, D12:D39))/(SUMIF(A12:A39,">"&B2,D12:D39))

where D3 contains $B_0 - P_0$. The SUMIF function evaluates the sum in the second term on the right-hand side of (10.15).

For the third bond, we repeat this procedure using $PD^0(1)$ and $PD^0(2)$ estimated from the first two bonds. The result, a stepwise constant PD structure, is returned in column G.

The quarterly PD from the settlement date (July 15, 2006) to the last default date before the maturity of the first bond (April 15, 2008) is 2.33%. The PD from that date until the last default date before the maturity of the second bond (Jan 15, 2011) is 1.54%; the PD for the time following is 2.16%.

We can copy the PDs contained in column G into column D of Table 10.4 to price the CDS with this new PD structure. The estimated spread is 5.48%, 16 basis points smaller than before. The reason is that the use of the three bonds leads to a lower average PD for the life of the CDS (1.88% versus 1.97%).

Finally, note that we would possibly have to adapt the formula if the maturities of the bonds, the chosen default date frequencies or other parameters changed. To increase sheet flexibility, we could increase the ranges in the formula (i.e., sum over A15:A65536 instead of A15:A39) and work with IF-conditions and other tricks.

MARKET VALUES FOR A CDS

So far we have discussed how to estimate a CDS spread from a PD structure. In many settings, however, we observe market CDS prices. With these prices at hand we can, for example, reverse Equation (10.14) to back out the market implied PD. Or we can use principles from financial mathematics to estimate the current value of an open CDS position, price a forward starting CDS contract or even an option on a CDS. We explore these three points in the remainder of this chapter.

Let us start with the market value of a CDS position. In the earlier section on CDS pricing (page 232), we saw that the value of a CDS is the difference between the present value (PV) of expected default payments and the present value of expected fee payments. At CDS inception, the spread is chosen such that the market value is zero. As time goes on, the contractual fee to be paid until default remains constant, but both the present value of expected default payments and the present value of expected fee payments can change if default probabilities or interest rates change. The valuation logic remains the same, however. The current market value of a CDS entered at some point in the past is obtained through

Market value of old CDS =
PV of expected default payments (at current PDs and interest rates) −
PV of expected fee payments (at current PDs and interest rates, for *contractual* spread)

Now consider a newly entered CDS with the same maturity and the same notional principal as the old CDS whose market value we want to determine. For such a new CDS, the market value is zero by convention. It therefore holds that

Market value of newly entered CDS = 0 =
PV of expected default payments (at current PDs and interest rates) −
PV of expected fee payments (at current PDs and interest rates, for *current* spread)

Note that the present value of default payments is identical for both CDSs. In the equation for the market value of the old CDS, we can therefore replace the present value of expected default payments with the present value of expected fee payments at current market conditions. This leads to

Market value of old CDS =
PV of expected fee payments (at current PDs and interest rates, for current spread) −
PV of expected fee payments (at current PDs and interest rates, for contractual spread)

To determine the market value of a CDS, we therefore do not need to determine the value of default payments. We simply need to evaluate the difference between the present values of two fee payment streams.

To do so, it is convenient to introduce an expression for the expected present value of a fee payment of 1 basis point. It is called the risky PV01 (Present Value of 01 basis point) and is obtained by discounting the expected fee payments with the risk-free rate. The expected fee payments are given as 1 (basis point) times the probability of surviving until the scheduled payment date. Let us denote today by t_0, each coupon date by t, the year fraction between coupon date t and the previous coupon date by Δ_t and maturity by T, and then the risky PV01 is given by

$$\text{RiskyPV01} = \sum_{t=t_0}^{T} \frac{1 - \text{PD}(t_0, t)}{(1+r)^{t-t_0}} \Delta_t \tag{10.16}$$

The PV01 is called 'risky' because the fee payments are uncertain; they are made only until default and default is uncertain. With the risky PV01 at hand, we can determine the market value of a CDS through

Market value of old CDS =
current spread × RiskyPV01 × notional principal −
contractual spread × RiskyPV01 × notional principal

which can be simplified to

Market value of old CDS =
(current spread − contractual spread) × RiskyPV01 × notional principal

To estimate Equation (10.16) we need to know the PD. One common approach is to use the hazard rate implied by the CDS spread. The hazard rate $h(t)$ is defined as the instantaneous default probability, conditional on survival until t. Assuming the hazard rate to be deterministic, which implies independence of the hazard rate and both the interest rates and the recoveries, the rate can be approximated from the CDS spread s_t with recovery rate R as[9]

$$h(t) = s_t/(1 - R) \tag{10.17}$$

We can extend this model to a continuous time default probability to time T conditional on surviving up to time t as

$$\text{PD}(T) = 1 - \exp\left(-\int_t^T h(s)ds\right) \tag{10.18}$$

Assuming further that the CDS spread is constant over time or piecewise constant between coupon intervals, we find the probability of default implied by a CDS spread of s_T as[10]

$$\text{Imp.PD}(s, T) = 1 - \exp\left(-\frac{s_T}{1-R}(T - t)\right) \tag{10.19}$$

Combining Equation (10.19) with (10.15), we obtain the risky PV01 at time t_0 as function of the CDS spreads s_τ at each coupon time t until maturity T:

$$\text{RPV01}(s, T) = \sum_{t=t_0}^{T} \frac{\exp\left(-\frac{s_t}{1-R}(t - t_0)\right) \Delta_t}{(1 + r_t)^{t-t_0}} \tag{10.20}$$

[9] This approximation can be considered as market standard; see the Appendix at the end of this for details.

[10] See, e.g., O'Kane and Turnbull (2003) for a discussion of the underlying assumptions.

As specification for the risk-free rate r, the International Swaps and Derivatives Association (ISDA), which provides the standard documents for CDS trading, uses swap rates. A user-defined function for the risky PV01 formula (10.16a) is straightforward with the tools already derived in this chapter. For the convenience of notation we will only mention the two arguments s and T when referring to the risky PV01 in the text; e.g., we will speak of RPV (500 basis points, 5 yr) even though the function has more than these two arguments.

```
Function RPV(startd, maturity, freq, r, s, Optional LGD)

If IsMissing(LGD) Then LGD = 0.6
Dim nperiod As Integer, i As Integer, efr, ps, cdates

'Calculate coupon dates
nperiod = coupnum(startd, maturity, freq)
ReDim cdates(1 To nperiod) As Date

'1st period
cdates(1) = coupncd(startd, maturity, freq)
efr = (cdates(1) - started) / 360
RPV = Exp(-INTSPOT(s, efr) * 1 + INTSPOT(r, efr)) ^ (-efr) _
        * (cdates(1) - startd) / 360

'For each coupon date estimate dayfraction, discount rate and surv prob
For i = 2 To nperiod
  cdates(i) = coupncd(cdates(i - 1), maturity, freq)
  efr = (cdates(i) - startd) / 360
  RPV = RPV + Exp(-INTSPOT(s, efr) / LGD * efr) * _
        (1 + INTSPOT(r, efr)) ^ (-efr) * (cdates(i) - cdates(i - 1)) /
360
Next i

End Function
```

In the RPV function we use Excel's COUPNCD function, described previously in this chapter, to estimate coupon dates. We then interpolate over the CDS spreads and risk-free interest rates using our INTSPOT function. With these interpolated numbers we estimate the survival probability according to Equation (10.19) and the risk-free discount factors. Multiplying both numbers with the year fraction between coupon dates and summing them up over all periods we arrive at the risky PV01.

Example

You have a CDS protection over five years at 100 bps on 10 million (mm) notional on the book. The current swap rate over five years is $r_5 = 3\%$, recovery rate is 40% and the market spread for this position is currently at 80 bps. The market value or mark-to-market (MtM) value of your position is

= (0.8%-1%)*RPV(TODAY(),TODAY()+5*360,4,0.03,0.8%)*10^7

which is −88,208.8. Note that the Excel function TODAY() returns the current date. With the assumed day count convention, adding 5*360 to TODAY gives a maturity of five years.

The RPV is a handy approximation that can be used in a variety of settings. We will apply the concept to the pricing of a pro-rata basket, but before that we discuss the conversion of running spreads, i.e., premiums paid quarterly, and upfront payments.

ESTIMATING UPFRONT CDS AND THE 'BIG BANG' PROTOCOL

The 2007–2009 credit crisis has not left the CDS market unaffected. After all it was the first real test of this young market and several adjustments have been and will be made due to the lessons learned. As an important example take the over-the-counter (OTC) nature of the market. Since CDS are traded between professional investors only outsiders do not observe trades or traded prices. Regulators are trying to reduce the opaqueness of CDS trading, e.g., by introducing a central counterparty. Hereby the counterparty risk shall be reduced and information efficiency increased. With such a central clearing facility, however, CDS had to be further standardized, e.g., by extending the upfront pricing of CDS indices to CDS single names.

With indices the difference between the deal spread, i.e., the spread at which the index started trading, and the current market spread is exchanged upfront. For example: as of March 1, 2010, the iTraxx Europe Series 12 index maturing Dec 2014 is trading at 85 bps; the deal spread of this series is fixed at 100 bps. Buying €100mm CDS protection leaves 71 days until the next quarterly premium payment of 25 bps (=100 bps/4 quarters). Thus, first, the accrued premium has to be exchanged: in this case it amounts to −€197,222 = 71 days accrued/ 360 days × 100 bps × €100 × 10^6. Furthermore the difference between the current spread and the deal spread is compensated, here −€674,001 = RPV(85 bps, 5) × (85 bps − 100 bps). So in total an upfront premium of −€871,223 is exchanged when the CDS is bought with the protection buyer receiving the money.[11] On the next quarterly payment date, June 1, 2010, the CDS protection buyer then pays a regular €250,000 = 100 bps/4 × €100 × 10^6 unless one or more of the index names defaulted.

This very principle was introduced to single name CDS with the so-called 'Big Bang' protocol starting in the US on April 18, 2009, and is now being used for the European CDS market as well. Here the deal spread of a CDS contract is fixed at 100 bps or 500 bps, depending on the credit quality of the name. Again the difference between the deal spread and the currently traded spread is exchanged upfront.

It is useful to convert upfront spreads in all-running spreads, and so we discuss a possible procedure in the following. Suppose the price for a CDS is split into an upfront payment u and a running-spread s. If the whole premium would be payable running the fair spread, i.e., the all-running spread, $s + x$ would be obtained. To find x we define the function

$$g(x) = u - \mathrm{RPV}(s + x, T)x$$

and find its root by using the solver to find the x that brings $g(x)$ to zero. Now $s + x$ is the all-running spread approximation corresponding to an upfront payment of u and a running spread of s. Table 10.6 gives an example. We found that this simple procedure yields useful

[11] Think about it in this way: you pay 85 bps for something worth 100 bps, and so in order to compensate you additionally pay an amount upfront.

Table 10.6 Calculating an all-running spread

	A	B	C	D
1	**Upfront to all-running conversion**			
2				
3	Upfront Premium u (%)	15%		
4	Running spread s (bps)	500		
5	Recovery Rate (%)	40%		
6	Value Date	4/15/2010		
7	Maturity	4/15/2015		
8	Swap Rate r (%)	2%		
9				
10	x (bps)	476	<- Solver changes B12 such that B11=0	
11	Function g(x)=x-RPV(s+x,T)*x	0%	=B3-RPV(TODAY(),B7,4,B8,(B10+B4)/10^4)*B10/10^4	
12				
13	All-running spread (bps)	**976**	=B10+B4	

results in most settings; the reader should bear in mind, however, that the calculation depends on the approximation quality of the risky PV01.

PRICING OF A PRO-RATA BASKET

In a pro-rata basket, such as a Credit Linked Note (CLN), the loss within the basket is divided proportional according to the lost proportion. As an example, take a basket with two assets, in which the first asset accounts for 80% of the basket's principal, the second for 20%. If the second asset defaults the pro-rata basket's loss will be 20% of the second asset's loss. The pro-rata basket is one of the plainest structures and a good application of our risky PV01 formula.

In Table 10.7 we estimate the price of such a pro-rata default basket. In our example there are ten different debtors each with a different CDS spread (column B9:B18). The CDS and the pro-rata basket are priced with a recovery rate assumption of 40% (cell B3), a maturity of five years (cell B4) and a current swap rate over this maturity of 3% (cell B5). In column C9:C18 we estimate the corresponding RPV for each debtor's CDS spread by applying formula (10.16). The second step is to estimate the weighted upfront pro-rata premium for the basket. For each obligor this is given as RPV times the CDS premium times the weights.[12] This weighted sum obtains in cell E6 by entering:

$$= \text{SUMPRODUCT(B9:B18,C9:C18,D9:D18)}$$

The fair value per annum for this basket is now given by finding a spread s^{basket} such that $\text{RPV}(s^{\text{basket}}, 5) \times s^{\text{basket}}$ equals the sum just estimated. We solve this problem by defining the error function in cell E5 as the scaled squared difference between E3 and E6. Applying the solver to minimize this error function by changing E3, the s^{basket} price, we find the fair price to this pro-rata basket to be 230 bps.

The most common pro-rata baskets are the iTraxx and CDX indices. These baskets are equally-weighted with respect to the defaults, i.e., if one of the 125 names in the iTraxx

[12] Since there are ten obligors in our example, we weight each position by 1/10th.

Table 10.7 Pricing a pro-rata basket

	A	B	C	D	E	F	G
1	**Pro-rata basket**						
2							
3	Recovery Rate	40%		Price	2.30%	<-- Solver	
4	Maturity	5					
5	Swap Rate	3%		Error function	0.00	=(RPV(TODAY(),EDATE(TODAY(),12*B4),4, B5,E3)*E3-E6)^2*10^10	
6				Weighted sum	9.79%	=SUMPRODUCT(B9:B18,C9:C18,D9:D18)	
7							
8	Debtor #	CDS	RPV01	Weight			
9	1	1.00%	4.498	C9:=(RPV(TODAY(),EDATE(TODAY(),12*$B$4),4,$B$5,B9))			
10	2	1.50%	4.404	0.1			
11	3	1.80%	4.349	0.1			
12	4	2.10%	4.294	0.1			
13	5	2.20%	4.276	0.1			
14	6	2.40%	4.241	0.1			
15	7	2.80%	4.171	0.1			
16	8	2.90%	4.154	0.1			
17	9	3.00%	4.137	0.1			
18	10	3.10%	4.053	0.1			
19							
20							
21							
22							
23							
24							
25							
26							
27							
28							
29							
30							

defaults the notional position is reduced by 1/125. However, the fair price of the index is estimated in the way of a pro-rata basket, i.e., the individual spreads enter the basket's price by their RPV weights. Although our procedure can be used to estimate the iTraxx or CDX indices' fair prices, they will seldom match the observed index prices. The indices are traded as a basket and their price is obtained by demand and supply for the basket protection. The difference between the traded and the fair price is called (index-) skew.

FORWARD CDS SPREADS

With the development of the CDS market traders subsequently introduced products giving them more freedom in putting different trading ideas to work. Moving from spot CDS spreads to forward CDS has been the first step. A forward CDS is a spot CDS starting at a future point of time. This product can be used to hedge future risk positions; for example, when the loan officer knows of a new syndicated loan becoming effective in six months, the risk management can buy protection via a 'regular' spot CDS or rather buy a forward CDS that becomes effective when the loan's exposure sets in. In normal times the CDS term structure is upward sloping, i.e., longer protection is more expensive than shorter protection, and so in the case of buying CDS protection one has to outweigh the higher forward CDS premium against the premium saved. The opposite holds for selling protection.

To find the fair price of a forward CDS consider the following situation. You want to have protection in t years over T years, and so you buy a spot CDS maturing in $T + t$ years at s_{T+t} and sell a CDS maturing in t years at s_t. The market value of this position is

$$\text{RPV}(s_{T+t}, T + t) \times s_{T+t} - \text{RPV}(s_T, T) \times s_T$$

Now let us look at the market value of a forward CDS position starting in t years over T years. Denoting the forward spread by s_T^t, the appropriate RPV weight is given by the difference between the risky PV01 over $T + t$ years and the risky PV01 over t years: $(\text{RPV}(s_{T+t}, T + t) - \text{RPV}(s_t, t)) \times s_{T+t}$. Since both market values – the one using the replication and the forward CDS one – have to be equal, we can find the forward CDS spread as

$$S_T^t = \frac{RPV(s_{T+t}, T + t)s_{T+t} - RPV(s_t, t)s_t}{RPV(s_{T+t}, T + t) - RPV(s_t, t)} \tag{10.21}$$

So with the CDS spreads today over t years, s_t, and over T years, s_T, plus the corresponding swap rates r, we can easily estimate the forward CDS spread.

Example

Let us illustrate this with an example. In the following quote you see Goldman Sachs' CDS spreads on March 1, 2010:

1yr 86/96; 2yr 100/110; 3yr 105/115; 5yr 122/128; 10yr 124/134

The left-hand number of each year's tenor gives the bid price at which CDS protection can be sold, while the right number gives the ask price at which protection can be bought. The most liquid contract is always the 5yr quote, which you also notice here when looking at the bid-ask spread. You can go protect yourself against Goldman risk until June 20, 2014, for 128 bps or you could go for the 10yr contract paying as little as 6bps more for an additional 5yr. So what about 5yr protection in five years then? With the current ISDA swap rates at hand we apply the forward formula to find 119/150.[13] So you pay 16 bps more for the forward protection, however, you save 670 bps (= 134 bps for the ten year protection, paid over five years) on your notional if you do not need Goldman protection right away.

PRICING OF SWAPTIONS

In contrast to forward CDS spreads, there is a more liquid market in CDS options, so-called *swaptions*. Swaptions are traded on the CDS indices, mainly on the investment grades ones, i.e., iTraxx Europe Main and CDX IG.

[13] Note that the ask forward price is calculated using the ask price of the 10yr CDS and the bid price of the 5yr CDS, whereas the bid forward price uses the bid price of the 10yr CDS and the ask price of the 5yr CDS. We used a constant swap rate of 2.51%, the average of the 5yr and 10yr spot rate at the time we are writing.

The swaptions work similarly to ordinary stock options, the terminology is just a bit different and more related to interest options. The right to buy protection is called *payer*, because it is the right to pay the CDS premium under the option. *Receiver* is the name of the right to sell protection.

To understand the market lingo, consider the following run for the iTraxx Main from March, 1:

Strike	Payer	Delta	Receiver	Delta	Vola%
60	141/151	−85.8	10/20	14.1	69.0
70	115/125	−77.4	23/33	22.6	69.3
80	92/102	−68.0	41/51	31.4	70.0

Sep 10, Ref: 81.5, prices in cts, no knock-out, European option

These are quotes for an option expiring September 15, 2010, which is six months until expiry. The reference spread of the underlying, i.e., the quote upon which the dealers agreed at that morning, is at 81.5 bps. The reference spread is used as the basis for calculating the options. This number is fixed throughout the day. The majority of swaptions are traded with delta-exchange where the option is bundled with the delta-position in the index. For example you want to have the right to buy 250mm protection at 80 bps at September 10. You pay 2.55m = 102cts × 250mm for the option. The option's delta is at 68%, and so you sell 170mm CDS protection against it. This is the option package you could purchase.[14]

So much for the practice, now we move on to the theory of swaption pricing. Assume the duration of the option is t, the duration of the underlying CDS is T and the forward spread is s_T^t. Denote the strike by K and the spread volatility by σ. The prices are then given as

$$Payer = \frac{RPV01(s_T^t, T)}{(1+r_t)^{-t}}\left(s_T^t\Phi(d_1) - K\Phi(d_1 - \sigma\sqrt{t})\right) \tag{10.22a}$$

$$Receiver = \frac{RPV01(s_T^t, T)}{(1+r_t)^{-t}}\left(K\Phi(\sigma\sqrt{t} - d_1) - s_T^t\Phi(-d_1)\right) \tag{10.22b}$$

with

$$d_1 = \frac{\log\left(\frac{s_T^t}{K}\right) + 0.5\sigma^2 t}{\sigma\sqrt{t}}.$$

Equations (10.22) are obtained in analogy to the common option pricing framework of Black and Scholes. Here a long payer position corresponds to a long call and a long receiver swaption to a long put option.

In Table 10.8 we put these formulae to work. In the first part A3:B6 we specify the characteristics of the underlying CDS. In this case we use the iTraxx Main Europe Series 12 with a maturity of Dec 2014 (B6). This series has a deal spread of 100 bps (B3) and is trading at 81.5 bps (B4) as of March 15th 2010. Next we specify the swaption in the area A9:B14.

[14] If, for example, the index rallied at that day to 70 bps, the swaptions would still be quoted with the reference price of 81.5 bps and the delta-exchange would take place at that price as well.

Table 10.8 Pricing a CDS swaption

	A	B	C	D	E	F	G	H
1	**Swaption Pricer**							
2	Underlying			t	Spot Rate		t	CDS Spread spot
3	Deal Spread (bps)	100		0.08	0.42%		0.5	0.80%
4	Current Spread (bps)	81.5		0.25	0.66%		1	0.80%
5	Recovery Rate	0.4		1	1.22%		2	0.80%
6	Maturity	12/20/2014		2	1.45%		3	0.80%
7				3	1.83%		5	0.85%
8	**Swaption**			5	2.45%		7	1.00%
9	Type	P		10	3.00%		10	1.10%
10	Start Date:	3/1/2010						
11	Expiration Date	9/15/2010						
12	Amount (mm)	100						
13	Strike (bps)	80						
14	Volatity (%)	69%						
15								
16	Time to Expiration t	0.54	=YEARFRAC(B10,B11,0)					
17	Time to Maturity T	4.80	=YEARFRAC(B10,B6,0)					
18								
19		t	t+T					
20	CDS Spreads (%)	0.80%	0.88%	=INTSPOT(G3:H9,B17+B16)				
21	Swap rates (%)	0.87%	2.49%	= INTSPOT (D3:E9,B17+B16)				
22	RPV	0.56	4.28	=RPV(B10,B6,4,D3:E9,G3:H9)				
23								
24	Forward CDS (%)	0.89%	=(C20*C22-B20*B22)/(C22-B22)					
25	Forward Swap (%)	2.67%	=((1+C21)^(B17+B16)/(1+B21)^B16)^(1/B17)-1					
26								
27	d1	0.34	=(LOG(B24/(B13/10^4))+B14^2*B16*0.5)/(B16^0.5*B14)					
28	Premium	0.902%	=RPV(B10,B6,4,B25,B24)/(1+B21)^(-B16)*IF(B9="P",1,-1)*(B24*NORMSDIST(IF(B9="P",1,-1)*B27)-B13/10^4*NORMSDIST(IF(B9="P",1,-1)*(B27-B16^0.5*B14)))					
29	Price	902,313	=B28*B12*10^6					
30								

The first input is the type of swaption in cell B9. A capital ‘P’ marks a payer option, whereas any other input reverts to a receiver option. The start date of the swaption is usually set to the next working day; note that forward pricing of a swaption is not included in this setting. In cell B11 we specify the expiration date, in this case September 15. Cell B12 contains the amount in million, B13 the strike spread in basis points and B14 the volatility in percentage points. When market quotes for the volatility are unavailable the common practice is to use daily spread changes over a history of three months.

Now all that is left to specify is the term structure of spot rates in D3:E9 and CDS spreads in G3:H9. For the spot rates the ISDA spot should be used. For the CDS term structure one uses either market quotes or assumptions on the term structure. With this setup we start the calculation. In cells B16 and B17 we use the previously mentioned YEARFRAC() function to estimate the time to expiration of the option and the time to maturity of the underlying; both numbers are needed later to estimate the forward rates. To interpolate the theoretical spot rates for the time to expiration and maturity, we use the INTSPOT() function described above. In cell B20 we thus interpolate over the range G3:H9, which contains the CDS spreads. The time parameter is given in cell B16. CDS spreads are given in basis points, to match the spot rates we convert them to percentage points, and so B20 reads

B20=INTSPOT(G3:H9,B16)/10^4

The second CDS spread in C20 interpolates over $t + T$ and thus uses B16+B17 as second parameter. The swap rates in B21 and C21 are estimated accordingly; here the first argument of the INTSPOT() function is changed to the array D3:E9.

Now we employ the RPV function defined above to estimate the corresponding present values of the CDS. The forward CDS spread starting at time t going over T periods is simply given by applying formula (10.17) to the numbers just calculated.[15] Cell B24 gives the forward CDS spread. The forward interest rate in cell B25 is then calculated by the following formula:

$$r_t^T = \sqrt[T-t]{\frac{(1+r_T)T}{(1+r_t)^t}} - 1 \tag{10.23}$$

where r_t^T denotes the forward rate starting at t going until T and r_xs are the spot rates until x. Applying formula (10.19) in cell B25 gives the corresponding forward rate.

Now we can continue to price the swaption. To keep things less messy we separate the calculation of d1 in cell B27 (see footnote 15). The premium is then estimated by combining formulae (10.21). Let ξ be an indicator function, which is 1 if the swaption is a payer and -1 otherwise. Then

$$\text{Premium} = \frac{\text{RPV}(s_T^t, T)}{(1+r_t)^{-t}} \left(\xi \left(s_T^t \Phi(\xi d_1) - K\Phi\left(\xi(d_1 - \sigma\sqrt{t})\right)\right)\right)$$

is the combination of both formulae. The ξ is simply an IF-statement IF(B9="P",1,-1), the rest is corresponding to the right cells, and so the premium in B28 reads

```
=RPV(B10,B6,4,B25,B24)/(1+B21)^(-B16)*
IF(B9="P",1,-1)*(B24*NORMSDIST(IF(B9="P",1,-1)*B27)-
B13/10^4*NORMSDIST(IF(B9="P",1,-1)*(B27-B16^0.5*B14)))
```

Now the premium is a percent number, and so the price is given by multiplying this number with the amount in B12 and scaling to million by 10^6. Here we estimate a premium of 0.922% or 92.2cts on the Euro, just as the bid side on the swaption run above. The price for 100 million of this protection is €921,567.

Note that our pricing routine is only valid in the absence of a knockout in the swaption's contract. With a knockout the swaption is cancelled if the underlying suffers from a credit event. Market standard is the absence of a knockout for index swaptions and the inclusion for single-name options.

[15] Of course one can use the formulae of cells B22 and C22 directly within B24's calculation.

NOTES AND LITERATURE

CDS designs and variations are manifold and it is beyond the scope of this chapter to provide an overview. For practical design issues the reader is referred to the webpage of the International Swaps and Derivatives Association (`www.ISDA.org`).

The PD estimation and CDS valuation in this chapter follows the methodology discussed in Hull, J. and White, A., 2001, Valuing credit default swaps I: No counterparty default risk, *Journal of Derivatives*, 8, 29–40. For generalizations, see Hull, J. and White, A., 2001, Valuing credit default swaps II: modeling default correlations, *Journal of Derivatives*, 8, 12–22. Textbook treatments can be found, among others, in: Duffie, D. and Singleton, K., 2003, *Credit Risk,* Princeton University Press; and Lando, D., 2004, *Credit Risk Modeling. Theory and Applications*, Princeton University Press. For details on risk-neutral valuation and pricing of derivatives, see Bingham N.H. and Kiesel, R., 2004, *Risk-Neutral Valuation, Pricing and Hedging of Financial Derivatives*, second edition, Springer.

Two textbooks with details on the RPV estimation and forward spreads are: Sundaresan, S., 2001, *Fixed Income Markets and Their Derivatives*, Academic Press; and Bomfim, A., 2004, *Understanding Credit Derivatives and Related Instruments*, Academic Press. An introduction to swaptions is given by Tucker, A. and Wei, J., 2005, Credit default swaptions, *Journal of Fixed Income*, 15, 88–95. A derivation of the hazard rate for CDS with discrete coupon payment is found in Berndt, A. and Obreja, I., 2010, Decomposing European CDS returns, *Review of Finance*, 14, 2, 189–233.

For a discussion of the underlying assumptions when finding the probability of default implied by a CDS spread, see O'Kane, D. and Turnbull, S., 2003, Valuation of credit default swaps, *Quantitative Credit Research Quarterly*, June, Lehman Brothers.

APPENDIX

Deriving the hazard rate for a CDS

We start with the CDS pricing formula (10.14), where the CDS spread is found such that the expected fee payments equal the expected default payments, bringing the present value of the CDS to zero. Denote the risk-neutral probability of survival over the next T periods by $q(T)$ and denote the time-constant default intensity (hazard rate) by h; then $q(T,h) = \exp(-hT)$ and thus $\mathrm{PD}_t^0 = 1 - q(T,h)$. We use this expression in formula (10.14). For illustration purposes we look at a one period setup ($T = 1, \mathit{freq} = 1$) and arrive at

$$\frac{s}{\mathit{freq}} = (1-R)\left(\exp\left(\frac{h}{\mathit{freq}}\right) - 1\right)$$

Solving this for the hazard rate h we get

$$h = \mathit{freq}\ln\left(1 + \frac{s}{\mathit{freq}(1-R)}\right)$$

Now note that we can approximate $\ln(1+x)$ by x, for small x, giving us

$$h = \frac{s}{(1-R)}$$

which is formula (10.17) from the text.

11

Risk Analysis and Pricing of Structured Credit: CDOs and First-to-Default Swaps

In structured credit transactions, pay-offs depend on the default performance within a portfolio. In a first-to-default swap, for example, a payment is made upon the first default that happens within a group of issuers. *Collateralized debt obligations* (CDOs) are claims on a debt portfolio that differ in their seniority. A CDO is only affected if the portfolio loss exceeds some threshold level: the more senior the obligation, the higher the threshold level.

In this chapter, we clarify the basic concepts and methods for analyzing structured credit transactions. We first show how to determine the risk structure of CDOs both by simulation and analytically. For the latter we rely partly on the large homogenous portfolio (LHP) approximation, in which the CDO portfolio is proxied by a portfolio with an infinite number of loans that are uniform in their risk parameters. Then we simulate correlated default times over several periods. In each step, we make heavy use of concepts from Chapter 6 and of simulation tools developed in Chapter 7.

Finally, we create pricing routines for CDOs. We show how to use the LHP approximation for the pricing of multi-period CDOs, and then we develop a simulation-based pricing routine.

ESTIMATING CDO RISK WITH MONTE CARLO SIMULATION

Consider a portfolio with N loans that mature in one year with exposure totaling 100. Now issue three obligations: the most senior obligation has a principal of 93, the mezzanine obligation has 4 and the junior obligation 3. At the end of the year, the loan repayments from the portfolio are distributed to the obligations. First, the senior obligation is served and then the remaining funds are used to serve the mezzanine obligation. What is left is paid to the holders of the junior obligation.

This simplified structure illustrates the mechanics of CDO transactions. They are called CDOs because debt portfolios serve as collateral for the issued obligations. Reflecting the fact that the portfolio principal is sliced into pieces, individual obligations are often called *tranches*. Their cut-off points are usually expressed as percentage of the total exposure. The lower cut-off of a tranche is its attachment point and the upper cut-off is its detachment point. In our example above, the mezzanine tranche has an attachment point of 3% and a detachment point of 7%. The most junior tranche is usually called the equity tranche because holders of the junior tranche receive the residual cash flows, very much like equity holders in a corporation do.

CDO structures are often used by financial institutions when selling parts of their loan portfolio to the capital market. The repackaging in the form of tranches serves to cater to different investor preferences. As we will see later on, senior tranches can have a default probability corresponding to an AAA rating, even though the underlying portfolio may contain speculative grade investments.

Table 11.1 Information required for the simulation analysis of CDO tranches

	A	B	C	D	E	F	G	H	I
1	**Simulation specifications**						**Simulation results for tranches**		
2							Attachment	PD	EL
3	# trials		1 000 000				0.000%		
4							3.000%		
5							7.000%		
6									
7									
8	**Portfolio**								
9	Loan	PD	LGD	EAD	w				
10	1	1%	50%	100	0.3				
11	2	1%	50%	100	0.3				
12	3	1%	50%	100	0.3				
...	...	...	...	...	...				
125	125	1%	50%	100	0.3				

CDO structures are also used in the derivative market, where they are called *synthetic CDOs*. In a synthetic CDO, buyers and sellers agree on a portfolio and the tranching without putting up a portfolio of actual loans or bonds. Synthetic CDOs are very flexible instruments for investing, hedging and speculating.

Real-life CDO structures are more complex than the one sketched above. In particular, one has to set up rules on how cash flows accruing before maturity (e.g., coupon payments) are distributed. We nevertheless stick to the simplified, one-period structure with no interim payments in the first part of this chapter. This helps us to focus on the key modeling issues. In the second part of this chapter, we successively adapt our models to real-life.

The risk of CDO tranches is usually evaluated by estimating their probability of default or their expected loss. The probability of default is the probability that portfolio losses are so high that the tranche cannot be served in full. The expected loss is the percentage of the tranche principal that on average is lost due to default. To determine these risk measures, we need the distribution of portfolio losses. Abstracting from interest earned on tranches we can say that a tranche with attachment point of 10% will default if portfolio losses are larger than 10% of the portfolio principal. A tranche's probability of default is then identical to the probability that portfolio losses exceed its attachment point.

In Chapter 7, we used the asset value approach and a one-factor model to simulate the distribution of portfolio losses. We use the same approach and also build on tables and macros developed in Chapter 7. We believe that it is in the interest of the reader if we refrain from summarizing the modeling steps explained in previous chapters.

Similar to Chapter 7, we collect the portfolio risk parameters in the sheet. In Table 11.1, we can see the data necessary to analyze a CDO on a portfolio of 125 loans.[1] For each loan, we specify the probability of default PD, the loss given default LGD, the exposure at default EAD and the factor sensitivity w. The attachment points of the tranches are listed in column G, starting in cell G3. We have three tranches with attachment points 0%, 3% and 7% respectively.

[1] We choose 125 because this is the number of obligors in a synthetic CDO of the iTraxx or CDX family, which we will price later in this chapter.

In cell C3, we fix the number of trials for the Monte Carlo simulation whose output will extend over the range H3:I5.

We then modify the macro simVBA from Chapter 7 to simulate the probability of default and expected loss of each tranche. In the first lines, we input the number of simulations (M), the number of loans in the portfolio (N) and the number of tranches (K). The latter two are found by counting the elements in the ranges reserved for those items. (The macro assumes that no irrelevant entries are made at some other place in those columns.) After declaring and dimensioning variables, we record the attachment points in the array `attach` and write the sum of individual loan exposures into the variable `sumEAD`.

In a `For i=1 to N` loop, we write the loan parameters into arrays. The only difference from the macro in Chapter 7 is that we convert the exposures to percentage exposures. This facilitates the computation of tranche losses, because the tranches' attachment points are stated in percentage terms.

The portfolio loss in one trial of the Monte Carlo simulation is determined in exactly the same way as in Chapter 7. We first draw a factor (the function NRND() introduced in Chapter 7 returns a standard normal random number), and then implement the factor model and sum the individual loan losses to get `loss_j`, the percentage portfolio loss in trial *j*.

The entire code of the macro reads as follows:

```
Sub simCDO()

Dim M As Long, N As Long, K As Integer, i As Long, j As Long, a As
  Integer
M = Range("c3") 'Number of simulations
N = Application.Count(Range("B10:B65536")) 'Number of loans
K = Application.Count(Range("G3:G65536")) 'Number of tranches

Dim d(), LGD() As Double, EAD() As Double, w() As Double, w2() As Double
Dim tranchePD() As Double, trancheEL() As Double, attach() As Double

Dim factor As Double, loss_j As Double, sumEAD As Double

ReDim d(1 To N), LGD(1 To N), EAD(1 To N), w(1 To N), w2(1 To N)
ReDim tranchePD(1 To K), trancheEL(1 To K), attach(1 To K + 1)

'Read in attachment points and sum of loan exposures
For a = 1 To K
    attach(a) = Range("G" & a + 2)
Next a
attach(K + 1) = 1
sumEAD = Application.Sum(Range("D3:D65536"))

'Write loan characteristics into arrays and sum EADs
For i = 1 To N
    d(i) = Application.NormSInv(Range("B" & i + 9))
    LGD(i) = Range("C" & i + 9)
    EAD(i) = Range("D" & i + 9) / sumEAD
```

```
    w(i) = Range("E" & i + 9)
    w2(i) = ((1 - w(i) * w(i))) ^ 0.5
Next i

'Conduct M Monte Carlo trials
For j = 1 To M
    factor = NRND()
    'Compute portfolio loss for one trial
    loss_j = 0
    For i = 1 To N
        If w(i) * factor + w2(i) * NRND() < d(i) Then
            loss_j = loss_j + LGD(i) * EAD(i)
        End If
    Next i

    'Record losses for tranches
    a = 1
    Do While loss_j - attach(a) > 10 ^ -15
        tranchePD(a) = tranchePD(a) + 1 / M
        trancheEL(a) = trancheEL(a) + Application.WorksheetFunction.Min_
                     ((loss_j - attach(a)) / (attach(a + 1) _
                                            - attach(a)), 1) / M
        a = a + 1
Loop

Next j
Range ("H3:H" & K + 2)=Application.WorksheetFunction. _
      Transpose(tranchePD)
Range ("I3:i" & K + 2)=Application.WorksheetFunction. _
      Transpose(trancheEL)
End Sub
```

Tranche losses are recorded in a `Do While` loop. In doing so, we start at the equity tranche, which has index `a=1`. Tranche `a` suffers a loss if the percentage portfolio loss is larger than tranche `a`'s attachment point. We could check this via `loss_j>attach(a)`. However, in order to avoid potential problems arising from numerical imprecision, we allow for some very small tolerance and record a default only if `loss_j - attach(a) > 10 ^ -15`.

If a tranche is affected by the portfolio loss, we increase the variable `tranchePD` by `1/M`, the probability of an individual trial. After completing the *M* trials, `tranchePD` therefore contains the probability of default. To determine the expected loss, note that a tranche's principal is the difference between its detachment and attachment points. In the VBA macro, this is `attach(a+1) - attach(a)`. The percentage that is lost is the difference between the portfolio loss and the attachment point, divided by the principal, and capped at one (we do not need a floor at zero because we leave the loop when the loss is smaller than the attachment point):

```
Application.Worksheetfunction.Min _
       ((loss_j - attach(a)) / (attach(a + 1) - attach(a)), 1)
```

Table 11.2 Simulation analysis of CDO tranches in a one-period setting

	A	B	C	D	E	F	G	H	I
1	**Simulation specifications**						**Simulation results for tranches**		
2							Attachment	PD	EL
3	# trials		1 000 000				0%	59.3312%	16.480%
4							3%	0.7333%	0.1331%
5							7%	0.0050%	0.0000%
6									
7									
8	**Portfolio**								
9	Loan	PD	LGD	EAD	w				
10	1	1%	50%	100	0.3				
11	2	1%	50%	100	0.3				
12	3	1%	50%	100	0.3				
...	...	...	...	...	...				
125	125	1%	50%	100	0.3				

Run macro simCDO to return the PD and EL for tranches in H3:I5

Dividing this loss by M, and summing it up over the M trials leads to the expected loss.

Finally, we write the `tranchePD` and `trancheEL` arrays into the sheet as the results of the simulation. Since these arrays are row vectors within VBA, we transpose them to convert them into column vectors that fit into the structure of our sheet.

The results shown in Table 11.2 vividly illustrate the effects of tranching: the default probability decreases from 59% (equity tranche) over 0.73% (mezzanine) to 0.005% (senior). The latter corresponds to an AAA rated corporate bond – even though the default probability in the underlying portfolio is 1%.

When rating agencies assign a rating to a CDO tranche, they follow approaches very similar to the one used here. Based on a credit portfolio model, they determine a tranche's probability and/or expected loss, and assign a rating accordingly.

We can play around with the parameters to explore the tranches' sensitivity to the characteristics of the underlying portfolio. For example, if we set all factor sensitivities to 0.5 and re-run the Monte Carlo simulation, the default probability of the senior tranche increases to 0.34%. The default probability of the equity tranche by contrast is reduced to 43%. The reason for this is that an increase in correlation makes it more likely to experience either zero losses or very high losses.

Finally, note that simulation accuracy is an important issue, especially for the senior tranches with low default probabilities. This is why we used 1,000,000 trials here. They take roughly one minute for the 125 loan portfolio. For other portfolios, they may take much longer – and they may not even be sufficient to reach an acceptable degree of accuracy. We would then consider more sophisticated simulation approaches such as the ones discussed in Chapter 7.

THE LARGE HOMOGENEOUS PORTFOLIO (LHP) APPROXIMATION

Although Monte Carlo simulations can be structured such that they require little computing time, it is useful to have a direct, analytical method for determining the risk of CDO tranches. If we are willing to make some simplifying assumptions, such a solution can indeed be derived.

The solution is built on the concept of conditional default probability within the one-factor asset value approach. Recall from Chapter 6 that the default probability of an individual exposure i conditional on a factor realization Z is

$$p_i(Z) = \Phi\left[\frac{\Phi^{-1}(p_i) - w_i Z}{\sqrt{1-w_i^2}}\right] \tag{11.1}$$

where p_i is the default probability (the PD), and w_i is the factor sensitivity. The first assumption that we make is that the underlying portfolio is homogenous in the sense that PDs, LGDs, EADs and factor sensitivities are uniform across debt instruments. In Equation (11.1), we can therefore drop the subscript i. The resulting $p(Z)$ is the default rate in the portfolio that we expect for a given Z.

The second assumption is that the portfolio is large – really large indeed. We assume that it contains loans from an infinite number of obligors. By the law of large numbers, it follows that the realized default rate is equal to the conditional default probability $p(Z)$.

The conditional percentage portfolio loss, denoted by Loss(Z), can be directly obtained as LGD times conditional default probability:

$$\text{Loss}(Z) = \text{LGD} \cdot \Phi\left[\frac{\Phi^{-1}(p) - wZ}{\sqrt{1-w^2}}\right] \tag{11.2}$$

We now move on to describe the distribution of losses. The probability that the loss is larger than some value λ can be expressed as the probability that the factor Z is smaller than some critical value $d(\lambda)$. To obtain $d(\lambda)$, set Loss(Z) $= \lambda$ in Equation (11.2) and solve for Z:

$$\text{Prob}(\text{Loss} \geq \lambda) = \text{Prob}(Z \leq d(\lambda)) = \Phi[d(\lambda)]$$

$$d(\lambda) = \frac{\Phi^{-1}(p) - \sqrt{1-w^2}\,\Phi^{-1}(\lambda/\text{LGD})}{w} \tag{11.3}$$

With this result, we have made an important step towards determining the expected loss of CDO tranches. For the calculations, it is convenient to express the expected loss as a percentage of the portfolio notional, not as a percentage of the tranche principal as introduced above. For an equity tranche with attachment point 0 and detachment point λ, the expected loss as percentage of the portfolio notional can be written as

$$\text{E}(\text{Loss}_{(0,\lambda)}) = \text{LGD} \cdot \text{E}\left[\Phi\left(\frac{\Phi^{-1}(p) - wZ}{\sqrt{1-w^2}}\right) I\{Z > d(\lambda)\}\right] + \lambda\Phi(d(\lambda)) \tag{11.4}$$

The second term on the right-hand side captures factor scenarios where the portfolio loss is larger than the detachment point λ; in this case, the entire tranche principal, which is λ times the portfolio notional, is lost. The first term is the expected loss for factor scenarios that do not have a loss greater than λ. This restriction is captured by the indicator variable $I\{Z > d(\lambda)\}$, which takes the value 1 if Z is above $d(\lambda)$ – so losses are below λ – and zero else. As shown in the Appendix at the end of this chapter, there is a closed-form solution for the expectation

Table 11.3 Applying the LHP model to determine the expected loss of CDO tranches in a one-period setting

	A	B	C	D	E
1	**LHP assumptions**				
2	PD	LGD	w		
3	1.00%	50%	0.3		
4					
5	**LHP analysis**				
6	Attachment λ	d(λ)	E(Loss(0, λ))	Tranche expected loss	
7					
8	0%	-2.81062798	0.49842%	16.61415%	
9	3.00%	-4.31929635	0.49999%	0.03923%	
10	7.00%		0.50000%	0.00001%	
11	100.00%				
12					
13					
14					
15					
16					
17					
18					

B8: =NORMSINV($A$3)/$C$3-(1-$C$3^2)^0.5/$C$3*NORMSINV(A9/B$3)
(can be copied into B9)

C8: =IF(A9<1,B$3*BIVNOR(NORMSINV($A$3),-B8,-C$3)
+A9*NORMSDIST(B8),A$3*B$3)
D8: =(C8-C7)/(A9-A8)
(can be copied down to row 10)

in the first term, which leads to

$$\mathrm{E}(\mathrm{Loss}_{(0,\lambda)}) = \mathrm{LGD} \cdot \Phi_2\left(\Phi^{-1}(p), -d(\lambda), -w\right) + \lambda\Phi(d(\lambda)) \tag{11.5}$$

where $\Phi_2(x, y, \rho)$ denotes the cumulative standard bivariate normal distribution function with correlation ρ. It is not available as a standard Excel function, but in Chapter 6 we already used a user-defined function BIVNOR.

Importantly, the formula can also be used to determine the expected loss of a tranche with nonzero attachment point λ_1 and detachment point λ_2. We make use of the following, general relation:

$$\mathrm{E}(\mathrm{Loss}_{(\lambda_1,\lambda_2)}) = \mathrm{E}(\mathrm{Loss}_{(0,\lambda_2)}) - \mathrm{E}(\mathrm{Loss}_{(0,\lambda_1)}) \tag{11.6}$$

For the senior tranche with detachment point $\lambda_2 = 1$, we can set $\mathrm{E}(\mathrm{Loss}_{(0,1)}) = \mathrm{LGD} \times \mathrm{PD}$.

In Table 11.3, we use the LHP model to determine the expected loss for the tranches from Table 11.1. We write the attachment points in column A, including the detachment point 1 for the most senior tranche. In column B, we determine the thresholds $d(\lambda)$; in column C, we implement formula (11.5). Finally, in column D we determine the tranches' expected loss as a percentage of the tranche principal. Recall that the expected loss formulae from above are not expressed as a percentage of the tranche principal. This is why we divide by the difference between a tranche's detachment and attachment points.

Looking at the results, we see that the expected loss of the junior tranche is fairly close to the result that we obtained in the Monte Carlo simulation (see Table 11.2). For the mezzanine tranche, however, the LHP leads to a considerably smaller loss. The reason for this is that the LHP blends out firm-specific risk, which has a relatively strong impact on the risk of the mezzanine tranche here. If the number of the obligors in the portfolio increases, the quality of the LHP approximation improves as well. Other parameters affecting the quality of the approximation are the magnitude of the factor sensitivity and the heterogeneity of the portfolio.

With the LHP model, we can easily assess the effects of parameter uncertainty. As demonstrated in Chapter 7, we can treat parameter uncertainty as an additional risk factor. Say we want to model errors in the estimation of the factor sensitivity. Based on an assumption about the distribution of the true factor sensitivity w, we can draw a random w, plug it into cell C3 of Table 11.3 and record the resulting expected loss figures. When we do this many times, we get a distribution of loss figures. This distribution can be used to perform stress scenario analyses or to correct biases arising from parameter uncertainty.

Here, we do not spell out such an analysis because it is straightforward to apply the procedure of Chapter 7 to the simulation analysis of the previous section or the LHP analysis of this section. We only illustrate the possible effects with a simplified example. Assume that you do not know whether the factor sensitivity is 0.2, 0.3 or 0.4. Inserting the values into cell C3 of Table 11.3, we obtain the following expected loss figures:

	Expected loss for different ws		
Tranche	$w = 0.2$ (%)	$w = 0.3$ (%)	$w = 0.4$ (%)
[0, 3%]	16.66638	16.61415	16.21695
[3, 7%]	0.00022	0.03923	0.32251
[7%, 100%]	0.00000	0.00001	0.00064

Note the asymmetry. An increase in the factor sensitivity from 0.3 to 0.4 has a larger impact than a decrease from 0.3 to 0.2. Assuming that the three factor sensitivities are equally likely, the correct estimate of the expected loss is obtained as a simple average. For the mezzanine [3%, 7%] tranche, for example, the correct expected loss would be 0.12065%, three times as large as the one obtained with the average factor sensitivity of 0.3. This shows that an incorporation of estimation risk can be essential for a correct analysis of CDOs. In most applications, however, estimation risk used to be ignored. One likely reason why the risk of CDOs was underestimated before the 2007–2008 financial crisis is therefore the neglect of parameter uncertainty.

The LHP model is often used to back out correlation assumptions implicit in market prices of CDOs. If we use risk-neutral default probabilities instead of actual ones (see Chapter 10 for the distinction between the two), we can value a CDO tranche by discounting the expected cash flows, which we can determine with the LHP model, with the risk-free rate. We explore this method in a latter section of this chapter (see page 263). Conversely, if we have a market price for a CDO tranche and assumptions about PD and LGD in the portfolio, we can find the factor sensitivity w that levels the LHP model price with the market price. Since the square of the factor sensitivity is the asset correlation in the asset value approach, this leads us to estimates of market-implied correlation.

SYSTEMIC RISK OF CDO TRANCHES

Examining the PD or expected loss of CDO tranches is the common way of assessing their risk. Still, one should not conclude that a CDO tranche with a default probability of 0.1%

carries the same risk as a corporate bond with a default probability of 0.1%. The two can dramatically differ in their systematic risk, i.e., their sensitivity to overall market conditions.

An intuitive way of measuring systematic risk is to examine an instrument's default probability in a bad state of the world. In the one-factor approach used here, it is the default probability conditional on a bad factor realization.

With the simulation tool from the first section, we could obtain conditional default probabilities by fixing the factor in the simulation at some value, say −3.09 (−3.09 is a scenario that is worse than 99.9% of all possible scenarios).

If the portfolio is homogenous in PDs, LGDs, EADs and factor sensitivities (or if we are willing to assume this as an approximation), we can assess systematic risk analytically. As in the previous section, we could also assume the portfolio to be large – but this is not really necessary. Consider again the conditional default probability

$$p(Z) = \Phi\left[\frac{\Phi^{-1}(p) - wZ}{\sqrt{1-w^2}}\right] \tag{11.7}$$

We now determine the exact conditional default probability of a homogeneous tranche with attachment point λ_1. Let N be the number of issuers in the portfolio, while D denotes the number of defaults in the portfolio. A tranche attachment λ_1 is hit if the following holds true:

$$\frac{D \times \text{LGD} \times \text{EAD}}{N \times \text{EAD}} > \lambda_1 \tag{11.8}$$

The left-hand side gives the percentage portfolio loss, which is compared to the attachment point. Simplifying and rearranging yields:

$$D > \lambda_1 \times N/\text{LGD} \tag{11.9}$$

In the asset value model, defaults are independent conditional on a factor realization. The number of defaults D thus follows a binomial distribution with success probability equal to the conditional default probability. The probability that a tranche is hit is therefore given by

$$1 - \text{Binom}\,(\lambda_1 \times N/\text{LGD}, N, p(Z)) \tag{11.10}$$

where Binom(x, N, q) denotes the cumulative probability of observing x or fewer successes in N trials with success probability q. In Excel, it is available through the function BINOMDIST(x, N, q, 1), where the logical value 1 tells Excel to return the cumulative distribution rather than the density.

In Table 11.4, we compute conditional default probabilities for the mezzanine tranche from the previous tables as well as for an individual bond with the same default probability as the mezzanine tranche.

If times get rough, the risk increase is much stronger for the CDO than for the bond. For a moderately bad scenario ($Z = -2$), the default probability of the tranche is almost three times as high as the default probability of the bond. If times get really rough ($Z = -3$), the ratio increases to 6.5.

In credit portfolio modeling, one should not treat CDO tranches as bonds with a standard factor sensitivity. This could lead to severe underestimation of portfolio risk. When comparing

Table 11.4 Conditional default probabilities of a CDO tranche and a standard corporate bond with the same PD

	A	B	C	D	E	F
1	**Homogeneous CDO portfolio**					
2	PD	1%				
3	LGD	0.5				
4	factor sensitivity	0.3				
5	# issuers	125				
6						
7	**CDO tranche**					
8	Attachment	3%				
9	PD	1.00%	(from Table 10.2)			
10						
11	**Conditional PDs**					
12	Factor Z	Tranche	Bond with same PD as tranche			
13	-3.1	67.93%	5.67%			
14	-3.0	61.17%	5.32%			
15	-2.9	54.12%	4.98%			
16	-2.8	47.01%	4.67%			
17	-2.7	40.06%	4.37%			
18	-2.6	33.47%	4.09%			
19	-2.5	27.42%	3.82%			
20	-2.4	22.01%	3.56%			
21	-2.3	17.31%	3			
22	-2.2	13.35%	3			
23	-2.1	10.08%	2			
24	-2.0	7.47%	2			
25	-1.9	5.42%	2			
26	-1.8	3.86%	2			
27	-1.7	2.70%	2			
28	-1.6	1.85%	1			
29	-1.5	1.25%	1			
30	-1.4	0.82%	1			
31	-1.3	0.53%	1			
32	-1.2	0.34%	1			
...	...	...				
44	0.0	0.00%	0.53%			

B13: =1-BINOMDIST(B$8/B$3*B$5,B$5, NORMSDIST((NORMSINV(B$2)-B$4*A13)/(1-B$4^2)^0.5),1)

C13 : =NORMSDIST((NORMSINV(B$9)-B$4*A13)/(1-B$4^2)^0.5)

(can be copied into B13:C44)

the spreads of bonds and CDO tranches with the same rating, one should bear in mind that spreads reflect differences in systematic risk, whereas ratings do not (if they are based on default probability or expected loss).

Apparently, many market participants were not aware of this before the 2007–2008 crisis, which can explain why the losses on CDOs and other instruments caught many investors by surprise. (We would like to note that the above warning concerning the large systematic risk was already given in the first edition of this book, published in May 2007.) The high systematic risk of tranches can also contribute to explaining why rating agencies heavily downgraded many CDOs at the same time. If a shock hits the economy, an individual tranche will react very strongly due to its high systematic risk; and tranches from different transactions will react in a very similar fashion because they depend on the same systematic risk factors.

Of course, there are other explanations why rating agencies produced overly optimistic ratings, which were then lowered dramatically. Possible reasons include neglected risk factors, optimistic assumptions about model inputs, use of flawed models and conflicts of interest. Ongoing academic research addresses the question of which of the explanations is most important. Recent work, for example, suggests that it was not primarily the models themselves that led to overoptimistic ratings; rather, model adjustments made by analysts (which are part of the standard rating process) seem to have contributed to the prevalence of AAA ratings.

DEFAULT TIMES FOR FIRST-TO-DEFAULT SWAPS

In standard, single-name credit default swaps (CDS), which we covered in Chapter 10, payment is made upon the default of the issuer to which the CDS refers. To value the CDS, we need default probabilities of this reference issuer over the maturity of the swap. In a first-to-default swap, payments are triggered by the first default that occurs in a portfolio of issuers. We therefore need the probabilities that the first default occurs over the life-time of the contract.

As before, we start the analysis by specifying individual risk parameters for the obligors in the portfolio. In particular, we require individual default probabilities of the issuers in the basket to which the first-to-default swap refers. If the goal is to value the swap, we would take risk-neutral default probabilities, e.g., ones backed out from bond prices (see Chapter 10). If the goal is to assess the risk of the swap, we would take actual default probabilities, e.g., estimated from past default rates. An example for the latter is the following default frequencies for A-rated issuers from Moody's (2006, Exhibit 35):

Cumulative PDs				
1 year	2 years	3 years	4 years	5 years
0.022%	0.114%	0.271%	0.418%	0.563%

Next, we have to model correlations. Again, the straightforward way would be to take the asset value approach coupled with a one-factor model. In a one-year analysis, we would record a default if the normally distributed asset value falls below $\Phi^{-1}(\text{PD}_1)$, where Φ denotes the standard normal distribution function and PD_t denotes the cumulative default probability over t years. In the multi-year setting, we record a default in year t if the asset value ends up between $\Phi^{-1}(\text{PD}_t)$ and $\Phi^{-1}(\text{PD}_{t-1})$.

In the literature, one would describe this as an application of a Gaussian copula. Copulas provide a very flexible tool for modeling dependence. The choice of the copula is not obvious, and can lead to dramatic changes in dependence. We will stick to the Gaussian copula in this chapter, however the implementation of other copulae in our setting is straightforword.

In Table 11.5, we assemble a basket of 125 loans. The basket parameters are recorded from row 10 onwards. We require factor sensitivities as well as default probabilities for each period that we want to analyze. In the macro we are about to write, we will require inputs in the form of cumulative default probabilities; the number of periods, however, can be chosen freely within the column number constraint of Excel. In the example shown in Table 11.5, we

Table 11.5 Information required for the time of the first default in a basket of 125 obligors

	A	B	C	D	E	F	G	H
1	**Simulating 1st to default times**							
2	# trials		100 000					
3	**Simulated probabilities for 1st default**							
4								
5		in period t						
6		cumulative until t						
7	**Basket**							
8		Factor sensi-	Cumulative PDs over period t					
9	Obligor	tivity w	t=1	t=2	t=3	t=4	t=5	
10	1	0.3	0.108%	0.313%	0.572%	0.902%	1.241%	
11	2	0.3	0.108%	0.313%	0.572%	0.902%	1.241%	
12	3	0.3	0.108%	0.313%	0.572%	0.902%	1.241%	
13	4	0.3	0.108%	0.313%	0.572%	0.902%	1.241%	
14	5	0.3	0.108%	0.313%	0.572%	0.902%	1.241%	
15	6	0.3	0.108%	0.313%	0.572%	0.902%	1.241%	
16	7	0.3	0.108%	0.313%	0.572%	0.902%	1.241%	
17	8	0.3	0.108%	0.313%	0.572%	0.902%	1.241%	
18	9	0.3	0.108%	0.313%	0.572%	0.902%	1.241%	
19	10	0.3	0.108%	0.313%	0.572%	0.902%	1.241%	
...	...	...	...	...	...	...	...	
134	125	0.3	0.108%	0.313%	0.572%	0.902%	1.241%	

determine cumulative default probabilities for five years. For each obligor, we assume PDs to be given by Baa default rates (parameters could also be heterogeneous).

The macro simTIME builds on the macro simVBA from Chapter 7. The main modifications are as follows. In contrast to the previous analyses, we now have multiple default thresholds for each obligor – one for each period. Therefore, we define the array `d` as a matrix with N (= number of obligors) rows and K (= number of periods) columns.

Depending on the source of our default probability estimates, we may have estimates of zero. In such a case, the NORMSINV function returns an error value. A simple fix then is to set the threshold to a large negative number, e.g., −(10^10).

In a trial `j` of the simulation, we first simulate the factor and then loop through the obligors. Having drawn an asset value `x` for obligor `i`, we use a `Do while` loop to determine whether the obligor defaulted, and if so, in which period. If the default happens in the first period, the loop would lead us to compare the asset value `x` to the zero element of array `d`, which we have not defined. We thus exit the loop when we reach the element `a=0`.

Next, we write the default time into a variable `deftime_j`. It records the period of the first default in trial `j`, and so we only change it if the default of borrower `i` happened earlier than any previous default in this trial. This is accomplished in

```
If a + 1 < deftime_j Then deftime_j = a + 1
```

Note that we have to increment the default period counter `a` by one because the preceding top checking loop overshoots the index `a` by 1. Once we have gone through all obligors, we add `1/M` in position `deftime_j` of the array `deftime`. (`1/M` is the probability of an individual trial.) Note that `deftime_j` takes the value `K+1` if no default occurred within the specified time horizon. To prevent the index from running out of range, we have chosen the dimension (1 to K+1) for the array deftime.

Finally, we write the output into the sheet. We copy the period dates from the basket data and write the array deftime into the sheet. Deftime contains the probability that the first default occurs within period *t*. To also obtain the cumulative probability that the first default occurs before or within period *t*, we just sum up the period by period default probabilities. This is done with appropriate spreadsheet formula that the macro writes into the sheet.

```
Sub simTIME()

Range("C4:IV6").Clear 'Clear output range in sheet

Dim M As Long, N As Long, K As Integer, I As Long, j As Long, _
  a As Integer
M = Range("C2") 'Number of simulations
N = Application.Count(Range("B10:B65536")) 'Number of obligors
K = Application.Count(Range("C10:IV10")) 'Number of default dates

Dim d() As Double, w() As Double, w2() As Double, deftime() As Double
Dim factor As Double, x As Double, deftime_j As Integer

ReDim w(1 To N), w2(1 To N), d(1 To N, 1 To K), deftime(1 To K + 1)


'Write issuer characteristics into arrays (d=default points,
' w=factor sensitivity)
For i = 1 To N
    w(i) = Range("B" & i + 9)
    w2(i) = ((1 - w(i) * w(i))) ^ 0.5
   For j = 1 To K
        If Cells(i + 9, j + 2) > 0 Then
             d(i, j) = Application.NormSInv(Cells(i + 9, j + 2))
        Else: d(i, K) = -(10 ^ 10)
        End If
   Next j
Next i

'Conduct M Monte Carlo trials
For j = 1 To M
    factor = NRND()
    deftime_j = K + 1

    'Determine first default for this trial
    For i = 1 To N
        x = w(i) * factor + w2(i) * NRND()
        a = K
        Do While x < d(i, a)
```

```
            a = a - 1
            If a = 0 Then Exit Do
        Loop
        If a + 1 < deftime_j Then deftime_j = a + 1
    Next i
    deftime(deftime_j) = deftime(deftime_j) + 1 / M

Next j

'Add headers, write output into sheet, and cumulate default times
Range("C4:IV4") = (Range("C9:IV9"))
Range(Cells(5, 3), Cells(5, 2 + K)) = deftime
Range("C6") = Range("C5")
Range("d6") = "=C6+D5"
Range(Cells(6, 4), Cells(6, 2 + K)).FillRight

End Sub
```

Simulation results are shown in Table 11.6. As in the case of CDOs, it is interesting to compare the risk-structure of the first-to-default instrument to the one of an individual bond. The cumulative first-to-default probability over 1 year is 9.39%, well below the average one-year default probability of C-rated bonds, which is 14.42% as reported by Moody's (2006). Over five-years, however, the first-to-default probability is 59.76%, well above the 37.70% reported for C-rated bonds.

Table 11.6 Simulated first default times for a basket of 125 obligors

	A	B	C	D	E	F	G	H
1	**Simulating 1st to default times**							
2	# trials		100 000					
3	**Simulated probabilities for 1st default**							
4			t=1	t=2	t=3	t=4	t=5	
5		in period t	9.39%	14.42%	13.52%	12.81%	9.61%	
6		cumulative until t	9.39%	23.81%	37.33%	50.15%	59.76%	
7	**Basket**							
8		Factor sensi-	Cumulative PDs over period t					
9	Obligor	tivity w	t=1	t=2	t=3	t=4	t=5	
10	1	0.3	0.108%	0.313%	0.572%	0.902%	1.241%	
11	2	0.3	0.108%	0.313%	[illegible]	[illegible]	[illegible]	
12	3	0.3	0.108%	0.313%	[illegible]	[illegible]	[illegible]	
13	4	0.3	0.108%	0.313%	[illegible]	[illegible]	[illegible]	
14	5	0.3	0.108%	0.313%	[illegible]	[illegible]	[illegible]	
15	6	0.3	0.108%	0.313%	0.572%	0.902%	1.241%	
16	7	0.3	0.108%	0.313%	0.572%	0.902%	1.241%	
17	8	0.3	0.108%	0.313%	0.572%	0.902%	1.241%	
18	9	0.3	0.108%	0.313%	0.572%	0.902%	1.241%	
19	10	0.3	0.108%	0.313%	0.572%	0.902%	1.241%	
...	...	...	...	...	...	...	...	
134	125	0.3	0.108%	0.313%	0.572%	0.902%	1.241%	

Run macro simTIME to return the probabilities in C5:G6

CDO PRICING IN THE LHP FRAMEWORK

The tools developed for the risk analysis of the previous sections provide a good basis for pricing CDOs. We will leave the simplifying one-period analysis behind and provide routines that are able to price real-life, multi-period CDOs. In the example applications, we will use the capital structure that is standard for synthetic CDOs. Tranche definitions differ between the European and the US market with respect to the attachment points and tranche thickness as illustrated by the following table:

	Attachment – Detachment	
Tranche	US	Europe
Index (0–100%)	CDX family	iTraxx family
Equity	0–3%	0–3%
Mezzanine junior	3–7%	3–6%
Mezzanine senior	7–10%	6–9%
Senior junior	10–15%	9–12%
Senior	15–30%	12–22%
Super senior	30–100%	22–100%

Box 11.1 gives example market quotes for iTraxx and CDX tranches. The collateral portfolio of synthetic CDOs such as the ones considered here is a portfolio of credit default swaps (CDS). The buyer of a CDO tranche receives regular premiums as long as the tranche is not wiped out; if a CDO tranche is hit, the buyer pays the loss amount to the seller of the CDO. Unlike in the CDOs examined in the previous sections, there is no principal repayment at the maturity of the CDO. Thus, cash flow streams of synthetic CDOs are very similar to those of CDSs.

Box 11.1 CDO pricing. Market standard in 2010

Let us have a look at a typical tranche run:

Tranche	Upfront (%) bid/ask	Running (bps) bid/ask	Fixed/deal spread (bps)
0–3	$24^1/_2/24^7/_8$		500
3–6	$-4^5/_8/-4^1/_4$		300
6–9	$-4^1/_8/-3^7/_8$		100
9–12		93/97	100
12–22		37/40	100
22–100		14/15.5	25

Tranche run as of April 15 for iTraxx Europe S9, 5y.

Consider buying protection in the equity tranche (0–3). You would pay $24^7/_8$ of the notional upfront, i.e., three days after purchase, and a fixed spread of 500 bps on the notional per year. Buying the 3–6 tranche you *get* 4.25% of the notional upfront and pay 300 bps per year. Starting with the 9–12 tranche the quotes become running quotes. Consider the ask price of the 9–12 tranche of 97 bps. For this price you buy a tranche with a fixed spread of 100 bps. The difference of the quoted price and the fixed spread (i.e., 97–100 bps) times the expected present value of one basis point of the tranche gives the upfront payment.

For US indices all tranches are quoted in percent upfront. A major shortcoming of this notation is that you cannot directly determine the overall cost of a tranche. However, traders often include a conversion into implied all-running spreads. The following CDX run illustrates this:

Tranche	Upfront (%)	Fixed spread (bps)	Implied all-running spread (bps)
0–3	38/38.5	500	2373
3–7	1.75/2.25	500	579
7–10	−8/−7.625	500	202
10–15	−0.5/−0.2	100	87
15–30	−1.95/−1.85	100	28
30–100	−2.32/−2.222	100	39

Tranche run as of April 15 for CDX S9, 5y.

Note the difference between the fixed coupons between the EU and US, e.g., the 3–7% tranche is quoted at a fixed coupon of 500 bps whereas the 3–6% iTraxx tranche is quoted with a coupon of 300 bps.

In what follows, we show how to estimate fair prices of synthetic CDO tranches based on the CDS spread of the underlying index as well as on assumptions about recovery rates and asset correlation. We start by using the large homogenous portfolio LHP framework with the Gaussian copula. The LHP framework was already used for the risk analysis of CDOs.

Before delving into the methodology, we specify CDO parameters and prepare the calculations. In Table 11.7 we start with the (constant) risk-free rate in cell B4, the number of coupon payments per year in cell B5 and the valuation date (i.e., the day on which the CDO is to be priced) in cell B6. The next cell B7 contains the maturity date of the CDO. We choose a CDO with a Sept 2014 maturity, e.g., a synthetic CDO of the iTraxx or CDX family. The asset correlation parameter in B8 is set to 20%. For the loss given default of the CDO, or the average LGD of the underlying CDSs, we choose the market standard of 60% (cell B9). The spread of the index (0–100% tranche) is entered in basis points in cell B10. The corresponding hazard rate is calculated in cell B12 as the index spread over the loss given default (see Chapter 10 for details on the hazard rate).

The capital structure of the CDO is entered in the range D5:E10, with the tranches in column D and their attachment points in column E. We use the European tranche system of six tranches. starting with the equity tranche in D5:F5 to the super senior 22–100% tranche in D10:F10.[2]

[2] Note that market conditions might lead to the case of tranches other than the equity tranche to be quoted upfront. In this case you need to adjust the upfront/running conversion for those tranches analogously to the equity tranche in our example. See Box 11.1 for more information about the current (as of Q2 2010) market conditions.

Table 11.7 Multi-period CDO pricing in the LHP framework

	A	B	C	D	E	F	G	H	I	J	K	L	…	Q	R	S	…	X
1	**Multi-Period CDO Pricing in the LHP framework**																	
2																		
3	**Deal Parameters**			**Capital structure**														
4	Risk-free (%)	2%		Tranche	Attachment	Tranche Size	Spread	Fixed coupon (bps)	Fixed leg	Accrued leg	Default leg							
5	Coupons p.a.	4		Equity	0%	3%	52.04%	500	2.43	0.08	66.36%							
6	Value Date	4/15/2010		Mezz J	3%	3%	6.99%		3.78	0.03	26.67%							
7	Maturity Date	9/20/2014		Mezz S	6%	3%	2.78%		4.11	0.01	11.46%							
8	Correlation	20%		Senior J	9%	3%	1.21%		4.22	0.01	5.12%							
9	Loss-Given-Default (LGD)	60%		Senior	12%	10%	0.28%		4.28	0.00	1.19%							
10	Spread of Index (bps)	82		Super Senior	22%	78%	0.00%		4.22	0.00	0.01%							
11				Index	0%	100%	0.82%		4.16	0.01	3.42%							
12	Implied Hazard Rate (bps)	136.67	=B10/B9															
13	# Periods	18	=COUPNUM(B6,B7,B5)															
14					**Marginal Losses**													
15	Date	Cum. PD	Disc fac	Δt	Equity	Mezz J	Equity	Senior J	Senior	S Senio								ior
16	6/20/2010	0.25%	0.996	0.183	4.953%	0.047%	0.004%	0.001%	0.000%	0.000%								9%
17	9/20/2010	0.60%	0.991	0.256	6.561%	0.335%	0.047%	0.009%	0.001%	0.000%								7%
18	12/20/2010	0.94%	0															5%
19	3/20/2011	1.28%	0															3%
20	6/20/2011	1.62%	0															2%
21	9/20/2011	1.97%	0									0.000%		0.176%		67.0%		99.0%
22	12/20/2011	2.30%	0									0.000%		0.173%		62.6%		98.8%
23	3/20/2012	2.64%	0									0.000%		0.173%		58.6%		98.6%
24	6/20/2012	2.98%	0									0.000%		0.174%		54.8%		98.5%
25	9/20/2012	3.32%	0									0.000%		0.173%		51.3%		98.3%
26	12/20/2012	3.65%	0									0.000%		0.171%		48.1%		98.1%
27	3/20/2013	3.98%	0									0.000%		0.169%		45.2%		98.0%
…	…																	
33	9/20/2014	5.96%	0.915	0.256	1.953%	2.059%	1.224%	0.663%	0.187%	0.002%		0.000%		0.169%		31.14%		96.9%

A16: =COUPNCD(B6,B7,4,0)
A17: =IF(ROW()<16+$B$13,COUPNCD(A16,$B$7,$B$5,0),"") (can be copied down to A33)

B16: =1-EXP(-$B$12/10^4*(A16-$B$6)/360) (can be copied down to B33)

C16: =(1+$B$4)^(-1*(A16-$B$6)/360) (can be copied down to C33)

D16: =(A16-$B$6)/360
D17: =(A17-A16)/360 (can be copied down to D33)

S16: =1-SUM(E$16:E16)-SUM(L$16:L16) (can be copied down to S16:X33)

={(LHP_LR(B16:B33,$B$8,B9,$E$5:$E$10))}
(applies to E16:Q33)

I5: =SUMPRODUCT($C$16:$C$33,S16:S33,$D$16:$D$33)
J5: =SUM(0.5*(E16:E33+L16:L33)*$C$16:$C$33*$D$16:$D$33)
K5: =SUMPRODUCT($C$16:$C$33,E16:E33)

G5: =IF(H5>0,(K5/(I5+J5)-(H5/10^4))*I5,K5/(I5+J5))
(can be copied to G11)

I11: =SUMPRODUCT(I5:I10,$F$5:$F$10) (can be copied to K11)

Next we determine the future coupon dates. To start, we estimate the number of periods before maturity in cell B13 using Excels COUPNUM function:

=COUPNUM(B6,B7,B5)

The first coupon date is calculated in A16 using Excel's COUPNCD function:

=COUPNCD(B6,B7,4,0)

To obtain the subsequent coupon dates we again use COUPNCD but now refer to the previous coupon date. Also, we check whether we have reached the last coupon date and leave the cells empty afterwards:

=IF(ROW()<16+$B$13,COUPNCD(A16,$B$7,$B$5,0), "")

The function can be copied down.

For each coupon date we estimate the cumulative default probability of a borrower in the collateral portfolio. The cumulative default probability PD^C from today to time t is given by one minus the probability to survive until time t and is calculated as

$$PD^C = 1 - \exp(-s/LGD(t - t_0)) \tag{11.11}$$

where s is the CDS index spread and LGD the loss-given-default.[3] Thus cell B16 reads

=1−EXP(−$B$12/10^4*(A16−$B$6)/360)

which can be copied down to B33. The term (A16–$B$6)/360 in this formula gives the number of days elapsed since the value date in cell B6.

The next parameter needed for the CDO pricing is the discount factor for each coupon date. We assume a flat interest rate curve,[4] and so cell C16 reads

=(1+$B$4)^(−(A17−$B$6)/360)

Another piece of information that we will need is Δt, the length of time between coupon dates, measured in years. The first Δt is given by the number of days between the value date (B6) and the first coupon date (A16) and is obtained through =(A16–B6)/360 in cell D16. The formula for the next day count refers to the previous coupon date, and so cell D17 reads =(A17–A16)/360. It can be copied down to D33.

Having prepared coupon date information we can now turn to the pricing itself. In Chapter 10 we argued that in order to avoid arbitrage the expected fees received from a CDS have to

[3] See Chapter 10 for details.

[4] It is straightforward, however, to implement a time structure into the discount factors, e.g., by using our INTSPOT function of Chapter 10.

equal the expected default payments. Synthetic CDOs are priced in much the same way. To price a tranche we need to determine the value of default losses – known as *default leg* in modelers' jargon – and the value of coupon payments, which is known as *fixed leg* because coupon payments are fixed. The fixed leg can be split in the coupon leg, which contains the regular (quarterly for synthetic CDOs) coupon payments, and the accrued leg, which collects accrued coupons in periods with a default. Denoting the CDS spread by s, the risk-free discount rate by r, the time between two coupon periods by Δt, the coupon payments dates as $t = 1, \ldots, T$, the notional at time t by N_t, the loss at time t by L_t, and assuming default to take place between two coupon payment dates,[5] the legs are defined as follows:

$$\text{Coupon leg} = s \sum_{t=1}^{T} \frac{\Delta t E_0[N]_t}{(1+r)^t} \tag{11.12a}$$

$$\text{Accrued leg} = s \sum_{t=1}^{T} \frac{\Delta_t E_0[N_t - N_{t-1}]}{2(1+r)^t} \tag{11.12b}$$

$$\text{Fixed leg} = \text{Coupon leg} + \text{Accrued leg} \tag{11.13}$$

$$\text{Default leg} = \sum_{t=1}^{T} \frac{E_0[L_t - L_{t-1}]}{(1+r)^t} \tag{11.14}$$

Note that each leg is computed per tranche. The key difference to the pricing of a CDS is that the notional of a tranche can change over time. If an index constituent defaults, the CDO notional is reduced by the notional principal of the defaulter, not just by the actual loss. This is made to ensure that the CDO's notional is equal to the notional of the underlying CDS index. It is important to correctly model how this is done. The loss arising in period t, which we will call marginal loss, reduces the notional of the most junior tranche still in existence. The recovery, i.e., (1 – loss given default) times the notional of the defaulter, reduces the notional of the most senior tranche still in existence.

Once the fixed leg and the default leg are determined, simply equate them and solve for the spread s. To implement the formulae, we need expected losses and expected recoveries for each future coupon date. They can be determined analytically with the tools from the section in which the LHP was introduced. We perform a large part of the calculations in our function LHP_LR(*pd*, *correlation*, *LGD*, *attachment*, [*rrec*]), which returns the expected losses for each tranche and each coupon date.

In Table 11.7 we apply the function to the range E16:Q33. Its input parameters are the cumulative PD (`pd`) from cells B16:B33, the correlation from cell B8, the loss given default (`LGD`), which is given in B9, and the attachment point structure (`attachment`) from cells E5:E10, and so in total the range E16:Q33 reads:

={LHP_LR(B16:B33,B8,B9,E5:E10)}

[5] This assumption affects the accrued leg only. If you want to model another assumption simply change the $\Delta_{t/2}$ in the formula and the VBA code.

Our LHP_LR function starts with some self-explanatory variable definitions:

```
Function LHP_LR(pd, correlation, LGD, attachment)

pd = pd: attachment = attachment 'Convert input
Dim i As Integer, Q As Integer, k As Integer, PDDm As Variant, r As _
  Integer
Dim j As Integer, lambda() As Double, d, w, trs, output
Dim loss, tr, mLoss, rec, mrec, notional, EL0, ER0

w = correlation ^ 0.5 'correlation parameter
Q = UBound(pd, 1) 'Number of dates
k = UBound(attachment, 1) 'Number of tranches


ReDim loss(1 To k, 0 To Q): ReDim mLoss(1 To k, 1 To Q) 'Loss variables
ReDim rec(1 To k, 0 To Q): ReDim mrec(1 To k, 1 To Q) 'Rec variables
ReDim output(1 To Q, 1 To 2 * k + 1)
ReDim notional(1 To k, 1 To Q): ReDim lambda(0 To k + 1)
ReDim EL0(0 To k, 1 To Q): ReDim ER0(0 To k + 1, 1 To Q)

For tr = 1 To k 'convert tranches
 lambda(tr) = attachment(tr, 1)
Next tr
 lambda(0) = 0: lambda(k + 1) = 1
```

The function's core consists of two loops, one over the number of periods, the second over all tranches within each period. For each tranche, we separately calculate the base loss, which is the loss for an artificial tranche with attachment point zero and detachment point equal to that of the tranche under analysis. This is done according to (11.3) and (11.5). The formula cannot be applied if the LGD is smaller than the detachment point λ. In such a case, however, the expected loss can easily be determined as LGD times PD. (If LGD is smaller than λ, tranches with attachment point larger than λ can never be hit and so the overall expected loss is completely allocated over the $0,\lambda$ tranche under analysis.) The results are stored in the variables `d` and `EL0()` respectively. For your convenience, we state the relevant formulae below the code:

```
For r = 1 To Q 'Periods
        For tr = 1 To k ' 'Loss calculation
   EL0(0, r) = 0: loss(tr, 0) = 0: ER0(0, r) = 0: ER0(k + 1, r) = 0
   If lambda(tr + 1) < LGD Then
   d = Application.NormSInv(pd(r, 1)) / w - ((1 - w ^ 2) ^ 0.5) / _
      w * Application.NormSInv(lambda(tr + 1) / LGD)
   EL0(tr, r) = LGD * bivnor(Application.NormSInv(pd(r, 1)), -d, -w) _
     + lambda(tr + 1) * Application.NormSDist(d)
        Else
   EL0(tr, r) = LGD * pd(r, 1)
   End If
```

$$d(\lambda) = \frac{\Phi^{-1}(p) - \sqrt{1-w^2}\Phi^{-1}(\lambda/\text{LGD})}{w}$$

$$\text{E}(\text{Loss}_{(0,\lambda)}) = \text{LGD} \cdot \Phi_2\left(\Phi^{-1}(p), -d(\lambda), -w\right) + \lambda\Phi(d(\lambda))$$

In the same way as in Table 11.3, we then calculate the tranche's loss and write it into the variable `loss()`. The `mLoss()` variable records the marginal losses between two pricing periods, i.e., the additional loss you should expect when moving from $t-1$ to t.

```
    loss(tr, r) = (EL0(tr, r) - EL0(tr - 1, r)) / _
                   (lambda(tr + 1) - lambda(tr))
mLoss(tr, r) = loss(tr, r) - loss(tr, r - 1)
output(r, tr) = mLoss(tr, r)
Next tr
```

Now we turn to the recoveries. We can apply the LHP formulae above to determine expected base recovery, i.e., expected recovery in a tranche that takes all recoveries until λ. The equation reads:

$$\text{E}(\text{Recovery}_{(0,\lambda)}) = (1-\text{LGD}) \cdot \Phi_2\left(\Phi^{-1}(p), -d_r(\lambda), -w\right) + \lambda\Phi(d_r(\lambda)) \qquad (11.15)$$

with

$$d_r(\lambda) = \frac{\Phi^{-1}(p) - \sqrt{1-w^2}\Phi^{-1}(\lambda/(1-\text{LGD}))}{w}$$

Note the changes compared to the $\text{E}(\text{Loss}_{(0,\lambda)})$ formula: LGD is replaced by (1 − LGD). When applying the equation in the function, remember that recoveries are assigned to the most senior tranche. Thus, compared to the expected loss calculations, everything is turned upside down. We start with the most senior tranche and then move on to the junior tranches. This is done through a `For tr = k To 1 Step -1` loop. Importantly, the λ in the above formula is not given by the tranche's attachment point. The super senior tranche has an attachment point of 22% but since we start from the top, the super senior tranche can absorb recoveries amounting to (1 − 22%) = 78% of the portfolio notional. Therefore, the λ required for $\text{E}(\text{Recovery}_{(0,\lambda)})$ is given by 1 – attachment point. The implementation reads:

```
For tr = k To 1 Step -1 'Recovery calculation
   If 1 - lambda(tr) < 1 - LGD Then
    d = Application.NormSInv(pd(r, 1)) / w - ((1 - w ^ 2) ^ 0.5) / _
        w * Application.NormSInv((1 - lambda(tr)) / (1 - LGD))
    ER0(tr, r) = (1 - LGD) * bivnor(Application.NormSInv(pd(r, 1)),
-d, -w) _
                + (1 - lambda(tr)) * Application.NormSDist(d)
    Else
     ER0(tr, r) = (1 - LGD) * pd(r, 1)
    End If
```

```
    rec(tr, r) = (ER0(tr, r) - ER0(tr + 1, r)) / _
      (lambda(tr + 1) - lambda(tr))
    mrec(tr, r) = rec(tr, r) - rec(tr, r - 1)
    output(r, tr + k + 1) = mrec(tr, r)
  Next tr

Next r

LHP_LR = output

End Function
```

We are now finished with the estimation of marginal losses and recoveries and can turn back to the spreadsheet of Table 11.7 to estimate the tranche spreads. The coupon is paid on the remaining notional of the tranche only. So we first need to calculate the notional of each tranche at each coupon date. We do this in S16:X33. The notional is one minus the sum of marginal losses and marginal recoveries up to this coupon date, and so cell S16 reads:

=1–SUM(E$16:E16)–SUM(L$16:L16)

With the absolute references properly set we can copy this formula down to S33 and to the right to X33.

The coupon leg of the equity tranche (ignoring the spread for which we want to solve) in cell I5 is calculated by

=SUMPRODUCT($C$16:$C$33,$D$16:$D$33,S16:S33)

Note that the last argument of the formula has to be adjusted for each tranche and cannot directly be copied into the other cells.[6] The accrued leg is calculated according to Equation (11.12b). For the equity tranche in cell J5 this reads

{=SUM($C$16:$C$33*$D$16:$D$33*0.5*(E16:E33 + L16:L33))}

and is entered as an array function pressing [ctrl]+[shift]+[enter]. Note that the change in the tranche's notional that shows up in Equations (11.12a,b) can be determined by adding up marginal losses and marginal recoveries. In the above expression, this is done through (E16:E33+L16:L33).

Finally, the expected loss is calculated in K5:K10. The expected loss is the sum of the discounted expected marginal losses per tranche. For the equity piece in cell K5 it is found by

=SUMPRODUCT($C$16:$C$33, E16:E33)

Again the formula has to be manually adjusted when copied to K10. After filling the formulae down we are ready to calculate the tranche prices. To show how to take fixed coupons for

[6] An alternative is the use of Excel's OFFSET function, which, however, makes the function less traceable.

some tranches into account we enter the fixed spread of 500 bps for the equity tranche in cell H5, while cells H6 to H10 are empty. In cell G5 we thus calculate an upfront payment for the equity tranche, while cells G6:G10, in our example, contain all-running spreads. The formula, however, is always the same. The raw running spread is found by dividing the expected losses per tranche by the sum of coupon leg and accrued coupon. The raw spread for the equity tranche would therefore equal K5/(I5+J5). In the case of a fixed spread, we subtract the running spread from this raw spread and multiply by the coupon leg to obtain the upfront premium. So the full formula of G5, which can be copied down to G10, reads

=IF(H5>0,(K5/(I5+J5)−(H5/10^4))*I5,K5/(I5+J5))

Usually one would quote the upfront spreads in percent and the running spreads in basis points. Our estimates are 52.04% upfront payment for the equity tranche, 6.99% for the junior mezzanine and down to 0.002% for the super senior. See Box 11.2 for an assessment of the sensitivity of the estimation to the correlation parameter.

Box 11.2 Sensitivity of tranche prices to correlation and spread

An increase in correlation makes it more likely to experience either very small or very large portfolio losses. Since the equity tranche benefits from small portfolio losses but is not affected by the magnitude of losses once they are larger than its attachment point, the price of the equity tranche is decreasing in the correlation. In contrast, the senior tranche's price increases with increasing correlation. Typically, the mezzanine tranche behaves like the equity tranche. The following graph shows the equity and super senior tranches' price from the model estimated in Table 11.7 for various correlation assumptions.

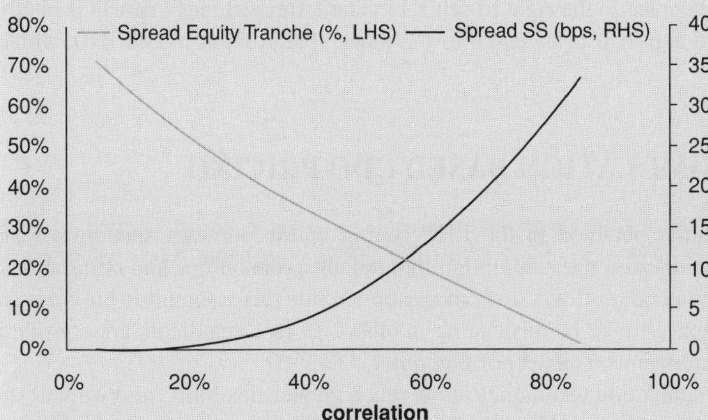

While the graph above holds the spread of the index constant, the following picture illustrates the nonlinearity of tranche prices (=spreads) to changing index spreads (=default probabilities).

Box 11.2 (Continued)

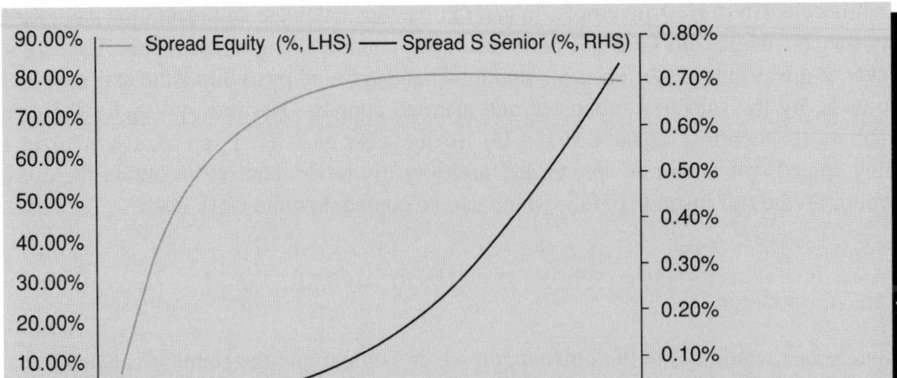

Lastly, as a cross check of the model and our implementation we calculate the index's spread. The coupon leg, default leg and accrued leg of the index tranche are obtained as the weighted sum of the tranches' legs, with the weights being the tranches' thickness. We estimate the tranche size in F5:F10 as difference between the next tranche's attachment and this tranche's attachment point, and so F5 reads =E6–E5. For the size of the super senior tranche the formula reads =1–E10.

The coupon leg of the index is obtained in cell I11 through

=SUMPRODUCT(I5:I10,$F$5:$F$10)

This formula can be copied to the right to cell K11. The estimated index spread is obtained in cell G10. We would expect it to be equal to the index spread input in cell B10, which is indeed the case.

SIMULATION-BASED CDO PRICING

The closed form solution obtained in the LHP setting of the previous section is fast to evaluate. However, it hinges on the assumption that default probabilities and correlations of the borrowers in the collateral portfolio are homogenous. While this assumption provides good results in many situations, it may be misleading in others. In fact, regulators are considering requiring the use of heterogeneous asset correlations.[7]

Monte Carlo (MC) simulation techniques allow much greater flexibility, and we will show how to use them for pricing CDOs. Often, the factor model structure used in previous sections would be sufficient to capture correlations. To increase the application potential, however, we show how to build simulations on an arbitrary correlation matrix. We will continue to use the

[7] Bank of International Settlements, *Strengthening the resilience of the banking sector*, Consultative Document 164, December 2009; see Chapter 12.

Gaussian copula but note that an extension to other copulas is straightforward (see Chapter 7 for an implementation of a *t* copula).

Let us start by examining how to generate correlated random survival times. The steps involved are as follows:

1. Generate normally distributed random numbers.
2. Impose an arbitrary correlation structure on these numbers.
3. Transform the correlated random numbers into survival times.

An efficient algorithm for the first step was discussed in Chapter 7, where we implemented the polar method for generating normal variables in the function NRND().

For the second step we first need to specify a correlation matrix. On its main diagonal the matrix has ones, the other entries are given by the pair-wise correlation coefficients. For a CDO with three obligors the matrix could look as follows:

$$\mathbf{A} = \begin{pmatrix} 1 & 0.24 & 0.2 \\ 0.24 & 1 & 0.18 \\ 0.2 & 0.18 & 1 \end{pmatrix}$$

To impose such a heterogeneous correlation structure in the copula approach, we can use the Cholesky decomposition of the correlation matrix. This procedure decomposes the correlation matrix $\mathbf{A}$ into the product of a lower triangular matrix $\mathbf{C}$, i.e., a matrix that has zeroes above the main diagonal, and the transpose of this triangular matrix. It therefore holds that $\mathbf{A} = \mathbf{CC}^{\mathrm{T}}$. To impose the correlation matrix in $\mathbf{A}$ on a vector $\mathbf{z}$ of standard normally distributed variables, simply determine $\mathbf{Cz}$.

The Cholesky decomposition of our example correlation matrix $\mathbf{A}$ is given by

$$\mathbf{C} = \begin{pmatrix} c_{11} & 0 & 0 \\ c_{21} & c_{22} & 0 \\ c_{31} & c_{32} & c_{33} \end{pmatrix} = \begin{pmatrix} 1 & 0 & 0 \\ 0.24 & 0.97 & 0 \\ 0.20 & 0.14 & 0.97 \end{pmatrix}$$

The Cholesky matrix can be determined recursively based on $\mathbf{CC}^{\mathrm{T}} = \mathbf{A}$. In the example from above, determine c_{11}, the upper left element, by $c_{11} \cdot c_{11} + 0 \cdot 0 + 0 \cdot 0 = 1$, which yields $c_{11} = 1$. Move one to determine c_{21} through $c_{21} \cdot c_{11} + c_{22} \cdot 0 + 0 \cdot 0.24$, and so forth. Our VBA implementation of the Cholesky decomposition is found in the Appendix at the end of this chapter; the function is called CHOLESKY(A) and takes a symmetric matrix A as argument.

For simulation-based CDO pricing, we need a random number for each obligor. Denote the number of simulation runs by *M* and the number of obligors by *N*. We suggest a user-defined function that assembles all random numbers needed for the simulation in a matrix with *M* rows and *N* columns:

```
Function Normalcopula(M, N, Cholesky, Optional untransformed)
Dim A, b, i As Long, j As Long, tmp, sum As Double, jj As Long
ReDim A(1 To M, 1 To N): ReDim b(1 To M, 1 To N): Cholesky = Cholesky
For i = 1 To M
```

```
    For j = 1 To N
        A(i, j) = NRND() 'Obtain Normal random numbers
    Next j

    For j = 1 To N
        sum = 0
        For jj = 1 To N
            sum = sum + A(i, jj) * Cholesky(j, jj)
        Next jj
        b(i, j) = sum
    If untransformed = False Then b(i, j) = Application.NormSDist(sum)
    Next j
Next i
Normalcopula = b
End Function
```

We draw random standard normal numbers for simulation run i and then multiply these numbers with the Cholesky matrix. To return correlated default indicators, which can be compared to default probabilities in order to determine survival times, we apply the cumulative normal distribution function. Note that the function includes an optional parameter untransformed. If set to true the function returns the untransformed, correlated standard normal variables. This feature is useful in the implementation of the pricing procedure later.

To translate default indicators generated with NORMALCOPULA() into correlated default times, we need information about possible default dates and individual default probabilities at those dates. We assume defaults to take place only between coupon dates. The individual default probabilities at these dates are calculated using CDS spreads for each obligor. As before, we assume a constant CDS spread over time, but an extension to a CDS term structure is straightforward. The CDS spreads translate into a PD by applying the hazard rate model described in Chapter 10:

$$\mathrm{PD}_{i,t} = \exp(-\mathrm{CDS}_i/\mathrm{LGD}_i(t - t_0))$$

The function PDMATRIX(*recovery*, *spread*, *cpdates*, *startd*, [*ninv*]) found in the Appendix to this chapter returns the corresponding matrix with default probabilities for each obligor i and each coupon date t.

With the preliminaries finished we can start calculating the tranches' spreads. Table 11.8 replicates the basic setup of Table 11.7 while adding some additional parameters. In the range A1:B13 we enter the basic inputs, such as the value date (B6), the maturity date (B7) and the spread of the index associated with the CDO, i.e., the spread of the 0–100% tranche. The discount rate in cell B4 is modeled as constant over time and tranches. A generalization allowing for term structures over time and over tranches is possible but beyond the educational scope of this presentation.

The copula parameters consist of the number of Monte Carlo trials (cell B11) and the correlation (cell B12). For the correlation we allow two options. If we enter a number larger than 0% and smaller than 100% in cell B12 we will model a homogenous asset correlation between all obligors. On the other hand we will program our function such that an entry of 0%

Table 11.8 CDO pricing with copula and Monte Carlo

	A	B	C	D	E	F	G	H	I	J	...	W
1	CDO tail risk										...	
2											...	
3	**Deal Parameters**			**Capital structure**							...	
4	Discount Rate (%)	2%		Tranche	Attachment	Spread	Running spread	Coupon Leg	EL	Accrued	...	
5	Coupons p.a.	4		Equity	0%	43.90%	500	2.32	59.07%	0.15	...	
6	Value Date	4/15/2010		Mezz J	3%	7.64%		3.56	27.71%	0.07	...	
7	Maturity Date	9/20/2014		Mezz S	6%	3.09%		3.90	12.16%	0.03	...	
8	Index Deal Spread (bps)	82		Senior J	9%	1.42%		4.02	5.71%	0.01	...	
9				Senior	12%	0.32%		4.09	1.30%	0.00	...	
10	**Copula Parameters**			Super Senior	22%	0.01%		4.10	0.02%	0.01	...	
11	Simulation trials	5000		Index	0-100%	0.81%		4.02	3.28%	0.02	...	
12	Correlation	20%										
13	Position of correlation matrix	CMatrix!C3:DW127										
14												
15	# Loans	125	=COUNTA(A24:A65536)									
16	# Periods	18	=COUPNUM(B6,B7,B5)									
17	Notional ($)	125,000	=SUM(B24:INDIRECT("B"&(23+B15)))								...	
18	Avg. LGD	0.60	=1-AVERAGE(C24 :INDIRECT("C"&(23+B15)))								...	
19	Avg. Spread (bps)	82	=AVERAGE(D24:INDIRECT("D"&(23+B15)))								...	
20	Implied Hazard Rate (bps)	136	=B19/B18								...	
21											...	
22	**Pool**					PD Structure					...	
23	Obligor Id	Notional	Recovery	CDS spread (bps)	...	6/20/2010	9/20/2010	12/20/2010	3/20/2011	6/20/2011	...	9/20/2014
24	Accor SA	1000	40%	131	...	0.4%	1.0%	1.5%	2.0%	2.6%	...	9.4%
25	Adecco SA	1000	40%	121	...	0.4%	0.9%	1.4%	1.9%	2.4%	...	8.7%
26	Aegon NV	1000	40%	112	...	0.3%	0.8%	1.3%	1.7%	2.2%	.	8.1%
...	...	...	...	...	...	...	...	...	...	...	...	...
147	Xstrata PLC	1000	40%	117	...	0.4%	0.8%	1.3%	1.8%	2.3%	...	8.4%
148	Zurich	1000	40%	84	...	0.3%	0.6%	1.0%	1.3%	1.7%	...	6.1%

9/20/2010

F5: =IF(G5>0,(I5/(H5+J5)-(G5/10^4))*H5,I5/(H5+J5))
(can be copied to F10)

F24:AA148 ={pdmatrix(C24:C148,D24:D148,F23:W23,B6)}

F23:W23: See Table 11.7, A16, A 17 for construction of the dates.

Table 11.9 Modeling a heterogeneous asset correlation

	A	B	C	D	E	...	DV	DW
1			0.20	0.20	0.20		0.20	0.20
2	Asset Correlation	Obligor Id	Accor SA	Adecco SA	Aegon NV		Xstrata PLC	Zurich Insurance
3	0.20	Accor SA	1.00	0.2				
4	0.20	Adecco SA	0.2	1.00				
5	0.20	Aegon NV	0.2	0.2				
6	0.20	Volvo AB	0.2	0.2				
7	0.20	Akzo Nobel NV	0.2	0.2	0.2			
8	0.30	Allianz SE	0.24	0.24	0.24		0.24	0.30
...								
126	0.20	Xstrata PLC	0.2	0.2	0.2		1	0.24
127	0.30	Zurich Insurance	0.24	0.24	0.24		0.24	1.0

C1:DW1 ={TRANSPOSE(A3:A127}

C3: =IF(ROW()=COLUMN(),1,($A3*D$1)^0.5)
(can be copied to all cells)

in cell B12 leads to the use of a user-defined correlation matrix. The position of the correlation matrix is entered in cell B13; here we refer to the worksheet 'CMatrix', which is shown in Table 11.9.

The second block of Table 11.8 consists of the CDO's capital structure in the range E5:E10. We use the same capital structure as in Table 11.7. In the range H5:I5 the simulation function will return the prices.

The obligor information storage starts in cell A24 with the id of the first obligor in the collateral portfolio of the CDO. We demonstrate the pricing with the iTraxx Europe series 9 universe of 125 European investment grade companies. Column B, starting in row 24, contains the notional invested in each obligor, while column C gives the recovery rate in percent and column D the CDS spread in basis points. The information you find in the sheet is data from April 15, 2010, with CDS spreads being mid spreads and recovery rates according to the market practice.

Before we estimate the individual PDs of each obligor, we obtain the coupon dates in cells F23:AA23 using the previously-described method (see Table 11.7). The PDs are found by applying the PDMatrix() function to the range F24:AA148 ={PDMatrix(C24:C148,D24:D148,F23:W23,B6)}.

As arguments, the PDMatrix function takes the individual recovery rates in C24:C148, followed by the CDS spreads in D24:D148, the coupon dates from F23:W23 and the start date in cell B6, which is needed to calculate the number of days elapsed at each coupon date.

In cell B15 we count the number of obligors. Since the obligor id can consist of names, as in our example, we use the COUNTA() function, which in contrast to COUNT() also counts non-numeric entries, over the range A24:A65536. The number of coupon dates in cell B16 is found by counting over the coupon dates in F23:W23. The total notional of the CDO is the sum of the notional values of the obligors. We could either sum over B24:B65536 or, since we know the number of obligors, use the INDIRECT() function. The INDIRECT function returns the cell specified by a text string, and so INDIRECT("B"&(23+B15)) returns the value of cell B148, because the value of B15 is 125 in our example. In full, cell B17 reads =SUM(B24:INDIRECT("B"&(23+B15))).

Using the same function we calculate the average LGD (B18), the average spread (B19) and the implied hazard rate as ratio of the average spread and the average LGD (cell B20).

Let us start the heavy part, the simulation process itself. The basic steps for each Monte Carlo trial are

1. Simulate default events using individual time-varying PD_{it}.
2. Calculate tranche losses.
3. Store the discounted loss per tranche.

Once the Monte Carlo simulation is finished, we calculate the expected loss and the fixed leg (=coupon leg + accrued leg) of each tranche. Dividing the former by the latter we finally arrive at the spreads.

We call our simulation tool MCpriceCDO() and start by obtaining information from the spreadsheet and defining the variables needed in the simulation process:

```
Sub MCpriceCDO()

Dim M As Long, n As Integer, k As Integer, Q As Integer, A As Integer,
Dim i As Integer, j As Long, tr As Integer, r As Integer
Dim cdates, choleskym, RndN, d(), RR() As Double, EAD() As Double, pd
Dim CDS() As Double, default As Boolean, lleft As Integer
Dim attach() As Double, attach_cum() As Double, sumEAD As Double

M = Range("B11") 'Number of simulations
N = Range("B15") 'Number of obligors
k = 6 'Number of tranches
Q = Range("B16") 'Number of Periods

ReDim RR(1 To N, 1), EAD(1 To N, 1), CDS(1 To N, 1)
For i = 1 To N 'Write obligor characteristics into arrays
    RR(i, 1) = Range("C" & i + 23) 'Recovery
    EAD(i, 1) = Range("B" & i + 23) 'Exposures
    CDS(i, 1) = Range("D" & i + 23) 'CDS spreads
Next i
sumEAD = Range("B17").Value 'Sum of exposures
```

Then we read in the attachment points and convert them to notional values:

```
ReDim attach(1 To k + 1), attach_cum(1 To k + 1), tr_size(1 To k + 1)
attach(k + 1) = 1 'Last tranche's attachment
For a = k To 1 Step -1 'Read in attachment points
  attach(a) = Range("E" & a + 4).Value
  tr_size(a) = (attach(a + 1) - attach(a)) * sumEAD
Next a

For a = 2 To k 'Convert into notional values
   attach_cum(a) = attach_cum(a - 1) + tr_size(a - 1)
Next a
attach_cum(k + 1) = sumEAD 'Last cumulative tranche attachment
```

In our example with a total exposure of €125,000 this leaves us with the following entries:

a	attach()	attach_cum()	tr_size()
1	0	0	3750
2	3%	3750	3750
3	6%	7500	3750
4	9%	11,250	3750
5	12%	15,000	12,500
6	22%	27,500	97,500
7	100%	125,000	

Now we determine the default probabilities and the discount factors.[8] We transform the survival probabilities with the cumulative standard normal distribution function because we will later compare them with random normal numbers in order to determine the default times:

```
'Obtain inverse PS's and Coupon dates
cdates = Range(Cells(23, 6), Cells(23, 6 + Q)))
PS_inv = pdmatrix(RR, CDS, cdates, Range("B6"),True)

Dim discount, dday: ReDim discount(1 To Q): ReDim dday(1 To Q)
discount(1) = Exp(Range("B4") * ((cdates(1, 1) - Range("B6")) /
  360))
dday(1) = (cdates(1, 1) - Range("B6")) / 360 / discount(1)

For r = 2 To Q 'Obtain discount rates & discounted time
 discount(r) = Exp(Range("B4") * ((cdates(1, r) - Range("B6")) /
  360))
 dday(r) = ((cdates(1, r) - cdates(1, r - 1)) / 360) / discount(r)
Next r
```

The next step is the definition of the correlation structure. Our simulation routine is capable of either using a homogenous correlation structure if a number larger than zero and smaller than one is entered in cell B12, or using a user-defined heterogeneous correlation structure. For the latter the value of B12 is not used, but the correlation matrix is obtained from the reference given in cell B13. Here we call the correlation matrix's sheet 'CMatrix', the matrix itself starts in cell C3 of that sheet and goes to cell DW127 (see Table 11.9):

```
If IsEmpty(Range("B13")) = False Then 'Obtain heterogeneous
  correlation
 choleskym = Cholesky(Range(Range("B13").Value))
Else 'Build homogenous correlation matrix
 Dim corrm: ReDim corrm(1 To n, 1 To n)
 For i = 1 To n
  For j = 1 To i
   corrm(i, j) = Range("B12").Value
   If (i = j) Then corrm(i, j) = 1
  Next j
 Next i
 choleskym = Cholesky(corrm)
End If
```

[8] A straightforward extension here would be the inclusion of discount factors using a term structure over time and tranches.

With the Cholesky matrix at hand we draw the correlated random numbers and write them into the array RndN:

```
Application.StatusBar = "Drawing Random Numbers"
RndN = Normalcopula(M, n, choleskym, True) 'Normal Copula
```

With this information stored we begin the simulation process itself, after defining the variables needed:

```
'Variable Definitions
Dim loss, loss_cum, rec, rec_cum 'losses per simulation
ReDim loss_cum(1 To Q): ReDim rec_cum(1 To Q): ReDim loss(1 To Q)
ReDim rec(1 To Q)

Dim loss_q, rec_q: ReDim loss_q(1 To Q): ReDim rec_q(1 To Q) ' per quarter
Dim loss_tr, CL_tr, acc_tr, loss_tr_total ' per tranche
ReDim loss_tr(1 To M, 1 To k): ReDim CL_tr(1 To k): ReDim acc_tr(1 To k)
  ReDim loss_tr_total(1 To k)
```

Now the Monte Carlo trials start. In each round we begin by simulating the default times for each obligor:

```
For j = 1 To M 'Conduct M Monte Carlo trials
Application.StatusBar = "Trial " & j & " / " & M
   For i = 1 To N 'For each obligor
     default = False: lleft = Q
     Do While (RndN(j, i) >= PS_inv(i, lleft)) 'Simulate default times
      default = True
      lleft = lleft - 1
      If lleft = 0 Then Exit Do
     Loop
   If default = True Then 'Compute loss per obligor and trial
    loss(lleft + 1) = loss(lleft + 1) + ((1 - RR(i, 1)) * EAD(i, 1))
    rec(lleft + 1) = rec(lleft + 1) + RR(i, 1) * EAD(i, 1)
     End If
    Next i
```

The variables `loss()` and `rec()` store the sum of losses and recovery rates over all obligors for each trial by their occurrence of the default in time.[9] These quarterly losses within one trial are now cumulated across time:

```
loss_cum(1) = loss(1): rec_cum(1) = rec(1)
For r = 2 To Q 'cumulate losses over periods Q
  loss_cum(r) = loss(r) + loss_cum(r - 1)
  rec_cum(r) = rec(r) + rec_cum(jr - 1)
Next r
```

[9] Note that we would not need to store them for each trial separately because this information is directly processed by the following waterfall. However, we experienced this as being faster than resetting the quarterly vectors in each simulation trial.

The variables `loss_cum()` and `rec_cum()` contain the sum of `loss()` and `rec()` over the periods. Consider the following illustration for one trial. Each row represents one period, i.e., quarter in our spreadsheet; however, in this example we use a maturity of six quarters for demonstration:

$$loss^T = \begin{pmatrix} 2400 \\ 0 \\ 4800 \\ 600 \\ 1400 \\ 0 \end{pmatrix} \quad loss^T_{cum} = \begin{pmatrix} 2400 \\ 2400 \\ 7200 \\ 7800 \\ 9200 \\ 9200 \end{pmatrix}$$

The application of the waterfall structure is the last step in the simulation process. Within each tranche we compare the tranche's specification with the cumulative loss over all periods, assuming defaults to appear at the end of the previous period.

```
For tr = 1 To k 'Apply waterfall

  loss_q(1) = Application.Min(Application.Max(0#, loss_cum(1) _
     - attach_cum(tr)), attach_cum(tr + 1) - attach_cum(tr))
  rec_q(1) = Application.Min(Application.Max(0#, rec_cum(1) _
     - (sumEAD - attach_cum(tr + 1))), tr_size(tr))

  For r = 2 To Q
   loss_q(r) = Application.Min(Application.Max(0#, loss_cum(r) _
             - attach_cum(tr)), attach_cum(tr + 1) - attach_cum(tr))
   loss_tr(j,tr) = loss_tr(j,tr) + _
                   (loss_q(r) - loss_q(r - 1)) / discount(r)
   rec_q(r) = Application.Min(Application.Max(0#, rec_cum(r) _
             - (sumEAD - attach_cum(tr + 1))), tr_size(tr))
   CL_tr(tr) = CL_tr(tr) + dday(r) _
      Application.Min(Application.Max(0, attach_cum(tr + 1) - _
      loss_cum(r) - rec_q(r)), tr_size(tr))
   acc_tr(tr) = acc_tr(tr) + dday(r) * (loss_q(r) - loss_q(r - 1)) + _
             (rec_q(r) - rec_q(r - 1)) * 0.5

 Next r
```

To see what is happening, consider the variable `loss_q()` and the following two cases for the third tranche (6–9%). In the first case the cumulative loss in this period is larger than the cumulative attachment point, e.g., `loss_cum()`= 8000 and the cumulative attachment point of this tranche is 7500. The tranche suffered a partial default, because the loss is smaller than its size (3750). We thus record a partial loss of 500 for this tranche, period and trial. In the second case the loss is smaller than the cumulative attachment point, and thus the tranche is not affected and a zero goes to the record of losses. But what about the recoveries and the coupon payments? As long as the tranche's principal is not defaulted the holder of the CDO receives coupon payments. We sum them up in the `CL_tr()` variable over all tranches.

The accrued payment in the case of a default is stored in the `acc_tr()` variable, while the variable `loss_tr()` holds all discounted tranche losses over all quarters for one simulation trial and `loss_tr_total()` sums up `loss_tr()` over all trials:

```
      loss_tr_total(tr) = loss_tr_total(tr) + loss_tr(j,tr)
    Next tr
  ReDim loss(1 To Q): ReDim rec(1 To Q): ReDim loss_cum(1 To Q) ) 'Reset
  ReDim rec_cum(1 To Q) 'Reset
Next j
```

While the above procedure is repeated in each trial, all that is left to do at the end of the simulation is to calculate the coupon leg and accrued coupon as the average of the coupon payments and accrued payments, respectively, over all simulations as well as the total expected loss per tranche. We return these variables to the range H5:J10 in the spreadsheet (see Table 11.8):

```
Application.StatusBar = False
For tr = 1 To k 'Output
  Range("H" & tr + 4) = CL_tr(tr) / M / tr_size(tr) 'Coupon leg
  Range("I" & tr + 4) = acc_tr(tr) / M / tr_size(tr) 'Accrued leg
  Range("J" & tr + 4) = loss_tr_total(tr) / M / tr_size(tr) 'Default leg
Next tr
```

And we are done. The simulation script outputs the coupon leg to H5:H10, the accrued leg to I5:I10 and the expected loss to J5:J10. The tranches final spread in F5:F10 take the running spreads of G5:G10 into account, and so the equity tranche's spread in F5 is obtained as =IF(G5>0,(J5/(H5+I5)-(G5/10^4))*H5,J5/(H5+I5)). This formula can be copied down to F10.

We calculate the legs of the index by weighting the tranche's legs by the tranche size, just as we did in the previous section. Comparing the estimated index spread of 0.81% with the average CDS spread of 82 bps (see cell B19 of Table 11.8) the convergence of this demonstration with just 5000 Monte Carlo trials is good. Though we did not aim to make the simulation procedure as fast as possible, it took less than one minute to run 5000 simulations on our desktop computer.

NOTES AND LITERATURE

For an overview of CDO risk analysis, see Fender, I., and Kiff, J., 2004, CDO rating methodology: Some thoughts on model risk and its implications, Working paper, Bank for International Settlements.

A discussion of the risks of structured finance instruments is provided by Coval, J., Jurek, J. and Stafford, E., 2009. The economics of structured finance, *Journal of Economic Perspectives* 23, 3–25. The accuracy of CDO rating models is an active research field: see, for example, Griffin, J. and Tang, D., 2009, Did subjectivity play a role in CDO credit ratings? Working paper.

For a description of the LHP analysis of CDOs, see Berd, A., Engle, R. and Voronov, A., 2005, The underlying dynamics of credit correlations, *Journal of Credit Risk*, 3, 27–62.

The Gauss copula for simulating default times is described in Li, D., 2000, On default correlation: A copula function approach, *Journal of Fixed Income*, 9, 43–54. Multi-year default frequencies of rated bond issuers can be obtained from rating agency default studies, e.g., Moody's, 2006, *Default and recovery rates of corporate bond issuers*, 1920–2005, Special comment, Moody's.

Implied correlation is in depth discussed by O'Kane, D. and Livesey, M., 2004, Base correlation explained, Working paper. Implementing issues of different CDO models are covered by Picone, D., Shah, P., Stoeckle, M. and Loddo, A., 2008, CDO models: Opening the black box. A good textbook covering most of the material presented in this chapter is Tavakoli, J., 2008, *Structured Finance and Collateralized Debt Obligations: New Developments in Cash and Synthetic Securitization*, Wiley.

APPENDIX

Closed-form solution for the LHP model

We show how to derive Equation (11.5) from (11.4). The challenging part within (11.4) is the expectation:

$$E\left[\Phi\left(\frac{\Phi^{-1}(p)-wZ}{\sqrt{1-w^2}}\right)I\{Z>d(\lambda)\}\right] \tag{11.16}$$

It can be evaluated through the following integral:

$$\int_{d(\lambda)}^{\infty}\Phi\left(\frac{\Phi^{-1}(p)-wZ}{\sqrt{1-w^2}}\right)\phi(Z)dZ \tag{11.17}$$

where ϕ is the standard normal density. Introducing $a=\Phi^{-1}(p)/\sqrt{1-w^2}$ and $b=-w/\sqrt{1-w^2}$, we rewrite (11.17) as

$$\int_{d(\lambda)}^{\infty}\Phi\left(a+bZ\right)\phi(Z)dZ \tag{11.18}$$

Next, introduce $y=-bZ+u$, where u is standard normal and independent from Z, and note (conditional on Z, y has mean $-bZ$ and variance 1, and so Prob($y \leq a|Z$) = Φ[a – ($-bZ$)])

$$\int_{d(\lambda)}^{\infty}\Phi(a+bZ)\phi(Z)dZ=\text{Prob}(y\leq a,\ Z>d(\lambda)) \tag{11.19}$$

The joint probability in (11.19) can be evaluated with the bivariate normal distribution Φ_2. Since the variance of y is $\sqrt{1+b^2}$ and the correlation between y and $-Z$ is $b/\sqrt{1+b^2}$, we get

$$\text{Prob}(y\leq a,\ Z>d(\lambda))=\text{Prob}(y\leq a,\ -Z\leq -d(\lambda))=\Phi_2\left(\frac{a}{\sqrt{1+b^2}},\ -d(\lambda),\ \frac{b}{\sqrt{1+b^2}}\right) \tag{11.20}$$

From our definitions of a and b, note that

$$\frac{a}{\sqrt{1+b^2}}=\frac{\Phi^{-1}(p)/\sqrt{1-w^2}}{\sqrt{1+w^2/(1-w^2)}}=\Phi^{-1}(p) \tag{11.21}$$

and

$$\frac{b}{\sqrt{1+b^2}} = \frac{-w/\sqrt{1-w^2}}{\sqrt{1+w^2/(1-w^2)}} = -w \tag{11.22}$$

The integral (11.18) can thus be evaluated to

$$\Phi_2\left(\Phi^{-1}(p), -d(\lambda), -w\right) \tag{11.23}$$

Cholesky decomposition

Our implementation of the Cholesky decomposition CHOLESKY(A) takes a matrix **A** and estimates the decomposition by finding the elements of the matrix **C** in $\mathbf{A} = \mathbf{CC}^{\mathrm{T}}$. Since **A** is a lower triangular matrix, each element on the main diagonal of **C** is found as

$$c_{ii} = \sqrt{\left(a_{ii} - \sum_{k=1}^{i-1} \left(c_{ik}^2\right)\right)}$$

where x_{ij} is the ith row and jth column entry of the matrix **X**. Off-diagonal elements are given by

$$c_{ji} = \left(a_{ji} - \sum\nolimits_{k=1}^{i-1} (C_{jk}C_{ik})\right) / c_{ii}$$

```
Function Cholesky(A)

Dim C() As Double, n As Integer, j As Integer, s As Double, _
  k As Integer, _ i As Integer
A = A: n = UBound(A)
ReDim C(1 To n, 1 To n)

'Cholesky Decomposition
For j = 1 To n
 S = 0
 For k = 1 To j - 1
   S = S + C(j, k) ^ 2
 Next k
 C(j, j) = A(j, j) - S
 If C(j, j) <= 0 Then Exit For
 C(j, j) = (C(j, j)) ^ 0.5

For i = j + 1 To n
  S = 0
  For k = 1 To j - 1
    S = S + C(i, k) * C(j, k)
  Next k
```

```
  C(i, j) = (A(i, j) - S) / C(j, j)
  Next i
 Next j

Cholesky = C

End Function
```

Estimating PD structure from a CDS

Our PDMATRIX() function uses the recovery rate (`reco`), the CDS spread (`spread`), the coupon dates (`cpdates`) and the startdate (`startd`) to estimate a PD for each coupon date. The optional parameter `ninv` returns the inverse of the standard normal distribution of the PD. This assumes a constant CDS spread over different maturities. A straightforward extension is the use of a CDS term structure, e.g., by implementing our INTSPOT() function.

```
Function pdmatrix(Reco, spread, cpdates, startd As Date, _
Optional ninv As Boolean)
'PD matrix with n rows & k columns, Obligor i in rows, Date j in columns
Dim rec, CDS, cdates, n As Integer, k As Integer, j As Integer, _i As
  Integer

rec = Reco: CDS = spread: cdates = cpdates 'Convert input
n = UBound(rec) 'Obtain obligors
k = UBound(cdates, 2) 'Obtain dates
Dim pd: ReDim pd(1 To n, 1 To k)

For j = 1 To k
 For i = 1 To n
  pd(i, j) = 1 - Exp(-(CDS(i, 1) / 10 ^ 4) / (1 - rec(i, 1)) * _
              ((cdates(1, j) - startd) / 360))
'Transformation of PD into inverse Normal
   If ninv = True Then pd(i, j) = Application.NormSInv(pd(i, j))
  Next i
 Next j

pdmatrix = pd

End Function
```

12
Basel II and Internal Ratings

To secure a minimum level of solvency even in adverse conditions, regulators require banks to hold a certain, specified amount of equity capital which serves to cushion losses from risky activities. These capital requirements are a cornerstone of bank regulation.

Credit risk, which is the main driver of risk for many banks, can differ substantially across individual loans and credit-risky instruments. The rules set out in the Basel I accord from 1988, however, showed little differentiation in the capital required to be held against loans. For every dollar lent to a corporation, regardless of whether it was rated AAA, CCC or unrated, banks were required to hold 8 cents in equity.

Therefore, one key motivation for reforming the Basel I accord was to make capital requirements more sensitive to the risk of an individual exposure. The new Basel II framework allows several approaches for measuring this risk. In the standardized approach, individual risk is measured through external agency ratings; each rating commands a certain risk weight that determines capital requirements. In the internal ratings-based (IRB) approach, which has a foundation and an advanced variant, individual risk is measured using banks' internal ratings.

In this chapter, we first show how to program the key formula of the IRB approach, which represents capital requirements as a function of a loan's default probability, loss given default and maturity. Subsequently, we explore the question of how boundaries for internal rating grades should be set in order to minimize capital requirements and maximize the discriminatory power of the rating system.

At the time of writing, possible changes to the Basel II regulations are being discussed. Since they have not been finalized, we decided not to include them. We are confident that it will be unproblematic to incorporate any changes into the functions presented in this chapter.

CALCULATING CAPITAL REQUIREMENTS IN THE INTERNAL RATINGS-BASED (IRB) APPROACH

To determine how capital requirements should vary with the risk of a loan, the Basel Committee employs a one-factor model of portfolio credit risk (see Chapter 6). In this model, defaults are triggered by a continuous latent variable, which is often interpreted as the borrower's asset value. Borrower i's asset value A_i is taken to depend on one systematic factor Z and an idiosyncratic factor ε_i:

$$A_i = w_i Z + \sqrt{1 - w_i^2}\varepsilon_i, \quad \operatorname{cov}(\varepsilon_i, \varepsilon_j) = 0, i \neq j;\ \operatorname{cov}(Z, \varepsilon_i) = 0_i \forall i \tag{12.1}$$

where Z and ε_i are standard normal variables; by construction, A_i is also standard normal. The default event is triggered if $A_i < \Phi^{-1}(\text{PD}_i)$, where PD_i is the default probability; $\Phi(\cdot)$ denotes the cumulative standard normal distribution function. To verify that this specification preserves the specified PD, consider:

$$\text{PD}_i = \text{Prob}\left(A_i \leq \Phi^{-1}(\text{PD}_i)\right) = \Phi\left(\Phi^{-1}(\text{PD}_i)\right) = \text{PD}_i \tag{12.2}$$

The factor sensitivities w_i determine asset correlations and therefore default correlations. The asset correlation between two borrowers is $w_i \times w_j$. If two borrowers have an identical factor sensitivity w, their asset correlation is w^2.

Capital requirements are set according to the expected loss in a stress scenario. A stress scenario is defined as an extreme, negative realization of the factor Z. Based on (12.1), the expected default probability conditional on a factor realization Z is given by

$$\begin{aligned} \text{PD}_i(Z) &= \text{Prob}\left(A_i \leq \Phi^{-1}(\text{PD}_i)|Z\right) \\ &= \text{Prob}\left(w_i Z + \sqrt{1-w_i^2}\varepsilon_i \leq \Phi^{-1}(\text{PD}_i)\right) \\ &= \text{Prob}\left(\varepsilon_i \leq \frac{\Phi^{-1}(\text{PD}_i) - w_i Z}{\sqrt{1-w_i^2}}\right) \\ &= \Phi\left[\frac{\Phi^{-1}(\text{PD}_i) - w_i Z}{\sqrt{1-w_i^2}}\right] \end{aligned} \tag{12.3}$$

A scenario with a low value of Z (such as –2) is 'bad' in the sense that it is associated with a high conditional default probability. If the stress scenario is taken to be one with the property that only α of all scenarios are worse, its value is $\Phi^{-1}(\alpha)$ in our notation. Further assuming a loss given default (LGD), we arrive at the (percentage) expected loss in the stress scenario of

$$\text{E}\left[Loss \mid Stress\right] = LGD \times \Phi\left(\frac{\Phi^{-1}(PD) - w_i \Phi^{-1}(\alpha)}{\sqrt{1-w_i^2}}\right) \tag{12.4}$$

Equation (12.4) is the cornerstone of the Basel II formulae for capital requirements. It is used in the regulations for different types of loans. The capital requirement formula for corporate, sovereign and bank exposures is shown in Box 12.1. Note that the capital requirement is expressed as a percentage of a given exposure at default (EAD).

In the following table, we compare our notation to the Basel one:

	This book	Basel II
Factor sensitivity = square root of correlation	w	$R^{0.5}$
Cumulative standard normal	Φ	N
Inverse cumulative standard normal	Φ^{-1}	G
Stress scenario for factor	$\Phi^{-1}(0.001)$	$-G(0.999)$

Important aspects of the formulae in Box 12.1 are as follows:

- The α chosen to define the stress scenario is 0.1%. This is equivalent to the statement that there is a confidence of $1 - \alpha = 99.9\%$ that realizations are better than the stress

Box 12.1 Formula for risk-weighted assets for corporate, sovereign and bank exposures (from: Basel Committee on Banking Supervision International, 2005, *Convergence of Capital Measurement and Capital Standards. A Revised Framework*. Basel, pp. 59–60)

271. The derivation of risk-weighted assets is dependent on estimates of the PD, LGD, EAD and, in some cases, effective maturity (M), for a given exposure. Paragraphs 318 to 324 discuss the circumstances in which the maturity adjustment applies.

272. Throughout this section, PD and LGD are measured as decimals, and EAD is measured as currency (e.g. euros), except where explicitly noted otherwise. For exposures not in default, the formula for calculating risk-weighted assets is:

Correlation (R) = 0.12 × (1 – EXP(–50 × PD))/(1 – EXP(–50)) + 0.24 × [1 – (1 – EXP(–50 × PD))/(1 – EXP(–50))]

Maturity adjustment (*b*) = (0.11852 – 0.05478 × ln(PD))^2

Capital requirement (K) = [LGD × N[(1 – R)^ – 0.5 × G(PD) + (R/(1 – R))^0.5 × G(0.999)] – PD × LGD] × (1 – 1.5 × b)^ – 1 × (1 + (M – 2.5) × b)

70 Ln denotes the natural logarithm.

71 N(x) denotes the cumulative distribution function for a standard normal random variable (i.e. the probability that a normal random variable with mean zero and variance of one is less than or equal to x). G(z) denotes the inverse cumulative distribution function for a standard normal random variable (i.e. the value of x such that N(x) = z). The normal cumulative distribution function and the inverse of the normal cumulative distribution function are, for example, available in Excel as the functions NORMSDIST and NORMSINV.

- scenario. Since the normal distribution is symmetric, $-\Phi^{-1}(\alpha)$ in formula (12.4) is the same as $+\Phi^{-1}(1-\alpha)$. Accordingly, $-\Phi^{-1}(0.001)$ is the same as $+G(0.999)$.
- The correlation is made dependent on the PD; it varies from 0.12 for high PDs to 0.24 for low PDs.
- The factor model captures only losses from default, but the maturity adjustment serves to adjust the capital requirements in such a way that they also reflect losses from deteriorations of credit quality. The longer the maturity of a loan, the higher is the price impact of a given deterioration. The adjustment depends on the PD because borrowers with a lower PD have more potential of being downgraded than do borrowers that already have a higher PD.[1]
- The unconditional expected loss, given by LGD × PD, is subtracted from the expected stress scenario loss, reducing capital requirements. The motivation is that banks routinely provision against the unconditional expected loss, and so it does not jeopardize their solvency in case it materializes.

[1] The form of the maturity adjustments has been derived by applying a credit risk model that incorporates the value effects of credit quality changes.

The three parameters that have to be specified for the capital requirement formula are PD, LGD and the maturity M. We could enter the formula directly into the sheet, but it is more convenient to provide a user-defined function that returns the capital requirement. Such a function CAPREQ could look as follows:

```
Function CAPREQ(PD, LGD, M)
Dim rpd As Double, bpd As Double
rpd = 0.12 * (1 - Exp(-50 * PD)) / (1 - Exp(-50)) _
    + 0.24 * (1 - (1 - Exp(-50 * PD)) / (1 - Exp(-50)))
bpd = (0.11852 - 0.05478 * Log(PD)) ^ 2

CAPREQ = (LGD * Application.WorksheetFunction.NormSDist(_
    (Application.WorksheetFunction.NormSInv(PD) _
    + rpd ^ 0.5 * Application.WorksheetFunction.NormSInv(0.999)) _
    / (1 - rpd) ^ 0.5) _
    - PD * LGD) _
    * (1 + (M - 2.5) * bpd) / (1 - 1.5 * bpd)
End Function
```

Similarly, one can provide functions for other capital requirement formulae (e.g., for retail exposures) as defined in the new Basel accord.

ASSESSING A GIVEN GRADING STRUCTURE

In the internal ratings-based (IRB) approach, PDs used in the capital requirement formula are usually determined as follows: borrowers are assigned rating grades and the average PD of each grade is estimated. The average PD-estimate for a grade is then used as the PD for all borrowers within the grade.

Regulators admit three possible ways of estimating grade PDs: (i) internal default experience of borrowers; (ii) default rates of external rating systems to which the internal ones are mapped; and (iii) average predicted default probabilities from statistical default prediction models. For (i) and (ii), one would use the methods discussed in Chapter 3; statistical default prediction models are discussed in Chapter 1.

Box 12.2 Selected requirements for rating structure (from: Basel Committee on Banking Supervision, 2005, *International Convergence of Capital Measurement and Capital Standards. A Revised Framework.* Basel, p. 87)

403. A bank must have a meaningful distribution of exposures across grades with no excessive concentrations, on both its borrower-rating and its facility-rating scales.

404. To meet this objective, a bank must have a minimum of seven borrower grades for non-defaulted borrowers and one for those that have defaulted. Banks with lending activities focused on a particular market segment may satisfy this requirement with the minimum number of grades; supervisors may require banks, which lend to borrowers of diverse credit quality, to have a greater number of borrower grades.

Banks have some leeway in the design of the grading system. The essential requirements laid out by the regulators require a bank to have at least seven grades for non-defaulting borrowers and to avoid undue concentrations in the distribution of borrowers across grades (see Box 12.2).

To assess the pros and cons of different grading systems, we should try to assess the economic consequences of system design. Some consequences will be difficult to measure. Consider an example: with many grades, prices can be better tailored to individual risk, which should help increase the bank's profits. However, competition or other forces may restrain the pricing flexibility of the bank, something that is difficult to foresee and to quantify.

Two effects that can be measured for a given distribution of individual PDs in a straightforward way are the following:

- The grading structure affects capital requirements.
- The grading affects the discriminatory power of the system (see Chapter 8 for measures of discriminatory power).

Let us start with the impact of the grading system on capital requirements. The capital requirement function is concave as a function of the PD. As illustrated in Figure 12.1, this implies that capital requirements are reduced if the fineness of the grading structure increases. Assume that a particular grade collects borrowers with PDs between 0.2% and 3%. For simplicity, further assume that there are just two borrowers that fall into this grade, with individual PDs of 0.5% and 2.5%. The grade PD is obtained as the average of the individual ones, which is 1.5%. The solid circle in Figure 12.1 marks the average capital requirement with this rating system. Now assume that the grade is divided into two, one ranging from 0.2% to 1.5%, the other one ranging from 1.5% to 3%. The PDs of the two new grades are 0.5%

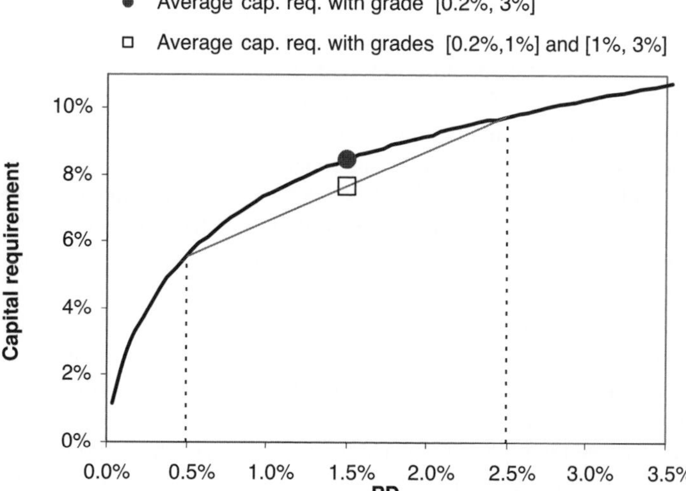

Figure 12.1 How a finer grading reduces capital requirement: simplified example with two borrowers (PD1 = 0.5%, PD2 = 2.5%)

and 2.5%, respectively. The new average capital requirement can be obtained by connecting the capital requirements associated with those new PDs, and selecting the middle point of this line segment. It is marked with a square in the figure.

A system with many grades exploits this concavity better than a system with few. For a given number of rating grades, however, it does depend on the definition of the grades. The curvature of the capital requirement function varies with the PDs; to better exploit the concavity effect, the grading system should depend on the curvature of the function. In addition, the distribution of borrowers across PDs matters. Rating grades should be finer over PD regions with many borrowers.

Like capital requirements, discriminatory power is affected by both the number of grades and the distribution of grade boundaries. In a rating system that discriminates well, borrowers with lower PDs should have better grades. Intuitively, this is easier to achieve with a large number of grades. Just think of a grading system that has a grade collecting PDs from 1% to 50%. By construction, it does not discriminate between PDs of, say, 2% and 20%, even though the difference in PDs is dramatic. To see why the choice of boundaries matters for a given number of grades, compare the following two rating systems:

	Lower PD boundaries (in %) for grade						
	1	2	3	4	5	6	7
System A	0	0.05	0.08	0.12	0.5	2.5	15
System B	0	0.05	0.08	0.1	0.15	0.25	0.5

Both systems have seven grades. System A closely follows the grading system of major rating agencies. System B is much finer in the low PD region, at the cost of putting all borrowers with a PD larger than 0.5% into one grade (grade 7). In a typical loan portfolio, a substantial fraction of borrowers has medium to high risk with PDs larger than 0.5%. Due to their large PD, those borrowers make up the bulk of defaults. System B, however, does not discriminate between medium and high-risk borrowers, and will therefore perform badly in standard tests of discriminatory power.

In Table 12.1 we explore the consequences of grading structure for a given distribution of individual PDs. The example data comprises 1500 borrowers. Columns A and B contain the portfolio data on exposure at default (EAD) and PDs. We have chosen the PDs such that the portfolio composition is representative for commercial banks.

Lower PD boundaries for rating grades are specified in the range F4:F20. In the current set-up, up to 17 grades are possible. If a rating system has less, we define the lower boundaries by starting in F4 and then leaving blank the remaining cells. The grade numbers are recorded in G4:G20. Having specified the grades, borrowers are graded based on their PD. In the range C4:C1502, this is done via the function VLOOKUP(). After grading the borrowers, we determine the distribution of borrowers across grades so that we can check for undue concentrations. In H4:H20, we first use COUNTIF to determine the number with a given grade, and then divide by the overall number of borrowers in the portfolio, which we obtain by applying the function COUNT to column A.[2]

In I4:I20, we estimate the grade PD by averaging the PDs of the borrowers within a grade. This can be done by coupling the function AVERAGE with an encapsulated IF-condition. Note that we divide by 100 because the PDs in column B are stated in percent. The capital

[2] Depending on the purpose of the analysis, it might also be interesting to compute the EAD-weighted portfolio share.

Table 12.1 Average capital requirement (CR) for a given grading system

	A	B	C	D	E	F	G	H	I	J	K	L	M
1	**Portfolio structure**					**Grading structure and calculations**							
2	EAD	PD(%)	Grade	CR		Lower PD (%)	Grade	Portfolio	Grade	Grade			
3	100	30.85	7	19.3%		bound		Share	PD	CR			
4	100	30.18	7	19.3%		0	1	3.1%	0.04%	1.5%			
5	100	29.56	7	19.3%		0.05	2	5.5%	0.06%	1.8%			
6						.08	3	10.9%	0.12%	2.6%			
7						.15	4	29.0%	0.30%	4.3%			
8						.5	5	28.3%	1.01%	7.4%			
9	100	27.49	7	19.3%		2	6	19.0%	5.57%	12.4%			
10	100	27.04	7	19.3%		15	7	4.2%	21.08%	19.3%			
11	100	26.62	7	19.3%			8	0.0%	0.00%	0.0%			
12	100	26.21	7	19.3%									
13	100	25.83	7	19.3%									
14	100	25.46	7	19.3%									
15	100	25.11	7	19.3%									
16	100	24.77	7	19.3%									
17	100	24.45	7	19.3%			14	0.0%	0.00%	0.0%			
18	100	24.13	7	19.3%			15	0.0%	0.00%	0.0%			
19	100	23.83	7	19.3%			16	0.0%	0.00%	0.0%			
20	100	23.54	7	19.3%			17	0.0%	0.00%	0.0%			
21	100	23.26	7	19.3%									
22	100	22.98	7	19.3%									
23	100	22.72	7	19.3%		**Summary statistics for specified grading structure**							
24	100	22.46	7	19.3%		CR							
25	100	22.21	7	19.3%		6.95%	=SUMPRODUCT(A3:A1502,D3:D1502)/SUM(A3:A1502)						
26	100	21.96	7	19.3%									
27	100	21.73	7	19.3%									
28	100	21.50	7	19.3%									
29	100	21.27	7	19.3%									
30	100	21.05	7	19.3%									
.	.	.	.	.									
1502	100	0.04	1	1.5%									

C3: =VLOOKUP(B3,F$4:G$20,2,1)
D3: =VLOOKUP(B3,F$4:J$20,5,1)

(can be copied down to row 1502)

G4: =G3+1
H4: =COUNTIF(C$3:C$1502,"=" &G4)/COUNT(A$3:A$1502)
I4: {=AVERAGE(IF(C$3:C$1502=G4,B$3:B$1502,""))/100}
J4: =CAPREQ(I4,0.45,2.5)

(can be copied down to row 20)

requirement for a grade directly follows by applying the function CAPREQ (defined in the previous section) to the grade PD, which is done in J4:J20; LGD and maturity are set to the default values used by the Basel committee, which are 0.45 and 2.5, respectively. In column D, we then assign the capital requirement to individual borrowers, similar to the way we looked up the grade PD.

At this stage, we can already compute the average capital requirement of the portfolio, which is done in cell F25. In the example, we have chosen a uniform EAD for all borrowers, but in practice, EADs might systematically differ across grades. Accordingly, it is sensible to calculate an EAD-weighted capital requirement. Applying the function SUMPRODUCT to columns A and D gives the minimum capital measured in dollars; dividing by the sum over the exposures we arrive at the average capital requirement as a percentage of EAD. The capital requirement for our example portfolio (and for the chosen grading system) is 6.95%, somewhat less than the 8% that would result from Basel I.

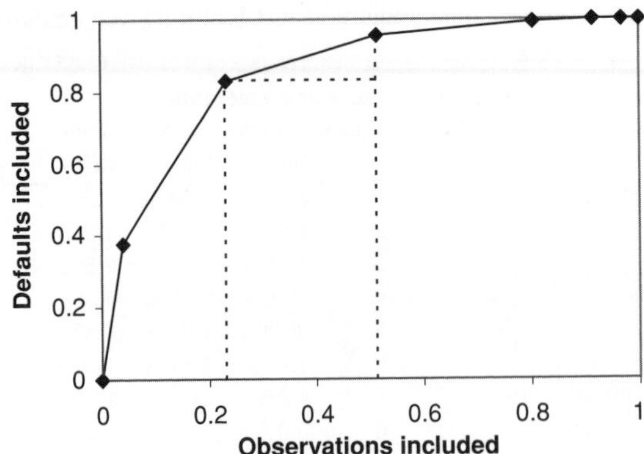

Figure 12.2 The cumulative accuracy profile as the basis for calculating accuracy ratios

Discrimination, by contrast, is usually analyzed on a borrower basis, and so the EADs do not enter the formula. The measure that we are going to calculate is the accuracy ratio (AR, see Chapter 8, which also gives more computational details than this chapter). For a given portfolio and a given observation period, the AR is a random variable because it depends on the realized distribution of defaults, which are random. To decide how to structure the grading system, we would like to know what the average associated AR will be. One straightforward way is to calculate the AR under the assumption that the number of defaults in each rating grade is equal to the expected number of defaults. Let us call this AR the *expected accuracy ratio*. Assuming the estimated PDs to be correct, the expected number of defaults is quite simply (grade PD) × (number of borrowers in the grade).

In Figure 12.2 we briefly recap the construction of the cumulative accuracy profile (CAP). Starting with the worst rating grade, we plot the fraction of all defaulters with grade *i* or worse against the fraction of all borrowers with grade *i* or worse. The AR is (Area under the CAP – 0.5) / (Area under the CAP for a perfect rating system – 0.5). In a perfect rating system, the worst rating grade contains all defaulters, and only those. The area under its CAP is therefore (default rate/2 + (1 – default rate)).

To calculate the expected accuracy ratio, which we do in Table 12.2, let us start with the area under the expected CAP of our rating system. It is easily computed grade by grade. For each grade, the associated area under the curve is made up of a triangle and a rectangle. The baseline is the portfolio share that we have already computed in H4:H20 in Table 12.1. The altitude of the triangle is the grade's share of expected defaults; it is calculated in K4:K20. We exploit the following relationship, where N_i is the number of borrowers in grade *i*, *N* is the overall number of borrowers and PD is the average default rate of the entire portfolio:

$$\text{Grade } i\text{'s share of defaults} = \frac{\text{PD}_i \cdot N_i}{\text{PD} \cdot N} = \frac{N_i}{N} \cdot \text{PD}_i/\text{PD}$$
$$= \text{Portfolio share}_i \cdot \text{PD}_i/\text{PD}$$

The average PD that we need for this formula is determined in G22. Note that the ISERROR() function is used in K4:K20 to return zeros for grades that are either non-defined or have no borrowers assigned to them. Otherwise, we could get error values that inhibit the computation of the accuracy ratio.

Table 12.2 Average capital requirement (CR) and accuracy ratio (AR) for a given grading system

	A	B	C	D	E	F	G	H	I	J	K	L	M
1	**Portfolio structure**					**Grading structure and calculations**							
2	EAD	PD(%)	Grade	CR		Lower PD (%)	Grade	Portfolio	Grade	Grade	Exp. share	Area under	
3	100	30.85	7	19.3%		bound		Share	PD	CR	of defaults	CAP	
4	100	30.18	7	19.3%		0	1	3.1%	0.04%	1.5%	0.06%	3.13%	
5	100	29.56	7	19.3%		0.05	2	5.5%	0.06%	1.8%	0.15%	5.53%	
						0.08	3	10.9%	0.12%	2.6%	0.54%	10.81%	
						0.15	4	29.0%	0.30%	4.3%	3.69%	28.25%	
						0.5	5	28.3%	1.01%	7.4%	12.27%	25.28%	
9	100	27.49	7	19.3%		2	6	19.0%	5.57%	12.4%	45.33%	11.52%	
10	100	27.04	7	19.3%		15	7	4.2%	21.08%	19.3%	37.96%	0.80%	
11	100	26.62	7	19.3%			8	0.0%	0.00%	0.0%	0.00%	0.00%	
12	100	26.21	7	19.3%			9	0.0%	0.00%	0.0%	0.00%	0.00%	
13	100	25.83	7	19.3%			10	0.0%	0.00%	0.0%	0.00%	0.00%	
14	100	25.46	7	19.3%									
15	100	25.11	7	19.3%									
16	100	24.77	7	19.3%									
17	100	24.45	7	19.3%									
18	100	24.13	7	19.3%									
19	100	23.83	7	19.3%									
20	100	23.54	7	19.3%			17	0.0%	0.00%	0.0%	0.00%	0.00%	
21	100	23.26	7	19.3%		**General**							
22	100	22.98	7	19.3%		Average PD	2.3%	=AVERAGE(B3:B1502)/100					
23	100	22.72	7	19.3%		**Summary statistics for specified grading structure**							
24	100	22.46	7	19.3%		CR	AR	Grading structure					
25	100	22.21	7	19.3%		6.95%	72.3%	0-0.05-0.08-0.15-0.5-2-15----------					
26	100	21.96	7	19.3%		**Saved results**							
27	100	21.73	7	19.3%		6.84%	78.9%	0-0.04-0.05-0.07-0.09-0.11-0.13-0.18-0.25-0.35-0.5-0.8-1.2-2-5-8-15					
28	100	21.50	7	19.3%		6.95%	72.3%	0-0.05-0.08-0.15-0.5-2-15----------					
29	100	21.27	7	19.3%									
30	100	21.05	7	19.3%									
…	…	…	…	…									
…	…	…	…	…									
1502	100	0.04	1	1.5%									

C3: =VLOOKUP(B3,F$4:G$20,2,1)
D3: =VLOOKUP(B3,F$4:J$20,5,1)

(can be copied down to row 1502)

G4: =G3+1
H4: =COUNTIF(C$3:C$1502,"=" &G4)/COUNT(A$3:A$1502)
I4: =AVERAGE(IF(C$3:C$1502=G4,B$3:B$1502,""))/100
J4: =CAPREQ(I4,0.45,2.5)
K4: =IF(ISERROR(I4)=FALSE,H4*I4/G$22,0)
L4: =H4*(SUM(K5:K$21)+K4/2)

(can be copied down to row 20)

F25: =SUMPRODUCT(A3:A1502,D3:D1502)/SUM(A3:A1502)
G25: =(SUM(L4:L20)-0.5)/((G22/2+(1-G22))-0.5)
H25: =F4&"-"&F5&"-"&F6&"-"&F7&"-"&F8&"-"&F9&"-"&F10&"-"&F11&"-"&F12&"-"&F13&"-"&F14&"-"&F15&"-"&F16&"-"&F17&"-"&F18&"-"&F19&"-"&F20

Finally, areas of the CAP segments are calculated separately for each grade in L4:L20. In cell L4, for example, the formula reads:

$$= H4^*(SUM(K5:K\$21)+K4/2)$$

H4 is the baseline (the grade's portfolio share); SUM(K5:K$21) is the share of defaults occurring in worse rating grades, which gives the altitude of the rectangle in Figure 12.2; K4 is the current grade's share of defaults, which gives the altitude of the triangle in Figure 12.2.

The segment areas are summed up in G25, together with the other steps necessary to arrive at the AR.

When experimenting with different grading structures, the ability to save the key results of grading structures is certainly an advantage. Capital requirements and accuracy ratio are already provided in F25:G25; we complete the information by condensing the grade boundaries into one cell. Using &, we concatenate the boundaries from F4:F20 and, separated by hyphens, write them into H25. Now we can easily save the key facts of the grading system by copying the range F25:H25 to another range in the worksheet. Cells F27:H28 contain the results for two grading systems whose boundaries mimic the default rates of external ratings. The first system has seven grades corresponding to the seven letter ratings of agencies, the second has 17, corresponding to the number of modified grades for which the agencies publish statistics. The results show that the increase in the number of ratings from 7 to 17 leads to a considerable increase in the accuracy ratio. In terms of capital requirements, the 17-grade system is also superior, but the improvement seems to be less pronounced than in terms of accuracy.

TOWARDS AN OPTIMAL GRADING STRUCTURE

Experimenting with the sheet shown in Table 12.2 can already give valuable insights into grading structures, but simple experimentation may not reveal the structure that best meets the bank's objectives. In this section, we therefore show how to systematically search for attractive grading structures.

The attractiveness of a grading structure could be made operational by defining an objective function, for example

$$\text{expected accuracy ratio} - \gamma \times \text{capital requirement}$$

and imposing constraints on the maximum number of grades and other aspects of the grading system. One could then use appropriate techniques to find the grade boundaries that maximize this function. An alternative approach that is quicker to implement is to randomly simulate grading systems and then examine those that perform well on the dimensions in which we are interested. This is the strategy that we pursue here. It may take some computing time, but the same problem applies to a numerical optimization. And several minutes do not matter much for a decision that is typically meant to last for several years, as is the choice of a grading system.

Table 12.3 is built upon Table 12.2. The key difference is that we make the grading system random. In doing so, we impose some restrictions. For example, a bank may not tolerate a grading system where the best grade comprises PDs from 0% up to 5%. We can model such restrictions by specifying maximum values for the upper boundaries of rating grades. In the table, this is done in E4:E20. The simulation of grades is based on the function RAND(), which returns random numbers that are uniformly distributed over the interval (0, 1). To arrive at the lower boundary for grade i, we take the simulated lower boundary of grade $i-1$ and add RAND() times the maximum for grade i minus the simulated lower boundary of grade $i-1$. This is done in cells F4:F20. Using the function ROUND(x, n) we also round the random numbers to two digits because round numbers are often preferred in practice. Though we simulate the grades such that their number is fixed (to seven), the sheet could easily be adapted such that we also have a random number of grades.

Each time the sheet is recalculated (e.g., because of a change in the sheet or a keypress of F9), a new random grading system is chosen and its characteristics are summarized in F25:H25. To find attractive ones via simulation, we use the following macro:

```
Sub gradesim()
Application.ScreenUpdating = False
Application.Calculation = xlCalculationAutomatic
```

Table 12.3 Average capital requirement (CR) and accuracy ratio (AE) for a given grading system (built on Table 12.2)

	A	B	C	D	E	F	G	H	I	J	K	L	M
1	**Portfolio structure**					**Grading structure and calculations**							
2	EAD	PD(%)	Grade	CR	Max	Lower PD	Grade	Portfolio	Grade	Grade	Exp. share	Area under	
3	100	30.85	7	19.3%		bound (%)		Share	PD	CR	of defaults	CAP	
4	100	30.18	7	19.3%		0	1	3.1%	0.04%	1.5%	0.06%	3.13%	
5	100	29.56	7	19.3%	0.2	0.12	2	5.5%	0.06%	1.8%	0.15%	5.53%	
6	100	28.99	7	19.3%	0.5	0.25	3	10.9%	0.12%	2.6%	0.54%	10.81%	
7	100	28.46	7	19.3%	2	1.47	4	29.0%	0.30%	4.3%	3.69%	28.25%	
8	100	27.96	7	19.3%	10	4.57	5	28.3%	1.01%	7.4%	12.27%	25.28%	
9	100	27.49	7	19.3%	20	8.62	6	19.0%	5.57%	12.4%	45.33%	11.52%	
10	100	27.04	7	19.3%	25	12.47						0.80%	
11	100	26.62	7	19.3%								0.00%	
12	100	26.21	7	19.3%			9	0.0%	0.00%	0.0%	0.00%	0.00%	
13	100	25.83	7	19.3%			10	0.0%	0.00%	0.0%	0.00%	0.00%	
14	100	25.46	7	19.3%			11	0.0%	0.00%	0.0%	0.00%	0.00%	
15	100	25.11	7	19.3%			12	0.0%	0.00%	0.0%	0.00%	0.00%	
16	100	24.77	7	19.3%			13	0.0%	0.00%	0.0%	0.00%	0.00%	
17	100	24.45	7	19.3%			14	0.0%	0.00%	0.0%	0.00%	0.00%	
18	100	24.13	7	19.3%			15	0.0%	0.00%	0.0%	0.00%	0.00%	
19	100	23.83	7	19.3%			16	0.0%	0.00%	0.0%	0.00%	0.00%	
20	100	23.54	7	19.3%			17	0.0%	0.00%	0.0%	0.00%	0.00%	
21	100	23.26	7	19.3%		**General**							
22	100	22.98	7	19.3%		Average PD	2.3%						
23	100	22.72	7	19.3%		**Summary statistics for specified grading structure**							
24	100	22.46	7	19.3%		CR	AR	Grading structure					
25	100	22.21	7	19.3%		6.97%	74.0%	0-0.12-0.25-1.47-4.57-8.62-12.47----------					
26	100	21.96	7	19.3%		**Saved results**							
27	100	21.73	7	19.3%		6.84%	78.9%	0-0.04-0.05-0.07-0.09-0.11-0.13-0.18-0.25-0.35-0.5-0.8-1.2-2-5-8-15					
28	100	21.50	7	19.3%		6.95%	72.3%	0-0.05-0.08-0.15-0.5-2-15----------					
29	100	21.27	7	19.3%		**Results for simulated grading systems**							
30	100	21.05	7	19.3%		6.88%	74.9%	0-0.18-0.48-0.95-1.91-6.9-13----------					
31	...	...	...	...		6.88%	74.9%	0-0.19-0.49-0.79-1.8-6.23-13.47----------					
...	...	...	...	...		6.88%	74.4%	0-0.16-0.39-0.83-1.82-8.4-12.74----------					
...	...	...	...	...		...	...	...					

F10: =F9+ROUND(RAND()*(E10-F9),2)
(can be copied into F5:F9)

```
Dim imax As Long, i As Long

imax = 5000
For i = 1 To imax
  Application.StatusBar = i
  Range("F" & i + 29 & ":H" & i + 29) = (Range("F25:H25"))
Next i

Range("F30:H" & 29 + imax).Sort Key1:=Range("F31"), _
  Order1: =xlAscending
End Sub
```

Essentially, the macro loops over random grading structures and saves the result into the sheet. The way the macro is written requires the option *automatic calculation* to be activated, and the second line of the macro makes sure that it is. `Application.ScreenUpdating= False` speeds up the calculation because it prevents Excel from displaying the change in numbers associated with newly-drawn rating boundaries. Since the macro may run several minutes, it is useful to see its current progress in the status bar, which is achieved by typing `Application.StatusBar=i`. The line below writes the key information on the simulated system into the sheet. After completing the loop, we sort the output according to the capital requirements (in ascending order). This brings the best to the top, and therefore facilitates our inspection of the results. In the example, we set the number of iterations to 5000.

The results suggest that 5000 is indeed sufficient. The top systems are all in relatively close proximity to one another when measured against either of the two criteria, and so it is not very likely that there should exist other highly superior systems which were not drawn during the course of the simulation. Comparing the simulated grading systems with those corresponding to external agency grades, it is evident that we can significantly improve upon a standard seven-grade system. We can easily have lower requirements, *and* increase expected accuracy ratios by more than two percentage points. As seen here, system design can really matter. With the criteria and the portfolio examined here, it is key to differentiate across medium- and high-risk borrowers. Having more than one grade for default probabilities between 0 and 0.15% does not improve the criteria, even though external ratings reserve three grades (AAA, AA and A) for this region.

To conclude, Table 12.4 shows the figures for two 'realistic' rating systems derived from the simulations. Banks prefer round figures, and so boundaries are based on key patterns of the top-performing simulated systems, but are once more rounded. This is exemplified in the first row of the table. In the second system, we add another grade for low-risk borrowers because banks may require a fine structure among low-risk borrowers for other reasons. For comparison, we also report the results for the systems that mimic external grades.

As can be seen from the first row, additional rounding does not matter much; capital requirements and accuracy ratio are very close to the best ones from Table 12.3, and nor does the addition of another low-risk grade lead to significant improvements.

Table 12.4 Capital requirements (CR) and expected accuracy ratios (AE) for different grading systems

Lower grade boundaries (in %)	# grades	CR (%)	AR (%)
0-0.15-0.5-1-2-7-15----------	7	6.88	74.9
0-0.05-0.15-0.5-1-2-7-15---------	8	6.88	74.9
0-0.05-0.08-0.15-0. 5-2-15----------	7	6.95	72.3
0-0.04-0.05-0.07-0.09-0.11-0.13-0.18-0.25-0.35-0.5-0.8-1.2-2-5-8-15	17	6.84	78.9

NOTES AND LITERATURE

The regulatory details of the IRB approach are set out in Basel Committee on Banking Supervision, 2005, *International Convergence of Capital Measurement and Capital Standards. A revised framework.* Basel.

A detailed explanation of the capital requirement formula can be found in Basel Committee on Banking Supervision, 2005, *An Explanatory Note on the Basel II IRB Risk Weight Functions.* Basel.

Appendix A1
Visual Basics for Applications (VBA)

MACROS AND FUNCTIONS

In this book, we use VBA (Visual Basic for Applications) to write macros and user-defined functions. Macros and functions are routines for running a series of commands specified by the user. The key differences between macros and functions are as follows:

- User-defined functions can be used like standard spreadsheet functions, e. g., we can type =OURFUNCTION(*arguments*) into a cell (or range of cells in the case of an array function) of the spreadsheet. The function will be run and the result will be returned in the sheet. Macros have to be called by some action that we take outside a cell.
- The output of a function extends only to the cells in the sheet that it applies to; a function cannot be used to change other cells. For example, if we type =OURFUNCTION(*arguments*) into cell A1, we cannot make this function fill B3 with some value. With a macro, we can change any cell in the worksheet, move to other sheets and so on.

WRITING A NEW MACRO OR FUNCTION

To start writing a macro or function, open the VBA editor: the short-cut would be pressing [alt]+[F11]. Although this shortcut works in all Excel versions, the alternative menu path differs. Prior to Excel 2007 select Tools→Macro→Visual Basic Editor. In Excel 2007 you find the Visual Basic item on the Developer tab. If the Developer tab is not shown, click on the Office button (the round symbol in the upper left), click Excel Options, then Popular and select 'Show Developer tab in the Ribbon'. In Excel 2010 there is no longer an Office button. Here you access the Options menu in the File tab. Click on 'Customize Ribbon' on the left side, then select 'Popular Commands' in the 'Choose commands from' dialog box on the left side. Now turn to the right side, select 'Main tabs' in the 'Customize the ribbon' menu and check 'Developer'.

In VBA, macros are encompassed by two lines with the following structure:

```
Sub MYMACRO()
    ...
End Sub
```

Similarly for functions:

```
Function MYFUNCTION()
    ...
End Function
```

The VBA editor will automatically provide the end statement and the parentheses behind the name that we supply.

A first macro, a first function

Imagine that we want to write the number 156 into cell A3 using VBA. We could use the following function:

```
Function FIRSTFUNCTION()
      FIRSTFUNCTION=156
End Function
```

Type = FIRSTFUNCTION () into A3, and you will see 156 in A3.

We could also write the following macro:

```
Sub FIRSTMACRO()
      Range("A3")=156
End Sub
```

and run it. Two possible ways of running a macro are as follows:

- While in the worksheet, press [alt]+[F8], select the macro of your choice from the list and press 'Run' (Excel <2007: Tools→Macro→Macros; Excel ≥2007: Developer Ribbon→Macros).
- While in the VBA editor, point the cursor to some place within the macro text, and press F5 (or press the play button).

In the macro FIRSTMACRO, we have already seen a way of referring to a cell within VBA. The next section gives more details.

Referencing cells

In this book, we use two ways of referencing worksheet cells in VBA: the A1 method and the index method. Here are two examples:

A1 method	Index method	Refers to
`Range("A3")`	`Cells(3,1)`	A3
`Range("A1:B3")`	`Range(Cells(1,1),cells(3,2))`	`A1:B3`

This is probably self-explanatory. In the A1 method, we first state the column letter, immediately followed by the row number. In the index method, we first state the row number; the column number follows, separated by a comma.

In programming, the cells to which we refer often depend on some variable. Assume that we use the variable `col` to define the column number, and the variable `row` to define the row number. The following are then examples for referencing:

A1 method	Index method	col	row	Refers to
`Range("A" & row)`	`Cells(row,1)`		3	A3
`Range("A1:B" & row)`	`Range(Cells(1,1), cells(row,2))`		3	A1:B3
`Range("A" & col & ":B3")`	`Range(Cells(1,col), cells(3,2))`	1		A1:B3

Declaring variables

Declaring variables means that we explicitly tell VBA that we are going to work with a variable named xxx. By default, we do not need to declare variables. We can, however, force ourselves to do so by writing

```
Option explicit
```

right at the very top of a module in the VBA editor.

Variables are usually declared through a `Dim` statement, e. g.,

```
Dim i
```

declares a variable named i.

Data types and arrays

VBA variables can have one of several data types which differ in the range of values they support. Table A1.1 shows a list of important data types.

When we do not assign a specific data type, VBA works with the data type variant, i.e., the one consuming maximum memory. Assigning appropriate data types can reduce the memory needed and thus speed up computations.

For example, if we use a variable `col` to define the column number of a worksheet cell, we would choose the data type *Integer* because the number of worksheet columns is below 32.767. For a variable `row` that defines the row number of a cell, the data type *Long* would be appropriate.

Table A1.1 Data types in VBA

Data type	Memory	Possible values
Byte	1 Byte	Integers from 0 to 255
Boolean	2 Bytes	True or False
Date	8 Bytes	0:00:00 (midnight) on January 1, 0001 through 11:59:59 p. m. on December 31, 9999
Integer	2 Bytes	Integers from –32.768 to 32.767
Long	4 Bytes	Integers from –2.147.483.648 to 2.147.483.647
Double	8 Bytes	–179769313486231E308 to 94065645841247E-324; 494065645841247E-324 to 179769313486232E308
Variant	16 (numerical values)	Numerical values as for Double; strings possible

To assign the data type *Byte* to a variable x, we would type

```
Dim x as Byte
```

We can assign the other data types in a similar way.

An array is a variable that contains a group of values with the same data type, e. g., a vector or a matrix. To declare an array with values of data type double, we write

```
Dim x() as Double
```

where the () tells VBA that x is an array. In the declaration, we could also specify the dimension of x, i.e., how many elements it has:

```
Dim x(1 to 10) as Double
```

For example, would declare a (row) vector with 10 elements, the first having the index 1. In this book, however, we always use a separate statement to fix the dimension, the `Redim` statement:

```
Dim x() as Double
ReDim x(1 to 10)
```

One reason for using `Redim` is that the `Dim` statement does not accept variables for determining the dimension. Consider the situation where a variable *N* contains the dimension that we want to assign to array x. We cannot type `Dim x(1 to N)`, but we can type `Redim x(1 to N)`.

By default, the index of an array runs from 0 to the number we state in `Redim` or `Dim`. `Redim x(10,3)` would create a matrix with 11 rows and 4 columns. As already seen above, we can let the index start at 1 by using Redim (1 to..., 1 to...). Alternatively, we could tell VBA to let the index start at 1 by default. To this end, write

```
Option base 1
```

at the top of a module in the VBA editor. In this book, we let the index start at 1 because this gives nice correspondences to the formulae in the text.

Loops

In order to repeat a similar command within VBA, we can use loops. If the number of repetitions is known in advance (e. g., when conducting a Monte Carlo simulation), a *for* loop is convenient:

```
For i=1 to 1000
   ...
Next i
```

By default, the counter (here a variable called `i`) is increased by 1 in each loop. But we are free to choose any other step size, or loop in the reverse direction. Here is an example with step size 0.01:

```
For i=1 to 1000 Step 0.01
   ...
Next i
```

And here is another one where we loop from 1000 to 1 with step size 1:

```
For i=1000 to 1 Step -1
   ...
Next i
```

In other situations, we may prefer a loop that is only left once a certain condition is met. The top-checking variant would be

```
Do while deviation>10^-10
   ...
Loop
```

And here is the bottom-checking variant:

```
Do
   ...
Loop until deviation<=10^-10
```

Of course, we would have some operation that changes the variable `deviation` within the loop.

If-statements

A simple if-statement has the following structure:

```
If condition Then
      ...
End If
```

which can also be written as

```
If condition Then ...
```

If-statements can be expanded by Else-statements, e. g.,

```
If condition Then
      ...
Else
      ...
End If
```

Table A1.2 Selected VBA functions

Abs(*number*)	Returns the absolute value of number.
Dateserial(*year*, *month*, *day*)	Returns a variable of type date containing the serial date, i.e., the number of days since December 1, 1900.
Day(*serialdate*)	Returns the day of *serialdate*.
EXP(*number*)	Returns 'e' raised to the power of number.
IIF(*expression*, *truepart*, *falsepart*)	Returns *truepart* if expression is true, *falsepart* else.
Int(*number*)	Returns number with decimals removed
IsMissing(*argument*)	Returns true if argument is not defined and false else.
LBound(*array*)	Returns the lowest index of *array*.
LOG(*number*)	Returns the natural logarithm of number.
Month(serialdate)	Returns the month of *serialdate*.
Rnd	Returns uniform random number between 0 and 1.
UBound(*array*)	Returns the highest index of *array*.
Year(*serialdate*)	Returns the year of *serialdate*.

Functions within VBA

Table A1.2 presents a selection of VBA functions that we use in the book.

In VBA, we can also use (most) EXCEL spreadsheet functions. However, we have to call them with the prefix `Application.Worksheetfunction` (or just `Application`). To compute the sum of the elements in the array `x`, for example, we would type

```
sum_x = Application.WorksheetFunction.Sum(x)
```

An important thing to note is that the result of an array function can only be written to a variable with data type variant:

```
Dim z() as double
z = Application.WorksheetFunction.MMult(x, y)
```

for example, does *not* work, whereas

```
Dim z()
z = Application.WorksheetFunction.MMult(x, y)
```

works (if `x` and `y` are properly defined).

As an alternative to analyzing data with functions, we can, in some cases, make VBA return us some property of the data. To count the number of rows in the matrix `x` that we read in as an argument of some function, for example, we can type

```
Rownum = x.rows.count
```

Finally, in other cases, we may expect that there is a straightforward solution, but then we fail to find one. For example, we might expect to be able to add up two arrays `x` and `y` by typing `z=x+y`. This is not possible. Nor is there a function for adding two arrays. A way out is to loop through the elements of the arrays. If `x` and `y` are matrices with *N* rows and *K* columns, we could use

```
For i = 1to N
       For j = 1to K
              z(i, j) = x(i, j) + y(i, j)
       Next j
Next i
```

Code editing

To insert a comment, use an apostrophe:

```
'This is a comment
x = Log(y) / 2 'And this is another comment
```

To spread a statement over several lines of code, use an underscore preceded by a space:

```
area = Application.WorksheetFunction.NormSDist(0.01) _
  + Application.WorksheetFunction.Sum(x)
```

To use several statements in one line of code, use colons:

```
For i = 1 To N: x(i) = y(i): Next i
```

Macro recording

A very useful feature is available through Tools→Macro→ Record New Macro (Excel <2007) or Developer tab→Record Macro (Excel ≥2007). Having started recording, each step you perform in the spreadsheet is translated into VBA and stored in a macro until you stop recording. You can then run or change this recorded macro, or examine it to learn how a task can be performed in VBA.

Troubleshooting

When we use a function in the worksheet, you may run into problems when calling the same function within another function. Most commonly this is caused by the difference between arrays and ranges. Consider the following function

```
Function fun1(range1)
 fun1=range1.rows.count
End function
```

This function returns the number of rows of `range1`. So if you type =FUN1(A1:A10) in the worksheet, the function returns 10. However, if you type =FUN1({1,2,3,4,5,6,7,8,9,10}) so that `range1` is an array, the above function returns an error. As a solution, you can consider an alternative to `rows.count`, for example `application.worksheetfunction.COUNT()`.

Now consider the case of fun2, which uses an array as input:

```
Function fun2(array1)
 fun1=Ubound(array1)
End function
```

This function returns the highest index of `array1`. When you call this function in the worksheet, e. g., = fun2(A1:A10), it returns an error; the function works, however, when you input an array.

Avoiding this problem is simple. We just add `array1=array1` to convert any range into an array:

```
Function fun2(array1)
 array1=array1
 fun1=UBound(array1)
End function
```

Now fun2 works both with ranges and arrays.

The way in which variables are referenced might also cause problems. Without going too deeply into technical details, VBA treats variable names as references by default. Consider two functions:

```
Function fun3(number1)
 Dim tmp
 tmp=fun4(number1)
 fun3=number1
End function

Function fun4(number1)
 number1=number1*10
End function
```

If you call, for example, fun3(10), then the function does not return 10, but 100, because the argument `number1` is changed by function fun4. To circumvent this problem, we can pass arguments by their value. This can be simply achieved by putting a `ByVal` before the argument. In the above example we would write

```
Function fun3(number1)
 Dim tmp
 tmp=fun4(number1)
 fun3=number1
End function

Function fun4(ByVal number1)
 number1=number1*10
End function
```

Now fun3(10) returns 10.

Appendix A2
Solver

The Solver is a tool for finding numerical solutions to various kinds of problems. We can use it to maximize or minimize a function or to set a function to some specified value.

Before we start demonstrating the use of the Solver, we have to ensure that the Solver Add-in is installed. In Excel versions prior to 2007, you just open the Add-In item from the Tools menu. For Excel 2007, you first press the Office button in the upper left of Excel (or press [alt] then [d]), then you choose Excel Options (or press [i]). In Excel 2010, you find the Excel Options menu under the File tab ([alt]+[f]). In both cases you now choose Add-ins on the left side of the dialog box, choose Excel Add-ins from the drop-down menu ([alt]+[a]) on the lower right part of the dialog box and press Go ([alt]+[g]). In any Excel version you should see a picture similar to the following:

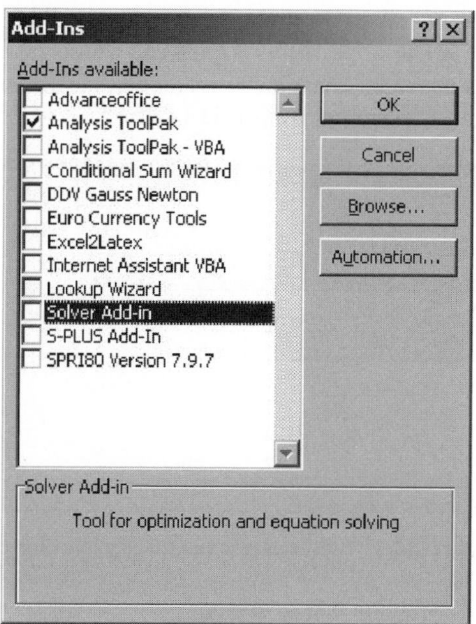

Figure A2.1 Installing the Solver Add-in

Here check the box next to the entry 'Solver' and confirm by pressing OK.

If the Solver Add-in does not show up in this list, your Excel installation does not contain the Solver Add-in. To install it use the item Detect and Repair from the Help menu to initialize the setup routine. If you believe that the Solver Add-in is installed, you can try to add the reference manually in the Add-In item from the Tools menu by pressing Browse.

The Solver Add-in is typically located in the following directory:

<Program Files>\Microsoft Office\OFFICExx\Library\SOLVER

where <Program Files> points to the standard directory for programs, e.g., C:\Program Files, and xx gives the office version. For Office XP xx equals 10, for Office 2003 xx is 11, for Office 2007 xx is 12 and for Office 2010 it is 13.

Now we are ready to look at an example to demonstrate the use of the Solver. Assume that you want to maximize the following function:

$$y = \left(\sqrt{x} - \frac{x^{1.5}}{3}\right) \tag{A2.1}$$

Straightforward calculus would tell us that y is maximized for $x = 1$, but let us use the Solver to determine this value.

We guess some value for x (here 0), write it in cell A2 and type the functional relationship (A2.1) into another cell, here B2:

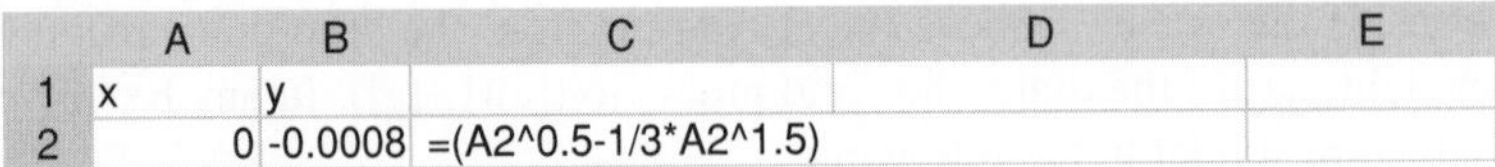

	A	B	C	D	E
1	x	y			
2	0	-0.0008	=(A2^0.5-1/3*A2^1.5)		

Then we open the Solver window via Tools→Solver (Excel$<$2007) or choose Solver from the Data tab (Excel$\geq$2007). Our target cell is B2, the cell whose value we want to maximize. We thus tick Max (see Figure A2.2). Changing cells are cells that the Solver considers changing in order to reach the set goal. In our case, this is just cell A2.

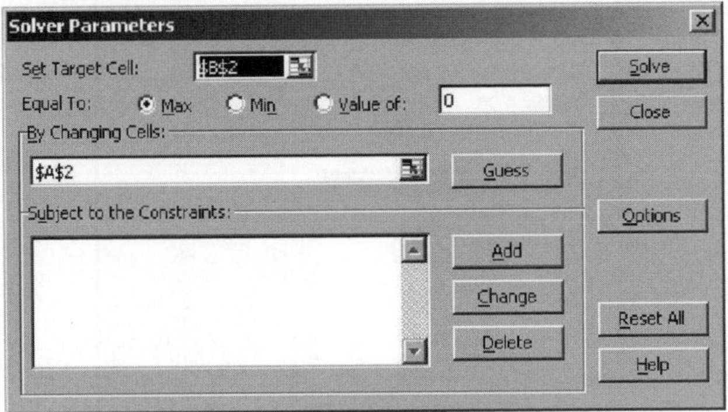

Figure A2.2 Solver parameters for example problem

We press Solve and get the solution that we expect:

	A	B	C	D	E
1	x	y			
2	1	0.666666667	=(A2^0.5-1/3*A2^1.5)		

Now let us consider some cases that require troubleshooting. Assume that our initial value was 10 rather than 0:

	A	B	C	D	E
1	x	y			
2	10	-7.37864787	=(A2^0.5-1/3*A2^1.5)		

We run the Solver as above and get

	A	B	C	D	E
1	x	y			
2	-6	#NUM!	=(A2^0.5-1/3*A2^1.5)		

During its search procedure, the Solver considered the value −6, and got trapped because -6ˆ0.5 produces an error value. Since we know that negative values of x are not admissible in this particular problem, we can tell the Solver not to consider them. In the Solver main window shown above, we could enter the constraint A2>0, but there is a quicker way. Press the button Options in the window above and then tick 'Assume Non-Negative' as shown in Figure A2.3:

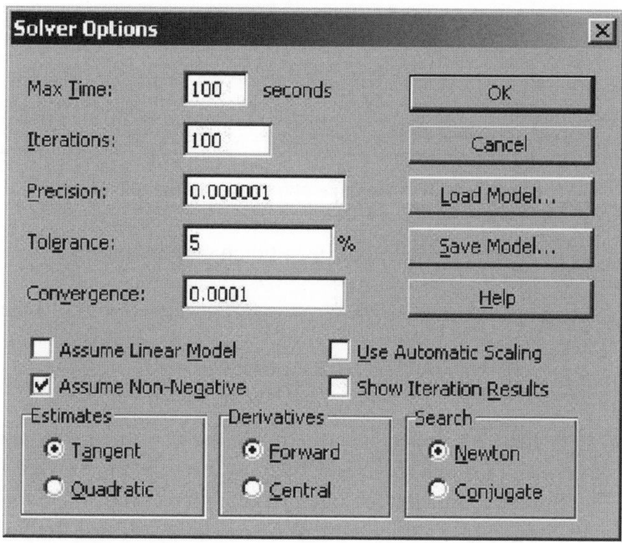

Figure A2.3 Solver options for example problem

With this change, the Solver finds the solution with the starting value 10 as well.

Information on this and other Solver options can be obtained via the Help button. Here we only comment on two more options. Precision sets the accuracy that Solver tries to achieve: the smaller the number, the higher the targeted precision of the result. In our example, the precision is set to the default value of 0.000001. The solution was not exactly 1, but it came very close. For the starting value 0, the Solver presented the solution 1.00000003191548. If we had set the precision to 0.5, for example, the Solver would have presented the solution 1.05997857962513.

Now consider the problem of maximizing the following function:

$$y = \left(\sqrt{x} - \frac{x^{1.5}}{3} + 100000\right)^{11} \tag{A2.2}$$

Inspecting the function, we see that its maximization is equivalent to maximizing our previous function (A2.1). But the Solver does not simplify functions algebraically, and so let us see what happens. We set the initial value to zero:

	A	B	C	D	E
1	x	y			
2	0	1E+55	=(A2^0.5-1/3*A2^1.5+100000)^11		

and call the Solver with the settings from above. The returns are shown in Figure A2.4:

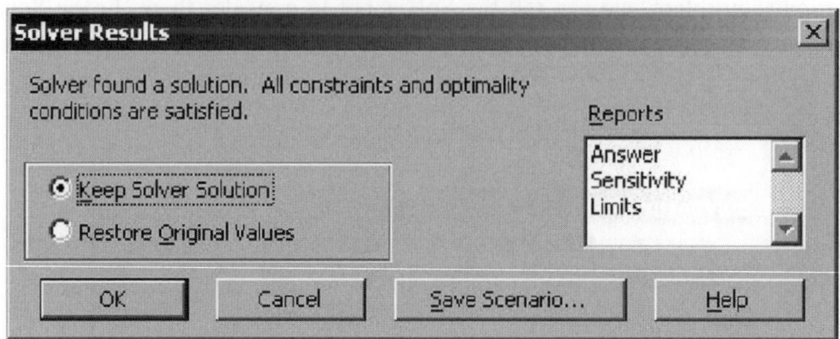

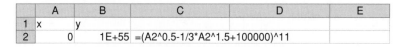

Figure A2.4 Message upon running the solver

But this message is misleading. There has been no change in the sheet:

	A	B	C	D	E
1	x	y			
2	0	1E+55	=(A2^0.5-1/3*A2^1.5+100000)^11		

What causes trouble is that the dimension of the changing cell is very different from the dimension of the target cell (around 1E+55). Changing x has a very small effect on the value of the target cell. The Solver is thus led to conclude that there is no scope for maximization.

In cases like this, the option Use automatic scaling can help, because the Solver will then try to internally scale changing cells and target cells. There is no guarantee that this works. Here it does. Having ticked the option in our example, the Solver converges to the correct solution, which is again the value of 1.

The Solver can be run in macros, but it cannot be run in user-defined functions (a function cannot be made to change cells in the worksheet, but this is what the Solver requires to work). The VBA code for the last run of the Solver that we just discussed would read

```
SolverOk SetCell:="$B$2", MaxMinVal:=1, ValueOf:="0", ByChange:=
  "$A$2"
SolverOptions MaxTime:=100, Iterations:=100, Precision:=0.000001,
AssumeLinear _
     :=False, StepThru:=False, Estimates:=1, Derivatives:=1,
SearchOption:=1, _
     IntTolerance:=5, Scaling:=True, Convergence:=0.0001,
AssumeNonNeg:=True
SolverSolve
```

An easy way to get this code is to record a Macro (see Appendix A1). While recording the Macro, open the Solver main window from the sheet, open the Solver option window, go back to the main window and run the Solver.

We mention below three important things for using the Solver in VBA:

- Running the Solver in VBA requires that we have set a reference to the Solver via Tools→References in the VBA editor (this is the same for all Excel versions although the ways to open the VBA editor differ; see Appendix A1 or simply press [alt]+[F11]).
- To run the Solver in VBA, it is not necessary to specify the complete Solver settings in VBA. For choices not explicitly specified, VBA takes the active specifications (i.e., the ones from the last run) or the default settings. By typing SolverReset right at the start, we can set everything to the default setting, e.g., because we want to prevent ourselves from unwittingly using some unwanted settings.
- If we run the macro with just SolverSolve, we will be asked to confirm the solution before it is written in the sheet. In many situations, e.g., when calling the Solver within a loop, this is inconvenient. We can skip it by having Userfinish:=True behind the SolverSolve statement.

To conclude, we provide an example of a macro that solves our problem and that specifies only the option settings that differ from the default settings:

```
Sub RUNSOLVER()

SolverReset
SolverOk SetCell:="$B$2", MaxMinVal:=1, ValueOf:="0", _
  ByChange:="$A$2"
SolverOptions Scaling:=True, AssumeNonNeg:=True
SolverSolve UserFinish:=True

End Sub
```

Appendix A3
Maximum Likelihood Estimation and Newton's Method

The maximum likelihood method is a way of inferring parameter values from sample data. Parameters are chosen such that they maximize the probability (=likelihood) of drawing the sample that was actually observed. We can split the procedure into two main steps:

1. Set up a likelihood function that describes how the probability of a given sample depends on the parameters.
2. Based on step 1, determine the parameters that maximize the likelihood of the sample at hand.

Let us work through a simple example. Consider a sample of three numbers

$$x_1 = -1, \quad x_2 = 5, \quad x_3 = 2$$

which are derived from a normal distribution with unknown mean μ and unknown variance σ^2. The likelihood of observing a single value x_i is given by the density of a normal distribution:

$$L_i = \frac{1}{\sqrt{2\pi}\sigma} \exp(-(x_i - \mu)^2/(2\sigma^2)) = (2\pi\sigma^2)^{-1/2} \exp(-(x_i - \mu)^2/(2\sigma^2)) \tag{A3.1}$$

In many cases, we have good reasons to assume that individual draws are independent. The likelihood of the entire data set then can be obtained by multiplying the individual likelihoods. In our case this leads to (recall $\exp(x)\exp(y) = \exp(x + y)$):

$$\begin{aligned} L &= \prod_{i=1}^{3} (2\pi\sigma^2)^{-1/2} \exp(-(x_i - \mu)^2/(2\sigma^2)) \\ &= (2\pi\sigma^2)^{-3/2} \exp\left(-\sum_{i=1}^{3} (x_i - \mu)^2/(2\sigma^2)\right) \end{aligned} \tag{A3.2}$$

For the simple example, we can easily graph the likelihood function L: it is shown in Table A3.1. The function PI() returns π. To compute the sum of squares $\Sigma(x_i - \mu)^2$ we could type (here for cell B8):

```
($B$2-$A8)^2+($B$3-$A8)^2+($B$4-$A$8)^2
```

but as shown in the table, we can also use an array function

```
{SUM(($B$2:$B$4-$A8)^2}
```

Table A3.1 Likelihood for a sample of three normally distributed numbers

	A	B	C	D	E	F	G	H	I
1	**Data**								
2	x_1	-1							
3	x_2	5							
4	x_3	2							
5									
6	**Likelihood**								
7	μ / σ²	2	4						
8	-4	4.7E-16	1.1E-09	1.2E-0					
9	-3	1.8E-12	7.1E-08	1.9E-0					
10	-2	1.5E-09	2.1E-06	1.8E-0					
11	-1	2.9E-07	2.9E-05	1.0E-0					
12	0	1.2E-05	1.9E-04	3.5E-0					
13	1	1.2E-04	5.7E-04	7.5E-0					
14	2	2.5E-04	8.4E-04	9.6E-0					
15	3	1.2E-04	5.7E-04	7.5E-04	7.6E-04	7.0E-04	7.0E-04	7.3E-04	
16	4	1.2E-05	1.9E-04	3.5E-04	4.3E-04	4.5E-04	4.5E-04	4.4E-04	
17	5	2.9E-07	2.9E-05	1.0E-04	1.7E-04	2.1E-04	2.1E-04	1.9E-04	
18	6	1.5E-09	2.1E-06	1.8E-05	4.5E-05	7.4E-05	7.4E-05	6.0E-05	
19		=(2*PI()*B$7)^(-3/2)*EXP(-SUM(($B$2:$B$4-$A18)^2)/(2*B$7))							
20		*(can be copied into B8:H18)*							

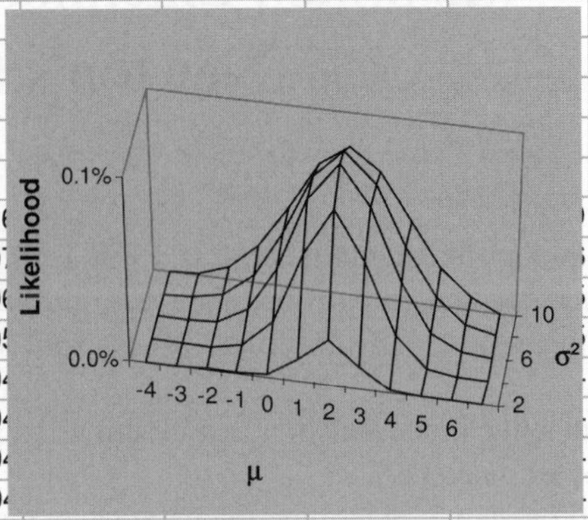

For the discrete parameter values that we specified, the likelihood is maximized for $\mu = 2$ whatever the value of σ^2. (Note that 2 is also the arithmetic average over the three observations.) The overall maximum is obtained for $\mu = 2$ and $\sigma^2 = 6$.

In typical situations, of course, we will not be able to maximize the likelihood by visual inspection – nor would it be efficient to do so. As in other maximization problems, we can compute the first derivative of the likelihood, and then find the parameter values that set the derivative equal to zero. In some cases, we quickly get an analytical solution to this problem; in others, we resort to numerical procedures.

In doing so, it is more convenient to work with the logarithm of the likelihood. For the likelihood (A3.2) of the example from above, we get the following log-likelihood (recall $\ln(x^a) = a \cdot \ln(x)$, $\ln(xy) = \ln(x) + \ln(y)$, $\ln(\exp(x)) = x$):

$$\ln L = \ln \prod_{i=1}^{3} (2\pi\sigma^2)^{-1/2} \exp(-(x_i - \mu)^2/(2\sigma^2))$$

$$= -\frac{3}{2}\ln(2\pi) - \frac{3}{2}\ln\sigma^2 - \sum_{i=1}^{3}(x_i - \mu)^2/(2\sigma^2) \tag{A3.3}$$

Its first derivative with respect to μ is

$$\frac{\partial \ln L}{\partial \mu} = \sum_{i=1}^{3}(x_i - \mu)/\sigma^2 \tag{A3.4}$$

Setting (A3.4) to zero yields a formula for the maximum likelihood (ML) estimator of μ:

$$\sum_{i=1}^{3}(x_i-\mu)/\sigma^2=0 \Leftrightarrow \sum_{i=1}^{3}x_i-\sum_{i=1}^{3}\mu=0 \Leftrightarrow \sum_{i=1}^{3}x_i-3\mu=0$$

$$\Rightarrow \mu_{ML}=\frac{1}{3}\sum_{i=1}^{3}x_i \tag{A3.5}$$

which is also the formula for the arithmetic average and evaluates to 2, confirming our observation from above. Similarly, we could differentiate the log-likelihood with respect to σ^2 to get the following maximum likelihood estimator for the variance:

$$\frac{\partial \ln L}{\partial \sigma^2}=-\frac{3}{2\sigma^2}+\frac{1}{2\sigma^4}\sum_{i=1}^{3}(x_i-\mu)^2=0 \tag{A3.6}$$

$$\Rightarrow \sigma^2_{ML}=\frac{1}{3}\sum_{i=1}^{3}(x_i-\mu_{ML})^2 \tag{A3.7}$$

which evaluates to 6 for our data.

When there are no analytical solutions, we can use numerical procedures to find the root to the first derivative. In many cases, Newton's method is easy to implement and reliable. Let us explain this method for the case in which we look for a scalar x that set $f(x)$ equal to zero. Starting with a guessed value x_0 we search for x_1 that brings us closer to $f(x)=0$. With a first order Taylor expansion, $f(x_1)$ can be expressed as

$$f(x_1)=f(x_0)+f'(x_0)(x_1-x_o) \tag{A3.8}$$

Our goal is to find x_1 such that $f(x_1)=0$, and so we set (A3.8) to zero and solve for x_1:

$$\begin{aligned} f(x_1)&=f(x_0)+f'(x_0)(x_1-x_o)\overset{!}{=}0 \Rightarrow \\ x_1&=x_0-f(x_0)/f'(x_0) \end{aligned} \tag{A3.9}$$

With the x_1 obtained through this rule, we evaluate $f(x_1)$ and check whether it is zero (or reasonably close). If yes, we have a solution. If not, we continue the iteration process, taking x_1 as our new guess and determine a new estimate x_2 analogously to (A3.9).

When applying this procedure to likelihood maximization, ensure that you get the correspondences right. We want to set the first derivative of the likelihood function to zero, and so $f(x)$ corresponds to the first derivative of the log-likelihood, $f'(x)$ to its second derivative.

The Newton procedure can also be applied when there are several unknown parameters. We will illustrate this for the example from above. Collecting the two unknown parameters in a column vector θ

$$\theta=\begin{bmatrix}\mu\\ \sigma^2\end{bmatrix} \tag{A3.10}$$

we can set up the following rule:

$$\theta_1 = \theta_0 - \left[\frac{\partial^2 \ln L}{\partial \theta_0 \partial \theta_0'}\right]^{-1} \frac{\partial \ln L}{\partial \theta_0} \tag{A3.11}$$

The first derivative is a column vector with one row for each parameter, the second derivative is a symmetric square matrix with the number of columns and rows being equal to the number of parameters. For our example, its elements are

$$\frac{\partial^2 \ln L}{\partial \theta_0 \partial \theta_0'} = \begin{bmatrix} \dfrac{\partial^2 \ln L}{\partial \mu \partial \mu} & \dfrac{\partial^2 \ln L}{\partial \sigma^2 \partial \mu} \\ \dfrac{\partial^2 \ln L}{\partial \mu \partial \sigma^2} & \dfrac{\partial^2 \ln L}{\partial \sigma^2 \partial \sigma^2} \end{bmatrix} \tag{A3.12}$$

Table A3.2 Applying Newton's method to a sample of three normally distributed numbers

	A	B	C	D	E	F	G
1	**Data**						
2	x_1	-1					
3	x_2	5					
4	x_3	2					
5		**Parameters**		**1st derivatives**		**2nd derivatives of lnL**	
6	**Iteration**	θ=[μ σ²]'		**of lnL (gradient)**		**(Hessian)**	
7	0	0		6.0000		-3.000	-6.000
8		1		13.5000		-6.000	-28.500
9	1	1.818		[illegible]		[illegible]	-0.229
10		1.091					-12.681
11	2	1.959					-0.024
12		1.580					-3.967
13	3	1.991		[illegible]		[illegible]	-0.003
14		[illegible]		[illegible]		-0.003	-1.285
15						-0.963	0.000
16						0.000	-0.441
17	5	2.000		0.0002		-0.727	0.000
18		4.126		0.1651		0.000	-0.168
19	6	2.000		0.0000		-0.587	0.000
20		5.108		0.0513		0.000	-0.078
21	7	2.000		0.0000		-0.520	0.000
22		5.769		0.0104		0.000	-0.049
23	8	2.000		0.0000		-0.501	0.000
24		5.983		0.0007		0.000	-0.042
25	9	2.000		0.0000		-0.500	0.000
26		6.000		0.0000		0.000	-0.042
27	10	2.000		0.0000		-0.500	0.000
28		6.000		0.0000		0.000	-0.042

D7: {=SUM(B$2:B$4-B7)/B8}
D8: {=-3/(2*B8)+SUM((B$2:B$4-B7)^2)/(2*B8^2)}
(can be copied down to row 28)

F7: =-3/B8
F8=G7: {=-SUM(B$2:B$4-B7)/B8^2}
G8: {=3/(2*B8^2)-SUM((B$2:B$4-B7)^2)/B8^3}
(Can be copied down to row 28)

B9:B10: {=(B7:B8)- (MMULT(MINVERSE(F7:G8),(D7:D8)))}
(Can be copied down to row 28)

which are given by

$$\frac{\partial \ln L}{\partial \mu \partial \mu} = -3/\sigma^2$$

$$\frac{\partial \ln L}{\partial \mu \partial \sigma^2} = \frac{\partial \ln L}{\partial \sigma^2 \partial \mu} = -\sum_{i=1}^{3}(x_i - \mu)/\sigma^4 \tag{A3.13}$$

$$\frac{\partial \ln L}{\partial \sigma^2 \partial \sigma^2} = 3/(2\sigma^4) - \sum_{i=1}^{3}(x_i - \mu)^2/\sigma^6$$

The vector of first derivatives is often called the gradient vector $g(\theta)$, whereas the matrix of second derivatives is called the Hessian matrix $H(\theta)$. With this notation, we can rewrite (A3.11) as

$$\theta_1 = \theta_0 - H(\theta_0)^{-1} g(\theta_0) \tag{A3.14}$$

In Table A3.2, we apply this procedure to our sample data. Note that the calculations for one iteration spread over two rows. Our starting values are $\mu = 0$ and $\sigma^2 = 1$, input in cells

Table A3.3 Using the solver to maximize the likelihood for a sample of three normally distributed numbers (based on Table A3.1)

	A	B	C	D	E	F	G	H	I
1	**Data**								
2	x_1	-1							
3	x_2	5							
4	x_3	2							
5									
6	**Likelihood**			**Ln likelihood**					
7	μ / σ²	6.000		-6.944	=ln(B8)				
8	2.000	9.6E-04							
9		=(2*PI()*B$7)^(-3/2)*EXP(-SUM(($B$2:$B$4-$A8)^2)/(2*B$7))							

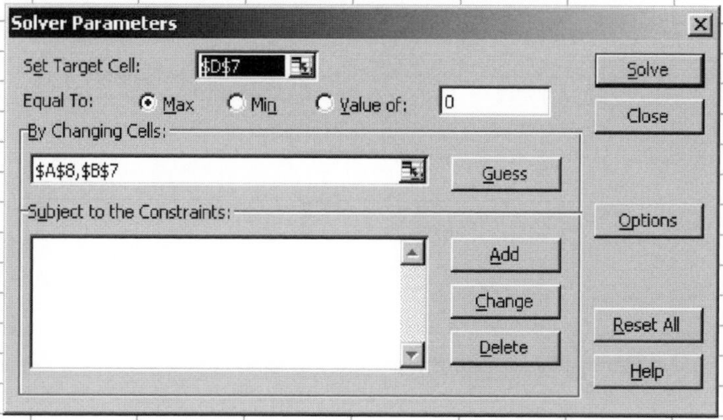

Solver Parameters

Set Target Cell: $D$7

Equal To: Max / Min / Value of: 0

By Changing Cells: $A$8,$B$7

Subject to the Constraints:

Solve | Close | Guess | Options | Add | Change | Delete | Reset All | Help

B7:B8. The gradient vector is evaluated in D7:D8 using (A3.4) and (A3.6), the Hessian matrix in F7:G8 using (A3.13). The first iteration following (A3.14) is performed in B9:B10. In each case we use array functions, and so we have to input the formula using [ctrl]+[shift]+[return]. Even though the starting values are not close to the ML estimates, the iteration converges quickly. After nine iterations, there is no visible change in parameters, and the first derivatives of the likelihood equal zero at the displayed precision.

To make sure that the solution we have found is actually a maximum of the likelihood function, we can inspect the second derivatives. In some applications of the ML procedure, this step is not necessary because the likelihood function is globally concave.

In some situations, derivatives of the likelihood function are difficult to evaluate analytically. We can then, for example, use a quasi-Newton procedure. It uses the same iteration rule as in (A3.14) but computes the gradient and the Hessian through discrete approximations rather than analytically. In Excel, such a numerical procedure is available through the Solver. Again, we use our example with the three observations. In Table A3.1, we have already computed the likelihood for a set of parameters. We copy everything to Table A3.3, but then keep only the likelihood function for one combination of parameters specified, namely the ones specified in cells A8 and B7. We could now try to maximize the likelihood in cell B8, but it is advisable to perform maximization on the log-likelihood. (The likelihood value is very small in absolute terms, and so we would have to take great care in making sure that the Solver is sensitive enough to changes in the likelihood.)

We therefore write the logarithm of the likelihood in cell D7 and call the Solver to maximize D7 by varying A8 and B7. Table A3.3 shows the Solver input window as well as the results from applying the Solver (initial values were set to A8 $= \mu = 0$ and B7 $= \sigma^2 = 1$). Again, we obtain the by now familiar solution $\mu = 2$ and $\sigma^2 = 6$.

Appendix A4
Testing and Goodness of Fit

In many situations, we examine data to get an estimate of unknown parameters. Examples for such parameters are the mean of a distribution, the variance of a distribution or the weights b that we apply in combining variables x into a prediction of another variable y.

In this book, we mainly employ the maximum likelihood and the least-squares estimation principles. The maximum likelihood principle is described in Appendix A3. In least squares, we choose the estimate such that the squared differences between observed values and our predictions are minimized. As an illustration, consider the case where we want to estimate the mean m of a sample of N observations x_i. In the least squares approach, our prediction for a single observation will be just the mean m we are looking for, and so we minimize:

$$\text{Sum of squared errors} = \sum_{i=1}^{N} (x_i - m)^2 \rightarrow \min_{m}! \tag{A4.1}$$

We can solve this problem by taking the first derivative with respect to m:

$$\frac{\mathrm{d}(\text{Sum of squared errors})}{\mathrm{d}m} = -2\sum_{i=1}^{N} (x_i - m) \stackrel{!}{=} 0 \tag{A4.2}$$

Solving for m yields the estimator $\hat{m}$:

$$\hat{m} = \frac{1}{N}\sum_{i=1}^{N} x_i \tag{A4.3}$$

that is, the arithmetic average of our observed xs.

Standard errors

Once we have arrived at some estimate b, we would like to know about the estimate's precision. Precision can be measured by the standard error (SE), the square root of the estimator's variance (var):

$$\mathrm{SE}[b] = \sqrt{\mathrm{var}(b)} \tag{A4.4}$$

In standard least-squares problems, we just plug the formula for our estimator into (A4.4) and try to get a handy expression for SE[b]. For the estimate of the mean m this would give the following ($\sigma(x)$ denotes the standard deviation of x):

$$\begin{aligned}
\text{SE}[\hat{m}] &= \sqrt{\text{var}\,[\hat{m}]} = \sqrt{\text{var}\left[\frac{1}{N}\sum_{i=1}^{N} x_i\right]} = \sqrt{\frac{1}{N^2}\text{var}\left[\sum_{i=1}^{N} x_i\right]} \\
&= \sqrt{\frac{1}{N^2}\sum_{i=1}^{N}\text{var}(x_i)} \\
&= \sqrt{\frac{1}{N^2}N\,\text{var}(x)} \\
&= \frac{\sigma(x)}{\sqrt{N}}
\end{aligned} \tag{A4.5}$$

Moving from the first line to the second, we assume that the x_i are independent; moving from the second to the third, we assume that they have identical variance. The result conforms to intuition: our estimate is more precise (i.e., has a lower standard error) if we have more observations N and if the variable that we want to predict is less dispersed. Note that we would have to estimate the standard deviation $\sigma(x)$ in order to get an estimate of our standard error SE[m].

In maximum likelihood (ML) estimation, the standard error can be estimated as the negative inverse of the second derivative of the log-likelihood with respect to the parameter, evaluated at its ML estimate. Thus, the standard error for some estimate b_{ML} would be

$$\text{SE}[b_{\text{ML}}] = \sqrt{-\left[\frac{\partial^2 \ln L}{\partial b_{\text{ML}}^2}\right]^{-1}} \tag{A4.6}$$

To get an intuition, look at Table A4.1. We separately estimate the means for two samples of normally distributed variables. With ML estimation, we get a mean of 2 and a variance of 6 for each sample. But the second sample has twice as many observations as the first, and so we would expect the mean of the second sample to be more precisely estimated. How is this reflected in the second derivatives of the log-likelihood? In the table, we graph the log-likelihoods for both samples. We vary the mean and keep the variance at the ML estimate of 6. Both likelihoods are concave, which means that their second derivatives with respect to μ are negative. But the likelihood for the larger sample is more highly curved. Carefully examining (A4.6), note that a higher curvature (e.g., the second derivative is –1 rather than –0.5) leads to a smaller standard error. Why should this be so? The higher the curvature, the more likelihood is lost when moving from the ML estimate to the left or to the right; therefore, with a high curvature, we are relatively sure that our ML estimate does the best job rather than some other value in the neighborhood.

t-tests

Once we have an estimate b and its standard error SE[b] we can test hypotheses. We would like to know whether the estimate is statistically different from some other value (our null

Table A4.1 Likelihood functions for two samples of normally distributed variables

	A	B	C	D	E	F	G	H	I
1	**Data**								
2		Sample 1	Sample 2						
3		-1	-1						
4		5	5						
5		2	2						
6			-1						
7			5						
8			2						
9	**Likelihood**								
10	μ / σ²	6	6						
11	0	-7.94	-10.44						
12	0.25	-7.71	-9.						
13	0.5	-7.51	-9.						
14	0.75	-7.34	-9.						
15	1	-7.19	-8.						
16	1.25	-7.09	-8.						
17	1.5	-7.01	-8.						
18	1.75	-6.96	-8.						
19	2	-6.94	-8.						
20	2.25	-6.96	-8.						
21	2.5	-7.01	-8.						
22	2.75	-7.09	-8.						
23	3	-7.19	-8.						
24	3.25	-7.34	-9.						
25	3.5	-7.51	-9.57						
26	3.75	-7.71	-9.98						
27	4	-7.94	-10.44						
28									
29									
30									
31									

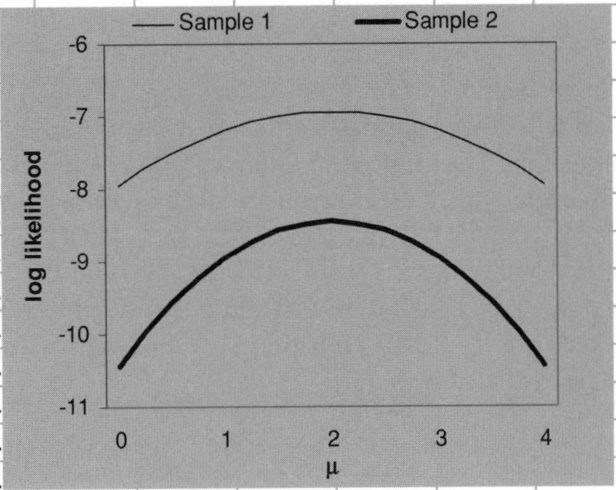

```
B27: =LN((2*PI()*B$10)^(-3/2)*EXP(-SUM((B$3:B$5-$A27)^2)/(2*B$10)))
C27: =LN((2*PI()*C$10)^(-3/2)*EXP(-SUM((C$3:C$8-$A27)^2)/(2*C$10)))
Formulae can be copied in B11:B26 and C11:C26, respectively.
```

hypothesis). Such a test can be based on the t-ratio:

$$t = (b - b^h)/\mathrm{SE}[b] \tag{A4.7}$$

where b^h is our null hypothesis. The t-ratio tells us how far our estimate is away from the hypothesized value, where distance is measured in multiples of standard error. The larger the t-ratio in absolute terms, the more distant is the hypothesized value, and the more confident we can be that the estimate is different from the hypothesis.

To express confidence in a figure, we determine the distribution of t. Then we can quantify whether a large t-ratio should be attributed to chance or to a significant difference between our estimate and the null hypothesis.

Table A4.2 Testing the hypothesis of a zero mean for a sample of normally distributed variables

	A	B	C	D	E	F	G	H
1	**Data**		**Estimates and tests**					
2	0.35567		mean	0.890	=AVERAGE(A2:A11)			
3	-0.08808		SE(mean)	0.305	=STDEV(A2:A11)/COUNT(A2:A11)^0.5			
4	3.08575		t (H_0=0)	2.914	=D2/(D3)			
5	0.93212		p-value	0.017	=TDIST(ABS(D4),COUNT(A2:A11)-1,2)			
6	1.19826							
7	0.52357							
8	0.47544							
9	-0.23522							
10	0.95054							
11	1.70372							

In applications of the least-squares approach, it is common to assume that the coefficient estimate follows a normal distribution, while the estimated standard error follows a chi-square distribution. The t-ratio then follows a t-distribution if the null hypothesis is true; the degrees of freedom of the t-distribution are given as the number of observations minus the parameters that we estimated. Given some t-ratio for a model with DF degrees of freedom, we look up the probability that a t-distributed variable with DF degrees of freedom exceeds the t-ratio from our test. Usually, we perform a two-sided test, that is, we examine the probability of exceeding t or $-t$. This probability is called the p-value. In Excel, the p-value of a t-value t^* can be evaluated with

=TDIST(abs(t*),DF,2)

The p-value is the probability of making an error when rejecting the null hypothesis. When it is low, we will tend to reject the null hypothesis. This is usually formulated as: we reject the null hypothesis at a significance of <p-value>.

Let us examine an example. Assume that we have sampled 10 normally distributed numbers. In Table A4.2, they are listed along with the estimate for the sample mean (see Equation (A4.3)), its standard error (A4.5), the t-ratio for the null hypothesis that the mean is zero (A4.7) as well as its associated p-value.

We obtain a mean of 0.89 with a standard error of 0.305. The t-statistic is fairly high at 2.914. We can reject the hypothesis that the mean is zero with a significance of 1.7%.

When we use maximum likelihood to estimate a nonlinear model such as logit (Chapter 1) or Poisson (Chapter 4), we cannot rely on our coefficient estimates following a normal distribution in small samples. If the number of observations is very large, however, the t-ratio can be shown to be distributed like a standard normal variable. Thus, we refer the t-ratio to the standard normal distribution function, and we usually do so even if the sample size is small. To avoid confusion some programs and authors therefore speak of a z-ratio instead of a t-ratio. With the normal distribution, the two-sided p-value of a t-ratio t^* is obtained as

=2*(1-NORMSDIST(abs(t*)))

R^2 and Pseudo-R^2 for regressions

In a linear regression our goal is to determine coefficients b such that we minimize the squared differences between our prediction, which is derived from weighting explanatory variables x with b and the dependent variable y:

$$\sum_{i=1}^{N} [y_i - (b_1 + b_2 x_{i2} + b_3 x_{i3} + \ldots + b_K x_{iK})]^2 = \sum_{i=1}^{N} (\mathrm{e}_i)^2 \to \underset{b}{min}! \tag{A4.8}$$

where we introduce the shortcut e_i for the residual, i.e., the prediction error for observation i.

We can measure a regression's goodness of fit through the coefficient of determination, R^2 for short. The R^2 is the squared correlation coefficient between the dependent variable y and our prediction. Equivalently, we can say that it is the percentage of the variance of y that is explained by the regression. One way of computing R^2 is

$$R^2 = 1 - \frac{\sum_{i=1}^{N} (\mathrm{e}_i)^2}{\sum_{i=1}^{N} (y_i - \bar{y})^2} \tag{A4.9}$$

The nonlinear regressions that we examine in this book have the structure

$$\mathrm{Prob}(Y_i = y_i) = F\,(b_1 + b_2 x_{i2} + b_3 x_{i3} + \ldots + b_K x_{iK}) \tag{A4.10}$$

where Y is some random variable (e.g., the number of defaults) whose realization y we observe. F is a nonlinear function such as the logistic function. Having estimated regressions of the form (A4.10) with maximum likelihood, the commonly used analog to the R^2 is the Pseudo-R^2 proposed by Daniel McFadden. It is defined by relating the log-likelihood of the estimated model ($\ln L$) to the log-likelihood of a model that has just a constant in it ($\ln L_0$):

$$\text{Pseudo-}R^2 = 1 - \ln L/\ln L_0 \tag{A4.11}$$

To understand (A4.11), note that the log-likelihood cannot be positive. (The maximum value for the likelihood is 1, and $\ln(1) = 0$.) If the variables x add a lot of explanatory power to a model with just a constant, the Pseudo-R^2 is high because in evaluating $\ln L/\ln L_0$ we divide a small negative number by a large negative one, resulting in a small value for $\ln L/\ln L_0$. The Pseudo-R^2 cannot be negative because adding one or several variables can never decrease the likelihood. In the extreme case where the variables x are useless, the estimation procedure will assign them a zero coefficient, thus leaving likelihood unchanged.

In relation to this observation, note that the Pseudo-R^2 and the R^2 can never decrease upon inclusion of additional variables.

F-tests

An F-test is a generalization of a t-test for testing joint hypotheses, e.g., that two regression coefficients are jointly zero. An F-test can be constructed with the R^2s from two regressions: a regression without imposing the restrictions yielding R^2, and another regression that imposes the restrictions yielding R_0^2:

$$F = \frac{(R^2 - R_0^2)/J}{(1 - R^2)/DF} \tag{A4.12}$$

where J is the number of restrictions implied by the hypothesis, and DF is the degrees of freedom of the unrestricted regression. If the hypothesis is not valid, imposing it will lead to strong decrease of R^2, and so F will be large. Thus, we can reject the hypothesis for large values of F. The associated p-value is obtained by referring the F-statistic to an F-distribution with degrees of freedom J and DF. In Excel, this can be done using

=FDIST(F*,J,DF)

When testing the hypothesis that all coefficients except the constant are equal to zero, we can construct the F-test with just one regression because the R_0^2 in (A4.12) is then the R^2 from a regression with just a constant, which is zero.

Likelihood ratio tests

For a model estimated with maximum likelihood, one analog to the F-test is the likelihood ratio (LR) test.[1] In the F-test, we compare the R^2s of unrestricted and restricted models; in the likelihood ratio test, we compare the log-likelihood of unrestricted ($\ln L$) and restricted ($\ln L_0$) models. The likelihood ratio statistic LR is constructed as:

$$\text{LR} = -2\,[\ln L_0 - \ln L] = 2\,[\ln L - \ln L_0] \tag{A4.13}$$

Thus, the more likelihood is lost by imposing the hypothesis, the larger will be the LR statistic. Large values of LR will thus lead to a rejection of the hypothesis. The p-value can be obtained by referring LR to a chi-squared distribution with J degrees of freedom, where J is the number of restrictions imposed:

=CHIDIST(LR,J)

We should bear in mind, though, that the LR statistic is only asymptotically (i.e., for a large number of observations) chi-squared distributed. Depending on the application, it might be advisable to explore its small sample properties.

[1] The other two are the Wald test and the Lagrange-Multiplier test.

Appendix A5
User-defined Functions

Throughout this book we use Excel functions and discuss user-defined functions to perform the described analyses. Here we provide a list of all these functions together with their syntax and short descriptions. The source for original functions is Microsoft Excel 2003's help file.

All the user-defined commands are available in the xls file accompanying each chapter and the lp.xla Add-in, both provided on the DVD. The Add-in is furthermore available for download on our website: www.loeffler-posch.com.

INSTALLATION OF THE ADD-IN

To install the Add-in for use in the spreadsheet, take the following steps in Excel:

1. Click on the item Add-Ins in the Menu Tools.
2. Click on Browse and choose the location of the lp.xla file.
   (a) If you are using the DVD, the file is located in the root directory, e.g., D:\lp.xla.
   (b) If you downloaded the Add-in from the Internet, the file is located in your download folder.

To install the Add-in for use within your own VBA macros, take the following steps in Excel:

1. Open the VBA editor by pressing [alt]+[F11].
2. Click on the item References in the Tools menu.
3. Click on Browse and choose the location of the lp.xla file.
   (a) If you are using the DVD, the file is located in the root directory, e.g., D:\lp.xla.
   (b) if you downloaded the Add-in from the Internet, the file is located in your download folder.

FUNCTION LIST

We developed and tested our functions with the international English versions of Excel 2003 and Excel 2007. If you run into problems with your version, please check that all available updates are installed. If you still encounter problems please visit our homepage for updates or send us an email to vba@loeffler-posch.com.

Shaded rows in Table A5.1 refer to user-defined functions available in the accompanying Add-in. Optional parameters are marked by []. ATP refers to the Analysis ToolPak Add-in; see Chapter 10 for details.

Table A5.1 Comprehensive list of functions with short descriptions

Syntax	Description	Chapter
ACI(*settlement*, *maturity*, *rate*, *freq*, [*basis*])	Returns the accrued interest at settlement of a bond maturing at maturity: *rate* gives the coupon rate of the bond and *freq* the coupon frequency (annual (1), semi-annual (2) or quarterly(4)).	10
AVERAGE(*number1*, *number2*, ...)	Returns the average (arithmetic mean) of the arguments.	1, 4, 6, 12
BETAINV(*probability*, *alpha*, *beta*, *A*, *B*)	Returns the inverse of the cumulative distribution function for a specified beta distribution. That is, if *probability* = BETADIST(x, ...), then BETAINV(probability, ...) = x.	7
BINOMDIST(*number_s*, *trials*, *probability_s*, *cumulative*)	Returns the binomial distribution probability.	3, 8, 11
BIVNOR(*d1*, *d2*, *r*)	Returns the bivariate standard normal distribution function with correlation *r*.	6, 11
BOOTCAP(*ratings*, *defaults*, *M*, *alpha*)	Returns bootstrapped confidence intervals for the accuracy ratio using simulated CAP curves. *M* is the number of trials and *alpha* the confidence level.	8
BOOTCONF(*id*, *dat*, *rat*, *M*, *toclass*, *confidence*)	Returns bootstrapped confidence intervals for transition to *toclass*. *M* is the number of repetitions and confidence the confidence level.	3
BRIER(*ratings*, *defaults*)	Returns the Brier score.	8
BSd1(*S*, *x*, *h*, *r*, *sigma*)	Returns d1 of the Black-Scholes formula	2
CAP(*ratings*, *defaults*)	Returns the Cumulative Accuracy Profile.	8
CAPREQ(*PD*, *LGD*, *M*)	Returns the capital requirement according to the Basel-II framework.	12
CG_CDS(*S*, *sigma_S*, *d*, *Lambda*, *sigma_B*, *t*, *Rec*, *r*)	Calculates the CDS spread in the CreditGrades model with *S* as stock price, *sigma_S* as its volatility and *d* as debt-by-share. *Lambda* is the parameter of the global recovery, *sigma_B* its volatility *Rec* is the recovery and *r* the risk-free yield.	2
CG_PS(*S*, *sigma_S*, *d*, *Lambda*, *sigma_B*, *t*)	Calculates the probability of survival up to time *t* in the CreditGrades model using *S* as stock price, *sigma_S* as its volatility and *d* as debt-by-share. *Lambda* is the parameter of the global recovery, *sigma_B* its volatility.	2

CHIDIST(*x*, *degrees_freedom*)	Returns the one-tailed probability of the chi-squared distribution.	1, 4, 9
CLINEST(*yraw*, *xraw*, *cl*)	Implements an estimator of the coefficients' standard errors that is robust to correlation within clusters. The function's output is organized in the same way as that of Excel's LINEST.	5
COHORT(*id*, *dat*, *rat*, [*classes*], [*ystart*], [*yend*])	Returns a transition matrix according to the cohort approach. If the optional parameters are omitted, they are calculated upon the supplied data.	3
COMBIN(*number*, *number_chosen*)	Returns the number of combinations for a given number of items.	6
CORREL(*array1*, *array2*)	Returns the correlation coefficient of the *array1* and *array2* cell ranges.	9
COUNT(*value1*, *value2*, . . .)	Counts the number of cells that contain numbers and also numbers within the list of arguments.	4, 9, 12
COUNTIF(*range*, *criteria*)	Counts the number of cells within a range that meet the given criteria.	1, 9, 12
COUPDAYS(*settlement*, *maturity*, *frequency*, *basis*)	Returns the number of days in the coupon period that contains the settlement date. (ATP Add-In)	10
COUPDAYSNC(*settlement*, *maturity*, *frequency*, *basis*)	Returns the number of days from the settlement date to the next coupon date. (ATP Add-In)	10
COUPNCD(*settlement*, *maturity*, *frequency*, *basis*)	Returns the next coupon date after the settlement date. (ATP Add-In)	10
COUPPCD(*settlement*, *maturity*, *frequency*, *basis*)	Returns the coupon date preceding the settlement date. Frequency is the number of coupon payments per year. (ATP Add-In)	10
CRITBINOM(*trials*, *probability_s*, *alpha*)	Returns the smallest value for which the cumulative binomial distribution is greater than or equal to a criterion value.	3, 6
DEVSQ(*number1*, *number2*, . . .)	Returns the sum of squares of deviations of data points from their sample mean.	9
EDATE(*start_date*, *month*)	Returns the serial number of the date that is the indicated number of months before or after the start date.	10, 11
EXP(*number*)	Returns 'e' raised to the power of number.	1, 2, 4, 7

(*Continued*)

Table A5.1 (*Continued*)

Syntax	Description	Chapter
GENERATOR(*id*, *dat*, *rat*, [*classes*], [*ystart*], [*yend*])	Returns the generator matrix.	3
HALTON(*j*, *base*)	Returns the *j*th Halton number of *base*.	7
IF(*logical_test*, *value_if_true*, *value_if_false*)	Returns one value if a condition you specify evaluates to TRUE and another value if it evaluates to FALSE.	2, 4, 10, 11, 12
INDEX(*array*, *row_num*, *column_num*)	Returns the value of a specified cell or array of cells within array.	9
INTSPOT(*spots*, *year*)	Uses the array *spot* to linearly interpolate the spot rate of *year*.	10
ISERROR(*value*)	*value* refers to any error value (#N/A, #VALUE!, #REF!, #DIV/0!, #NUM!, #NAME?, or #NULL!).	12
KURT(*number1*, *number2*, . . .)	Returns the kurtosis of a data set.	1
LINEST(*known_y's*, *known_x's*, *const*, *stats*)	Calculates the statistics for a line by using the 'least squares' method to calculate a straight line that best fits your data, and returns an array that describes the line.	4
LN(*number*)	Returns the natural logarithm of a number.	2, 6, 9
LOGIT(*y*, *xraw*, *constant*, *stats*)	Runs a logit (or logistic regression): *y* contains the binary response (0 or 1), *xraw* is a range of explanatory variables; *constant* and *stats* are optional parameters for inclusion of a constant in the model and return of statistics. The default is *constant*=true and *stats*=false.	1
LOSS(*settlement*, *maturity*, *rate*, *spots*, *notional*, *freq*, *compound*, *fromdate*, *R*, [*basis*])	Returns the expected loss: *spots* can be an array of spot rates; *R* gives the recovery rate.	10
MADD(*ByVal array1*, *ByVal array2*)	Returns the sum of two matrices.	3
MATCH(*lookup_value*, *lookup_array*, *match_type*)	Returns the relative position of an item in an array that matches a specified value in a specified order.	7
MAX(*number1*, *number2*, . . .)	Returns the largest value in a set of values.	1, 3, 4

MDIAG(*m As Integer*, *D As Double*)	Returns a symmetric $m \times m$ matrix with D on-diagonal and zeroes off-diagonal.	3
MEDIAN(*number1*, *number2*, ...)	Returns the median of the given numbers.	1
MEXP(*array1*)	Returns the exponential of *array1* using a truncated sum.	3
MEXPGENERATOR(*generator*)	Returns the exponential of *generator* assuming that generator is a valid generator matrix.	3
MIN(*number1*, *number2*, ...)	Returns the smallest value in a set of values.	1, 3
MPOWER(*array1*, *power*)	Returns *array1* raised to the power *power*.	3
MSMULT(*ByVal array1*, *ByVal array2*)	Returns the elementwise product of *array1* and *array2*: *array1* can be a scalar or an array.	3
MYPRICE(*settlement*, *maturity*, *rate*, *spots*, *notional*, *freq*, [*compound*], [*fromdate*], [*basis*])	Returns the price per $100 face value of a security that pays periodic interest; spots can be an array or a number.	10
NORMSDIST(*z*)	Returns the standard normal cumulative distribution function.	2, 4, 6, 8, 11
NORMSINV(*probability*)	Returns the inverse of the standard normal cumulative distribution.	6, 7, 8, 9, 11
NRND()	Returns a random normal number using the polar method algorithm.	7
OFFSET(*reference*, *rows*, *cols*, *height*, *width*)	Returns a reference to a range that is a specified number of rows and columns from a cell or range of cells.	4, 7
OOSTREND(*y*, *x*, *xnew*, *year*, *startyear*)	The first arguments are the same as in Excel's TREND() function. *Year* is a range that contains the observation date. *Startyear* is the first date for which an out-of-sample prediction is made; i.e., we run a regression with data from before *startyear*, and then use the estimated coefficients from this regression together with the new predictors (*new_x's*), to generate a prediction.	5
PERCENTILE(*array*, *k*)	Returns the *k*th percentile of values in a range.	1, 3
POIREG(*y*, *x*)	Runs a Poisson regression of *x* on *y*.	4

(Continued)

Table A5.1 *(Continued)*

Syntax	Description	Chapter
POISSON(*x*, *mean*, *cumulative*)	Returns the Poisson distribution.	4
POITREND(*y*, *x*, *xn*)	Returns predicted trend of a Poisson regression; refers to POIREG().	4
RHOSEARCH(*z1*, *z2*)	Performs a line search for the correlation coefficient between *z1* and *z2*. Both parameters are arrays which are assumed to be standard normal.	9
RAND()	Returns an evenly distributed random number greater than or equal to 0 and less than 1.	6, 7, 9, 12
ROC(*ratings*, *defaults*)	Returns the Receiver-Operator-Curve.	8
ROUND(*number*, *num_digits*)	Rounds a number to a specified number of digits.	12
RPV01(*startd*, *maturity*, *freq*, *r*, *s*, *Optional LGD*)	Calculates the present value of a basis-point using the discount rate *r*, the CDS spread *s* with coupon frequency *freq* starting at *startd* and going until maturity. The loss-given default LGD is optional and set to 60% if omitted.	10
SKEW(*number1*, *number2*, . . .)	Returns the skewness of a distribution.	1
SLOPE(*known_y's*, *known_x's*)	Returns the slope of the linear regression line through data points in *known_y's* and *known_x's*.	2
STDEV(*number1*, *number2*, . . .)	Estimates standard deviation based on a sample.	1, 2
SUM(*number1*, *number2*, . . .)	Adds all the numbers in a range of cells.	4, 6, 7, 12
SUMIF(*range*, *criteria*, *sum_range*)	Adds the cells specified by a given criteria.	1, 10
SUMPRODUCT(*array1*, *array2*, *array3*, . . .)	Multiplies corresponding components in the given arrays, and returns the sum of those products.	1, 4, 6, 9, 10, 12
SUMSQ(*number1*, *number2*, . . .)	Returns the sum of the squares of the arguments.	9
SUMX2MY2(*array_x*, *array_y*)	Returns the sum of the difference of squares of corresponding values in two arrays.	4

TRANSITION2GENERATOR(*array1*)	Returns the approximate generator of a transition matrix.	3
TREND(*known_y's*, *known_x's*, *new_x's*, *const*)	Returns values along a linear trend.	4
VARP(*number1*, *number2*, . . .)	Calculates variance based on the entire population.	9
VLOOKUP(*lookup_value*, *table_array*, *col_index_num*, *range_lookup*)	Searches for a value in the leftmost column of a table, and then returns a value in the same row from a column you specify in the table.	3, 9, 12
WINSOR(*x*, *level*)	Winsorizes *x* according to level.	1
XTRANS(*defaultdata*, *x*, *numranges*)	Transforms *x* into *numranges* according to the default frequency in each bin.	1
YEARFRAC(*start_date*, *end_date*, *basis*)	Returns the difference between two dates as fraction of a year. Basis specifies the day-count convention. (ATP Add-In)	10

Index

Index compiled by Terry Halliday